1946
LAST WAR OF INDEPENDENCE
ROYAL INDIAN NAVY MUTINY

PRAMOD KAPOOR, the founder and publisher of Roli Books (established in 1978), has over the course of his illustrious career, conceived and produced award-winning books that have proven to be game-changers in the world of publishing. Be it the hit *'Then and Now'* series and the seminal *Made for Maharajas*, or the internationally acclaimed *Gandhi: An Illustrated Biography*, which is published in eleven editions in most major languages worldwide.

In 2016, he was conferred with the Chevalier de la Legion d'Honneur (Knight of the Legion of Honour), the highest civil and military award in France, for his contribution towards producing books that have changed the landscape of Indian publishing. He is also a recipient of the Mahatma Award 2021 (an Aditya Birla Group initiative) for Lifetime Achievement for his contribution to publishing and literature in India.

This book is a result of his years of research and deep interest in the period and personalities who have left a mark in the subcontinent's history.

advertising executive in Lintas. I got acquainted with him when I joined the agency as a copywriter. It was then that I read his account of the Naval Mutiny which was later published under the title *Mutiny of the Innocents*.

'Pramod Kapoor's book is a comprehensive account of the Naval Mutiny. Thoroughly researched, it is an exciting account of what is commonly seen as a footnote in the history of the Freedom Movement. It may have been a footnote, but it certainly was the last straw that broke the colonial camel's back.'

SHYAM BENEGAL

'Pramod Kapoor has transformed a footnote into a book. This book is a major achievement based on incredible research. A must-read for anyone interested in the history of twentieth-century India and how common people made that history.'

RUDRANGSHU MUKHERJEE

'Could 1946 have turned into a rerun of the Great Uprising of 1857? Pramod Kapoor's remarkable research has shed important new light on a thrilling and critically important but partly forgotten story, and does so with great flair and panache.'

WILLIAM DALRYMPLE

'Pramod set out to unearth a forgotten and ignored chapter in our nationalist history and what an excellent job he has done. Meticulous research and fact-checking and digging out facts that are hidden and long forgotten. Our historians just brushed it aside… Pramod has once again brought it to the attention of the public, especially younger Indians. This is a document that fills a vital gap in our history.'

SIDHARTH BHATIA

First published in 2022

ISBN: 978-93-49474-24-6

Roli Books Pvt. Ltd.
M-75, Greater Kailash II Market, New Delhi 110 048
Phone: +91 (011) 40682000
E-mail: info@rolibooks.com
Website: www.rolibooks.com
Also at Chennai & Mumbai

Typeset in Bembo Std by Roli Books Pvt. Ltd

1946

LAST WAR OF INDEPENDENCE
ROYAL INDIAN NAVY MUTINY

PRAMOD KAPOOR

ROLI

3 BRITISH CABINET MINISTERS FOR IN[DIA]

PETHICK-LAWRENCE, CRIPPS & ALEXANDER IN MISSION

NEGOTIATIONS WITH POLITICAL LEADERS TO BEGIN BY END OF MARCH

DELEGATION GIVEN FREE HAND EXCEPT ON MATTERS OF MAJOR POLICY

LONDON, FEB 19—THREE BRITISH CABINET MINISTERS ARE GOING TO INDIA TO DIS-CUSS WITH LEADERS OF INDIAN OPINION THE FRAMING OF AN INDIAN CONSTITUTION. THEY ARE LORD PETHICK-LAWRENCE, SECRETARY FOR INDIA, SIR STAFFORD CRIPPS, PRESIDENT OF THE BOARD OF TRADE, AND MR ALBERT ALEXANDER, FIRST LORD OF THE ADMIRALTY. THIS WAS OFFICIALLY ANNOUNCED IN THE HOUSE OF LORDS TODAY BY LORD PETHICK-LAWRENCE.

The Prime Minister, Mr Clement Attlee, in making a similar statement in the House of Commons added that the mission would go to India towards the one of March.

DUTCH ATROCITIES IN JAVA

Indian Troops Threaten Direct Action

LONDON, Feb 19—British and Indian troops in Batavia have informed their officers that they intend to cease direct action against Dutch troops unless British Armed authorities act to prevent Dutch atrocities against Indonesians, according to a dispatch in the Melbourne Herald today by the paper's correspondent in Batavia.

It was stated that British and Indian troops objected to the "Old Batavia" district, along that newly arrived Dutch soldiers are carrying out a campaign of racial persecution against Indonesians. The dispatch added that he had been informed that British and Indian troops were seething with indignation and that the Arms authorities were reported to be instituting inquiries.—Reuter.

JAI PRAKASH MAY BE

PROCLAMATION OF INDEPENDENCE MUST COME FIRST

NEHRU OUTLINES COUNTRY'S DEMAND AFTER ELECTIONS

ALLAHABAD Feb 19—Reports that Lord Pethick-Lawrence and other officials were soon coming to India were met today by the comment from Pandit Jawaharlal Nehru that such a group might help to fill in the details of arrangements for independence, but the first requirement is "recognition and proclamation of India's right to full independence.

Pandit Nehru's statement was made in an interview outlining the course of events he believed would follow the conclusion of the elections in April.

At the same time, he said, popular ministries were required to meet the food crisis and issued a warning to weaponless that they would have no grave in India's government after the change-over to Indian control.

Pandit Nehru's comment was...

But the question of Indian independence cannot be referred to arbitration and will have to be accepted on the basis of conservation and agreement.

Attitude To Pakistan

Pandit Nehru said that he was convinced that Pakistan, as demanded by the Muslim League, was harmful to all concerned and to India as a whole, and was in no...

NIGHTMARE GRIPS BOMBAY

FRESH TROUBLE BREAKS OUT IN MANY PARTS OF THE CITY

Two Trains Set On Fire At

Unconditional Surrender of RIN Ratings

It was officially stated in New Delhi on Saturday that the ratings in Bombay have surrendered unconditionally. The surrender has been accepted.

A signal from the Strike Committee said the ships are ready to surrender at...

GOVERNMENT CENSURED ON RIN RISING

RACIAL DISCRIMINATION THE ROOT CAUSE

By 'Dawn' Gallery Correspondent

The Central Assembly censured the Government on Friday...

INDIAN RATINGS MUTINY AT TWO CENT[RES]

HEAVY EXCHANGES OF FIRE WITH BRITISH TROOPS

ULTIMATUM BY KARACHI REBELS: "TRUCE" AT BOMBAY

STRIKERS STILL IN COMMAND OF SEVERAL SHIPS

C.-IN-C. RUSHES REINFORCEMENTS TO TROUBLE SPOTS

Mutinies by R.I.N. ratings in Bombay and Karachi assumed grave proportions on Thursday with the mutineers opening fire on military forces sent out to lay them under siege.

In Bombay a "cease fire" was called in the afternoon, but in Karachi ratings from H.M.I.S. *Hindustan* lying offshore sent out a signal at 5 p.m. giving the following ultimatum: "If our demands are not conceded by 6 p.m. today we will open fire on the military." Their chief demand was the withdrawal of the military.

Seven hours after the time of expiry of the ultimatum, there was still no news of any fresh developments in the situation. The "Hindustan" lies in the harbour with all her guns mounted.

In Bombay, beside the shore establishment at Castle Barracks, 25 R.I.N. ships, including Vice-Admiral's flagship "Narbada" joined in the mutiny. In Karachi three ships and all the shore establishments with complements numbering over 1,500 men were involved.

Meanwhile, strong naval, military and air reinforcements are on their way to Bombay, Poona and Karachi, it is announced by the General Headquarters from New Delhi.

NAVAL C.-IN-C.'s WARNING

Govt. Will Not Brook Indiscipline

BOMBAY, Feb 21—The determination of the Government of India not to stop indiscipline in the ranks of the service and never to give in to violence was expressed by Vice-Admiral Godfrey, Flag Officer Commanding, Royal Indian Navy, in a broadcast to the ratings from the Bombay station today.

Vice-Admiral Godfrey warned the ratings: "To realise the struggle is at the height of fury when you take into account the overwhelming forces at the disposal of the Government at this time and which will be used to their utmost even if it means the destruction of the Navy of which we have been so proud.

"In the present regrettable state of indiscipline in the service, I have adopted this means of addressing the R.I.N. as being the way in which I can speak in the greatest number of you at one time.

"To start with, everyone of you must realise that the Government of India has no intention of allowing indiscipline to continue, or their methods to be influenced by threats or intimidation. The Government will use the most stringent methods to restore discipline, using the vast forces at its disposal if necessary. I ask you to bear this in mind in considering the other things which I have to say to you now.

Redress of Grievances

"As regards the troubles made up of those of you who worked on the Flag Officer Bombay, on Tuesday, February 19, you may be assured that all reasonable complaints or grievances, if any, will be fairly investigated. Demobilisation will proceed strictly in accord with the age and service groups, though you must realise that this will mean that the service will lose its trained ratings of experienced ratings, especially in the Communications branch.

"The whole question of pay, travelling allowances, and family allowances...

RUSSIA ADMITS RECEIPT OF SECRET ATOM INFORMATION

'IN CAMERA' INVESTIGATION INTO LEAKAGES

LONDON, Feb 21—Russia acknowledged in an official statement broadcast by Moscow Radio last night that Canadian citizens had given "some information of a confidential character" to the Soviet Military Attache in Ottawa.

The information, the broadcast stated, "could be found in the published works concerning radio location, etc. and also in the well-known American pamphlet 'Atomic Energy.'

"The Soviet Government said considered it necessary to make the statement because the Canadian Government had issued a statement on the subject on February 15...

ATTLEE ORDERS WARSHIPS TO INDIAN PORTS

LONDON, Feb 21—Certain vessels of the Royal Navy are proceeding towards Bombay, said Mr C. R. Attlee, Prime Minister in the House of Commons today after Mr Henderson Stewart (Lib. Nat.) had...

CANADA CONSULTING BRITAIN

OTTAWA, Feb 21—The Prime Minister, Mr Mackenzie King, acting as the dominion Foreign Minister was reported to be in steady consultation with the British Government last night after reports of the Russian...

Karachi Situation | 6-Hour Battle In

SECOND DAK EDITION

The Sunday
Hindusthan Standard

VOL. IX, NO. 143 — CALCUTTA :—FEBRUARY 24, 1946, FALGOON 12, 1352 B. S. — PRICE TWO ANNAS

BRITISH PARATROOPS IN ACTION AT KARACHI

ROYAL ARTILLERY & INDIAN SAILORS EXCHANGE SHELLS

200 KILLED IN BOMBAY BATTLE

SAILORS LAY DOWN ARMS ON SARDAR PATEL'S ADVICE

CONGRESS ASSURANCE TO TAKE UP

NATIONAL HERALD
ARMOURED CARS IN BOMBAY STREETS

MORE FIRINGS BY POLICE AND ARMY

Killed And Over 1,200 Injured

Another Day Of Widespread Disturbances

BOMBAY

SECOND DAK EDITION

Hindusthan Standard

VOL. IX, NO. 147 — CALCUTTA :—THURSDAY, FEBRUARY 28, 1946. FALGOON 16, 1352 B. S. — PRICE TWO ANNAS

NON-VIOLENCE RAISED INDIA FROM SLUMBER OF AGES

GANDHIJI ANALYSES ARUNA'S STATEMENT

STRUGGLE MUST NOT BE PRECIPITATED

NATION LOSES NOTHING BY WAITING ON EVENTS

POONA, FEB. 26.—Mahatma Gandhi in a statement issued today refers to Mrs. Aruna Asaf Ali's refutation of his statement on the happenings in Bombay and declares that she was entitled to say that the people "are not interested in the ethics of violence or non-violence, but the people were very much interested in knowing the way which would bring freedom to the masses".

"Aruna and her comrades," Gandhiji says, "have to ask themselves every time whether non-violent way had or had not raised India from her slumber of ages and created in them a yearning, very vague perhaps, for Swaraj". In Gandhiji's opinion there is only one answer.

Referring to Mrs. Aruna Asaf Ali's statement that she would "rather unite Hindus and Muslims at the barricade than on the constitutional front", Gandhiji says : "The barricade life has always to be followed by the constitutional. That front is not taboo for ever".

Gandhiji adds that "it betrays want of foresight to disbelieve British declarations and precipitate a quarrel in anticipation. Is the official deputation coming to deceive a great nation? It is neither manly or womanly to think so. The nation will gain by trusting. The deceiver loses when there is correct response from the deceived".

Urgency Of Indian Situation

India Secy. To Arrive A Fortnight Earlier

(From Our Political Correspondent)
CALCUTTA, FEB. 26.—I gather from sources just are generally reliable that Lord Pethick-Lawrence, Secretary of State for India, one of the members of the proposed British Cabinet Ministers' Mission to India, is arriving in India about a fortnight earlier than was originally planned, probably by the middle of March.

He is coming ahead of his two other colleagues. This has been arranged, it is stated, in view that Labour Government was made alive to the urgency of the Indian situation and that it was imperative to make an early and serious approach of making the problem. This will also enable the Secretary of State to gain a close study of the situation on the spot, specially after the recent turn of events, and to make soundings in influential political quarters.

NO SUPPRESSION OF NATIONAL SPIRIT

AZAD ON R.I.N. EPISODE

APPEAL FOR RESPONDING TO PUBLIC OPINION

NEW DELHI, FEB. 26.—"India is not in a mood to tolerate any action that may have even the semblance of the suppression of national spirit in any quarter," says Maulana Abul Kalam Azad, the Congress President commenting on the recent happenings in the R.I.N.

Recalling the writing on the wall, Maulana Azad urges for moderation in official measures and says:

"I earnestly appeal to the authorities concerned who seem to be anxious to secure efficient working of the services both during the interim period and in the future to try to see things from the Indian National point of view.

"The Congress President admits that it is true that discipline in the army is a matter of supreme importance.

"But, having regard to the entire chain of happenings in connection with

TRAGIC HAPPENINGS OF 4 DAYS IN BOMBAY

SARDAR PATEL'S STERN WARNING

WRONG LEAD RESULTS IN ANARCHY AND CHAOS

"BEWARE OF EXPLOITERS OF MASS AWAKENING"

BOMBAY, FEB. 26.—A stern warning to the people of India not to be misled by those who attempt to exploit the anti-imperialist feelings and political awakening of the masses and direct them into wrong channels was given by Sardar Vallabhbhai Patel, presiding over a mammoth meeting at Choupathi this evening.

Sardar Patel declared that such a step would lead to complete anarchy and chaos. After three days of complete anarchy in the city which was followed by the military shooting innocent people, it was time for all concerned to do a certain amount of heart-searching over the tragic happenings of the past four days in the city.

"I shall however refrain," continued Sardar, "from plain speaking, as the time for such plain speaking will soon come".

Sardar Patel said that those who committed ghastly crimes during disturbances would not go unpunished. Over 200 persons had lost their lives and over 1,000 had been injured.

BOMBAY COMPLETELY QUIET NOW

Patel & Nehru Go Round Hospitals

BOMBAY, FEB. 26.—Pandit Jawaharlal Nehru and Sardar Vallabhbhai Patel visited all the disturbed areas and the hospitals this morning. This enabled Pandit Nehru to get a first hand impression of the extent of the damage and loss of life and injury to persons caused during the four days disturbances in the city.

Situation in Bombay is completely quiet. A small force of military and police continue to patrol. Tram and bus services have been further extended. All schools, colleges, markets, shops, mills and factories have resumed normal work.

TOLL OF LIFE

What we all this suffering, toll of human life for? I cannot discover why the people should of an uprising against the Government when the Congress had set a call for revolt but we engage peaceful, constructive

CAPT. BURHANUDDIN TO UNDERGO SEVEN YEARS' R. I.

C.-IN-C.'S ACTION ON COURT MARTIAL'S VERDICT :
I. N. A. HERO FLOWN TO UNKNOWN DESTINATION

BOMBAY

Scale of Miles

0   ¼   ½   1   1½

CONTENTS

Charged with slogans of 'Jai Hind' and 'Swaraj is my birthright', young Indians rejoiced the success of Azad Hind Fauj and Netaji Subhas Chandra Bose, who was able to unite the people of India as never before. The trial of INA officers in the Red Fort was a watershed moment, bringing together the Congress, Muslim League and the Communist Party of India.

PROLOGUE
1946: LAST WAR OF INDEPENDENCE

I stumbled onto references to the 1946 Naval Uprising quite by accident. While researching for my book *Gandhi: An Illustrated Biography,* I speed-read all the 98 volumes of *The Complete Works of Mahatma Gandhi* and made my own five-volume selection. In volumes 89 and 90, I came across some statements and letters relating to the Royal Indian Navy (henceforth RIN) mutiny which I took note of, but could not fit into that book. After the draft of the Gandhi book was done, I re-read the RIN mutiny episodes and realized the magnitude of the event. The more I read, the more I was convinced that the courageous actions of these young men deserved a full narrative. I felt there was certainly more to it than what I was reading in passing.

I discovered hundreds of reports made by the British admirals, commanding officers of ships and shore establishments, cables and letters exchanged between London and Delhi, proceedings in the British parliament and debates in the Legislative Council in India. They were honest reports but they portrayed the British side of the story. To represent the Indian side, there were personal memoirs of those directly involved in the mutiny. A high-powered Commission of Enquiry gave opportunity to both sides, British and Indian nationalists, and recorded their testimonies faithfully.

The full report was not made public until well after Independence. Then there were hundreds of newspaper reports, both by British-owned newspapers such as the *Times of India*, the *Statesman,* etc., and nationalistic ones like the *Free Press Journal, Bombay Chronicle, Hindustan Times, Dawn,* etc., reporting the same event differently. For the first few months these papers presented themselves as part of an intricate puzzle.

That jigsaw kept me obsessively absorbed for over five years. Even as it seemed it would solve itself, the arrival of a bunch of papers belonging to Special Branch, Criminal Investigations Department, Bombay, changed the shape of the puzzle again. New slots had to be created in the jigsaw to fit in the latest details as Rishi Dev Puri, Madan Singh, Kusum and P.N. Nair's covert meetings in Flat No. 2, Riviera in Marine Drive, Bombay, made a startling appearance in the police reports. I had to weave these new characters and revelations into the narrative.

Just as dramatic and in the literal sense, even more so, was the entry of the Indian People's Theatre Association (IPTA) whose prominent members like Khwaja Ahmad Abbas, Salil Chowdhury, Pt Ravi Shankar, Balraj Sahni, Ritwik Ghatak, Prithviraj Kapoor, et al, encouraged and supported the ratings and their uprising. I owe sincere thanks to Prof. Deepak Rao and Dr Shekhar Krishnan, who provided the documents that gave me new insight into the inspiring story of these young ratings.

The first book I read about the mutiny was the protagonist, B.C. Dutt's very lucidly written autobiographical account, *Mutiny of the Innocents.* Balai Chand (B.C.) Dutt was then an accounts executive with the leading advertising firm, Lintas. Helping him write the book was an extremely bright young copywriter, Shyam Benegal.

Recalls Shyam, 'Balai was an irrepressible man with strong communist leanings. Highly spirited, he was full of stories about the naval mutiny. He believed more in Netaji Subhas Bose than Mahatma Gandhi. He later turned socialist and became a staunch follower of Ram Manohar Lohia. This led him to dedicate the rest of his life to social causes at the Yusuf Meherally Centre in Panvel.'

Though intelligently written with fine prose, the book as one might expect, presented the perspective of the lead character and underplayed others' contributions and glossed over many details. The author was actually in jail for a critical period just preceding the mutiny, and he also did not have access to much of the material which is now available to researchers.

The links with the Nairs; the use of their flat; the connection with Aruna Asaf Ali; the support Dutt got from the Ex-Services Association, which in turn was supported by IPTA; were less elaborately described.

Rishi Dev Puri (R.D.), Dutt's best buddy (in present terminology his *bestie*), who was his partner in crime when they were writing inflammatory slogans and pasting seditious pamphlets on the walls and dais of HMIS *Talwar* is described only as 'Deb' and not introduced formally as Rishi Dev Puri. Madan Singh, the elected vice president of the Naval Central Strike Committee (NCSC), is introduced to the reader as a disciplined sailor and man of principles, but important details of his active participation in the mutiny are missing.

A popular historical narrative should succeed in making the reader see and feel the prose as moving pictures. It was therefore important for me to walk through and receive a first-hand physical experience of locales such as HMIS *Talwar* and Castle Barracks, now known as the Naval Transport Pool and INS *Angre*, respectively.

I was introduced to Commodore Srikant Kesnur by Commander Anand Khandelwal with whom I became acquainted when he was on deputation to the Ministry of External Affairs. I must thank Anand profusely because Cmde Kesnur became my go-to person for any navy-related query that I was unable to find answers for.

Upon my request, Kesnur also arranged permission to have an extensive tour of INS *Angre*, the dockyard and practically all of Navy

Nagar. Even the gates of areas normally forbidden for civilians were opened for me. This tour helped me immensely in understanding the history and geography of the area where the uprising took place. I was also given permission to visit the Receiving Station (which was HMIS *Akbar* in 1946) in Thane. That also gave me the opportunity to go to Mulund and walk on the grounds where once stood the camp where the mutinous ratings were incarcerated after their surrender. I was fortunate enough to see the last Nissen hut which was specially constructed to hold the prisoners. Not very far from Mulund, was the camp at Kalyan, a harsher place surrounded by barbed wires which looked like a concentration camp. This was where the ringleaders were taken to keep them in isolation. It was indeed an emotional tour, as the agony of the young ratings came alive. I also visited the home of Commander Mohan Narayan, a naval history buff, whose detailed knowledge of the subject was of enormous help. For all this and much more, I remain indebted to Cmde Kesnur, who is now an affable friend.

For a non-fiction narrative of a historical event, research is as crucial as writing. I must admit my bias or partiality is towards the former. I firmly believe that 'if it exists, I can get it'. I set upon searching for the descendants of the main heroes of my story with much zeal and the enthusiasm of a sleuth. Some searches resulted in great revelations, some in disappointments.

Rishi Dev Puri turned out to be the flamboyant uncle of Aroon Purie and Madhu Trehan of *India Today* fame. I got a lot of details about RD's personality traits from them, and I also shared police documents that made Madhu and Aroon believe that the tall tales their uncle told had a solid basis in truth.

They also facilitated my meeting with their cousin Devendra Nath Puri, who was also close to RD, leading to a lot of new material and hitherto unknown facts. Thus, I got some fascinating details of the life and times of RD. My appreciation and thanks to Madhu, Aroon, and Devendra Nath.

A newspaper article published in the mid-1990s provided

a clue that Madan Singh's son-in-law is the director of a well-established and prestigious school in Dalhousie. I called practically every school in that region and then zeroed in on the one being run by a Sikh. I got through to a small school, repeated my request and mentioned that the school I am looking for has a naval mutiny connection. That helped, and the gentleman on the other side gave me the landline number of Dalhousie Public School. This led me to contact Mr Diler Singh, who promised to connect me with Dr G.S. Dhillon, the son-in-law. He became my conduit to Madan Singh's family – daughter Annurag Dhillon and sons, Ranjit Pender, who lives in Spain, and Vijay Pratap Singh, a senior doctor and administrator who lives in Sacramento, California, with Mrs Madan Singh. Through the exchange of emails, FaceTime, and long-distance calls over many months, I recorded several hours of conversation. This exclusive and invaluable personal information helped me to curate the fascinating personality of Sardar Madan Singh. I remain indebted to the family for sharing some of the most extraordinary stories.

Kusum and P.N. Nair's deep involvement in the mutiny was really not known. Their flat in Marine Drive was the hub where the mutiny was largely planned. It was here that young ratings met with Aruna Asaf Ali and members of the Ex-Services Association and the IPTA.

I set about looking for the Nairs with just three pieces of information: 1. *The Army of Occupation*, a book authored by Kusum Nair; 2. Her Bombay address, Riviera Marine Drive; and, 3. the Nairs' address in Jor Bagh, New Delhi, where they had moved in the early 1960s. In one of her obituaries, I discovered her daughter's name, Aruna (she was named after Aruna Asaf Ali).

Aruna, the daughter of the Nairs', was married to Barry Michie, Director International Program support, which included the Fulbright Scholar Program for India, at Kansas State University. I searched online and finally found their son, Chef Chetan Michie on Facebook. He had spent his school years at Woodstock,

Mussoorie, and my own connection with Woodstock helped establish a relationship of trust with the Michies.

A quick message on Messenger connected me to Chetan who introduced me to his father. Over the next six months, some exciting information and stories flowed in. For the first time, it was revealed that the Nairs had plotted to put stones in the dal served in the dinner the night before and thus triggered the mutiny that began the next morning. Though dal with stones was not unusual but that night it was all planned to instigate the ratings to rebel. I owe a big thank you to the Michies. Unfortunately, Aruna did not live to read about her mother. On the morning of 6 September 2021, I read a message, 'My mother, Aruna Nayyar Michie died peacefully. The sun was shining and she left without pain… From being born from parents who participated in the Naval Mutiny in 1946 in India, she rose… not stopping until being a professor of Political Science at Kansas State University… Night mom, I love you.' Chetan Michie.

In 2015 when I started the research, the family and descendants of B.C. Dutt were on top of my list. Through friends in Bombay, I was able to gather that Anusuya Dutt, the widow of BC, was an ace family lawyer practising in Bombay High Court. Through the Bombay lawyers' network, I got to know she lived in a flat opposite the Cricket Club of India in South Bombay. I met her in the presence of her son, Tanuj, for about half an hour with a promise that I could have a longer chat the next day. That was not to be. She was hospitalized the next day. She passed away in 2017. B.C. Dutt pre-deceased her and had passed away in 2009.

Newspapers tend to be good sources for day-to-day accounts of such events. Their authenticity can be checked by reports published in one newspaper against the other. The challenge, in this case, was that while British-owned papers such as the *Times of India* and the *Statesman* gave the imperial interpretation of the happenings, the *Bombay Chronicle*, the *Hindustan Times*, *Amrita Bazaar Patrika*, etc., gave the Indian side of the story.

The British imperial papers played down what could be construed as unfavourable reports towards British while Indian papers fanned the fire. Then there were the Communist-owned and left-leaning papers, such as the *People's Age*, owned by the Communist Party of India and *Blitz* owned by the mercurial left-leaning legend, R.K. Karanjia. His daughter Rita Mehta was of great help in getting copies of *Blitz* published during the fateful days of the mutiny. *Dawn,* founded by M.A. Jinnah and published from Delhi those days, carried pro-Muslim stories mostly, as expected. I was able to get copies of *Dawn* from the British Archives.

One paper that multiplied its circulation exponentially during the mutiny was the *Free Press Journal (FPJ)*, a fiercely nationalistic newspaper that not only devoted all of its front pages to screaming banner headlines during the course of the mutiny and for days after the uprising ended. Under its legendary owner-editor, Swaminathan Sadanand, it was the most vocal and broke anti-British stories not just during the continuance of the mutiny and the resultant riots (18–25 February 1946), but also ran edits and stories for months thereafter.

The British hated the *FPJ* and it was not exactly a favourite with centrist political parties like the Congress and Muslim League either. But it was perceived as the most authentic source for mutiny-related news. It was the go-to newspaper for the ratings themselves and for common citizens of Bombay.

I collected hundreds of issues of various newspapers while researching the book. Obviously, *FPJ,* 18–25 February were the most important dates. I looked for these dates at the Nehru Memorial Library, the National Archives, Maharashtra State Archives and, thanks to the present owner, Abhishek Karnani, I scanned through the archives of the *FPJ* several times.

Alas, I did not find these most important issues anywhere, including in their own archives. I suspect they were removed altogether. I left no stone unturned because I wasn't ready to give up. Finally, after looking high and low, my unending moment of joy came when I found copies across the seas in the National Maritime

Museum, Greenwich, across the Thames in London. Finally, I had the most authentic elucidation of day-to-day accounts.

I made several trips to London, often combining publishing work with visits to the British Library, the National Archive Kew, the Imperial War Museum, the National Army Museum, and the National Maritime Museum, Greenwich.

I will forever remember the help and assistance provided by Peter Day and Andrew Lewis. Both Peter and Andrew were of great help in relaying material from London. Two days before the Caird Room at the Imperial War Museum, which housed the papers of Admiral J.H. Godfrey (FOCRIN India at the time of the mutiny) and his ten-volume unpublished 'Naval Memoirs', was to close for years for renovation, taking these papers out of reach, Peter managed to email a copy of this most useful memoirs. Later of course, I learnt that these papers are also available at the Churchill Archive Centre, Churchill College, Cambridge.

A chance discovery of a file containing desperate cables exchanged between Prime Minister Clement Richard Attlee and Viceroy Lord Archibald Wavell at the height of the mutiny revealed the extent of fright and panic that had set in the British administration.

Indian archives are a rich source for the files relating to the RIN mutiny. The National Archive, Delhi, has hundreds of files on the subject. I would consider this a very valuable resource. I was able to obtain many issues of newspapers from the Nehru Memorial Library at the Teen Murti Bhawan, New Delhi, as well.

In Bombay, Deepti Anand accompanied me during my visit to INS *Angre*, Naval Dockyard, and naval establishments in Thane and Mulund. She also helped me with research and dug out some very useful material from the Maharashtra State Archives, the Asiatic Library, and the Maritime History Society in Bombay.

Commodore Odakkal Johnson was and remains very helpful. He made available some of the lesser-known resources of the Society, which were of immense use.

Conducting research across the border in Pakistan was most interesting. Despite the barricade, I was able to gather considerable material and confirm information. Aitzaz Ahsan, as usual proved to be a most helpful friend, often confirming my credentials to those who did not know me at all.

Through him I was able to connect with Admiral Mian Zahir Shah (retd), who generously allowed me to use portions from his books on Pakistan Navy, regaling me with most interesting anecdotes about how ships were divided between India and Pakistan at the time of Partition. It was not easy to find, or get across from Pakistan, copies of Admiral Shah's books in India. I am indebted to our former high commissioner to Pakistan, TCA Raghavan, for getting photocopies of these books.

Thanks to Aitzaz Ahsan I also made a friendly connection with Ms Turqain Zamaria, daughter of former chairman, Joint Staff Committee, Admiral Mohammad Shariff (1920–2020). This was a case of mistaken identity, when I was looking for the president of the Central Strike Committee, Mohammad Shuaib Khan (both had identical initials, MS). Turqain has been most cordial and helpful since our introduction.

I could pick up the phone and call Ameena Sayid at will, and she always responded with help via her enormous network of contacts. Thanks to her, I was able to connect with Nazish Brohi, a niece of Ali Ahmed Brohi, a rating whose knowledge and articulation of history of French and Russian revolutions while deposing in the Commission of Enquiry impressed me most, and I was keen to include his profile in the book. Thanks to Nazish, I got connected to Dr Muhammad Ali Shaikh, the son-in-law of Ali Ahmed Brohi. Dr Shaikh is a well-known academic and the author of one of the most widely read biographies of Benazir Bhutto. Because of him, I was able to put together an authentic profile of Brohi, a rating I admired most.

Hamid Haroon, an ever-reliable friend in Pakistan, was very supportive with his advice. His encouragement and suggestions from time to time were most useful. I consulted Aslam Khwaja, a leftist historian from Karachi, and borrowed from the pieces he wrote for *Mainstream*. Ahmad Saeed of Saeed Book Bank emailed across portions from the books that were not available here, and I must express my great appreciation for his friendship and help.

Extensive research of this nature has its pitfalls too. Agha Humayun Amin will remain unforgettable for leading me up the garden path. Since he had come to me with a reliable recommendation, I was taken in with his glib promises which continued for over a year. He promised the moon, benefited from false promises and disappeared all of a sudden into thin air, leaving no trace. I would like to believe that I would have traced Mohammad Shuaib Khan who remains elusive if I was not misled by Amin.

Narrating recent history can have its disappointments too. One often regrets not having written the book earlier. The mutiny itself happened in 1946. Most of the main protagonists were still alive until after the turn of the century. Ali Ahmed Brohi passed away in 2003, Madan Singh passed away in 2007, B.C. Dutt passed away in 2009, Rishi Dev Puri passed away in 2014, and Commander King in 2014. It's an exciting thought to have written the book after interviewing them. But that remains wishful thinking.

I was, however, fortunate to have a memorable lunch with the legendary Admiral Manohar Prahlad Awati, an icon of the Indian Navy. His insight into the service conditions at the time still resonates and helped me understand the subject so much better, especially since I was taking baby steps at the time. Admiral and Mrs Kripal Singh also invited me to their home in Gurgaon to one of the most charming lunches I have had in a long time. Besides insights into the RIN, I also gathered that they are the proud parents of celebrated journalist and friend Prabha Chandran.

Talking to both these admirals who were in their nineties, I gathered extensive insight and thought I must have multiple meetings with them, which would have oriented me so much better. Alas, that was not to be. Both sadly passed on during the writing of the book.

The story of my missed meeting with Admiral V.A. Kamath is poignant. I was to meet him on an appointed day. I called on that day to confirm my meeting when I was told that he was not feeling too bright and would like to meet me next week. I was all ready to leave home on that day at the appointed time and made a last-minute call before I left home. His daughter answered the call only to inform me, 'Admiral Kamath passed away yesterday.'

I have experienced many different shades of hopes and despair in the process of putting together the book in the last six years. Being new to the subject has its own thrills; every headline in the newspapers of the time seemed like breaking stories. There were times when I could read through a thousand pages in a week, meticulously colour coding them according to the chapters I had planned.

There were the brightest shades of hope and happiness. Finding material in archives far and wide; bumping into the descendants of the protagonists; making the discovery that Ian Fleming, creator of James Bond, was an assistant to Admiral Godfrey and that the character of 'M' in the James Bond stories was actually based on the admiral himself, were bright spots.

The book went through periods of distress and despair too. Three surgeries, at least one of them life-threatening, set the book back by miles. Getting back into the book was not easy without the support of friends and family.

S. Prasannarajan has always been a big source of encouragement and he is my go-to man when in doubt and whenever I felt the narrative needed course correction. Tony Jesudasan, the ever-dependable friend, read some of the pieces and gave mature advice. Thank you, Prasanna and Tony.

Dilip Bobb, my trusted old friend, took over from where a very able Ashwin Ahmed had left. Dilip's ability to clean up and rewrite is remembered by his colleagues during his days in *India Today*. He can churn out the most lucid prose banging on the typewriter with his eyes closed. Thank you, Dilip for being such a support in times of need. Thanks are also due to another friend, Raju Santhanam, for having offered insightful advice from time to time.

My admiration and sincere thanks to my editor, Devangshu Datta, for making the book reader-friendly through his smart and meticulous editing. It was wonderful working with him. With his gentle and easy handling of the editing process, the book progressed smoothly.

Halfway through the book, the pandemic struck and I had to relocate myself from Delhi to Landour. I met Nita Roy and the illustrious Admiral Vasant Laxman Koppikar AVSM, over lunch at the lovely home of Preeti and Rati Puri. It indeed was a fortuitous meeting for Kiran and me.

We were looking for a homestay in Dehradun to escape the harsh winter and deep snow that we usually experience in our home, St Asaph, in Landour perched 7,500 feet above the sea. The admiral very graciously hosted us for nearly two months in his most extraordinary abode, set in the middle of a large orchard with sightings of barking deer, porcupines, wild boars and rumours of panthers. An admiral's idyllic home proved to be the most appropriate place to write a book relating to naval history. In two months, I managed to write five chapters. Knowledge about ships and their armaments came as a bonus while sitting in comforts in front of a lovely fireplace. At the end of two months, Admiral Koppikar had become Kopi to me. My sincere gratitude to Nita and Kopi.

Landour and Rajpur proved to be the most fitting places to write. Not just for me but for many other writers, the pandemic was the most propitious time to complete the unfinished job. But like the others, I too, had my own share of agony and pain.

I lost three of my close family members within a span of four days, which shut my mind down for months. The book is dedicated to my eldest brother, his wife, and another sister-in-law who treated me with the affection usually reserved for a blood brother. Kiran, my wife, lifted me up when I was down on my knees. I fondly remember all the love and affection given to me by Priya, Diya, Karam, and Kapil. They were my source of renewed energy.

I was greatly assisted by Neelam Narula, the ever-dependable managing editor, for her most useful suggestions and Sneha Pamneja, who designed a very fitting jacket for the book. Lavinia Rao who not just kept track of the manuscript but found portions of the material I would misplace in the long years since I started collecting them. Thanks are also due to our veteran layout experts of many years, Naresh Mondal and Bhagirath, for setting the text in style.

Nonica Dutta found rare books on the subject and most importantly introduced me to Pragya Gautam, who provided invaluable help in collating the database of already researched material and did the fact-checking. She is a very bright young research scholar. I wish her the very best in future. I must also thank Anisha Sehgal and Namrata Sarmah, who assisted me in my initial research.

The endorsements by Dr Ashis Nandy, Shyam Benegal, Dr Rudrangshu Mukherjee and William Dalrymple are great sources for reassurance and encouragement. My endless thanks to them.

I am also grateful to Sidharth Bhatia for reading the manuscript and sharing his valuable suggestions. His feedback is hugely appreciated.

The resilience developed over the years in publishing helped in abundance. I firmly believe, perhaps superstitiously, that suffering foretells success. My aspiration and ambitions for the book continue. Through thick and thin, I have given the subject my best. Hope it meets the expectations of the readers.

Last but everlastingly, I will remain beholden to the celestial inspiration that keeps me going from the first ray of sunrise, as I open my eyes in the morning, to the last light of sunset when I push the shut button of my iPad.

PRAMOD KAPOOR

St Asaph, Landour, November 2021

Huge crowds thronged Minerva theatre in Calcutta where Utpal Dutt's play Kallol, based on the naval mutiny of 1946, was released. The play, first performed in 1965, ran houseful despite press publicity and advertisement blocked by the then Congress government in power in West Bengal.

1946: SHIPS AND SAILORS, REBELLION AND RAJ

On 29 March 1965, a Bengali play by Utpal Dutt, *Kallol* (literally 'commotion' or 'hubbub') hit the boards at the legendary Minerva Theatre, on Beadon Street in North Calcutta. Dutt, a staunch communist, had dramatized the naval mutiny of 1946, taking it upon himself to act the part of Rear-Admiral Sir Arthur Rullion Rattray, Flag Officer Commanding, Bombay, who was one of the villains of the piece. The legendary Tapas Sen was director of lighting and Samir Majumdar, the assistant director.

The play lived up to its name as thousands lined up for tickets, causing pandemonium. Every show was houseful. Majumdar recalls: 'It was one of the finest productions. Utpal Dutt had created a wonder, the ship HMIS *Khyber*, was shown sailing in water on the stage.'

The play was highly critical of the role played by the Congress and the Muslim League, depicting famous politicians as duplicitous, and highlighting their role in persuading the young, nationalistic ratings to surrender. Dutt had deployed his gifts of satire masterfully, ridiculing stalwarts like Pandit Jawaharlal Nehru and Sardar Vallabhbhai Patel.

The Congress under Chief Minister Prafulla Chandra Sen ruled West Bengal at the time, and even twenty years after the actual event, the party tried to stall the production. They did not have the courage to ban it. But there were attempts to disrupt it by throwing bombs and sending goons to prevent people from entering the hall. The Communist Party of India (Marxist), or CPM, countered this by putting a ring of volunteers around the venue to ensure smooth entry.

In his book, *Towards a Revolutionary Theatre,* Dutt later wrote, 'Workers from the factories and students of several colleges took turns to stand guard outside the theatre... Youth Congress strongmen who had come prepared to attack the theatre, beat a hasty retreat seeing the CPM *bandobast.* Comrade Subhash Chakraborty (later sports minister of West Bengal) led the protecting volunteers at Minerva...

'Under pressure from Congress, no newspaper or periodical published news or reviews. The theatre critic of *Ananda Bazar Patrika* (ABP), a pro-Congress paper, bought tickets and smuggled himself in. ABP wove a review centred around one question: Why has the play not been banned immediately? But as the crowds at the box office grew larger and larger, ABP lost its sangfroid and wrote an editorial, calling for a social boycott of the actors and technicians.'

The *Statesman* was the only newspaper that praised the play in its review. It also published a sarcastic opinion piece headlined 'The Mutiny on Beadon Street'. Dutt writes, 'One day, all newspapers excluding the *Statesman,* refused to print our advertisements. That they were acting in concert and under instructions from the Congress bosses and police chiefs was obvious to all.'

To counter the absence of media, CPM volunteers made posters and pasted them across Calcutta. Some of these read in Bengali, '*Apni kon dol ey — jara Kallol dekhechhey na jara Kallol dekheini*' which roughly translates to 'On which team are you, – those who have seen *Kallol* or those who haven't?'

Street corners across Bengal boldly displayed posters saying '*Cholchhe, Cholbe*', – 'Whatever is happening will carry on happening' – in an apparent reference to attempts to stop the play. That slogan has since been used in every, yes every, sort of demonstration in Bengal. *Cholchhe, Cholbe* in Bengal became like *Inquilab Zindabad* elsewhere.

Dutt was arrested in September 1965. He was picked up in a midnight raid and detained without trial in the Presidency Jail. He was only released in March 1966, in an event celebrated with much fanfare and a special performance of the play.

But while the Congress did not succeed in bringing down the curtain on *Kallol*, it did succeed, over the decades, in downplaying mentions of one of the most important and seminal events of the independence struggle. Instead of being enshrined in public memory alongside the Salt March, Jallianwala Bagh, etc., the naval mutiny of 1946 tends to be relegated to just a footnote, except in scholarly works written by historians, for the benefit of other historians.

So, what was the naval mutiny – what was this event, which made the ruling Congress so nervous that it wanted to shut down even fictional references?

In February 1946, ratings – common sailors of the Royal Indian Navy (RIN) – many of whom were veterans of the Second World War, staged a mutiny. These young men, all aged between sixteen and twenty-five, were simmering due to failed promises made at the time of recruitment, horrible living conditions, unpalatable food and abhorrent racial discrimination. They were also politically charged and inspired by the Indian National Army (INA) and thus, hungry to play a part in India's independence movement.

Within 48 hours of the start of the mutiny, 20,000 ratings took over scores of ships and many shore establishments and presented a charter of demands. They were joined by civilians all across India, particularly those in Bombay and Karachi, and by servicemen in the army and air force.

The ratings pulled down the White Ensigns of the Royal

Pamphlets and advertisements to recruit young sailors in the Indian Navy offered 'splendid opportunities'. These were promises and assurances that turned out to be false.

Navy and replaced them with three entwined flags – the tricolour of the Congress, the green of the Muslim League and the red of the Communist party – on every ship and shore establishment they controlled. They declared themselves the *Azad Hindis*, and raised patriotic slogans.

Their demands included the release of all Indian political prisoners and of soldiers who had fought in the Azad Hind Fauj, as well as the withdrawal of Indian troops from places like Indonesia and Egypt, where they had been deployed to suppress uprisings by local independence movements against colonizers. That charter makes it very clear that, apart from legitimate demands related to better service conditions, the ratings were also imbued with nationalistic fervour.

There was a direct connection to the INA trials, which were ongoing at the time. The Second World War ended in August 1945. The subsequent trials of officers and men of the INA, or

Azad Hind Fauj focused attention on their deeds, and the ratings were inspired by these men.

The untimely and unexplained death of the charismatic Netaji Subhas Chandra Bose, who forged the INA, had actually made him a more powerful icon for those who craved independence.

Even the Mahatma, who would never negotiate about his creed of non-violence, issued a public statement at the height of the naval uprising on 23 February 1946: 'The hypnotism of the INA has cast its spell upon us. Netaji's name is one to conjure with. His patriotism is second to none…' This was published prominently in major newspapers and also in Mahatma Gandhi's own periodical, *Harijan*.

The revolt did not last very long. It was put down in a matter of days by the British, who used a combination of brute force and guile. Despite the mutiny being initiated on a footing of non-violence, pitched battles soon erupted in Bombay and Karachi when the British attempted to storm establishments that the ratings controlled. In addition, street battles in Bombay between civilians supporting the ratings and troops extracted a huge toll. The British were forced to call in white troops to conduct these operations because Indian soldiers were reluctant to fire on their comrades.

The politicians of the Congress and the Muslim League did not however, emerge from this episode, with any credit. Sardar Patel and Jinnah helped persuade the ratings to surrender, and the politicians later reneged on their promises to protect the mutineers from punitive action. Only the Communists and some of the Young Turk socialist elements of the Congress backed the revolt.

Although the mutiny ended quickly, the British realized that fateful week in February marked the beginning of the end for their nearly two centuries of rule. After this incident and the INA trials, the British felt they could never again rely on Indian *faujis* to help put down another insurrection.

Documents from British archives make it clear that the ratings' mutiny accelerated the rush towards freedom, and India achieved

Independence just a-year-and-a-half later. In his book, *Last Years of British India*, Michael Edwards, an imperialist historian, says: 'The British had not feared Gandhi the reducer of the violence, they no longer feared Nehru, who was rapidly assuming the lineaments of statesmanship... but the ghost of Subhas Bose like Hamlet's father, walked the battlement of Red Fort and his suddenly amplified figure overawed the conferences that were to lead to independence.'

This was because of 'A complete psychological transformation of the British officers and men of the British armed forces – from being pro-British mercenaries to fiercely militant nationalists.' Edwards concludes that the final, fatal blow to British rule was inflicted by Bose.

Sadly, the role of the young ratings, some of them just teenagers, in bringing about *azadi* has never received appropriate acknowledgement. This momentous event, a revolt by Indian naval personnel which shook the foundations of the empire, was largely edited out of our pre-independence history, and has never been given the importance it deserved.

While 1857 may be called the First War of Independence, the 1946 uprising by naval ratings was the last. In his book *RIN Strike*, Subrata Banerjee writes: 'If the year 1857 marked the beginning of the organized participation of the Indian soldiers in the fight for independence, the year 1946 saw its culmination.'

The role of established Indian politicians during this episode can only be described as inglorious. They actually helped the British put an end to the uprising, despite widespread sympathy for the ratings across the nation.

The Indian National Congress, which had led the freedom movement for over four decades, was unwilling to risk rocking the boat at a time when independence seemed imminent, through non-violence rather than revolt.

As Dr Anirudh Deshpande explains in his book, *Hope and Despair: Mutiny, Rebellion and Death in India, 1946,* 'Who would start, lead, control and end Satyagraha was important to the Gandhian leadership of the Congress. Movements which were not started by the Congress or could not be kept firmly under Congress control were not only discouraged but also actually disowned, condemned and finally left to the mercy of the colonial state.'

Long months of deep research, including interviews, reading the biographies of those involved, lengthy correspondence and conversations with family members of some of the key mutineers, and delving through newspaper archives, back up that conclusion. I also strongly believe that Partition would have been less bloody if the political leaders had tried to build upon the communal unity created by the events of February 1946, instead of ignoring it.

I hope this book will bring to light the sacrifices made by these brave souls, who risked their lives and were then summarily dismissed from service in a spiteful manner. The leaders of the Congress and the Muslim League persuaded the ratings to surrender at a time when they were prepared to battle on. The promises Indian leaders made while asking the ratings to surrender were never kept. Instead, they were literally left on the streets with no money and no future.

Even more telling was the fact that after Independence, successive Congress governments in India and Muslim League governments in Pakistan refused to re-employ these men in the services, or even to acknowledge them as freedom fighters. Every effort was made to blot out the memory of the mutiny post-Independence. Even two decades later, plays like *Kallol* faced obstruction and unofficial censorship.

The military historian Ronald Spector, who teaches at George Washington University, says, 'Few aspects of the Indian struggle for independence have attracted as much controversy (and as little historical research) as the Royal Indian Navy strike of 1946.'

In *The Almost Revolution, Essays in honor of S.C. Sarkar*, leftist historian Gautam Chattopadhyay says, 'Had the leaders wanted it, they could have had a revolution. The division of the country could have been averted, but the leaders of the Congress and the

Muslim League turned a blind eye to the Hindu-Muslim unity created in the course of this struggle.'

The British, who were usually past-masters at 'Divide and rule', seriously erred in conducting the open trial of Prem Kumar Sahgal, Shahnawaz Khan, and Gurbaksh Singh Dhillon – three stalwart officers of the INA. All three had been commissioned into the Indian Army, and then opted to join the INA. At the time of their surrender, Khan held the rank of major general, commanding an INA division, while Dhillon and Sahgal were colonels.

Putting a Hindu, a Muslim and a Sikh jointly on trial at the Red Fort, Delhi, at a time when most Indians were already deeply sympathetic to the INA meant that three major communities stood unitedly behind the call for Independence.

The trial led to an uproar. According to Sumit Sarkar in *Modern India 1885–1947*: 'Very foolishly, the British initially decided to hold the public trial of several hundreds of the 20,000 INA prisoners, as well as dismissing from service and detaining without trial, no less than 7,000. They compounded the folly by holding the first trial in the Red Fort, Delhi, in November 1945, and putting in the dock together a Hindu, a Muslim and a Sikh.' Unwittingly, at the street level the British united them.

Most of the Congress leadership had been imprisoned since the Quit India movement of 1942 and released only after the end of the war. They rallied to protect the soldiers of the INA. Jawaharlal Nehru donned his black robes after years, and a defence committee headed by a legal luminary, Tej Bahadur Sapru, appeared on behalf of the INA. This support of the soldiers by the top political leadership also encouraged the nationalistic fervour of the ratings.

An Intelligence Bureau (IB) note dated 20 November 1945 admitted that 'there has seldom been a matter which has attracted so much Indian public interest.' Journalist B. Shiva Rao, interviewed the Red Fort prisoners and reported that 'There is not the slightest feeling among them of Hindu and Muslim.'

The mutineers too were equally united across religions, ironically due to the miserable conditions in which they were quartered. Their meals presented a perfectly secular picture. Irrespective of religion, caste, creed or class, they had to circle around a huge round wooden vessel, which was filled with watery, stone-infested dal. They were doled out coarse rotis, which they would dip into this communal vessel.

B.C. Dutt, one of the protagonists of the mutiny says, 'The cook lent us an aluminium mug from which all of us drank water. The first meal removed at one stroke the barriers from which the society we came from suffers.'

They were not Hindu, Muslim or Sikh; they were brothers-in-arms. The force was truly secular and it would stand unitedly for the religious rights of one another against the foul-mouthed, tyrannical British officers. It's worth noting that a Hindu-majority force chose a Muslim, Mohammad Shuaib (M.S.) Khan, to head the Strike Committee.

Gandhiji in an obvious reference to the united revolt, condemned what he called 'The unholy combination of Hindus and Moslems for a violent purpose'. 'I might have understood it if they had combined from top to bottom. That would, of course, have meant delivering India over to the rabble. I would not want to live up to 125 to witness that consummation. I would rather perish in the flames,' he wrote in *Harijan* on 7 April 1946.

Belying the old adage 'history is written by the winner', the history, in this case was never allowed to be written in detail. The ratings found themselves trapped between two sets of rulers: one hoping to leave with their reputation and discipline intact, and the other in a tearing hurry to take over the reins of governance. Recording this event in all its dimensions for posterity was not in the interest of either.

Yet, despite the attempts to wipe it out of public memory, many historians believe that this mutiny was actually the decisive event – the final straw that convinced the British it was time to leave India.

The revolt had its roots in the deceitful manner in which the ratings were recruited and treated. But it morphed into much more. The Second World War led to a rapid mobilization of the armed forces. As in the First World War, India was the most fertile ground for recruitment.

From 3 September 1939, when hostilities began with Germany, to Victory over Japan Day on 15 August 1945, when the war officially ended, the strength of the Royal Indian Navy grew from 40 boats to 132, and from 1,700 sailors to 27,000.

Recruitment ads were plastered across massive billboards and thousands of pamphlets were distributed across India promising a dream life in the navy. In their very first day in a barrack, new recruits learnt how utterly false the advertising was.

Attracted to the Royal Indian Navy by grand-sounding advertisements, they felt hopelessly let down once they boarded ships and shore establishments since the realities were starkly different. The ratings lived in wretched overcrowded barracks, experienced racial abuse, ate unpalatable food, and took orders from foul-mouthed white officers. They had been promised long careers and permanent employment. But by 1946, it was clear that many of them would soon be demobilized, receiving only a pittance.

While the RIN gave a good account of itself during the war, by 1946, the ratings could hardly remain unaffected by the growing chorus for freedom. Their nationalistic sentiments surfaced as is evident from their charter of demands. The nationwide support for the INA enhanced the nationalistic determination of the ratings. They knew public sympathy for them had been eroded due to their participation in the Second World War on behalf of the British. There was a common perception that they were traitors or servants of the British who would never support the freedom movement, and they were very strongly motivated to prove this perception wrong.

The exact timing of the naval revolt was the result of a

combination of factors, but given the tinderbox conditions of the subcontinent, something like it was bound to happen sometime. Anger at racial discrimination and wretched service conditions had been simmering. The passion to free the motherland from tyrannical foreign rule had also taken hold as the INA trials progressed.

The fuse was lit. The explosion came on Monday, 18 February 1946, when the ratings from signal school HMIS *Talwar*, ignoring the sound of the morning pipe, struck work. The signal ratings ensured that the morse coded message reached across all naval establishments in India and beyond. News of the rebellion soon reached the common man. Sumit Sarkar in *Modern India* says: 'The afternoon of 20 February saw remarkable scenes of fraternisation, with crowds bringing food for the striking ratings to the Gateway of India and shopkeepers inviting them to take whatever they needed.'

Congress rebel Aruna Asaf Ali saluted the ratings for refusing to 'submit sheepishly to the hectoring and swearing of their British rulers'. Hailing the courage of the young ratings, she said, 'It was a welcome sign that Indian people had plucked up enough courage to face bullets from machine guns... there was a time when our people shuddered at lathi blows but those days were of the past.'

The mutiny started in *Talwar*, a signal school located in Colaba, Bombay and soon escalated to involve 78 ships, 21 shore establishments, and over 20,000 ratings. In less than 48 hours, it completely crippled one of the most formidable navies of the Second World War. Naval ships were taken over, armouries broken open and officers, British and Indian, ordered to leave their posts. Even the flagship of the Flag Officer Commanding RIN, Admiral John Henry Godfrey's, was taken over and converted into a control centre. The Union Jack and the White Ensign of the Royal Navy were pulled down and replaced with the tricolour of the Congress, the green flag of the Muslim League, and the red of the Communist Party.

When the British made a show of force, and threatened the ratings with low-level sorties by fighter aircraft, the ratings retaliated by training their ships' guns on iconic Bombay landmarks, such as the Yacht Club, the Naval Dockyard, and the Gateway of India, with the warning that these would be blown up if the action escalated.

★ ★ ★

This explosion threatened to engulf all three arms of the defence forces and the world was also watching this colossal revolt. It had all the elements necessary to administer a final push towards toppling the Raj.

As the British scrambled to douse the flames, they felt trepidation that this could turn into a repetition of 1857. And, unlike in 1857, public awareness, and aspirations for Independence were significantly more widespread and intense by 1946.

Gautam Chattopadhyay claims: 'Three days later, Sir Claude Auchinleck, C-in-C of Indian armed forces sent a desperate secret warning to PM Attlee: "We may be faced with complete rebellion, supported by the whole of the Indian armed Forces".'

In 1946, the Indian defence forces had more men in uniforms than Britain itself and all three arms contained battle-hardened veterans of the Second World War, led by an experienced officer cadre. The INA experience also indicated there were no guarantees the officers would hold to their oaths of allegiance to the British monarch.

The ratings' mutiny found allies in the air force and was threatening to spread to the army. Soldiers from the army had made contact on several occasions with the leaders of the ratings and Mahratta, Garhwali and Gurkha troops had all proved reluctant to fire on the ratings.

Barely 24 hours into the mutiny, the British hustled to announce a Cabinet Mission which was to travel to India and discuss the transfer of power with Indian stakeholders. This was announced by Prime Minister Attlee in the British Parliament on the very day he received news of the naval mutiny.

The high-powered mission included A.V. Alexander, the First Lord of the Admiralty as a member, as well as Lord Pethick-Lawrence, secretary of state for India. It was to be led by Sir Stafford Cripps, president of the Board of Trade, and an old India hand.

As the British pressed the panic button, cables flew between the viceroy's office in Delhi and the prime minister's office in Westminster. The desperation and anxiety was evident as different government departments blamed each other for tardy responses.

A weekly intelligence summary on 25 March 1946 admitted that units of the Indian army, navy and air force were no longer trustworthy, and for the army 'only day to day estimates of steadiness could be made'. If it came to the crunch where wide-scale public unrest took shape, the armed forces could not be relied upon to support counter-insurgency operations as they had, during the 'Quit India' movement of 1942. The mutiny was therefore deemed as a 'point of no return'.

The fire was fanned by screaming media headlines across the globe. The UK's *Daily Mail* said: 'INDIAN NAVY MUTINY: HAUL DOWN OUR ENSIGN', while London's *Daily Telegraph* followed suit with 'NAVY RATINGS ATTACK BRITISH IN BOMBAY.' The *Manchester Guardian* carried a front-page banner headline: 'INDIAN MUTINEERS SEIZE SHIPS.' The *New York Times*, had a front-page banner, 'BOMBAY SWEPT BY FLAMES—59 DEAD REPORTED—FIRES RAKE BOMBAY'.

General Shahnawaz issued a public statement that 'We, the INA people, were coming to help the naval mutineers.' The pro-British *Times of India* called the mutiny the 'Result of the extravagant glorification of the INA following the trials in Delhi'. Historians generally agree that the ratings were responding to the temper of the times. The urgent desire for freedom, according to S. Gopal, author of Nehru's three-volume biography, 'had finally penetrated even the British created armed forces... the event demonstrates... that the iron wall that the Britishers created between the Indian army and the Indian people had collapsed...'

★ ★ ★

Sadly, the Indian political leadership, namely the Congress and Muslim League, were hobbled by their own personal aspirations and egos, and opted to negotiate a peaceful transfer of power rather than backing the mutineers. After years of continuous conflict, the British, the Congress and the League found themselves on the same side trying to diffuse the mutiny purely out of self-interest.

Only the Communists backed the ratings and their call for a Bombay strike in support of the naval ratings saw nearly 300,000 mill workers, students, members of transport and unions take to the streets to stage violent anti-British protests. For the Communists, the uprising was a rare opportunity to emerge from the shadows of the Congress and Muslim League and to expand their base. It was also a way to make up for the lost time and regain some power by organizing bloody anti-British demonstrations in support of the ratings.

A few weeks after the mutineers were persuaded to surrender, an extract from a New Scotland Yard Report No. 319, dated 13 March 1946 comments on Rajani Palme Dutt, the Communist ideologue, who lived in London: 'Secret... R Palme Dutt states that the present events in India are a warning signal to the people of Britain. The strike of Indian Naval ratings, which began as a protest against indefensible discrimination, is only part of the nationwide revolt against the British rule and the condition it has brought about. The Indian people are united in their support of the Naval ratings...'

Prof. Bhagwan Josh, a Communist turned Gandhian in an interview to the author said, 'Innocent and inspired people make fantastic material to be misused.' The Communists viewed the naval mutiny as an opportunity to drive Indian independence in a more revolutionary direction, which is why they called for a Bombay-wide *hartal* in support of the mutineers. This eventually took a violent turn.

With over three lakh protestors on the streets, the British panicked and ordered armoured cars onto the streets of Bombay to crush public support for the ratings, which had turned violently anti-British. As a consequence, nearly 400 people were killed and over 1,500 wounded over two days of mayhem and street-fighting. A cyclostyled leaflet written in Hindi found at Victoria Terminus on 25 February called upon Indians to 'Kill every white man… take his weapons and his life… When we, Hindus and Muslims, are fighting together for the freedom of our motherland, there is no power on earth that will stop us from achieving the same. Today on our side are the Navy, Air Force… either perish yourself or abolish slavery. Jai Mazdoor. Jai Hind.' Such anonymous pamphlets were taken very seriously by the British.

The initial response came from a familiar playbook – use force to crush any uprising. The commander-in-chief of the army in India, Field-Marshal Sir Claude Auchinleck, after hurried consultations with the Viceroy Lord Wavell and PM Attlee, ordered the warship HMS *Glasgow* to sail full steam ahead from Trincomalee to Bombay to crush the rebellion.

Admiral Godfrey, chief of the navy in India, threatened the destruction of the Indian Navy and ordered several low flying sorties by fighters over the Bombay Dock area as a warning. The supply of water and food to the barracks was cut off. Agitating sailors were fired upon by British soldiers after Mahratta and Garhwali soldiers refused to open fire on their brothers.

The panic in the British high command escalated as the initial efforts to crush the rebellion by force, failed. Admiral Godfrey had worked closely with Winston Churchill. He had an impeccable reputation as one of Britain's finest diplomats and strategists. But he was forced to retire prematurely due to his perceived blunders in handling the uprising.

Rebellious Indian sailors supported by the common man were on the cusp of something that had the potential to change the narrative. All they needed and asked for, was leadership and directions from the political class. That was not to be.

Yet, this momentous event does not find the place it deserves in the history of the freedom movement.

★ ★ ★

Rakesh Krishnan Simha, in the article 'The Forgotten Mutiny that Shook the British Empire', quotes from a dispatch dated 22 March 1946 to King George VI from Viceroy Lord Wavell. 'The last three months have been anxious and depressing. They have been marked by the continuous and unbridled abuse of the government, of the British, of officials and police, in political speeches in practically the whole of the press, and in the assembly; by serious rioting in Bombay; by a mutiny in the RIN, much indiscipline in the RIAF, some unrest in the Indian army... by a general sense of insecurity and lawlessness. It is a sorry tale of misfortune and of folly...'

Sir Stafford Cripps in 1947, speaking in the House of Commons during the debate to grant independence to India, described the alarming situation. 'The Indian Army in India is not obeying the British officers... in these conditions if we have to rule India for a long time, we have to keep a permanent British army for a long time in a vast country of four hundred millions. We have no such army...'

His fears were responded to in India by the parliamentarian Minoo Masani in an emergency session of the Central Assembly. Pointing towards the British members, Masani loudly declared: 'I make an appeal to you to go while there is still an army, a navy and an air force in this country intact. And the sooner you go, the better for this country...' His, unfortunately, was a minority political voice in support of the ratings.

Outside the Assembly, only younger Congress workers like Jayaprakash Narayan, Ram Manohar Lohia, Acharya Narendra Dev and, most importantly, Aruna Asaf Ali, were willing to back the ratings. Most of the leaders of the Congress and Muslim League were as alarmed as the Britishers.

Differences between Aruna Asaf Ali, the firebrand socialist radical, and Gandhi surfaced during that fateful February. Aruna had spent four years underground with a price on her head running an underground radio station, after raising the flag at Gowalia Tank Maidan in August 1942. She had offered covert encouragement and guidance for several months to the ratings.

Meanwhile, sticking to his creed of non-violence, Gandhi denounced the rebels. He and Aruna argued bitterly in public, and their spat was splashed across the front pages of prominent newspapers.

Other differences and ego clashes surfaced between Sardar Patel and Nehru. Patel was infuriated when he heard about Nehru's arrival in Bombay to intervene on behalf of the rebels. He dashed off a letter to Gandhi which read: 'I advised him [Jawaharlal Nehru] not to come. Yet he is reaching here… the fact that he comes here on account of Aruna's telegram is sorrowful indeed!' Nehru was finally persuaded by Patel not to meet the ratings.

Gandhi's was the voice that mattered most and he came out most vocally against the ratings. He issued a number of statements against them. 'In resorting to mutiny they were badly advised… if they mutinied for freedom of India, they were doubly wrong… they were thoughtless and ignorant if they believed that by their might they would deliver India from foreign domination.'

His criticism was echoed by Patel, the most prominent Congress leader, who condemned the ratings' revolt, terming it 'nothing but hooliganism', adding 'the ship of freedom was coming close to the shore of India; people should not go out and sink it'.

On behalf of the Muslim League, Jinnah also advised the ratings to surrender. Hence, Patel, helped incongruously by Jinnah, managed to persuade the ratings to surrender on 23 February, giving an assurance that national parties would prevent any victimization – a promise he had no authority to give, nor the power to deliver upon. Nor was it kept.

Both Patel and Nehru while persuading the ratings to surrender assured them that no one would be victimized. When the president of the Strike Committee, M.S. Khan asked Patel to give an assurance in writing, Patel flared up, saying: 'When you don't trust my words, how can you trust my writing? I assure you on behalf of the Indian National Congress that not a single one of you will be victimised.'

However, Patel or for that matter, Jinnah and other political leaders, who had advised ratings to surrender promising that no victimization would take place, did not keep their promises. It was at the time, beyond their power. It is also worth noting that they did not try to make amends to the victimized mutineers even post-Independence.

In a letter to Andhra Pradesh leader Vishwanathan on 1 March, Patel wrote: 'Discipline in the army cannot be tampered with.' Eventually, the Congress, by not supporting the direct action on the streets of Bombay, lost the opportunity to unite Hindus and Muslims on one platform. It was a golden opportunity and perhaps the Partition that followed eighteen months later, would have been less bloody if the Congress had backed that show of communal unity against the foreign rulers.

Chris Madsen in an article titled 'British Officers and Striking Sailors: Mutiny in the Royal Indian Navy, February 1946', writes about Sardar Patel, who 'called upon sailors to surrender and promised Khan that there would be "no victimisation" of mutiny participants. With British warships menacingly arriving in force, Indian sailors prudently choose life over martyrdom'.

Madsen confirms that 523 sailors were summarily tried, and most were discharged with disgrace from the RIN as 'undesirable elements'. They were first incarcerated in a make-shift barbed-wired concentration camp in Mulund, in inhuman conditions. After summary trials and imprisonment, they were escorted to Kalyan railway station, given one-way third-class tickets to their homes and warned never to show their faces again in Bombay.

Young as they were, the ratings had entered the fight for independence with naive expectations. Eventually, when they became fully aware that the two major political parties, the Congress and Muslim League, were not with them, the ratings held a night-long meeting racked by anger, disagreements, words of heroism, and fearlessness. They wept like children, hugged one another, and finally agreed to surrender.

This suited the British who would rather sit at the negotiating table with political leaders they understood, than indulge in a display of open force, which risked uniting the three arms of the defence forces and the common people against them in a backlash. The British, the Muslim League and the Congress therefore, found common cause in helping to suppress the mutiny. The Muslim League wanted a separate Muslim state post-Independence and they could not risk supporting an open confrontation with the British with whom they, like Congress, were negotiating to find a peaceful common solution.

For both parties, the announcement of the Cabinet Mission to discuss the transfer of power was much more critical than a rebellion that could rock the boat. As one rating bitterly remarked: 'By then the political class was busy distributing cabinet berths among themselves'.

The sense that a transfer of power was imminent led the political leadership to adopt a conciliatory attitude with respect to the British. Dr M.R. Jaykar, prominent Congress leader and renowned lawyer, in a private letter to Tej Bahadur Sapru wrote: 'I often feel surprised at the wonderful change which has come over these big Congressmen. No hartals, no meetings, no processions, no closing of schools, no defiance… even the Mahatma now says that it is foolish to distrust the intentions of the British.'

The Congress and the Muslim League could sense public sympathy was with the ratings but the fear of upsetting the negotiations with the British meant they could not support the uprising openly. In his paper, 'The Royal Indian Navy Mutiny of 1946', John M. Meyer, of the University of Texas, wrote: 'Congress therefore in collaboration with Britishers made the ratings surrender.'

Subsequently, despite the enormity of such an event, the naval strike was dismissed in a few lines in the formal history of the Indian Navy and it is hardly a footnote in the standard textbooks. It was simply edited out of the history of the freedom movement and not allowed to become part of the national consciousness.

One striking element of the mutiny was that Indian naval officers did not, or perhaps could not, back the ratings and they stayed loyal to the Royal Indian Navy. As disciplined officers trained in unwavering allegiance and resolute faithfulness, it would perhaps, be unfair to expect them to betray their pledge and their basic training in order to support those who were resisting their superior officers.

Yet, their devotion to their country remained beyond reproach. They were simply fulfilling their oaths of commission and carrying on their duty. Many of them turned out to be brilliant officers who took the Indian Navy post-Independence to new heights and success, performing great deeds in the 1971 war. They are remembered fondly within the navy.

Rear Admiral Sadashiv Ganesh Karmarkar is a fine example. In 1945–46, he lived in the same navy complex where the conspirators met with Aruna Asaf Ali and planned the revolt. He spent months before the mutiny noting down their movements as was detailed in the Commission of Enquiry. But he also dedicatedly served the Indian Navy after Independence and rose to high rank due to his professional excellence.

Ronald Spector, a scholar with the U.S. Army Center of Military History says, 'The Indian commissioned officers of the navy, although themselves the victim of racism and discrimination, failed to make common cause with the ratings or provide them with effective leadership.' Adds Andrew Davies, British naval historian and author: 'The sailors of the RIN were neither wholly revolutionary, nor wholly obeisant.' I remember my conversation with the late Admiral Kripal Singh, who said: 'Indian officers were treated by the British differently in Britain but in India they always treated us with a sense of superiority.'

Ironically, after Pakistan and India obtained freedom on 14/15 August respectively, both countries opted to ask British admirals to continue heading their respective navies. Between 1947–1958, the Indian Navy was headed by four successive admirals of British nationality. The first Indian chief, Admiral Ram Das Katari took charge only in April 1958. The Pakistan Navy was also headed by a British admiral until 1953. That continuing relationship between the British and Indo-Pak navies may have also led the political class to distance themselves from showing sympathy, and reinstating the ratings who rebelled.

* * *

Despite the disdain shown by the political class, the ratings were openly supported by the common man and by the intelligentsia. Creative groups, largely left-leaning, aligned themselves openly with the strikers. Despite the official disapproval, echoes of the mutiny seeped into literature, art, and culture.

The Indian People's Theatre Association or IPTA had been formed in 1943, three years before the naval uprising. The IPTA was at the forefront of communicating the spirit of freedom through its cultural prism. The founding members included Utpal Dutt, Khwaja Ahmad Abbas, Balraj Sahni, Pt Ravi Shankar, Ritwik Ghatak, Salil Chowdhury, and Prithviraj Kapoor.

They not only supported the Ex-Services Association as a group but also lent their individual voices in support of the mutiny. In Karachi, A.K. Hangal was arrested for protesting against firing on the sailors. The famous artist Chittaprosad (whose painting is used as the cover of this book) displayed his paintings at a rally supporting the strikers. His ink drawings and prints on the mutiny were profusely used by the Communist Party paper, the *People's Age*.

Salil Chowdhury's *Dheu utchchhe, kara tutchhe* ('The waves of freedom are rising. The shackles of bondage and slavery are starting to crack'), the song written in July 1946, barely four months after the mutiny, resonates even 75 years later.

One of the most poignant episodes during the naval uprising was the sight of ratings with their heads covered in white shrouds after taking control of the ship HMIS *Kathiawar*, and reciting Josh Malihabadi's famous lines:

> *Kaam hai mera taghyur, naam hai mera shabab,*
> *Mera Naara, Inquilab, Inquilab, Inquilab…*
> (My mission is change, My name is youthfulness…
> My slogan is *Revolution, Revolution, Revolution)*

Sahir Ludhianvi also wrote powerful verses about the uprising.

> *Yeh jalte hue ghar kiske hain, yeh kat te hue tan kiske hain,*
> *Takseem ke andhe toofan mein, Lut te hue gulshan kiske hain,*
> *Badbakht phizayen kiski hain, barbad nashe man kiske hain,*
> *Kuchh ham bhi sune, humko bhi suna, Ye rahkar-e-mulk-o-kaum bata,*
> *Yeh kiska lahu hai kaun mara.*
> *Woh kaun sa jazba tha jis se, Farsuda-e-Nizame jeest hila,*
> *Jhulse hue veeran gulshan mein, ek aas ummeed ka phool khila,*
> *janata ka lahoo faujon se mila. Faujon ka lahu janata se mila.*

> What passion it was that made a moth–eaten system quiver
> What passion it was that caused a flower of hope to bloom in this
> dreary desiccated land

What passion it was that mingled the blood of people with the armies, the blood of armies with the masses.

The naval mutiny is also referenced in *Bhowani Junction*, a famous novel later turned into a multi-starrer movie, written by John Masters, a British Indian army officer. Salman Rushdie, in his novel *The Moor's Last Sigh* also devoted a large chunk to the mutiny. Amitava Ghosh's *Glass Palace* wonderfully details how young sons of peasants joined the navy at the beginning of the Second World War and then rebelled.

Utpal Dutt was so proud of the play, he named his home Kallol. The play ran for a record 850 shows. According to Samik Bandhopadhyay, a close associate and friend of Dutt, 'A massive rally was held at the *Maidan* (after he was released). A special stage was set up to show a truncated version of *Kallol*.' Jyoti Basu, Harkishen Singh Surjeet, B. T. Ranadive were present at the performance. The day was called the Kallol Vijay Utsav.

Two massive performances in the most extraordinary settings were produced after Utpal Dutt's death in 1993. An offshore set, which moved with the waves, was specially fabricated on the River Hooghly. Then in November 2005, over 50,000 people watched the play in Salt Lake Stadium, Calcutta. The stage resounded with cries of 'NO SURRENDER' every time it was staged.

★ ★ ★

The tragic epilogue to the mutiny was that the ratings who participated in the revolt were sent home with a third-class one-way ticket, and their salary dues were docked. They were escorted onto trains with the warning: Do not enter Bombay again.

They were out on the streets and got no support from the government even after Independence. Ratings who had approached the government hoping for reinstatement were curtly informed: 'Government of India has carefully considered… but regret their inability to reinstate in the armed forces, those personnel who were discharged or dismissed.'

A letter written to Nehru by one of the strike leaders bemoaned the fact that he had received no response, adding: 'If there is any law for those who have been dismissed for taking part in the freedom movement of the country that they cannot enter into their respective services, then I must ask you to explain why yourself being a leader of the Congress, a political party, should have the post of Prime Minister'.

The ultimate irony, as Masden wrote, was that 'Some Naval officers were censured for their conduct during the mutiny, but a court-martial acquitted Commander King charged of using the bad language that induced the mutiny.' That is truly shocking, considering the enormity of the events his abuse triggered and its context in the Independence Movement.

Weeks after the surrender, a Commission of Enquiry was announced, headed by Justice Fazl Ali, then Chief Justice of Patna High Court (he later became Chief Justice of India [CJI]) to look into the mutiny and its causes. It examined 229 witnesses.

Three months after the last hearing on 19 July 1946, the commission submitted a report to the government. It was ready for publication by 22 October, but it was not released to the press until 20 January 1947. It is not clear if the full report was ever released.

The 598 pages in the public domain catalogued numerous problems with the service conditions, administration and discipline in the over-expanded RIN. The report concluded: 'that sufficient evidence existed to support the claims of striking sailors about deplorable conditions and unfair treatment... the basic cause of the mutiny in the commission's opinion is the widespread discontent among the naval ratings arising primarily from a number of unredressed grievances, aggravated by the political situation.'

It was only in 1973 that the government granted freedom fighter status and pensions to those sailors discharged by the RIN after the mutiny. It was clearly a case of too little, too late. It was indeed India's forgotten mutiny. Sadly, this heroic saga is today just a footnote in our history and unknown to most Indians. A monument erected for these brave hearts at Colaba in Mumbai stands in mute testimony to their forgotten valour. Very few of the millions driving past this monument every day know what the memorial stands for.

B.C. Dutt wrote, 'The aftermath of a revolution is determined by the enormity of the change affected by it. The Indian revolution is itself an example, for despite the presence and influence of Mahatma Gandhi, blood did spill.'

The change, in this case, was that the British finally started to pack their bags. Independence came barely eighteen months later.

A shore-based logistics and support establishment of the Western Naval Command, INS Angre, is named after the bravest Maratha admiral ever, Kanhoji Angre. (Inset): Kanhoji Angre (1669–1729), admiral of the Maratha navy is believed to have never lost a sea battle and was a terror for European ships entering Indian waters.

NAVAL CLASHES: INDIAN PROWESS AT SEA

'*Jalaim Jasya, Valaim Tasya*' (He who rules the sea is all powerful.) This quote, which may be apocryphal is attributed to the great Maratha ruler Shivaji Maharaj (1630–1680). It is said to be a maxim he believed in.

In the mid-seventeenth century, as the Portuguese ranged up and down the Konkan coast, the warrior king set up the Maratha navy in 1654 and he established several naval bases along the Konkan to counter the Europeans.

By 1667, the Maratha navy had become a formidable force commanded by great admirals. One of them was Tukoji Angre, who commanded the Maratha fleet until 1689.

Tukoji was the founder of the imposing 'autonomous warrior-administrators' family of Angres. His brilliant son, the legendary Kanhoji Angre and his descendants practically controlled the Konkan waters until the mid-eighteenth century.

By the time of Shivaji's coronation on 6 June 1674, the strength of the Maratha navy consisted of around 5,000 men and fifty-seven warships. It operated out of the marine bases he had constructed all along the coast. Realizing the threat to their control over the Indian Ocean, the Portuguese sought to wrest control of the seas from the Marathas but met with little success.

The Portuguese were aided by the Siddis, a community descended from East African slaves imported to serve the Deccan sultanates. In time, the Siddis, with help from the Mughals, had become a naval power with their headquarters on the island fortress of Janjira off the coast of Raigad.

The latter part of the seventeenth century was a period of instability and political disorder with Janjira playing a major role. The Siddis and the Marathas continuously fought each other in order to acquire and hold the island.

The conflict between the Siddis and Marathas existed before Shivaji began a campaign to conquer Janjira. It was after taking control of Kalyan, Bhiwandi, Mahuli, Panvel, etc., that Shivaji came into direct conflict with the Siddis.

In the tussle between the Siddis and Shivaji, the former managed to garner allies and sympathizers like the Mughals, the English, and the Portuguese. Though the Europeans officially remained neutral towards the Marathas, they secretly helped the Siddis and some other feudal lords in order to restrain the naval activities of Shivaji.

The Maratha success at sea owed much to the ability of one of India's greatest naval warriors. Till his last breath, Kanhoji Angre (1669–1729) displayed the bravery, zeal and cunning needed to keep the Dutch, the British, and the Portuguese at bay. 'Kanhoji remained the quasi-independent Admiral of the Maratha Navy till his death in 1729,' says Anirudh Deshpande in his recently published book *The Rise and Fall of Brown Water Navy*.

It was under the tutelage of his father, Tukoji, that Kanhoji learnt the art of naval warfare. Thanks to the Angres, the Marathas dominated the Western Sea despite powerful adversaries such as the Siddis of Janjira, the Portuguese at Goa, the Dutch at Vengurla and, most significantly, the English.

Early on, Kanhoji Angre was dismissed in disparaging terms by the British. They called him 'a robber on land and pirate on the seas'. But he soon began to be acknowledged as a formidable naval tactician. His guile and his prowess at crafting brilliant counter-strategies made his fleet of fast-moving, smaller ships more than a match for huge, lumbering foreign ships.

Angre's tactics were simple but brilliant – surround big ships with fast-moving dhows and unleash a lethal attack from all sides with fireballs launched with unmatched accuracy at a stupefied, trapped enemy. Given the title of 'Grand Admiral', Angre's flotillas of ships ruled the seas from Surat along the Konkan coast, wreaking havoc on all colonial ships including the Dutch, Portuguese, and English.

Thanks to his expertise at sea, his fleet which began with just eight to ten galbats – small, fast-moving, warships – increased to forty galbats over a period of time.

Such was Angre's mastery that even many British historians rank him ahead of the British in the naval engagements of his time. The 'chief of the pirates' defeated the English, Portuguese and Siddis and remained undefeated until his death. He was appointed Sarkhel or Darya-Sarang (admiral), head of the Maratha navy in 1698.

The fear he caused amongst European fleets made the British send an armed squadron to protect their trade ships at an additional expense of tens of thousands of pounds. But Kanhoji continued to plunder English ships such as the *Diamond, Bombay, Success,* and *Otter.* French and Dutch ships, too, were not spared.

Angre's fierce resistance to the British came at a time when the East India Company was forging comprehensive treaties with the other, by now divided, Maratha rulers. But his bravery and skill were coupled with a stubborn refusal to succumb to the power of the British, who had gradually suborned or subjugated other Indian rulers. Tales of his legendary courage and his martyrdom, have secured a significant place in Indian maritime history.

The astonishing number of defeats that the British suffered at the hands of one man still defies belief. Repeated attacks on his main citadel Vijaydurg – ('Victory-fort') – achieved little.

Castle Barracks in 1940s is now known as INS Angre.

The British tried to take Vijaydurg in 1717 but failed. In 1719, they tried to take Khanderi Island, today known as Khanoji Angre Island, but again failed. Then in tandem with reinforcements sent by the Portuguese viceroy of Goa, the British sought to burn sixteen of Angre's vessels, but again could not capture the fort.

The naval successes of the Marathas would continue until Kanhoji's death in 1729. Even after his death, the Maratha navy remained a force to be reckoned with for another twenty years. But his passing was the beginning of the end for the Marathas as a naval sea force.

Infighting between his five sons allowed the European powers and Siddis to play one brother off against the other. However, one of his sons, Tulaji Angre, despite facing heavy odds, continued to battle on. From his stronghold at Vijaydurg, he continued to attack British ships, forcing them to use Royal Navy escorts and sail in staggered pairs.

Tulaji's Achilles heel was the Peshwas, particularly Nanasaheb Peshwa (also known as Balaji Baji Rao, 1720–61). Striking a deal with the British, Nanasaheb moved a 2,000-strong Maratha army into the area of Vijaydurg fort.

The British fleet, which also arrived there, was determined to seize the fort even as talks were taking place between Tulaji and the Peshwa, with the former willing to strike a deal. Thus, when the British opened fire on the fort on 12 February 1756, the talks were still on, and they were able to take the fort with little resistance.

They set fire to all of Angre's ships, going back on their word to the Peshwa, who also received no money as promised. With this, Vijaydurg, the last bastion of Maratha naval resistance, was taken thanks to British treachery.

Many buildings in Mumbai pay tribute to the Maratha naval warriors. Mumbai's first modern building, Manor House, earlier known as Castle Barracks, was renamed INS *Angre* (1959), after Kanhoji Angre. At one time, the Siddis captured most of Bombay Island and their stronghold, Bombay Castle, is now the Naval Barracks. The re-built Manor House in INS *Angre* is now the Office of the Flag Officer Commanding, Maharashtra Naval Area.

★ ★ ★

The seventeenth- and eighteenth-century naval battles between the Marathas and the Europeans were not, however, the first time India faced a threat from the sea. In fact, the threat started with the advent of the Portuguese explorers in the late fifteenth century.

The subcontinent has a very long coastline and many attached island archipelagos. It lies on important trade routes connecting Asia, Africa, Europe, and Oceania. India has a long maritime history dating back to the Harappan era, with trade connections to the Middle East and the Roman Empire, Indonesia, Cambodia, etc.

Trade brought the Europeans to India but right from the start, they attempted to dominate the seas and control the trade routes. As a result of this, India's independence came under threat from the sea.

One of the ironies of history is that it was an Indian who was directly responsible for the advent of the Europeans. The legendary Portuguese explorer Vasco da Gama set sail for India with four ships – the Sao Gabriel under his command, the Sao Raphael commanded by his brother Paulo da Gama, the Berrio under the command of Nicolas Coelho, and a 200-ton store ship on 25 March 1497.

They would never have made it to Indian shores had it not been for the services of an enterprising Kutchi Gujarati, Kanji Malam, about whom not much is known. The story of Kanji Malam is, in fact, recorded at the Naval Museum at INS Dronacharya in Kochi. Though there are some differences of opinion, scholars and historians from France, Italy, Portugal, China, and Singapore have reached a consensus that Kanji Malam, from the port town of Mandvi in Gujarat, which was well-known for its shipbuilding industry, guided Vasco da Gama to Calicut.

Kanji Malam reportedly met da Gama in the port town of Malindi in East Africa, and the Portuguese admiral took him on board as a guide. Malam guided da Gama to Calicut, or Kozhikode as it is now known.

The Portuguese promptly laid claim to these waters, a claim that received Papal sanction. This meant that they considered themselves to be the 'Lords of the Seas', and they justified the confiscation of merchandise traded through these waters.

THE KUNJALI MARAKKAR

Vasco da Gama pioneered and charted the ocean route for the Portuguese to reach India. The Portuguese then took measures to establish a monopoly over trade in Indian waters. They began to claim control of the waters for the Portuguese Crown and started attacking vessels without Portuguese permits. The Zamorin, the hereditary monarch of Calicut, resisted this. He dismissed the Portuguese claims to the sea, and a series of battles between the intruders and Zamorin troops allied with Arab traders took place with some decisive victories for the locals.

In 1500, when Admiral Pedro Cabral sought to occupy Calicut, eighty Zamorin ships manned by 1,500 sailors along with ships of a wealthy Arab trader, Khoja Amber, drove him away. A decisive role was played in this battle by Kunjali Marakkar.

The Marakkars, originally Muslim marine merchants, offered money, ships and men to the Zamorin when the Portuguese invasion began. They too fought and were so honoured that 'Kunjali Murakkar' was a title given by the Zamorin to designate his naval chief.

There were four Kunjali Marakkars who fought the Portuguese for over ninety years, and they were related by bloodline. Known for their fighting prowess, the Kunjali Murakkars struck terror into Portuguese hearts. Kunjali Marakkar II sank many Portuguese ships in his lifetime (one source claims that he sank fifty in one particular year). Their war strategy was like guerrilla engagements; they would surround large Portuguese ships with small ships and attack from all sides, crippling their manoeuvres. This was similar to the strategy Kanhoji Angre followed almost two centuries later.

So famous are the Marakkars in South India that a big budget Malayalam film, entitled *Marakkar: Arabikadalinte Simham* (Marakkar: The Lion of the Arabian Sea) – directed by noted director Priyadarshan and featuring the South Indian star Mohanlal – has been made on the life of the fourth and last Marakkar – Muhammad Ali Marakkar.

The film's release was delayed because of the pandemic. It was premiered on 2 December 2021. The story of the last Marakkar is particularly poignant because when he took charge in 1595, relations with the Zamorins were deteriorating. Historians say he was defeated and captured by the Portuguese only because they fed on the Zamorin's fears that the Marakkars were planning to dethrone him.

Troubled by these fears, the Zamorin's Nair soldiers fought

alongside the Portuguese forces to subdue these proud Marakkar soldiers, which they only managed after months of fighting.

Finally, in 1597, the last Marakkar surrendered to the Zamorin on the condition that his men's lives would be spared. Violating these terms, the Portuguese beheaded him and killed many of his men. Despite this treachery, the stories of the bravery of the Marakkars live on, and these show that, long before the freedom struggle and the First War of Indian Independence in 1857, Indians had selflessly given their lives to resist colonial invasions.

A TUSSLE BETWEEN COLONIAL POWERS

The first sign of the British interest in India was the founding of the Honourable Company of the Merchants Trading to the East Indies, better known as the East India Company, on 31 December 1600. A ship of the company called *The Hector* with Captain Hawkins as the commanding officer, arrived in Surat in 1608. From Surat, Hawkins travelled to Agra, arriving there on 16 April 1610 and he presented the Mughal Emperor Jehangir with a letter requesting permission to trade with India. This inevitably set Britain up for conflict with the Portuguese, and that development eventually gave birth to the Royal Indian Navy.

As Rear Admiral Satyindra Singh AVSM (retd) says in his book *Under Two Ensigns*: 'A squadron of warships, the *Dragon, Osiender, James* and *Solomon*, under the overall command of Captain Thomas Best, reached Swally, the roadstead of Surat, on 5 September 1612. This date is regarded by the British as the foundation day of the Royal Indian Navy, as the first arrival of their warships in India and the formation of the Indian Marine took place on this day.'

The Portuguese attacked Indian Marine warships on 29 October 1612 with four galleons and forty other craft but had to admit defeat. A second battle took place in 1614, where the Indian Marine emerged victorious and the East India Company received further trading rights from the Mughal emperor.

THE EVOLUTION OF NAVAL FORCES IN INDIA

1612   Indian Marine, also known as Honourable East India Company's Marine, comprising a squadron of ships, arrives in Swally, Surat, and are permanently anchored in India.

1686   Renamed Bombay Marine after commercial activity shifted to Bombay.

1829   Bombay Marine rechristened Bombay Marine Corps.

1830   Renamed His Majesty's Indian Navy, after King William the IV.

1858   Becomes Her Majesty's Indian Navy under Queen Victoria.

1863   The protection of Indian waters taken over by British Admiralty. Two branches created: Bombay Marine for Western Waters and Bengal Marine for Eastern Waters, after expiry of the Honourable East India Company and transferred to the Crown.

1871   The Indian Defence Force (IDF) is born.

1877   The IDF changes its name to Her Majesty's Indian Marine Force.

1892   Renamed Her Majesty's Royal Indian Marine under Queen Victoria.

1928   Becomes Royal Indian Navy (Combatant).

1934   **2 October.** Official birth date of the Royal Indian Navy (RIN). By coincidence, the day marks the birth of another celebrated Indian, Mahatma Gandhi.

1950   **26 January.** Becomes the Indian Navy (of independent India).

The most decisive battle though was the Battle of Swally in 1630, where the Portuguese were roundly defeated, and the East India Company took charge of the majority of the Portuguese ports in India. The British had now come to stay.

It was thus the East India Company established its base. After Swally, the British were poised to consolidate their hold in South Asia and Southeast Asia.

But it wasn't a smooth progression – they did not have everything going their way. In 1685, Sir John Child, then admiral of the East India Company's land and sea forces decided against the advice of the counsellors to adopt a more aggressive posture towards the Mughals. The result was the Anglo–Mughal war, or as some call it, 'Child's War'. The war lasted from 1686 to 1690 and this was the first attempt at British colonization of the Indian subcontinent.

The result of the war was that Emperor Aurangzeb, with the aid of the Siddis, captured most of Bombay Island and besieged Child in Bombay Castle (known today as the Naval Barracks). Peace was then restored and the siege of Bombay was lifted only when the British raiders paid 10,000 pounds in compensation and officers, according to reliable sources, were believed to have even prostrated themselves before the emperor. One of the conditions for peace laid down by the Mughals was that Child should be expelled. But he escaped this ignominy with his death in 1690.

Concurrently, there was naval warfare taking place in south western Konkan as well as the Marathas took on the Europeans.

The British had made their first attempt at colonizing India but Child's War had failed. Indeed, the maritime resistance would continue throughout the eighteenth century. This was where the Bombay Marine played a crucial role.

The primary function of the Bombay Marine was to defend the city from ongoing threats posed by the Siddis and Marathas. But it also served a larger purpose. Bombay port was crucial for establishing maritime supremacy in the Indian Ocean. The Royal

Navy, which was operating hundreds of miles away from home needed local logistical support and help to cater to Britain's commercial needs in the region.

As the consolidation of forces centred on the Bombay port helped the British dominate the seas, it wasn't surprising that the vision of an eastern empire grew. Indeed, the attitude of the East India Company underwent a radical change.

The Company's charter was modified by King Charles II in 1661, 'Power was given to the Company to seize and send home interlopers to wage war and conclude peace with non-Christian princes and to appoint governors, who in conjunctions with their councils, were to exercise civil and criminal jurisdiction at the various settlements.'

Through the charter, the British gave themselves licence to conduct war-like activities, annex territories and rule over enclaves in India for commercial gain. This could be seen in the use of the Bombay Marine ship units for the long maritime war against the Marathas, which ended in 1756, and in the Anglo-Burmese war, which began in 1824.

The 1824 war was fought between the British and Burmese empires for the control of north-eastern India. It saw the Bombay Marine fleet giving aid to land forces by sailing up the river Bassin resulting in the Burmese king suing for peace in 1826. The services of the Bombay Marine were duly recognized in 1830 when it was renamed His Majesty's Indian Navy. What this meant was that officers of the Bombay Marine would henceforth hold rank and pay equivalent to officers from the Royal Navy with neither service holding power of command over the other.

MOVING FROM SAIL TO STEAM

The First Indian War of Independence which started with the mutiny of sepoys in 1857, left Her Majesty's Indian Navy untouched. Yet, the naval historians recount that the two highest decorations ever to be awarded to the personnel of the Indian Navy before Independence were earned during the Great Rising in 1857.

Historians record that an Indian Naval Brigade comprising 78 officers and 1,740 men were assigned shore service during the mutiny. Guns and ammunition were provided from ships which arrived in Calcutta and the naval brigade is believed to have fought in Assam, and Dhaka.

Curiously enough, this is the only occasion when the Victoria Cross, the highest gallantry award, was given to Indian naval personnel – for operations conducted on land.

Following the quelling of the uprising, the British Crown took direct responsibility of governing India and the East India Company's rule ended. This also led to the restructuring of Her Majesty's Indian Navy. On 30 April 1863 it was reorganized as a non-combatant force with two branches in Bombay and Calcutta, which were respectively renamed the Bombay and Bengal Marines.

The late 1800s changed everything again. As the British started the expansion of their empire via the sea, the non-combatant role of the marines was changed in 1871. Two vessels, the *Magdala* and *Abyssinia,* were commissioned for coastal defence, which formed the nucleus of what was to be known as the Indian Defence Force.

They were also used as troop carriers as Britain went to war with Abyssinia, now the modern-day nations of Ethiopia and Eritrea, the same year. These events helped to prompt another name change with the navy being renamed Her Majesty's Indian Marine.

These naval forces were divided into Eastern and Western Divisions which were based in Calcutta and Bombay and respectively operated in the Bay of Bengal and Arabian Sea.

Apart from maintenance and patrolling of gunboats, H.M.'s Indian Marines were employed extensively in the Egyptian campaigns of 1882 and 1885 and especially in the third Anglo-Burma war in 1889. These campaigns were carried out by a squadron with an officer holding the rank of captain from the Royal Navy commanding the force. Though all officers were Europeans, a growing number of the crew were local Indian sailors. Indians were starting to make their presence felt in the British Navy. Though having a modest role, the service of these squadrons did not go unnoticed and, in 1892, Queen Victoria conferred upon them the title, 'The Royal Indian Marine' (RIM).

INDIANS SAIL ON WARSHIPS

On 2 October 1934, the Royal Indian Navy (RIN) came into being with a formal inauguration ceremony. Sardar K.M. Pannikar, statesman, diplomat and historian, highlighted the importance of establishing the Royal Indian Navy when he wrote: 'After the destruction of the Maratha naval power in 1751, Indians were sailing the seas for the first time in warships – small and insignificant units no doubt, but symbolic of the resuscitation of the old forces which had for at least two millennia held the mastery of the Indian seas.'

Despite the RIN allowing both Indians and Britishers to apply, Indian sailors remained few in number. It was a small force and this did not make it an attractive career prospect for many Indians.

The first Indian to join the RIM as an officer was Engineer Sub-Lieutenant D.N. Mukerji, commissioned on 6 January 1928. He rose to the rank of captain and took premature retirement from service in 1950.

Naval historians record that the RIN performed well even with limited resources, even receiving the King's Colour in 1935 for recognition of its services. These recognitions ensured the RIN developed into a small and efficient naval force between 1934 and 1939. However, there was clearly a need to expand.

It was felt that the RIN should be strengthened with an increase in ships and the opening and development of naval depots and training establishments. The rise of the RIN was a sign of hope, but Indian independence of the seas was still a few years away. It would only be on 26 January 1950 that India could truly call its navy, the Indian Navy.

REFERENCES

Anirudh Deshpande, 'Limitations of Military Technology: Naval Warfare on the West Coast, 1650–1800', *Economic and Political Weekly*, Vol. 27, No. 17 (25 April 1992), pp. 900–04.

B.K. Apte, 'Sovereignty of the Sea as Practised in the Maratha Period', Proceedings of the Indian History Congress, Vol. 29, Part I (1967), pp. 255–61.

Dolly Purohit, 'Relation between Marathas and the Siddis of Janjira in the17th century', Ph.D Research Scholar Centre for Historical Studies.

M.S. Naravane, *Battles of the Honourable East India Company: Making of the Raj*. New Delhi: A.P.H. Publishing Corporation, 2006, p. 99.

N.K. Mishra, 'Some Aspects of Piracy in Early Eighteenth Century Western India', Proceedings of the Indian History Congress, Vol. 32, Part II (1970), pp. 131–37.

P.L. Saswadkar, 'The Siddi's Tyranny Over the Hindus in 18th Century Konkan', Proceedings of the Indian History Congress, Vol. 37, 1976, p. 224.

Prof. A.R. Kulkarni, *Medieval Maratha Country*. Pune: Diamond Publications, 2008.

Rear Admiral Satyindra Singh AVSM (Retd), *The Indian Navy 1951–65 Blueprint to Bluewater*. Delhi: South Asia Books, 1992.

Ruby Maloni, 'The Angres and the English—Contenders for Power on the West Coast of India,' Proceedings of the Indian History Congress, Vol. 66 (2005–2006), pp. 546–51.

GALLANTRY AND BETRAYAL AT SEA

While the Indian Navy participated in the First World War, it was then used mainly as logistics support with Indian troops being transported to many sectors. The outbreak of the Second World War would be the first major test of the bravery and seamanship of Indian naval ratings and officers. They emerged with flying colours, literally.

Between 1939 and 1941, ratings of the RIN displayed outstanding courage and audacity in sea battles with many of them given gallantry awards. Archival dispatches from the Royal Navy reveal glowing accounts of the adventurous spirit of these young ratings who operated in the Red Sea, Gulf of Eden, and the Persian Gulf. Their brief was to patrol the sea lanes with the aim of protecting Allied shipping in the Gulf.

When the Second World War broke out, the RIN fleet comprised just five sloops, a survey vessel, a patrol ship, a depot ship, and a large number of smaller craft. The British Navy's role in the war extended from 1939 to 1945 and it remained a formidable force, undertaking a number of war operations critical to the Allied strategy. Much of that success can be attributed to the courage and enterprise shown by Indian sailors of the RIN who were involved in a number of operations and proved a great asset to the Allied Forces.

During the African campaigns between June 1940 and November 1941, the RIN played an important part in contributing to the downfall of the Italian forces in East Africa. The Italians had occupied British Somaliland and in its first joint operation with the Allied Forces, the RIN proved its mettle. Using a combination of guts and guile, they broke the Italian spirit, forcing them to surrender.

After Japan's entry into the war, the RIN was involved in numerous operations in Southeast Asia. In 1945, highly dangerous minesweeping jobs carried out by the Indian Navy enabled Allied troop landings, leading to the early capture of Rangoon. The top brass of the British Navy paid fulsome tributes to the role of Indian seamen for the part they played in the war, describing them as 'adventurous young men'.

The commanding officer, Lt General Sir Philip Christenson, was all praise for the officers and ratings of the RIN during the capture of Rangoon. He recorded that the RIN maintained high standards of cooperation and comradeship through the Burma campaign. Thanking all ranks of XV Indian Corps, he added: 'They demonstrated great skill, seamanship and courage. These qualities enabled us to carry out operations never before attempted by British forces.'

One such operation in the Persian Gulf involved the daring actions of Lt N. Krishnan, and this is now part of Indian naval folklore. In August 1941, as captain of *The Lawrence*, a relatively small tugboat with a crew of just twelve ratings, Krishnan's involvement in the capture of Khorramshahr, a port city in Iran, remains a source of pride and inspiration for the Indian Navy even today.

His tugboat was part of an Allied assault force in this port city where five German ships and three Italian ships lay in wait. Krishnan's tug not only provided advance warning to the Royal Navy ships behind him, but also forced the surrender of an enemy gunboat.

When he entered the port area under cover of darkness, his instructions were not to fire lest the approach of the Allied ships be exposed. Suddenly the Axis Naval vessels opened fire on his ship. Lt Krishnan decided that attack was the best form of defence. Along with four ratings with fixed bayonets and under covering fire from three other ratings, he closed in on the enemy barge. He was greeted with fire from all sides. Despite that, he wounded two men in the barge. The third dropped his rifle following which Krishnan boarded the barge. A fierce battle ensued in the dark. Lt Krishnan ran across the deck towards an open door from where there was continuous firing. After a brief encounter, in which he single-handedly took on the enemy, he forced them to surrender. In the process, Lt Krishnan was injured in the neck and shoulder but still managed to get the better of his adversaries.

In his autobiography, *A Sailor's Story,* Krishnan describes the action on the enemy boat: 'Hardly had I cleared one of the cabins leading to the foyer, I heard my consort shout "Look out Sir, on your left" …by instinct I swirled around firing both the revolvers… I felt a terrific thud and I felt my head had exploded into brilliant stars.' Continuing, he writes: 'My number had not yet been called… his bullet had struck my tin helmet high up and glanced off… Both my bullets had found their mark, one in the throat and one on the side of the chest of this hidden gunman… blood was literally sprouting from his neck and splashed on me as I knelt down to recover his rifle. He turned out to be the captain of the ship… By the time I got ashore, Khorramshahr was in Allied hands.' In that daring attack, four enemy seamen were killed and twenty seriously injured. This feat of bravery was all the more remarkable considering it was carried out by a small group boarding an enemy gunboat which had superior armament and almost four times the number of sailors. They overcame the enemy with only handguns as weapons, taking twenty prisoners. Among the dead was the captain of the enemy gunboat, gunned down by Krishnan in single-handed combat. Krishnan was awarded the

Distinguished Service Cross, becoming the first recipient of this prestigious medal in the RIN.

Lt Krishnan was not the only officer to show such bravery during the war. Equal courage and daring were shown by Engineer Lt Daya Shankar, who later rose to the rank of rear-admiral and controller general of Defence Production. In a sea battle in 1941, he boarded the Italian vessel *Cabot*, ran through a blazing deck at considerable risk to himself and captured the entire enemy crew. He too was awarded the Distinguished Service Cross.

The story of HMIS *Bengal* is equally inspiring. On 5 November 1942 she set out as escort to *MV Ondina*, a Dutch tanker, to Diego Garcia. A week into the sail she sighted a vessel coming straight towards her. About the same time another ship appeared over the horizon heading for her as well. Both ships, identified as enemy Japanese vessels, were considerably bigger than *Bengal*. The *Ondina* instructed *Bengal* to act independently, so *Bengal* moved to full speed. Admiral Satyindra Singh in his book *Under Two Ensigns*, describes the battle in the words of HMIS *Bengal* Commander W.J. Wilson. 'The raiders came up very fast and *Bengal* steamed straight ahead at her. The raiders also increased speed and opened fire at about 3,500 yards with her forward guns. We retaliated and hit first. At 3,000 yards we must have hit the raiders in the magazine because a great sheet of flame shot up astern, almost mast high. We then closed the range and fought the action at about 2,500 yards. Now the other Japanese raider came closer and started to fire at us continuously. The first ship we engaged carried on firing until, in a great sheet of flame, she blew up and sank. I estimate she fired over 200 rounds at us. We were running short of ammunition and our vessel was damaged fore and aft. The encounter lasted for over two hours but really the first three minutes had decided the issue… it was a matter of surprise that the *Bengal* emerged from this action without any serious damage. They had never been in action before, but when the action stations were sounded, everyone was perfectly calm, firm and disciplined and all hands were anxious to have a shot at the raiders…'

When *Bengal* reached Colombo, every ship in the harbour gave her a spontaneous, official reception. The height of acknowledgement came when they steamed into Bombay. While still outside the harbour, every RIN ship in the vicinity gave them a typical naval salute. The seventy-five officers and men were given a public reception and were honoured at a lunch in Sir Cowasjee Hall.

Besides the commanding officer of the ship, Lt Commander Wilson, two Indian ratings were also decorated. Leading Seaman Ismail Mohammad was awarded the Indian Distinguished Service Medal for gallantry and devotion to duty. Petty Officer Mohammed Ibrahim, captain of the 12-pounder gun, was awarded the Indian Order of Merit for setting an 'Excellent example of steadiness and resolution and using his weapons to the very best advantage even after *Bengal* had been hit by enemy gunfire.'

PRIDE FOR INDIA: HONOURED IN LONDON PARADE

After the end of Second World War a victory parade was held in London on 8 June 1946 in which representatives of the three Indian Armed Forces participated. The senior Indian Naval officer was Commander (later Rear-Admiral) A. Chakravarti and the naval contingent was led by Lieutenant (later Rear-Admiral) P.S. Mahindroo. In keeping with the inter-service seniority in which the navy was the senior service, the parade was led by the naval contingent. Reminiscing on this honour, Rear-Admiral Mahindroo, who later commanded our first aircraft carrier INS *Vikrant,* said: 'Needless to say, that as a turbaned officer leading the Naval contingent, I was most prominent and I must have given hundreds of autographs amongst thousands of spectators who probably slept on the pavement for one or two nights to witness this historic parade.'

Young boys outside 'RIN New Entry Camp': As the Second World War progressed, more such camps were organized to recruit sailors for the Royal Navy.

These accounts show that Indian seamen proved their mettle in warlike conditions. The ratings had fought tough battles on the high seas. In all these encounters, as many as 105 personnel of the RIN were killed, 27 of them being commissioned officers.

Considering that several ratings went on to win numerous gallantry awards and recognition for their bravery, it does beg the question: How did such brave, committed youngsters get involved in a mutiny? What were the reasons?

SEEDS OF THE MUTINY

Documented accounts show the seeds of the mutiny were sown on the very day the ratings were recruited. Till 1940, the focus had been on strengthening the army. When recruitment started in the navy, training facilities proved inadequate. The training establishments were overcrowded and staff shortages rampant. There were also large-scale desertions – as many as one-third of the recruits deserted after joining. The British made efforts to convince new recruits that life at sea would be a rewarding adventure but reports of ill-treatment had spread across the country, down to the villages.

From September 1939 to December 1945, as the war progressed, the efforts to increase recruits multiplied. The number of officers increased from 114 to 269, and 35 to 198 in the case of warrant officers.

While Muslims were initially recruited in large numbers, by 1945, there were an equal number of Hindus. By the end of the war, the strength of the RIN was 27,933, up from 1,722 in September 1939 at the start of the war. The RIN entered the war in 1939 with 2 sloops, 1 survey ship, 4 escort patrol vessels and 33 auxiliary class boats, a total of 40 boats on the water. At the end of the war in August 1945, this had increased to 7 sloops, 3 corvettes, 3 frigates, 19 fleet and motor minesweepers, 16 trawlers, 5 Persian

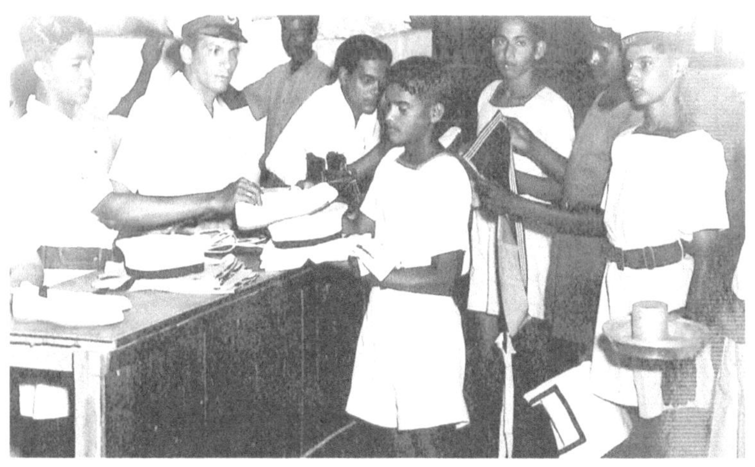

Most often the new recruits were as young as fourteen or fifteen years of age and joined the RIN with great expectations.

Typical RIN ratings in their impressive uniforms. The excitement of this new job and future though did not last long.

gunboats and 18 motor launches, a total of 132 boats on the water.

But the manner of recruitment left much to be desired. When the British found that not much interest was being shown by potential recruits, agents were commissioned to increase the numbers. There was massive advertising, and billboards were put up announcing that joining the navy meant finding oneself a secure job post-war. In reality, this promise was never fulfilled.

Hundreds of posters and pamphlets were distributed. A typical advertising slogan read as such: 'Permanent careers in the RIN. Earn while you leave. Promotion to Warrant Officers and Commissioned ranks… Pay during advanced training Rs 100 rising up to Rs 250.' A number of posters translated into several regional languages were also distributed to lure recruits.

One read: 'Be proud of your son. Let him join the RIN… The Navy will give him a good fellowship, good pay and plenty of food and good clothes.' This was accompanied by thirteen 'feel good' pictures of the recruits wearing impressive uniforms and outfits.

Most of the ratings had joined the service to secure a good job and future for themselves and their families. However, within months, disappointments set in.

Col A.A. Rudra, an officer deposing before the Commission of Enquiry which looked into the causes for the RIN mutiny, said the advertisements were blatantly misleading. 'As these are short service commissions, they cannot hope to rise even to the level of Warrant Officers, leave alone commissioned rank.'

Another officer, Lt Commander Shaw had this to say: 'By all accounts recruits were told glowing tales of life in the Navy by Recruiting Officers.' Another naval officer, Lt Rao, added: 'In some cases men were actually led by their hands and made to put their thumb impression on a piece of paper which brought them into virtual bondage as top-asses (menials) for some time.'

The other means of inducing recruits was through pamphlets. 'This,' said one pamphlet, 'is the story of Khalil and Kishore.' In a fictional tale designed to attract the interest of job seekers, the pamphlet read: 'Kishore runs away from home to join the Navy and gets a salary as Rs 60 per month as a Rating. Kishore persuaded Khalil to join the Ratings who earns even more than him. Khalil's parents are now convinced.'

The story extends further. Khalil says the contract is for ten years – a blatant lie. In the pamphlet, he tells his father: 'The Ratings will have a quick promotion from a starting pay of Rs 90 as an artificer to Rs 469. Facilities for good food, vegetarian and non-vegetarian, are available.' None of this was true.

It comes as no surprise to discover that a Royal Enquiry Commission actually found that no less than nine instances of mutinies had occurred before February 1946. These were:

- 3 March 1942, Bombay: Dissent over pay hike. Seven apprentices were court-martialled. All the accused were convicted and given jail terms from 3 to 15 months.
- 22 June 1942, Tobermory, UK: Complaints of rations. All seventeen ratings involved were sentenced to 90 days detention.
- September 1942, MIS *Orissa*, East London, South Africa. Frequent cases of indiscipline. Three ratings sentenced to prison from 3 to 7 years.
- September 1942, HMIS *Khyber*, UK: Six or seven greasers refused work since this was against their customs. Three men discharged. No action taken against greasers.
- 27/28 June 1944, HMIS *Akbar*: Religious outbreak among ratings. Action taken against *ganja* smokers.
- 30 July 1944, HMIS *Hamlawar*: A rating was found in a sitting position. When an officer arrived, the rating did not get up as he was praying. He was reading from the Holy Quran. The sub concerned was dismissed from the ship while thirteen other ratings who found the behaviour of the official objectionable were sentenced to various terms of imprisonment.
- 29, 30 & 31 July 1944, HMIS *Shivaji*: Seventeen Muslim sailors refused to eat since they believed that their meat was mixed with pork. Later, the seamen were assured that the meat was not contaminated. However, four seamen who had refused food were punished summarily.
- 16 March 1945, HMIS *Himalaya*, Karachi: Three leading seamen put in a request to attend afternoon prayers on shore.

They were refused permission despite which they left the ship to pray. The three were tried for disobedience and dismissed from service.

- 17 April 1945 and successive days, HMIS *Shivaji*: Direct entry ratings refused to clean the ship. There were Hindus, Muslims, and Sikhs. All gave religious reasons for refusal. Thirty-eight ratings were punished with 90 days rigorous imprisonment. Six more were awarded 90 days rigorous imprisonment but it was later suspended.

Lt Commander Soman, one of the witnesses who deposed before the Commission of Enquiry in May 1946, summed up the situation when he said, 'The higher authorities took no notice of the warning given as early as September 1942.'

One significant admission was a letter written by Commander Coverdale Smith on 23 April 1945: 'I am convinced that the refusal to clean ship is mainly an expression of dissatisfaction with the terms and conditions of the service about which they were misinformed when they were enrolled… their [ratings'] state of mind is such that they are prepared to go to jail rather than pinning any further faith in the possible redressal of their grievances by higher authorities.'

Treated like slaves

Indian ratings got a taste of what life would be like in the Royal Indian Navy from the day they joined. As a rating wrote in a letter home: 'Officers do not act according to printed regulations but make their own rules.' It was not just British officers. Even Indian officers treated them in the same way. Wrongdoers were not just punished but when they complained to an Indian officer, they were told that he could not take action against a white junior.

The indiscriminate use of abusive and foul language was seen a symbol of authority. 'Bastards', 'baboons' or 'swine' were common phrases heard in the navy along with 'bloody', '*behan chod*', 'blackies', and 'black bastards'.

Young ratings, barely out of their teens, were expected to be loyal to the Raj and forced to do even menial jobs.

Several times a day an Indian rating had to salute the Union Jack and chant 'God Save the King' but a British officer would fly into a rage if Indian music was played within his earshot. Indian naval officers generally sided with their British counterparts. Only one Indian officer, Lt Sobhani, rebelled and supported the ratings in their 1946 uprising.

The resentment related to several issues of discrimination. Indian ratings were forced to clean lavatories and pick up empty alcohol bottles and food after the onboard parties of British officers. Rating Mohd Ismail deposing before one of the enquiry commissions, said: 'The officers used to bring girls from the shore... booze during nights and make merry on the upper deck. This (deprived)... the ratings of their sleep. Some of us had to do boat pulling throughout the night for these officers and their girls.' After the parties, Indian ratings were ordered to clean the cutlery, dining hall or washrooms, writes Dilip Kumar Das in *Revisiting Talwar.*

To add to their problems, because of rapid enrolment, there was overcrowding in ships as well as shore establishments. Indian ratings were the ones who had to suffer this and on HMIS *Talwar,* it was worse. They were forced to sleep in messes and even on parade grounds.

As M.S. Khan, a leading telegraphist on *Talwar,* later president of the NCSC, said: 'Eighty per cent of the Indian ratings got no cots to sleep on... Ratings sleep on the floor and everywhere. No arrangements were made, no cots provided. They think Indians are sheep or goats to be herded... and bedding... two rough blankets and one pillow of straw, one bed cover, no bed sheets.' He added: 'The ships were meant for 100 or 120 people but in wartime or peacetime they (Indian ratings) were crowded to 200 or 220 people. Half of them had to sleep on the upper deck, half on the mess deck and when it rained, boys had no place to sleep. They had to shrink themselves and sit down all night.'

B.C. Dutt, a prime mover of the uprising, in his book *Mutiny of the Innocents,* writes about his first day in the navy: 'After a tiring day, I had fallen into a deep slumber... the rough blanket, hard pillow and the wooden deck did not trouble me... I was startled out of sleep by the shrill note from the pipe at 5 am... I stowed away the bed and then went to the lavatory. It was a bizarre sight. There were a dozen Indian style lavatories without doors. All were occupied in full view of the long queues in front of each of them. I just could not use it when my turn came...'

Lt Col Haq Nawaz, who was specially deputed to visit the establishments in Bombay and Karachi had this to say: 'The quarters which are meant for about 500 men are being used for 1,500. Admittedly there are difficulties in improving a temporary place like RIN Demobilisation Centre, but this last home that RIN gives to its ratings is by no means a happy place to be in... they leave with a bitter opinion.' He also attached copy of a leaflet, a bundle of which was actually found in the War Information Room of HMIS *Talwar.* It read as follows:

AN EYE HERE ALSO PLEASE

THE MOST GLORIOUS HELL IN BOMBAY

——VERSOVA ——

Or Demob Centre

Witness There

Our Sufferings:

HUNGER... INJUSTICE... OPPRESSION

Another broken promise was to do with medical facilities. Indian ratings were promised the highest medical facilities at par with their British counterparts. As M.S. Khan deposed during the Commission of Enquiry: 'I should like to give an example… when a man went to the doctor having pain in the stomach doctor gave him just salt to drink. When a man went having a pain in the foot he gave him the same mixture. If a man went with a headache he gave the same medicine. When a rating with a real stomach ache, the doctor instead of treating him, threatened him saying he was pretending and he wrote a chit to the commanding officer to get this man punished; in lieu of getting medical aid, he got two hours doubling [running in military slang] in the hot sun.'

According to documented accounts, another major reason for the disaffection and growing anger among Indian ratings was the quality of food they were supplied with on ship and shore establishments. Sub-standard rice full of stones, along with atta and dal so old they were infected with insects. The dal was also cooked with raw vegetables just thrown in without giving time for it to be properly cooked. If the cooks ran short of dal they would just add water and serve it. An inspection team that went to HMIS *Dalhousie* and *Talwar* confirmed that 'an offensive smell was given off by the issued parboiled rice and that it left a very bad taste in the mouth… further complaint of the large number of stones found in this rice.' The ratings were regularly served broken and burnt chapattis.

Since the meat was chopped on broken wood, often bits of wood went along with the bones into the curry. When the ratings complained to the cooks, they were told that with over 1,200 ratings to feed, there are only two galleys and ten cooks. The stones in the rice and dal were because they were not enough staff to wash them before cooking. Even the meat was cooked in under-staffed, cramped galleys by inexperienced helpers.

Deposing before the Commission of Enquiry, Khan said, 'While I was at sea, I starved on many occasions… while in Colombo on HMIS *Kathiawar*… the vegetables that came on board were old stinking pumpkins… brinjals and ladies fingers were full of worms…'When they complained, he was told,'Indian navy is only allowed to have B class vegetables and that A class is reserved for Royal Navy People (Britishers).We are given B class vegetables because we are Black people.'

On being asked by Gen. T.W. Rees, a British member of the commission, Khan said: 'It is down in the Eastern Fleet Communication order… that Indians because their colour was black were given these rations.Their work was not Black! I have to say another thing. One afternoon we were told that "Halal" meat could not be supplied to us.We were forced to take "Haram" meat – frozen meat from Australia.When I complained that as Muslim it is against our religion to eat Haram meat, we were told "If you do not eat it you should starve…We wondered we were so close to Colombo or India why couldn't Halal meat come from there? Why were we forced to eat frozen Haram meat from Australia!"'

An officer in charge in his confidential report did agree that 'Atta and rice is so full of stones and mud that it was fit only to be fed to animals, if the veterinary authorities permitted it!'

Demobilization was yet another factor that contributed to the mutiny. The end of the war saw rapid and ruthless demobilization for Indian ratings. The demobilization not only meant that the promises of stable careers, pensions, etc., were being broken. It was accompanied by infuriating regulations and demands to do with returning kits and uniforms.These had to be in pristine conditions or fines were levied.

The ratings, already tense and extremely stressed about their future after being asked to leave, found it impossible to keep their kit in perfect condition after many years of active service.As Kusum Nair in her book *The Army of Occupation* says, 'To expect a rating who is going out in the civilian street to shell out money for the Kit he has worn is to suck blood out of stone.'

A few months after the end of the war an anonymous letter was received in Naval Headquarters in Delhi… Some excerpts: 'Here we are, Sir, in hundreds living in the accommodation designed for fifty… Central Pay office reveal that they have not been able to settle the accounts of these ratings. They are drafted to central pool (coolie company) where all sorts of dirty work is sought from them even as to stone breaking and road building. The treatment is no better than of prisoners in jail… this is like a concentration camp…' Another letter said: 'Nearly two hundred rupees are due. So we refused to sign without getting paid in full. We were threatened with severe punishment. We were forced to sign to get released.' Lt McRae in a note submitted to the commission said: 'I have come across countless cases where ratings invalided from the service have for periods of anything up to ten months without receiving an anna of their disability pensions. Lal Din, a rating, was badly injured in a gunnery accident. He arrived in Delhi on discharge after 18 months in hospital without a penny of his back pay, no pension, nothing to show how his disability had been incurred or even to prove that he was an ex-serviceman and wearing only a cotton singlet and pants (the only naval kit he had been permitted to keep), although it was December and he was travelling to his home in Jammu… Ratings have been discharged in hundreds from the release centres with nothing but a dirty slip of paper to show they have served in the RIN.'

Resentments against the British which were fuelled by this inhuman treatment increased even further as debates about the larger issues involving the nation began to take place more frequently. The Quit India movement was in full force from 1942, and articles by fiercely nationalistic newspapers such as the *Free Press Journal*, *Bombay Chronicle* in English, *Pratap* and *Hindustan Dainik* founded by Madan Mohan Malaviya in Hindi, *Kesari*, founded by Bal Gangadhar Tilak and *Sudharak* in Gujarati, had raised nationalistic fervour.

This passion was further enhanced by the pamphlets circulated by members of Subhas Chandra Bose's Indian National Army, the Azad Hind Fauj. Mahatma Gandhi and Bose were heroes for their roles in the freedom movement and the INA soldiers were icons to these young men who saw these pamphlets as a call to arms.

Anger, discontentment, rage and hate fuelled by nationalistic passions ensured these young men were sitting on a tinderbox that would soon culminate in a rebellion. In February 1946, that tinderbox exploded.

REFERENCES

B.C. Dutt, *Mutiny of the Innocents*. Bombay: Sindhu Publications, 1971.

Biswanath Bose, *RIN Mutiny:1946*. New Delhi: Northern Book Centre, 1988.

Commander K. Shridharan, *Maritime History of India*. Delhi: Publications Division, Ministry of Information and Broadcasting, 1982.

Dr V.M. Bhagwatkar, *The Role of RIN Mutiny of Feb. 1946, (Royal Indian Navy Uprising), in the Indian Freedom Struggle*, 1989. PhD thesis approved for degree.

K.M. Pannikar, *India and the Indian Ocean*. London: Allen & Unwin, 1951.

Kusum Nair, *The Army of Occupation*. Delhi: Padma Publications, 1946.

Maj-Gen. Shahnawaz Khan, *My Memories of INA & its Netaji*. Delhi: Rajkamal Publications, 1946.

National Archives Files, Royal Indian Navy, 1943–1947, NAI.

Radha Kumud Mookherji, *A History of Indian Shipping*. Longman Green and Co., 1912.

Rear Admiral Satyindra Singh AVSM (Retd), *Under Two Ensigns:The Indian Navy 1945–1950*. New Delhi: Oxford and IBH Publishing Co., 1986.

Vice Admiral N. Krishnan, *A Sailor's Story: An Autobiography*. Gurugram: Punya Publishing, 2011.

*A charismatic and brave leader, Netaji Subhas Chandra Bose was
ideologically different from the Mahatma.*

THE GATHERING STORM

The first advance warnings of the brewing mutiny came on 1 February 1946. On that day, Rating R.K. Singh (whose full name is unknown) did something unprecedented. He resigned. In the RIN, you could be dismissed, demobilized or retire, but you could not resign.

What's more, Singh displayed his anger and defiance in the most blatant and provocative manner. Summoned by his British commanding officer (CO), he not only shouted out his resignation but carried out an action unthinkable at the time. He threw down his cap and kicked it in a show of open defiance, all the time looking his CO in the eye.

R.K. Singh's unprecedented act forcefully expressed his disgust and contempt for the British. He was jailed, but this act of rebellion carried a larger message.

It was the first indication that the Indian ratings were no longer willing to tolerate the treatment they were receiving from the British.

The first Indian seaman to submit his resignation as a mark of protest has been described by some as a 'dreamy youth'. It's obvious in hindsight that he was a patriot to the core. He subscribed to the

Gandhian way of open defiance and his defiance sent a message to his British officers and his fellow ratings.

His resignation was designed to encourage his peers to take action and he would lead the charge. This act of bravery sparked off cries for rebellion as news of his deliberate act of insubordination spread like wildfire through the barracks. What added fuel to the fire was his summary trial where he was sentenced to three months in Arthur Road Jail, a prison meant for criminals.

★ ★ ★

India's seamen were not immune to the widespread demands for change that were in the air. During 'liberty' (free time when ratings were allowed to leave anchored ships or shore establishments), they would read the newspapers, which carried reports of political activity and increasing nationalism. The ratings would also discuss the situation in the Far East with those who had returned, especially focused on the role and plans of Subhas Chandra Bose and the INA who had waged an armed struggle against the British. The daily reports of INA POWs being held by the British in the Red Fort infuriated those in the armed forces.

The Quit India call given by Gandhi four years earlier was still fresh in the minds of India's youth. India's leaders had also sharpened their rhetoric. At an All-India Congress Committee (AICC) meeting in Bombay on 7 August 1942, Gandhi said, 'Here is a mantra, a short one that I give you. The Mantra is "Do or Die". We shall either free India or die in the attempt.' His call for an open rebellion was echoed by Sardar Patel who announced: 'This time if a railway line is removed or an Englishman is murdered the struggle will not stop… This is going to be an opportunity of a lifetime.'

With emotions reaching fever-pitch, alarmed British officers were desperate to quench the fires of rebellion. By mid-August, all major leaders from the Congress, including Gandhi, were arrested. Gandhi's dramatic arrest on 8 August 1942 was a turning point for an already emotive nation. As *Time* magazine then reported, 'that arrest, though not Gandhi's first, served as a spark to tip the passive resistance he favoured into violent reaction.' Police stations and government buildings were set on fire, railway and telegraph services were disrupted and British government officials were openly assaulted by mobs chanting cries of 'Long Live Freedom'.

The arrest of prominent leaders led to the next level of young and inexperienced leadership rising to the challenge. Dubbed the 'heroine of the 1942 moment,' a young Aruna Asaf Ali, in an act of defiance, hoisted the Congress flag the next day (9 August) at the Gowalia Tank Maidan in Bombay. The British swiftly banned the Congress party but the torch of freedom had been lit and young leaders fanned the flames of revolution all over India. These young leaders like Aruna, Ram Manohar Lohia, Biju Patnaik, Sucheta Kriplani and other left-wingers in the Congress Party were more impatient and militant than their seniors. They triggered a wave of violence that engulfed the nation. On land, a wave of brutal arrests took place with over 1,00,000 Indian nationalists being jailed. In a letter to King George VI, Viceroy Lord Linlithgow termed it 'by far the most serious rebellion since that of 1857'.

Tragically, disagreements between the major political parties meant that freedom from British rule, which seemed so tantalizingly close, remained out of reach. The Muslim League declared that Independence could not be pursued until Congress agreed to the creation of Pakistan.

Organizations like the Rashtriya Swayamsevak Sangh (RSS) and the Hindu Mahasabha were not entirely against the British government. The Indian Communist Party too opted to stay neutral, thus preventing a united front in the battle for Independence.

Economically, the country was experiencing distress. The fall of the Indian rupee – deliberately devalued – led to mass inflation which destroyed the lives of many Indians, particularly the farming community.

The rising price of crops, hyperinflation and the creation of a black market led to the Bengal Famine – India's biggest recorded agrarian crisis. Largely dependent on agriculture, a huge number of people, mainly the rural poor, starved to death in 1942–43. An estimated two and a half to three million, out of a population of 60 million in the state of undivided Bengal, died. The British looked the other way as the crisis unfolded, in what was quite simply, a war crime.

Even this massive tragedy failed to douse the fire of rebellion. On the contrary, the desire to be free burned brighter and continued to resonate in the minds of Indians, particularly those in the INA led by the revolutionary from Bengal, Netaji Subhas Chandra Bose. Proud, strong and courageous, these young Indians were determined to free their country by any and all means necessary.

★ ★ ★

It is an ironic quirk of fate that one of the men who conceptualized the INA had first wanted to join the British Indian Army. But fate had other plans and it was just as well because Rash Behari Bose was born to be a revolutionary and he was committed to fighting for India's freedom, no matter the risk to his life. He was one of the brains behind the failed Ghadar mutiny of 1915 for which a bounty of Rs 1,00,000 was put on his head. After a thrilling cat and mouse chase with the police, he left India for Japan, never to return.

His exile proved to be India's gain. Despite being in a strange land (he married a Japanese woman) Rash Behari remained an Indian patriot. His persistent attempts to convince the Japanese authorities to stand with India against the British finally yielded results with the official birth of the INA.

The surrender of Singapore, led to the formation of the INA. It was a fighting force dedicated to the cause of India's Independence. Comprised of Indian POWs – soldiers who had surrendered to the Japanese when they captured Singapore – it was a formidable force of 50,000 men. The INA fired India's imagination as the

British and their allies began to lose battle after battle in the Far East in 1942.

The propaganda leaflets of an 'Indian Army' caught the fancy of Indians back home. Many Indian soldiers fighting for the British were willing to desert and join the army inspiring millions of Indians. Mohan Singh was one such soldier. A captain in the 1/14 Punjab Regiment, he was one of the POWs captured by the Japanese in Malaysia. The Japanese had assured him they had no territorial or economic ambitions over India, and said they would do all they could to rid India of its colonial masters.

On 15 February 1942, the dramatic day when Singapore fell to the Japanese, there were 45,000 Indian soldiers in the Allied garrison of 75,000 troops in Singapore. Major Iwaichi Fujiwara, who was in charge of Japanese Intelligence in that theatre, took control of the Indian POWs and dramatically announced that they would be reorganized under Mohan Singh and formed into the Indian National Army. This was finalized on 1 September 1942 when the INA was formally recognized and given official status.

The relationship between Netaji Subhas Bose and Gandhi was always complicated. They were divided ideologically. A charismatic leader in his own right, Bose could never have become Gandhi's follower in the same mould that Nehru had become. There was a fracturing of relations with Gandhi in the 1930s – and Bose would virulently criticize him for talking to British administrators, and the leaders of the Muslim League in 1944.

However, Netaji retained his reverence for the Mahatma to the end when he tragically died in an air crash in Taiwan (then called Formosa). His biographer and nephew Sisir Kumar Bose said that in his final words Netaji remarked on the great success of his army and said emotionally: 'Father of our Nation! In this holy war for Indian liberation we ask for your blessings and good wishes.'

On 4 July 1943, the INA was formally handed over to Netaji, and he accepted the charge with the two words that all Indians now use to salute their motherland: 'Jai Hind.'

'Dilli Chalo' was the next exhortation by Netaji as soon as he took over the INA. He understood men and his renaming the INA to the Azad Hind Fauj was a masterstroke. The rousing oratory of Netaji added to the fervour. *'Tum mujhe khoon do, main tumhe azadi doonga* (Give me blood and I promise you freedom)'*, he thundered, a slogan that reverberated through every corner of India.

The magnetism of Netaji and 'his' INA was such that it touched all India – men and women, Hindus and Muslims and Indians from all strata. General Mohan Singh was tasked with recruiting, and raising the Army Unit; Lakshmi Menon (later Sehgal) was given the responsibility of raising the women's corps which was named the Rani of Jhansi Regiment; General Shahnawaz Khan was given command of the Subhas Brigade; Colonel G.S. Dhillon was given command of the Nehru Brigade, and Captain Prem Kumar Sehgal was given command of No. 2 Infantry Regiment.

This was India's army and Netaji made sure every Indian knew it. That included the naval ratings. Literature, pamphlets and photographs found their way clandestinely to ships and shore establishments, ensuring no young rating was immune to the fervour of freedom. It helped to turn them into freedom fighters. It was hardly surprising that naval ratings who revolted in February 1946 called themselves Azad Hindi.

Netaji Subhas Bose spared no effort in exhorting all Indians serving the British Indian Army, Air Force and Navy to join the INA. Fiery slogans such as *'Qadam Qadam Badhaye Ja'* – the regimental quick march for the Azad Hind Fauj were printed on pamphlets stirring all Indians who heard it to action. It is today the regimental 'Quick March' of the Indian Army.

The defeat of the Axis powers forced the Japanese imperial army to withdraw from the Indo-Burma border in 1944–45. Sensing defeat, the INA too retreated in April 1945, but a large number were taken prisoner by the British. Determined to crush the spirit of Independence, the British looked to make an example of INA soldiers by trying them under court martial in an open trial in Delhi's Red Fort. The result was a public relations disaster for the colonizers.

★ ★ ★

This was undoubtedly one of the most famous trials in India's history. INA officers Prem Sehgal, Gurbaksh Singh Dhillon, and Shahnawaz Khan were tried together in open court for treason and 'waging war against the King'.

Trying INA soldiers – the lionized heroes of the country – was in itself, a grave mistake. But trying three soldiers of different faiths together was akin to lighting a stick of dynamite. India passions were roused and from then on, the British hold on the country would become more tenuous. The 1857 Mutiny that sparked the First War of Indian Independence had occurred when the British ignored religious sensitivities. They learnt another bitter lesson here – one that they would not be able to resolve.

The symbolic significance of trying a Muslim, Sikh and Hindu together not only gave the lie to the outdated policy of 'divide and rule' but it allowed Indians – already roused by patriotic ardour – to listen to men who had been prepared to give their lives to fighting for freedom. Their language was patriotic and simple. Responding to the charges of treason, Prem Sehgal said: 'The Indian Army had fought bravely against the heaviest odds, and in return, the British command had left them completely at the mercy of the Japanese. We felt that the British government had on its own cut off all bonds… and relieved us of all obligations.'

Dhillon reminded the military court of the words that were engraved in Chetwoode Hall in the Indian Military Academy in Dehradun. 'The honour, welfare and safety of your country comes first, always and every time. The comfort, safety and welfare of the men you command comes next. Your own safety and comfort comes last, always and every time.' These words aroused a sense of fearless commitment in the young ratings. Shahnawaz Khan told the packed courtroom: 'When I decided to join the INA, I decided to sacrifice my everything – my life, my home, my family and tradition of the force which pledged loyalty to the King.'

A battery of the best defence lawyers of the time, which included Bhulabhai Desai and Jawaharlal Nehru, fought their case in court but the might of the colonizers prevailed. On 29 December 1945, the trio were found guilty of waging war against the King and were sentenced to 'transportation for life'. This sentence was considered nearly equivalent to hanging. 'Transportation for life' meant that these brave men would be removed from mainstream India and transported to jail, probably in the remote Andamans.

The fact that a Hindu, Muslim and a Sikh officer had courageously defended their convictions in open court set the country afire. *'Lal Qile Ko Tor Do, Azad Hind Fauz Ko Chhor Do'* was the battle cry which reverberated around the country. Widespread unrest broke out.

S.A. Ayer, the INA's minister for publicity and a key defence witness during the trials, echoed the mood of the nation: 'The INA had literally burst on the country… from Himalayas to Cape Comorin it was aflame with an enthusiastic fervour unprecedented in its history…' he observed. Even Mahatma Gandhi, the apostle of non-violence, admitted 'the hypnotism of the INA has cast its spell upon us. Netaji's name is one to conjure with. His patriotism is second to none…' The battle cry for freedom reached the ships and more importantly, the largest signal school of the Royal Indian Navy, the HMIS *Talwar* in Colaba, Bombay.

★ ★ ★

The unjust manner in which the British had sentenced three brave officers had stirred anger, resentment, and hate. This was further fuelled by INA pamphlets procured secretly by the more educated ratings, which evoked a strong desire in them to stand up and fight for their country.

The signal school HMIS *Talwar* in Colaba, Bombay, was especially affected. The ratings there were more educated and thus, more aware of the rebellious activity taking place beyond the high walls of their barracks. Anger boiled over in men already incensed by the racist and demeaning behaviour of the British.

Heated debates had taken place in *Talwar* about the effectiveness of the 'Garam Dal' movement – the hard-line faction led by Lokmanya Tilak – which brooked no compromise with the British. The INA trial, along with the INA pamphlets and stories of numerous INA victories over British forces had brought a sense of confidence to all Indians. This was not misplaced. Though the Japanese had surrendered to the Allied Forces on 15 August 1945, the Azad Hind Fauj had done India proud.

Armed with stories, newspapers, documents and letters, Indian sailors shared with their counterparts the battles where the Fauj had more than held their own. These letters, stories and chapters praised Netaji and emphasized that on more than one occasion the Fauj had demonstrated its superiority over the British forces. The message was clear – it was time for Indians at home to rise and begin the war for freedom.

Salil Shyam became another catalyst for the revolt. Shyam was a rating who returned from the jungles of Malaya to India, where he spoke with wonder of the exploits of the Azad Hind Fauj to his friend Balai Chandra Dutt (B.C. Dutt), a fellow rating. Sharing photographs and literature and letters written by members of the Azad Hind Fauj addressed to Pandit Nehru and Sarat Chandra Bose, the elder brother of Netaji, he awoke dormant passions in his friend. Dutt experienced an irresistible urge to play his part in India's freedom movement.

In his memoirs – largely ignored by India's historians today – Dutt declares how he went about his plans for rebellion to fulfil the ultimate goal of freedom. He was a senior telegraphist on INS *Talwar* and was able to spread the word and also mobilize a number of fellow ratings whom he swore to secrecy. Thus, an underground movement was born.

Dutt and Salil knew all too well the consequences of their actions. If caught, they could be sentenced to high treason – a crime that could be punishable by hanging. But that did not deter them. The two ratings' roles went beyond being mere messengers.

Hushed meetings took place as to what would be the next course of action. The ringleaders Salil Shyam, B.C. Dutt, Madan Singh, Rishi Dev Puri alias 'Deb' and M.S. Khan were determined that a message needed to be sent to the British whatever the cost. All these men spread the word of revolution and freedom to their fellow ratings exhorting them to be ready to make the supreme sacrifice for the nation.

These meetings held in the hidden corners of the *Talwar* makes for poignant reading in Dutt's memoirs. The meetings of these underground 'patriots' became more frequent and their numbers started to swell. Calling themselves 'Azad Hindi', some exceptionally brave participants came to the fore. Rishi Dev Puri for instance, was a suave, sophisticated young man, who some later dubbed the 'Indian James Bond'. Puri and his fellow revolutionaries decided to target the soft spot in the British armour – their pride.

The saga unfolded most appropriately on Navy Day on 1 December 1945 and Indian naval ratings later recalled with pride how B.C. Dutt, R.D. Puri and other members of Azad Hindi humiliated the colonial powers on this most important day for the British Navy. For the first time, civilians including Bombay's Who's Who, were invited to witness the pomp and power of the RIN at the city's ship and shore establishments. The *Talwar* was the pride of the RIN and when the visitors entered the shore establishment, they saw something they found hard to believe.

Dutt himself describes the scene vividly in *Mutiny of the Innocents.* 'Navy Day would be a curtain raiser to our activities. The civil population was invited for the first time to visit the ships as well as the shore establishments. The authorities wanted to present a Navy of regular gentlemen – spick and span – and the ships dressed with flags and bunting.'

Dutt, Puri and their fellow conspirators worked tirelessly through the night to ensure that did not happen. There were challenges to be faced. The *Talwar* was never left unguarded and on that night, the security was extra-vigilant. There were permanent and regular sentries at the main gate and half a dozen more sentries patrolling the grounds and barracks.

The way to get round the sentries turned out to be shockingly easy. The main gate was armed by naval police but men from the barracks were selected for sentry duty every night. It so happened that one of the barrack leaders was part of Dutt's group. He and the underground group of men offered to take the midnight to 4 a.m. shift that nobody wanted. They made up half of the sentries. These sentries kept the other half of the sentries busy with chocolates, cigarettes, and chats. The result: Dutt and his men had full freedom to execute their plans. They worked tirelessly between 2 and 4 a.m. in the pitch-dark. Before the break of dawn, the plans for publicly humiliating the British was put into operation.

As Dutt recounts: 'The night became a witness to the organisational capacity of the ratings. By dawn the *Talwar*, meant as an exhibit before the admiring Bombay public, was in shambles. The parade ground was littered with burnt flag and buntings; brooms and buckets were prominently displayed from the masthead.' He added: 'The authorities guessed that this was not a one-man job. They tried every trick to track down the culprits but they could not pull off a single arrest. They were furious with impotent rage.'

The biggest embarrassment for the British was the political slogans. Etched in foot-high letters staring at each visitor from the corner of every wall, slogans like 'Quit India', 'Down with the Imperialists', 'Revolt Now', 'Kill the British', made the imperialists a laughing-stock of the whole of Bombay, and as nationalistic papers carried the news, of the rest of India as well. Nothing like this had ever happened before. The British were shaken. The deliberate and meticulously thought-out plan to disrupt Navy Day showed the organizational power and daring of the ratings. They would display this power, again and again.

★ ★ ★

The British ordered a change of guard and Commander Arthur Frederick King, a foulmouthed racist, was made the CO of *Talwar*, replacing Lt Commander ATJ Cole. In the eyes of the British, King would restore the discipline which had been missing under Cole. Cole's summary removal was an indication of how badly the empire had been shaken and it was no surprise that the ratings would strike again. The only question that remained was when.

King, who was made CO of HMIS *Talwar* on 21 January 1946, was anxious to assert his authority quickly. But he would face his first big test even before he had time to settle in. Eager to assure a sense of normalcy, the British announced that the commander-in-chief of British forces in India, Field Marshal Claude Auchinleck would be paying his first visit to the *Talwar* on 2 February, an occasion that the ratings were all too eager to seize upon. Commander King was determined that this would not be the case. The *Talwar* was spruced up and a special dais was erected from where the C-in-C would salute the guard of honour and then address the naval force. The visit was of great importance for the British and especially for King to ensure the embarrassment of Navy Day would not be repeated.

For this, foolproof security was put in place. Sentries and police were increased fourfold the previous night to ensure that every inch of the ground in *Talwar* was under surveillance. Floodlights were mounted on the parade ground and the lights of the verandas of the barracks were kept on.

But at the same time the ratings were determined to make a bigger and bolder statement than the one on Navy Day. As Dutt pointed out, tensions were rising by the minute and a showdown was imminent. This time though, the modus operandi had to be different. The tightened security meant that the plan the ratings had drawn up for Navy Day could not be followed. Dutt, however, was determined that they would continue, no matter the consequences. And so, without waiting for darkness, Dutt and Puri struck.

It was a mixture of luck and courage. As the gong for the call for supper went and other ratings rushed to the mess deck, Dutt and his men struck the 'first blow'. All the night sentries had not arrived by then and the two that did were new to the job. Handling them was easy as Dutt chronicles. Dusk was settling in and in that time the immortal words 'JAI HIND' and 'QUIT INDIA' had been painted on the very platform where the C-in-C would address the men. Despite being thought up on the spur of the moment, the plan was perfect. The ratings would certainly not be allowed to go near the platform at night and so Dutt, Puri and their men could be reasonably confident no one would notice what they had done until the C-in-C came to deliver his address. The sight of Britain's senior-most officer in India speaking from a platform etched with the words 'QUIT INDIA' on it would hit the British hard.

It did. Dutt was not done yet. As a senior telegraphist, he knew he could walk around the *Talwar* at night without being questioned. He made the most of this opportunity. Seditious leaflets had been smuggled into the *Talwar* earlier. Dutt pasted those on the walls and painted slogans as well.

Ironically, the message in the leaflets was from the Bible which said, 'No man can serve two masters; for either he will hate the one and love the other; or else he will hold on to the one and despise the other.' Calling for the ratings to 'hate' their masters, Dutt had written: 'Brothers this is a time for hate and this is a time for love. You must learn to recognise your enemy and hate him. You must love your mother, the land you were born in.' It was a powerful call to arms.

The patriotic graffiti was discovered only hours later at 5 a.m. Alarm bells sounded and all the ratings were ordered onto the parade ground. Even then, the brave telegraphist would have got away scot-free except for one glaring mistake. After nights of planning and outmanoeuvring sentries, he had forgotten to take the gum bottle located in their hideout and had instead taken the one in the wireless room.

Dutt's luck failed him. The steel-hearted telegraphist, who had never before been in any trouble with Commander King, was spotted by four trainees. A quick raid of his locker found seditious literature, diaries, copies of the leaflets and most damningly, copies of the *Indian Mutiny, 1857* by Asoka Mehta.

Dutt was arrested on 2 February 1946 and thrown into solitary confinement. It is most telling that once he was awakened, all thoughts of being a RIN rating left him. He thought of himself as an Azad Hindi – a proud citizen of Free India taking on the might of an empire. It was with this thought in mind that he answered Commander King's queries when the commander shouted at him in a bid to intimidate him.

King: 'Do you know the consequences?'

Dutt: 'Save your breath, Sir, I am ready to face your firing squad.'

REFERENCES

Andrew Davis, *Identity and Assemblage of Protest.*

B.C. Dutt, *Mutiny of the Innocents.* Bombay: Sindhu Publications, 1971, pp. 74–110.

Dilip Kumar Das, *Revisiting Talwar: A Study in the Royal Indian Navy Uprising of February 1946.* Delhi: Ajanta Publications, 1993, pp. 61–89.

Dr V.M. Bhagwatkar, *Role of R.I.N Mutiny of Feb. 1946 (Royal Indian Navy Uprising), in the Indian Freedom Struggle. 'Beginning of Strike'*, 2004, pp. 22–32, PhD thesis approved for degree.

Famine Inquiry Commission (May 1945). Report on Bengal. New Delhi: Manager of Publications, Government of India Press.

HMIS *Talwar*, National Archives.

INA Trial, Lal Salaam - A Blog by Vinay Lal.

Interview with B.C. Dutt.

John Jukes, *Mutiny.*

Lt. Cdr G.D. Sharma, VSM (Retd), *The Untold Story of Naval Mutiny: Last War of Independence.* Delhi: Vij Books, 2015, pp. 48–57, 76–95.

Naval Headquarters, File No. NL 9987/ Mutiny Petitions.

Navy Day Celebration, NAI.

Pail R. Greenough, 'Indian Famines and Peasant Victims: The Case of Bengal in 1942-44'. *Modern Asian Studies,* Vol. 14 (2) 1980, pp. 227–28.

Percy S. Gourgey, *The Royal Navy Strike of 1946.* Hyderabad: Orient BlackSwan, 1996.

'The Unsung Heroes of 1946', *Mainstream Weekly.*

Newspaper clippings (January–February 1946) (*Blitz, Free Press Journal*).

https://swarajyamag.com/columns/the-forgotten-naval-mutiny-of-1946-and-indias-independence

Riviera Building, Marine Drive. It was in Flat No. 2, home of Kusum and P.N. Nair, where the planning of the mutiny took place.

PLANNING THE MUTINY: THE SECRET HEROES

Flat number 2, Riviera Building, Marine Drive, Mumbai, was in a prime location, overlooking the Arabian Sea. From the balcony, one could see the warships of the British fleet flying the Royal Navy's ensigns. The building was used by the RIN to house Indian naval officers.

This was where the initial planning for the mutiny took place. Flat 2 was occupied by a young married couple, Pran and Kusum Nair. Kusum was a journalist who was very active in the underground freedom movement. Pran had actually served in various branches of the British Indian defence forces and was thus, privy to their psychology.

Their home was a safe haven for the ratings and the Nairs were friends with two of the key planners who became ringleaders – R.D. Puri and B.C. Dutt. Both of them had been inspired by the stories of heroism of Netaji and the INA.

In January 1941, Bose made a daring escape from house arrest in Calcutta and travelled overland to Germany via Afghanistan and the Soviet Union. From there, he made a journey by submarine to Japan and resurfaced dramatically as the inspirational new commander of the INA.

His feats made him a hero, and the INA was the pride of the nation. The average Indian saw the INA soldiers as role models. In contrast, those who had served in the armed forces commanded by the British were often taunted and humiliated for serving foreign masters.

Azad Hind leaflets and pamphlets urging Indians in the defence forces to rise and revolt had been smuggled into India. These writings found their way into the naval barracks and inspired many budding revolutionaries – young men and women – to revolt in an effort to finally put an end to British rule.

The core group of rebellious naval ratings including the flamboyant R.D. Puri and the master planner, B.C. Dutt became regular visitors to the flat, and close friends of the Nairs. Around end-1945, these young men would visit Nairs' flat in their 'liberty' time, almost every week.

In their meetings, they exchanged stories about the sacrifices made by the INA soldiers. They shared letters written by the INA soldiers to Indian political leaders describing their resistance and how they were waging battles for Independence on foreign soil.

The ratings also attended lectures at the flat, exhorting them to rise and work towards Independence. These lectures were addressed by well-known lawyer Purshottam Tricumdas, journalist Y.K. Menon, and possibly by Aruna Asaf Ali (the firebrand member of the socialist group within the Congress) too. Even earlier, these young men had been introduced to Aruna by an influential journalist and activist, Manohar Lal, from *Free Press Journal*.

These lectures inspired the youngsters with a burning desire to contribute towards the struggle for Independence. Like the other reasons, they also resented the poor living conditions, inedible food, and racial discrimination of the RIN.

Long months were spent plotting and inciting the ratings into taking the final step – an armed mutiny. A key group of leaders of the RIN ratings, namely Dutt, Puri, Salil Shyam, Madan Singh, and M.S. Khan – would form the core of this operation along with other politically minded youngsters, including Kusum and her husband Pran Nath Nair. B.C. Dutt, Puri, Madan Singh, Salil Shyam and Co. started to meet in restaurants around the Colaba area, where they planned for future acts of defiance.

In December, they painted seditious slogans across the walls of *Talwar*. Seeing the courage of these youngsters and their willingness to put themselves at risk, the Nairs encouraged them to clandestinely put stones in the dal served at the *Talwar* mess (on 17 February, the night before the mutiny began) in order to enrage and instigate all the ratings into open rebellion.

A large number of ratings were posted in and around Bombay in various RIN establishments and ships, and they worked at the heart of the military power of the British Empire – its navy. It was obvious to any revolutionary that crippling the Royal Navy would go a long way to curtailing the might of the British Empire.

Kusum was the more daring and adventurous of the couple. Devoted to social causes and absolutely fearless, she had naturally gravitated towards the cause of freedom. It was equally natural that their flat would serve as a base for discussing the key strategies on how to motivate the mass of ratings to take the ultimate step.

Now all they needed was a plan.

THE RINGLEADERS

Puri and Dutt – the two young leaders of the revolt –visited the Riviera flat every week, plotting ways and means to convince the ratings that the time had come to stage a final act of rebellion.

It fell on the Nairs to provide the political elements and to select the core team of the RIN mutiny. Kusum's role as a journalist gave her access and insight into the political thinking of the day. She was also close to Aruna Asaf Ali, a prominent, and rebellious member of the Congress.

Pran Nath had served in the army and later, been seconded to the navy, and was therefore, well acquainted with conditions in the defence services and understood the main issues of concern and complaints among the ratings.

Both of them were part of the Congress Socialist Movement, which brought them in close contact with stalwarts like Aruna Asaf Ali, Minoo Masani, Asoka Mehta and others. Kusum was especially close to Aruna, so much so that she and her younger sister addressed Aruna by her pet name 'Renee'.

Their home was also the hub where the Ex-Services Association was formed, with moral and financial support from IPTA, which included celebrities like Khwaja Ahmad Abbas, Balraj Sahni, Zohra Sehgal, Salil Chowdhary, Utpal Dutt, and Prithviraj Kapoor. For many of the ratings, the first lesson in revolutionary ideology and strategy was imparted at Riviera where they listened to prominent ideologues. Their activities had not gone unnoticed. The British typically used local inspectors from the CID to carry out surveillance on potential troublemakers. But in this case, they could conveniently call on the services of Sadashiv Ganesh Karmarkar, a naval officer who was living in the flat above the Nairs.

Karmarkar, under instructions from his British bosses was busy keeping notes on visitors to the flat. But knowing they would be under surveillance, the core group of conspirators who had named themselves 'Azad Hindi', took to clandestinely meeting in cafés, secluded corners on board ships, and shore establishments, as they planned their strategy. In addition, Puri and Kusum's younger sister Shaila had fallen in love, cementing what might otherwise have been a motley crew of conspirators.

Another man who played a leading role in making plans for a ratings' uprising was Mohammad Shuaib Khan (M.S. Khan), who later became the president of the NCSC.

BALAI CHANDRA DUTT

Generally, better known as B.C. Dutt, he was born in 1923 in a small village in Bengal. Enamoured by stories about life at sea, he joined the navy on 28 February 1941 after finishing his matriculation from Calcutta. He was then barely eighteen years of age.

He would, like many young men, soon be disillusioned with life in the navy. Dutt later said he had been lied to and seduced by promises made by Commander Bailey, who was then CO of the Signal School. He was told he could be a warrant officer in four years. But after five years in service, Dutt was still a Leading Telegraphist. Even his efforts to become a regular commissioned officer in the Indian Army were denied as he was six months older than regulations permitted.

Denied promotion, Dutt also recalled many stories of the racism he encountered during his career. In one instance, Dutt and his fellow ratings were returning exhausted from the war they had fought in Burma and their compartment was so tiny that they could not even sit, let alone lie down. The adjoining compartment

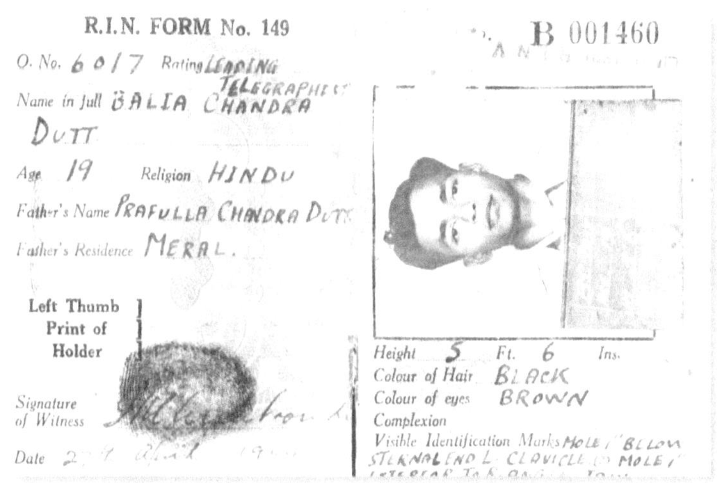

Identity card of B.C. Dutt. Leading Telegraphist in the RIN, he joined the service in February 1941 and was the protagonist of the mutiny.

reserved for Britishers was empty and could hold over a dozen people. Dutt complained to the RTO captain who told him to his face: 'You are Indians, you don't get a better place than what you have got already. Take it or leave it.' This, along with the fact that Dutt was pulled up by the CO of HMIS *Dalhousie* for writing about his disillusionment about naval life to his brother in 1941 drove him further along the revolutionary road.

However, it was a chance meeting with an old friend, Salil Shyam that led him to play a leading role in masterminding the mutiny. Shyam had just returned from the Far East when he met Dutt in Bombay where Dutt was serving at the HMIS *Talwar.* Shyam had brought letters written by members of Azad Hind Fauj addressed to Jawaharlal Nehru and Sarat Chandra Bose, and he was looking for a safe place to hide them before he could deliver them.

Dutt agreed to hide the letters in his locker. This was like a ticking bomb since such an act was considered high treason and could be punishable with discharge and even death. But Dutt had no hesitation in volunteering to help. Dutt had already displayed his rebellious streak during Navy Day (1 December 1945), when he painted 'Quit India' and 'Jai Hind' on the wooden platform from where the C-in-C was to address the officers and men.

Though Dutt was treated like a hero and lauded by the nationalist papers, the fallout was severe. His locker was opened, and it contained not just seditious literature but evidence of a larger conspiracy where other names, notably those of Kusum and Pran Nair, would feature. He would later write a book, *Mutiny of the Innocents*, where he elaborated upon his role and his relationship with the co-conspirators.

RISHI DEV PURI

If any of the ratings had to be typecast as a devil-may-care James Bond figure, it would have to be R.D. Puri, 'Harry' to his friends. He belonged to a wealthy and influential business family. His courage and charisma ensured he played a leading role.

R.D. was the son of Dasaundhi Ram Puri of Model Town, Lahore. His career choices were unusual. While he had devoted himself to a career in the armed forces, he shifted around. He moved from the army, to the air force, and then the navy.

His nonchalant attitude was in evidence when he took part in the precursor to the mutiny, by painting subversive slogans on RIN *Talwar* on Navy Day, alongside his friend and fellow Azad Hindi, B.C. Dutt. For his role in that episode, he was discharged from the navy.

R.D. was suspected; indeed, he was one of the main suspects. But the authorities could not find any evidence implicating him. Nevertheless, he was discharged from the navy.

R.D.'s intimacy with a wide circle of people and the trust they placed in him meant that he was privy to many confidential secrets about the strike, as well as personal gossip about people like Aruna Asaf Ali. His close relationship with Shaila, in particular, made him privy to many of the clandestine developments leading up to the mutiny and the subsequent fallout.

In a letter dated 3 March 1946, Shaila writes, 'I wanted to tell you something important about the strike. This morning, Commander Cole told Sachdev that he knew you were responsible for the Navy Day Show and that though Nair is a good man himself, his wife is a bad Communist. Kusum is definitely suspected of being involved in the strike. As for Karmarkar he is the absolute limit. He remains standing on his balcony and keeps a watch on who comes and goes to and from our flat. He told Hasan, "Either you can choose the Navy or you can go to Nair's place. You can't have it both ways."'

R.D. described his motivation in a letter to Shaila: 'I am not suited for the army under the imperial flag. My blood is for I.N.A. and if someone can take me now, I am out for it. Now I shall never join any force unless it is hundred per cent our own national force. Suppose there is a war now and I am called up again as I am still under the contract of ten years and temporarily released. I shall not join but prefer a cell behind the imperial bars.'

It is thanks to the interception of the couple's letters and internal intelligence reports, that we receive an understanding of R.D.'s actions and his relationship with Shaila, whom he affectionately called 'Kuku Baby'. We also get a sense of the rapid pace of events as these were taking place in Bombay during those hectic days.

Ironically, it was the Intelligence Bureau (IB) that made R.D. famous. The IB maintained constant surveillance on him and the Nairs and frequently intercepted their letters. Without the inputs from the snooping, R.D. would have flown under the radar and his role would never have been truly known except to his immediate friends and family.

A letter written by Assistant Director G.C. Ryan, IB Delhi, to Rao Bahadur M.N. Desai, MBE, deputy commissioner of Police, Bombay, said this: 'I write to inform you that the Punjab CID have discovered from further interceptions that "Kuku Baby" is Miss Shaila Prasad of 2 Riviera, Marine Drive Bombay. It appears that there is a romantic understanding between her and RD Puri. Between March 1946 and May1946 she wrote as many as 14 letters.'

R.D. was suspect in the eyes of Commander King, Lt S.M. Nanda and other officers. In a letter dated 20 May 1946, Shaila writes: 'This afternoon I went to the court. At that time Commander King was being cross examined… He said he was aware of the political consciousness in Talwar and when slogans were written on Navy Day, he would even place his finger on who the man was but unfortunately, he had no proof to offer… Here Iyengar was brilliant. He asked Nanda you said you could lay your finger on one man — who was that man?

'A: Dev, Rishi Dev.'

In the diary recovered from Dutt's locker, he had written: 'Deb [RD Puri]… one of the few most wonderful lads I have come in touch so far in my life… If I can be called idealist, he is certainly a realist. I shall take some time to get rid of his memories.'

R.D. would have carried on the struggle in some other way but his influential family persuaded him to pull back. R.D.'s elder

Rishi Dev Puri, a smart and suave rating in the RIN, was courageous to the core and played a leading role in starting the revolt that led to mutiny.

brother, V.V. Puri, convinced him to shift to Shimla where the family owned a famous nightclub called Davicos. R.D. took up playing the piano and entertained guests there every night, earning a name as a bon vivant. He lost touch with many of his naval friends in Bombay, and his family ensured he stayed out of further trouble.

MADAN SINGH

Born to Bhagvan Kaur and Sardar Ronak Singh, an unlettered farmer in Siahar village near Ludhiana in Punjab on 24 April 1920, Madan Singh's early life was a constant struggle. The eldest of five brothers, he was the only one who wanted an education. His stint at Arya High School meant walking many miles every day because it was far from his village.

He then went to Ludhiana, determined to join the navy. Asked why, at the post-mutiny Commission of Enquiry, he said: 'I joined

SECRET.

<u>Intercepted letter.</u>

Name and address of the sender. Rishi, Devico's Ltd.,
                                 Simla.
Date on letter.   3.4.46
Sent from   Simla.
Date of posting   5.4.46
Language.   English.
Name of the addressee.   Miss Shaila Prasad.
Address.   2 Rivera-Marine Drive,
                                 Bombay.
Date of receipt.   5.4.46.
Photographed or not.   not.
Detained or passed.   Passed.
Name of the examiner.   Hari Chand, Head Constable

    **   **   **

        If there is a movement, I willbe up there
before I dive in. Don't worry I will see you
before something happens.

    **   **   **

        I am not suited for the Army under
the Imperial flag. My blood is for I.N.A. and if
some one can take me now I am out for it. Now I
shall never join any force unless it is hundred
percent our own national force. Suppose there is
a war now and I am called up again as I am still
under the contract of ten years and temporarily
released. I shall not join but prefer a cell
behind the Imperial bars.

    **   **   **

R.D. Puri's letter to Shaila Prasad, intercepted by the IB, where he wrote:
'…shall never join any force unless it is hundred percent our own national force.'

R9.N° 3062/H
21-6-46.

No. 12/A.I./46-IV
Intelligence Bureau,
(Home Department),
Government of India,   18 JUN 1946

My dear Desai,

    Following is a copy of a letter dated
27-5-46, from Rishi Dev Puri, ex-R.I.N. rating, Simla
Bombay, to Miss Shaila Kumari, 10 Maskati Court,
Queens Road, Bombay, intercepted by the Punjab
C.I.D.   It seems to indicate that Puri will be
going to Bombay about the middle of this month.

    " I have got your letter. My parents
thought that I might play some more stunts
with the Navy business if I go to Bombay and
they therefore sent Puri Sahib to keep me calm
here.   I am sorry to have missed that golden
opportunity of meeting you and all others. Puri
Sahib did not want this hungry tiger to go out
of his cage just yet. You know I was dying to
give evidence in the Enquiry Commission and I
alone know how I was tied up here.

    I will be up there in the middle of
June. Remember it is a great secret. Do not
tell anyone that I am coming. "

    Yours sincerely,

(G.C. RYAN.)

Rao Bahadur M.N. Desai, MBE.,
Dy. Commissioner of Police,
Special Branch IB,
BOMBAY.

Copy of R.D. Puri's letter to Shaila 'Kumari', intercepted by the IB.

the Navy because I wanted to see the world and of course have my own interest of coming into the war because I felt it was my duty to do so.' Once disillusionment and discontent set in considering the degrading conditions in the service, he was persuaded to join the cause for freedom. As vice-president of the NCSC, he worked tirelessly with President M.S. Khan to unite the ratings against overwhelming odds.

On the objectives of the mutiny, Singh stated in an interview that they had a clear plan of action, first freeing Dutt and then obtaining arms from Bucher Island [where the armaments for the Bombay Presidency were stored] along with all telephone and wireless equipment near Pune. This meant that all naval ships could remain in constant communication and collective decisions, so crucial during the mutiny, could be made and broadcast faster and more efficiently.

According to his son Ranjit Pender, his father was involved in many heroic actions during the Second World War which showed not just his bravery but also his concern for his fellow men. In one such action, Madan Singh played a major role in rescuing survivors from his ship which had hit a mine and sunk near Port Blair.

As his son says: 'Dad did not belong to any political party and has always been fiercely independent. He often called politicians being as straight as *jalebi*. Sense of fairness meant a lot to him. In his eyes the British were unfair to Indians and therefore he fully supported Independence.' Singh earned a reputation as a strict disciplinarian among the ratings, a man of principles, and fiercely patriotic.

To a question at the Commission of Enquiry if he was happy in the navy, he responded: 'I realized that what my home can give no other place can. Initially I enjoyed when I was in HMIS *Baluchistan* and HMIS *Narbada* but later when I came to Castle Barrack, food conditions were awfully bad. There was corruption in those who supplied food to us. They would have good quality of food for themselves but give ratings poor quality. Also, those who paid Rs 3 per month to them underhand would get better food. They used to

A brave and principled ringleader, Madan Singh was involved in many heroic actions during the Second World War.

sell medicines that we were supposed to get free.'

He was, according to his son, involved in preventing an armed attack on pro-British newspapers. The ratings and their strike leaders had contacted leading newspapers regarding their support for the strike and most responded positively except a few British-owned papers, the most prominent of these being the *Times of India*.

Angered at the pro-British coverage, the ratings surrounded the offices of the paper in Bombay and demanded the editor face them personally. So petrified was the editor, Sir Francis Lyod that he escaped from the back door, fearing for his life. The ratings then decided to blow up the TOI building.

As Ranjit Pender recalls: 'Dad had to intervene and prevent ratings from doing any damage. The chief editor of TOI had frantically called *Talwar* saying that the ratings have lined up their guns towards the premises of TOI and were ready to blow it up. The message was given to dad who immediately proceeded towards the TOI building and met the head of the paper, then a prominent

Englishman. He assured the terrified head of TOI that no harm will be done and asked the ratings to clear the area.'

A major disaster was thus prevented. After riots broke out in the city, Pender recalls that his father 'met several senior Congress leaders to intervene in order for the strike to remain in control. These leaders assured that they will nominate a party leader to take up their cause but advised them to stop violence from spreading. Dad conveyed this to the NCSC of which he was nominated as vice president. The committee agreed to listen to their collective conscience but carry on the strike peacefully.'

MOHAMMAD SHUAIB KHAN

Better known as M.S. Khan, this blue-eyed Pathan belonged to a prominent family of lawyers in the Punjab. The family came from Daska near Sialkot, now in Pakistan. His passion was to join the navy, a move which was not approved by his family. So in 1939, when he was just thirteen, he ran away from home to begin life at sea. However, the romance of sea life soon wore off and in the very second month he resigned, disillusioned by the variance in promises made during recruitment and the actual conditions on board. His father refused to take him back so, a few months later, Khan decided to return to the navy in 1940 as an ordinary seaman. At the time of the mutiny he was drawing a salary of Rs 91 per month as a leading signalman.

Khan served in several ships and developed a reputation as a qualified, dependable seaman. During his service he had sailed and spent seventeen months in England, over a month in Africa, and sailed to Ireland, Scotland, and Burma serving alongside the Royal Navy. He took part in every theatre of war the RIN was involved in, in the Atlantic and the Mediterranean. He often did not sleep for several days and nights at a stretch – during the day, there were threats from aircraft and, at night, from submarines.

When he deposed before the Commission of Enquiry to probe

the RIN mutiny it was clear that he had strong views. He stated that he had a burning desire to end the blatant discrimination between Indian and British ratings. Naval authorities, he deposed, had given him false promises that he would be a warrant officer at the end of two years with a pay scale of Rs 350, which did not happen. While being grilled by the commission, he was asked as to why they were complaining about the service conditions when they were allowed the use of club facilities and dance with women. His reply was: 'Sir, you can't dance with water in your hand.' His reference was to Indian ratings being denied the consumption of alcohol in the club.

As a matriculate who spoke English well, he was a natural choice to become the president of the NCSC at the age of twenty-three because of his suave personality and his command over the English language. Having joined the *Talwar* just four days before the actual mutiny took place (he was on a 45-day leave prior to this) he was soon in the thick of the action serving as the principal negotiator between the authorities and the ratings.

KUSUM AND P.N. NAIR

Born in 1919 in Etah, now in Uttar Pradesh, Kusum was the first-born of Jwala Prasad Ashtana (1890–1962) and Manorama Saxena. Jwala Prasad was something of a rebel and Kusum was expected and encouraged to have an independent mind given her father's background. She certainly seems to have inherited her rebellious spirit from her father.

Jwala Prasad had rejected his family's attempts to arrange his marriage and run away from home. He became a teacher in Agra University and married a girl from a landed family, Manorama Saxena who was well educated – unusual at the time. Jwala then went to Cambridge where he made the acquaintance of a classmate, S. Radhakrishnan, who would become India's future president.

Radhakrishnan would become a regular at their home. Kusum called him 'uncle'. On his return to India, Jwala became the principal

FROM ... THE FLAG OFFICER, BOMBAY.

AT ... BOMBAY.

DATE ... 23RD MAY, 1946.

TO ... THE DIRECTOR INTELLIGENCE BUREAU, HOME DEPARTMENT, GOVERNMENT OF INDIA.

LT.COL. D.M. HENNESSY, KEVAL MAHAL, MARINE DRIVE, BOMBAY.

THE COMMISSIONER OF POLICE, BOMBAY.

SUBJECT :- **O.N.4988 LEADING SIGNALMAN M.S.KHAN**

The above mentioned rating, who was the principal spokesman and ring-leader in the February R.I.N. mutiny, was sentenced to dismissal with disgrace yesterday 22nd May and was put in a train to return to his home.

2. Arrangements were made with Bombay C.I.D. to follow the rating as far as Igatpuri to ensure that he leaves the Bombay area and to watch him if he returns to Bombay without going home. The police authorities in his district have been requested by the Deputy Commissioner, Special Branch, Bombay, to report on this man's movements.

3. As he was leaving Kalyan he made it quite clear to the Naval Officers escorting him that he intended returning to Bombay at some future date.

4. Particulars of this rating are as follows :-

Home address :- Vill: & P.O. Dhaska
Dist: Sialkot, Punjab.

Next of Kin :- Kurshed Jaw (wife)

Height :- 5' 9"

Hair :- Black.

Eyes:- :- Brown.

Complexion :- Brown.

Has a large mole one inch below mastoid process, right.

Date of birth :- 1st July, 1922.

5. As far as is known he is not connected with any political movement, but has expressed violent anti-British views on a number of occasions. During the mutiny he almost certainly came under the influence of subversive political elements. He has an unusual amount of control and command over large numbers of men and undoubtedly averted several outbreaks of violence during the mutiny.

Facsimile of a document with M.S. Khan's personal details and particulars from the Indian Navy records.

of Robertson College in Jabalpur where he mixed with an elite crowd which included the Nehrus. There are photographs of him at a college reunion, sitting next to Vijaya Lakshmi Pandit, Nehru's sister. This association may have fuelled his patriotic spirit even more. He was sacked by college authorities after he persuaded the students to sing *Vande Mataram* instead of 'God Save the King'. Clearly, his daughter Kusum, came from the same mould.

Father and daughter were of one mind when it came to doing what they thought was right politically. But it was quite a different story when it came to her husband, Pran Nath Nair/Nayyar, who was better known as 'Pano'. He was born into a Khatri family on 30 October 1913 in Kunjah, Gujerat District, in Punjab (now in Pakistan).

Pano's father, Mahesh Das Nair was a conservative man. It was unlikely that he and Kusum would ever marry, given the difference in attitudes of their fathers. If Jwala Prasad was a rebel, Mahesh Das who came from a large landowning family, remained a strict upholder of the law.

But romance blossomed when the two met and they continued to correspond as pen pals. They got married in 1937 in Jabalpur. Kusum was barely sixteen. Given the fact that it was a cross-caste and cross-ethnic marriage, one can imagine the stir it would have caused, especially on Pano's side of the family.

After moving to New Delhi, Pano started spelling his name 'Nayyar' because he was 'tired of being identified as a South Indian.' Kusum, however, was already established as an author with the 'Nair' spelling and she retained it, even after the couple split up in 1968. Kusum received her bachelor's degree in philosophy in 1941 from the University of Nagpur. She wasn't just quick-witted; she was athletic too. She soundly beat men at tennis as they moved around on postings to places like Belgaum and Karachi.

The couple then moved to Bombay and it was not long before they were heavily involved in the fight for freedom. Joining the Congress Socialist Movement, they rubbed shoulders with stalwarts such as Aruna Asaf Ali, Minoo Masani, Asoka Mehta and others in their Marine Drive home.

Kusum's closeness with these politicians grew, especially with Aruna Asaf Ali. Indeed, Kusum named her daughter Aruna. The Nairs were so determined to further the nationalist cause that wild schemes were hatched by them to help promote it. From holding not-very-successful poker games to raise money for the cause to Kusum's determination to sabotage the Raj from within by joining the army, they tried everything that was within their power that they could think of.

Kusum's dreams of sabotaging the Raj from within the army were dashed because she was appointed an office clerk which didn't hold much promise for furthering her revolutionary ambitions. Fed up, she went to her immediate supervisor and told her she was resigning. The supervisor told her she couldn't quit because she had signed up for the duration of the war. Kusum said she didn't care and insisted. Surprisingly, her resignation was accepted.

Given Pano's naval connections, it was natural that they would cultivate young radical seafarers. The Nairs planned and plotted to agitate and motivate sailors. One of their schemes was to ask the conspirators to mix bits of gravel in the food served to the ratings. This actually sparked off the strike in *Talwar* that led to the mutiny.

Kusum joined the army during the Second World War. Before taking a plunge into the fight for freedom, she became a close follower of Aruna Asaf Ali and was a conduit between the naval ratings and Aruna.

Kusum with husband, P.N. Nair. The couple played a major role in instigating the young naval ratings to revolt.

A few days before the mutiny, on 12 February 1946, the 'Indian Ex-Services Association' was formed with the well-known lawyer Purshottam Tricumdas nominated president, and Y.K. Menon general secretary, along with the Nairs on board. It was headquartered at the Nair's flat. According to a report published in the *Bombay Chronicle* on 22 February 1946, the Indian Ex-Services Association made its sympathies quite evident with the RIN ratings passing two resolutions, one of which stated, 'This Association greets the personnel of the Royal Indian Navy who have gone on strike and congratulates them on the exemplary solidarity and discipline they have maintained. This Association has full sympathy with the demands of the strikers and calls upon the authorities to concede the same as swiftly as possible. The Association strongly condemns the calling in of the police and the Indian Army for the purpose of coercing the RIN personnel.'

The British knew that the sailors had started mixing with political activists, and Kusum was under surveillance. During her interrogation at the enquiry commission post-mutiny, she was asked: 'Would you agree if anybody comes in contact with you or your writings, they would be liable to lose loyalty to the service?' Her answer was, 'If they are so influenced, I suppose, they would.'

Kusum was devoted to social causes and absolutely fearless. Pran's involvement stemmed from his experience as an officer in the Royal Indian Naval Volunteer Reserve (RINVR). In emails exchanged by the author with Kusum's son-in law Barry Michie, currently an academic in Kansas State University, he writes: 'I have many stories about the family, their relationships with nationalist leaders prior to the mutiny, how it was instigated on the *Talwar* (by Pran Nair) mixing a handful of gravel in the dal) to get the ratings worked up, the aftermath (she said at the enquiry they lied through their teeth saying it wasn't a mutiny but rather a strike), and that the purpose was to let the Brits know they couldn't rely on Indian forces any longer and that it was time for them to leave… My father-in-law was on the ship during the Mutiny and my mother-in-law, a journalist at the time, was a go-between with the Brits and the nationalist leaders. As you know, Gandhi and Nehru (who my in-laws knew well) were not pleased at all with the mutiny as it jeopardised their negotiations for Independence. For years, we were after my mother-in-law to write up the mutiny story but she was set on working on research on Indian rural development and agricultural economics and couldn't find the time… pity!'

Later, when she met the well-known Pakistani scholar Hamza Alavi in Michigan University, she confessed that the mutiny of 1946 was planned to the minutest details in her home in Bombay. From a study of documents found in B.C. Dutt's locker after the slogan-writing incident on Navy Day, the board of enquiry concluded that Dutt had some contact with Lieutenant P.N. Nair and a few others connected with the Ex-Services Association.

Y.K. MENON

A founder member of the Ex-Servicemen Association, who actively participated in the planning of the mutiny. Tricumdas and Menon founded the Ex-Services Association with Menon as general secretary and Tricumdas as chairman. The association was formed mainly to help the demobilized personnel of armed forces. But while operating in a clandestine manner, it guided the naval ratings in their revolt of February 1946.

Given his nationalistic leanings, it was no surprise that Menon would choose to get involved. A freelance journalist, Menon participated in the Quit India movement in 1942, and wrote stridently nationalistic articles. His active participation in the Quit India movement, and his vocation as a journalist meant that he had contacts with the top Congress leaders, including Mahatma Gandhi, Sardar Patel, and Jawaharlal Nehru.

Soon after his release from Nasik prison in 1945 (Menon was among the last 'Quit India freedom fighters' to be released) he became actively involved with the socialist elements of the Congress party like Jayaprakash Narayan, Aruna Asaf Ali, Minoo Masani and others. The first person he met after reaching Bombay, post his release was Lt P.N. Nair and his wife Kusum in Bombay. The Nairs alerted him about 'some boys in the navy they knew who were discontented and aggrieved with the treatment of the establishment and were imbued with patriotism.'

Menon remains a key figure to understanding the movement more so because he stood with it until the end, and also because he viewed it all from the sidelines, ensuring that he could provide as dispassionate a voice as possible.

Though Y.K. Menon did not himself write about the mutiny, a recorded interview explains just how the mutiny took off. Menon claims that it was at Nair's suggestion, that he started meeting with the more politically conscious boys during their free time. Some he claimed were 'emotionally unstable' for such organizational work but the educated boys at the HMIS *Talwar* – 'lent themselves to moulding politically speaking.'

Menon became directly involved when Commander King ordered the arrest of two ratings, he claimed had distributed seditious literature and pasted slogans such as 'Quit India' on the walls of the HMIS *Talwar*. A number of ratings landed up at Menon's home early morning on 17 February to complain about the arrests.

The contours of the mutiny became clear at this point. A committee was formed and leaders identified to liaise with the other ships and shore establishments to explain what was happening and gauge their reactions. The next day, there was mayhem in Bombay as ratings across the city took to the streets shouting slogans. The pivotal moment, it seemed, had come.

He says he tried to persuade Gandhi to meet the striking boys but the latter refused. He then met Nehru with Purshottam Tricumdas. Menon's account of the pre-mutiny period includes details of his meetings with leaders like Gandhi and Nehru. Asked about the role of the association, Menon claimed that among other things the main purpose of this association was to provide legal aid to all those who were court-martialled.

Asked as to whether the RIN mutiny could have led to a larger uprising, Menon believed it could and should have but the 'leaders of the national movement were venerable but tired old men who were not exactly eager to face any bloodbath'. Menon recalled how Mahatma Gandhi was staying overnight in Bombay en route to the Nature Cure Clinic at Uruli. He claims he led a delegation to meet the Mahatma who spoke with him alone in his bedroom but refused to meet the others. 'There are very few areas of discipline left in the country Kesu, and I do not want anyone to go about destroying those areas,' Menon quoted the Mahatma as saying.

PURSHOTTAM TRICUMDAS

Born in 1897 in Bombay, Tricumdas was educated in Bombay and Cambridge. He was a member of the Bombay Home Rule League and Joint Secretary, Bombay Unit of Swarajya Party, in 1924. In 1930, he participated in the Civil Disobedience movement and the Salt Satyagraha. In 1934, he was one of the founder members of the Congress Socialist Party and a member of its National Executive. A close aide of Mahatma Gandhi, he left the Congress Party in 1948 and was president at the Socialist Party's Nasik Conference where he was elected party's treasurer the same year. (He was elected to the Maharashtra Legislative Assembly in 1951.)

He was instrumental in getting Nehru to meet the ratings at his Malabar Hill residence, where Menon was also present. The meeting proved unfruitful because Nehru refused to get behind their cause. The delegation requested Nehru to meet with the viceroy and plead with him regarding the case of the Indian naval personnel. Nehru rejected this demand saying: 'How do you expect me to place this case before the Viceroy?'

Tricumdas was a lawyer by profession and practised at the Supreme Court, where he earned a reputation as a formidable legal brain. His most famous legal case was 'Emperor Vs Purshottam Trikam Das'. He authored several books, many of them published by Padma Publication, a publishing house founded and owned by Kusum Nair. At the Commission of Enquiry post the mutiny, he appeared as a lawyer on the side of the striking ratings.

ARUNA ASAF ALI

She was *the* inspirational figure in the 1946 naval mutiny, one of the few politicians from non-communist parties who dared to openly support the mutineers. Aruna Asaf Ali nee Ganguli was born to Ambalika Devi and Upendranath Ganguli in Kalka, Punjab (now in Haryana). Her father, a restaurant owner, hailed from Barisal district of Eastern Bengal but later settled in the United Province (now Uttar Pradesh). Her mother Ambalika, was a daughter of 'Biplabi' Trailokyanath Sanyal, a renowned Brahmo Samaj leader who composed many Brahmo hymns. Her paternal uncle, a university professor, was married to Rabindranath Tagore's only daughter, Mira Devi. Aruna's sister, Purnima Banerjee was a member of the Constituent Assembly. Little wonder then that she was imbued with both reformist zeal and an unbridled passion for India's freedom from British rule.

Aruna was educated at Sacred Heart Convent in Lahore and

then All Saints College in Nainital. After her graduation, she taught at Gokhale Memorial School in Calcutta. She met Asaf Ali, a Congress leader in Allahabad and got married in 1928, aged nineteen, defying opposition from the family on account of their different religious backgrounds and the fact that he was twenty-three years older. Her rebellious streak did not sit well with her paternal uncle who was Aruna's guardian at the time (her father had passed away by then) and he disowned her for her decision to marry a Muslim.

Aruna's husband Asaf Ali was a prominent politician and also an accomplished lawyer best known for defending Bhagat Singh. After her marriage, Aruna became a member of the Indian National Congress where Asaf Ali was a leading figure.

She participated in Gandhi's Salt Satyagraha and was arrested on the charge that she was a vagrant. Despite the government's decision to release all political detenues in 1931, she was not released because she was technically arrested for being a person without a permanent home. Her stature and popularity was such that other women prisoners refused to leave the jail until she was released. A public agitation and Gandhi's personal intervention secured her release.

In 1932, Aruna was again held prisoner at Tihar jail in Delhi where she undertook a hunger strike to protest the welfare of other women inmates. Her efforts resulted in improvements of conditions in Tihar but she was subsequently moved to Ambala and placed in solitary confinement.

Aruna took a very active part in the Quit India movement in 1942. Gandhi's call of 'Do or Die' was in line with her political thinking and action for attaining freedom. On 8 August 1942, when the Congress Party passed the Quit India resolution at the Bombay session, the British cracked down heavily and arrested all top leaders including Nehru and Mahatma Gandhi to stop the movement from gathering momentum.

This did not dampen the spirit of the firebrand young socialist. On the contrary, the arrests of top leaders motivated her to the extent that she presided over the remainder of the session on the

Young Aruna Asaf Ali in the late 1940s. Aruna was the prominent Congress leader who pledged an open and active support to the naval ratings.

following day, 9 August, and further defied the British by hoisting the Tricolour at Gowalia Tank Maidan (now Azad Maidan) in Bombay. Instead of courting arrest, as was the fashion, she went underground.

For the next three years she evaded the police, despite her property being seized and sold by the British Government. She refused to surrender, remained underground and continued to edit the Congress's monthly magazine *Inquilab*, along with another firebrand socialist, Ram Manohar Lohia. Months after going underground she started to broadcast on the Voice of Congress through Congress Radio from Bombay, a clandestine radio station that had started operations within two weeks from the day when Aruna went underground. It operated between 20 August 1942 and December that year during the Quit India movement.

The Congress Radio countered British propaganda disseminated through state-owned All India Radio, sarcastically named Anti India Radio by Congress leaders. Through the medium, she issued a call to the youth of India, asking them to avoid futile discussions on violence and non-violence and join the revolution. She and her comrades such as Jayaprakash Narayan and Ram Manohar Lohia were described as 'the political children of Gandhi, but recent students of Karl Marx.'

Several Congress leaders urged her to surrender but she was too independent-minded to listen to them. Even Mahatma Gandhi said:

'I have been filled with admiration for your courage and heroism. You are reduced to a skeleton. Do come out and surrender yourself.' But she was made of sterner stuff.

She eventually surfaced sometime in late 1945 when the reward on her head was withdrawn by the British. It was around this time that she was contacted by P.N. Nair, Kusum Nair, and Y.K. Menon. Young rebellious ratings like Dutt, R.D., and the group of other ratings who called themselves Azad Hindis, were put in touch with her by the Nairs to seek guidance and moral support for what they were planning. She pledged them active and open support. She became very close to the Nairs when Asaf Ali was in the hospital, as it was the Nairs who looked after him.

In her book, *Resurgence of Indian Women,* co-authored with GNS Raghavan, Aruna writes: 'With the raising of the level of political consciousness there was discontent among the Indian personnel of the armed forces...' Reaffirming her unstinting support for the uprising, she says: 'Had the revolutionary spirit shown by our people during the Quit India movement and the RIN Mutiny been mobilised for a final round of the struggle for freedom, the Subcontinent's partition might possibly have been averted.' She attacked the ageing leadership of the Congress saying 'ageing and tired Congress leaders whom the British released from the prison on 15 June 1945... were in no mood for a fresh struggle.'

Aruna Asaf Ali was more in agreement with Nehru, who had lauded the efforts of the naval ratings initially as opposed to the approach of Maulana Azad (then president of the Congress Party) and Sardar Patel who wanted the ratings to surrender. She also made her stand clear on the naval unrest saying the demand of the ratings were 'entirely legitimate'. She offered her services to the ratings as a peacemaker.

At the height of mutiny, she differed publicly with Mahatma Gandhi on the issue. She was openly in favour of 'the unconditional withdrawal of military patrols and immediate lifting of bans on civil liberties.' The history of the freedom movement and the naval mutiny of 1946 would be incomplete without mentioning her courageous, independent role.

She represented the bravery and courage of numerous young men and women and naval ratings whose revolutionary and sacrificial efforts need to be told. In 1946, a rebellion of this nature and extent seemed unthinkable until it happened. The odds against taking on the might of the British were overwhelming.

Yet, the fact that they succeeded in getting so far and caused widespread consternation in Westminster, offers testimony to their courage and commitment in the cause of freedom. Many naval historians, in fact, describe the 1946 RIN Mutiny as the spark that lit the way for the historic events that would follow in 1947, when India, in Nehru's words over All India Radio: 'Would Awake to Life and Freedom.'

REFERENCES

B.C. Dutt, *Mutiny of the Innocents*. Bombay: Sindhu Publications, 1971.

B.C. Dutt, Enquiry Report, NAI.

Copy of letter dated 29.4.46, from Kusum Nair to Aruna Asaf Ali, Secret document, Criminal Investigation Department, Delhi, 2 May 1946, File No. G-7.

Dilip Kumar Das. *Revisiting Talwar: A Study in the Royal Indian Navy Uprising of February 1946*. Delhi: Ajanta Publications, 1993.

INA Trial, Lal Salaam – A Blog by Vinay Lal.

Interview with B.C. Dutt, NAI.

John Adams, 'Obituary: Kusum Nair (1919–93)', *The Journal of Asian Studies*, Vol. 53, No. 3 (August 1994), pp. 1046–48.

'Lady Journalist appears before R.I.N. Commission', *Free Press Journal*.

Note on incidents connected with RIN Mutiny, NAI.

The Indian Annual Register (January–June 1946), Vol. 1., pp. 235, 289–98, 301–07.

Trotskiyst movement in India and Ceylon, RIN Mutiny.

Y.K. Menon, Eye-witness account recorded on 4.9.1969, NAI.

<u>NAIDU</u>. O.No.14029.

<u>JUBBAR</u>. O.No.21853.

<u>RODRIGUEZ</u>. O.No. 22913.

On the morning of 8th February, we were in our
barracks. There were about 14 or 15 people there.
I was combing my hair and pacing the locker. I
heard some shouts. I turned back and saw Comdr.
King standing at the door inside the barrack. Just
then I heard him saying "You sons of bitches stand
up". He also said "Whenever I come inside you must
all stand up". I also heard him using the words,
"You Junglies and Coolies". He asked one of them
to throw away his cigarette but actually there was
no cigarette in the hands of the rating.Next
morning we gave a complaint to our immediate officer
in O.O.O., who passed it on, and finally the
complaint was forwarded to Lt.Comdr.Shaw. My
complaint was taken by Mr. Asirvadam. I said I was
keen on my complaint being forwarded to higher
authorities. He said I should forgive and forget
but I did not agree to drop the matter. As to why
Comdr. King was using this abusive language, I did
not know the reason. I did not get any reply to
my complaints. Then we faced Comdr. King. He said,
"I cannot deal with this matter as it was against
himself but he said it was a false charge and he
will take heed of the matter. He gave me permission
to forward my request to higher authorities and we
did so but we got no reply.

SPARKS IN THE TINDERBOX

'Get up you sons of coolies, sons of bloody *junglees,* you sons of bitches.' That torrent of abuse was hurled by Commander King at the Indian ratings under his command, and it echoed across the barracks and corridors of HMIS *Talwar.* The abusive outburst would ignite a smouldering tinderbox and elicit a response, which would shake the British to the core and cause panic and consternation in faraway Whitehall.

The HMIS *Talwar* in Bombay was a strategically important naval establishment for the British forces in India. It was the second-largest signal school in all of the British Empire.

It became the platform for the launch of the naval mutiny of February 1946. There were close to 2,000 Indian naval ratings posted there, who had been subjected to the most degrading and inhuman service conditions. Their anger and frustration had reached boiling point, and it was further fuelled by stories of the nationalist movement and the heroic deeds of the INA.

The spark that lit the conflagration was supplied by the British themselves, namely, by Commander King. The British authorities made a cardinal mistake in appointing King as commander of HMIS *Talwar* in January 1946 – a time when emotions were running high in this important shore establishment.

Commander Arthur Frederick King was a racist officer. It was the foul language he used that sparked the mutiny in HMIS Talwar.

In his book B.C. Dutt described King as 'a large built man with a very small brain.' A racist, his hatred for 'Bloody Indians' was displayed openly. Not only was he a racist, he was also uncomfortable with educated ratings who could talk back to him. His dismal man-management skills led to him using bullying tactics to discipline the men under his command. The result was inevitable: he became the target for the ratings to vent their frustrations and growing anger at the mistreatment and blatant discrimination.

The ratings had deflated the tyres of his car and painted nationalist slogans like 'Quit India' on the vehicle, making King look foolish and incompetent. He became a laughing stock within the Bombay naval establishment and, by February 1946, his hold on command was tenuous. He was getting anonymous threatening letters that put him under extreme psychological pressure until he snapped, leading to the point of no return.

Commander Arthur Frederick King, who incidentally was born on 2 October (the same as Mahatma Gandhi) 1917 will forever be remembered as the man who lit the 'spark that kindled the fire' of the rebellion.

King's naval career started in 1934 when he applied for a cadetship in Royal Navy, but wasn't selected because he failed in the written exams due to his poor proficiency in French. He had, however, passed the admiralty interview and was invited to join the Royal Indian Navy. He underwent the same training given to seamen of the Royal Navy. He was involved in a salvage operation in the mid-Atlantic in the very first week of his joining the navy and earned appreciation for this.

King's first ship was the elderly sloop, HMIS *Clive*, which was operating in the Bay of Bengal searching for Japanese spies and for covert operations around the islands of the Andaman and Nicobar archipelago. He and his fellow seamen had to be disguised as pearl-fishermen for this mission. During the expansion years of the RIN in 1938, King was appointed to the training ship, HMIS *Dalhousie*. His first group consisted of forty boys from the Punjab who had never seen the sea, let alone board a ship. He had to learn Urdu to be able to communicate with them and pass his command exams.

In 1939, King was sent to Delhi to help set up the new Navy office. The following year, in 1940, he returned to England to qualify as a gunnery specialist. In 1941, he was appointed to HMIS *Jumna*, a new ship being built in Dumbarton, on the north coast of the River Clyde in Scotland. King visited nearby Glasgow frequently and met his future wife Anne there. In 1942, King spent a difficult, frustrating, and often exasperating year in Imperial Delhi, living in the Delhi Gymkhana Club. In 1943, he was transferred to England as first lieutenant because he despised the office work in Delhi. In 1944, while serving in HMIS *Cauvery*, then aged twenty-six, King was given the ship's command due to her captain falling sick. As captain of *Cauvery* he escorted convoys in the Atlantic and later hunted Japanese submarines in the Indian Ocean. His excellent record soon brought him to the commanding officer (CO) level.

Commander King took charge as CO of the troubled HMIS

Talwar on 21 January 1946. However, his task would be an uphill one. Taking charge as CO from Commander Cole was an onerous responsibility because Cole was hugely popular, particularly with the Indian ratings. This may have been a reason why Cole was seen as being too lenient and sympathetic towards Indians when the issue of writing anti-British slogans on the walls of HMIS *Talwar* became a concern.

The British wanted someone tough, and to them, King was a no-nonsense officer who would restore discipline to HMIS *Talwar.*

King wasted no time in enforcing his authority. On 8 February, a day after his car was painted with 'Quit India' slogans and its tyres deflated, he decided to make a surprise visit to the naval barracks early in the morning. The ratings ignored him and did not get up or salute him.

Enraged, he shouted, 'Get up, you sons of coolies,' and 'You sons of Indian bitches.' Discontent had been simmering for some months and this abuse was the last straw. The ratings complained orally to higher authorities, but their complaint was passed back to Commander King, who ordered them to take back their complaints or face serious consequences. For a week, no action was taken.

Earlier, on 2 February, B.C. Dutt had been arrested for writing seditious slogans on the walls of *Talwar.* That set off a chain reaction with ratings becoming more intransigent and King trying to impose his authority in a heavy-handed fashion.

8 FEBRUARY

King had received reports that the ratings had made cat-calls and whistled at women ratings WRINS (Women Royal Indian Navy). He felt his authority as CO was being undermined and he was determined to put these 'bloody Indians' in their place.

This was why he made a surprise visit to the barracks on 8 February. Here he met with a shocking display of insubordination.

The first parade for the Central Communications Office

(CCO) was at 9.15 a.m. But lying on their cots, smoking, and using abusive language, the ratings ignored him. The CO's standing had reached rock-bottom.

Enraged, King let loose a stream of foul, racially charged slur which would soon seal his fate. Storming out of the barracks, King summoned Lt Cdr Shaw, his second-in-command at the *Talwar*, and expressed his dissatisfaction with the behaviour of the ratings. King wanted action, and he wanted it without any delay.

Lt Cdr Shaw acted as directed. Calling each of the ratings in turn, he communicated King's displeasure to them. But on making further inquiries he found that the anger amongst the men was largely because of King's behaviour. Something had to be done and quickly. At 12.30, Shaw went to King's office and told him about his inquiry and the mood of the ratings. Lt S.M. Nanda, who would later become Chief of the Naval Staff, was present in the office at the time.

9 FEBRUARY

The next day, the ratings made their feelings clear to Lt Cdr Shaw as he met with fourteen of them individually. Each one said the same things during their one-on-one interactions. They then made an unprecedented move – filing a formal written complaint to Shaw against their CO! King had united all the ratings on the *Talwar* against him.

The crisis now escalated. All fourteen ratings who Shaw had spoken to, made formal complaints against the CO. It was a high-risk gamble. A joint complaint against a superior officer was considered mutiny, and even filing individual complaints was serious enough.

Shaken, Shaw tried to make the ratings see reason, even threatening them by saying their careers would be ruined. But these brave, proud young men had had enough. They had been subject to persistent 'humiliation and ill-treatment' and they would not pull back now. To do so would invite more ridicule and discrimination.

10 FEBRUARY

It was a precarious situation for Lt Cdr Shaw. He could not pass an order against his own boss (Commander King) but neither could he ignore the serious charges. Shaw sent a personal and confidential letter to his CO pleading with him to deal with the matter delicately, swiftly, and tactfully. If he did not, Shaw pleaded, they faced a crisis. A copy of this letter was sent to the Chief of Naval Staff in Bombay, Flag Officer Bombay (FOB), Rear-Admiral Arthur Rullion Rattray.

Shaw's letter should have stirred any right-minded CO to take swift action to pacify the ratings. But the arrogant Commander King still believed he was in control and immune to any resistance. These 'coolies', he felt, would fall back in line soon enough. So he pocketed the letter and did nothing.

Thus, in a most indifferent and capricious manner, King refused to heed his brother officer's advice. The matter would be decided through naval routine. This was called 'Request Men and Defaulters' – a naval unit court held by the CO once a week on Saturdays to dispense justice and hear complaints.

That meant the matter would be dealt with on 16 February – seven days after the incident. King's message was clear. This was not a serious issue. This was a further insult to the men who were already consumed by rage. Shaw's report stating the matter was 'serious' and pleading for 'immediate action' had been dismissed by his CO.

By now, *Talwar* was like a volcano waiting to erupt. Furious ratings; an arrogant and uncaring CO; and the head-in-the-sand attitude of naval staff in Bombay praying the problem would go away. The inevitable eruption was right around the corner.

Shaw tried his best to avert disaster. He repeatedly pleaded with King to hear the men before 16 February, but to no avail. King was blind to the crisis looming before his eyes. The result – justified anger gave way to blind fury. The gathering storm that built up between 9 and 16 February turned into open rebellion. King would pay dearly for the way he had spoken.

SATURDAY, 16 FEBRUARY 1946

On 16 February, King summoned the ratings and tried to bully them into submission. Ordering them to take back their charges against him, he gave them twenty-four hours to reconsider. 'No use of putting in this complaint,' he threatened. 'If you cannot prove it, you will only get into trouble.'

King was firm in his belief that the ratings would back down. Which Indian would dare go up against a white officer? But the angry ratings went ballistic. King was not only unapologetic, but he had also shown no interest in hearing them out and even accused them of filing false complaints. In effect, he was calling them liars, as well as troublemakers.

Aggravating the situation was the callous treatment meted out to B.C. Dutt, who was highly respected by his peers and had become a hero for writing seditious slogans on the eve of the FOCRIN's visit to *Talwar*. Tried by order of the FOB, Dutt was placed under open arrest in a cell located in one corner of the *Talwar*. (He was later moved to the residence of Commander King, who had moved out. Even here, Dutt was closely guarded, with two sentries inside and other four outside. The guards, however, were sympathetic to the cause and ensured Dutt remained in touch with the barracks and was privy to all news about the rising tension outside.)

According to Dutt in *Mutiny of the Innocents*, King came to him and asked to intervene and pacify the enraged ratings. Writes Dutt: 'King paid me an unexpected visit on the second night. He was quite friendly. He sent away the guards… invited me to sit with him on the soft grass of the lawn.' After some polite talk about Dutt's family, 'he tried his best to help me and see that my "young life is not ruined" by becoming a jailbird. He spoke to me for nearly an hour. He said he was speaking to me like a father and, in the absence of my own father he had to give me advice… Before leaving me he [Commander King]… did something that was unprecedented… As a prisoner I was not allowed to smoke. He offered the tin of cigarettes he was carrying… "Keep the tin."'

King then sent Dutt back to the barracks after informing him of the Government of India's decision to demote and discharge him from RIN. The papers officially announcing this would not be ready until Monday, this being the weekend. By allowing Dutt to spend the weekend in the barracks, King had hoped that he could calm the agitated ratings, but he had once again severely misjudged the situation. The rebellious mood had built to a point where a revolt was unstoppable – not that Dutt wanted to stop it anyhow. Dutt's advice 'not to stomach insults quietly but to protest' was enough incentive to the ratings. They stood their ground and would no longer be cowed. The ratings met that night with Dutt. As he wrote: 'We sat through the night, discussing and pondering… In the early hours of morning, we dispersed to study the situation more closely…'

SUNDAY, 17 FEBRUARY

At the previous night's meeting, Dutt and the ratings had decided to instigate the ratings on the issue of bad food. They should be provoked to refuse the food served to them. 'That would constitute a corporate offence – Mutiny.'

They sensed the atmosphere in *Talwar* was explosive enough to spark off an uprising. Dutt and his fellow agitators thought that their dream of 'capturing the navy and placing it at the disposal of the nation's leaders' was about to become a reality.

The plan was put into action on 17 February as the day began. A total of twenty-nine ratings in two messes refused to eat. As it is, the food was often unfit to consume. Moreover, the ratings were used to bad food and often, the rotis served to them were rock hard and simply inedible.

The indifferent cooks had not only mixed the dal with vegetables, but ratings also found gravel in the meal served to them. According to Kusum Nair, the gravel was deliberately added as planned, at the instance of her husband Pran, to instigate the agitated ratings even more.

Insult was added to injury when they complained to the duty officer. The duty officer was British, from the Royal Navy. He held the Indian ratings in contempt, and they, in turn, loathed him because he was incompetent and had been promoted over more deserving Indian ratings because of the colour of his skin.

His standard response to the Indian seamen's complaints was, 'Beggars can't be choosers.' There was also no attempt by him to report the matter to the CO, nor had there been any attempt to serve fresh food. Acting on the plan formulated the night before, the ratings refused the food served to them and went to bed hungry. This was a clear warning sign for the British – the situation had reached boiling point.

REFERENCES

Ajeet Jawed, 'The Unsung Heroes of 1946', 1 October 2008, *Mainstream.*

B.C. Dutt, *Mutiny of the Innocents.* Bombay: Sindhu Publications, 1971.

Dilip Kumar Das, *Revisiting Talwar: A study in the Royal Indian Navy Uprising of February 1946.* Delhi: Ajanta Publications, 1993.

Hyper War: The Royal Indian Navy (Chapter 1), https://www.ibiblio.org/hyperwar/UN/India/RIN/RIN-1.html.

Kusum Nair, *The Army of Occupation.* Delhi: Padma Publications, 1946.

Lt. Cdr G.D. Sharma, VSM (Retd), *The Untold Story of Naval Mutiny: Last War of Independence.* Delhi: Vij Books, 2015.

Ratnakar Sadasyula, 'The Forgotten Naval Mutiny of 1946 and India's Independence', 19 February 2016, *Swarajya Magazine.*

Rear Admiral Satyindra Singh AVSM (Retd), *Under Two Ensigns: The Indian Navy 1945–1950.* New Delhi: Oxford and IBH Publishing Co., 1986.

RIN, GoI, pp. 326–30: Resettlement/ Demobalisatoin (https://www.ibiblio.org/hyperwar/UN/India/RIN/RIN-15.html)

The Indian Annual Register (January–June 1946), Vol. 1., pp. 235, 289–98, 301–07.

https://www.indiannavy.nic.in/sites/default/themes/indiannavy/images/pdf/chapter1.pdf

The Times of India

ESTABLISHED 1838

NO. 43. VOL. CVIII.   BOMBAY: TUESDAY, FEBRUARY 19, 1946   PRICE TWO ANNAS   DO NOT PAY MORE

SOVIET TO DEMAND HIROHITO'S HEAD

General MacArthur's Bitter Opposition

TRIBUNAL TO TRY MAJOR JAP CRIMINALS FORMED

TOKIO, February 18.

GENERAL MacArthur, Supreme Allied Commander in Japan, today named Sir William Flood Webb, Chief Australian delegate and Chief Justice of Queensland, as President of the International Military Tribunal which is to try major Japanese war-crimes suspects.

General Kuzma Derevyanko, Soviet representative to the Four-Power Council which will rule Japan, today told General MacArthur that as soon as the Council operates Russia will press for Emperor Hirohito to be named as a war criminal, says the 'Globe.' General MacArthur bitterly opposes the demand for Hirohito's head.

He has repeatedly told Washington that the only way the Japanese can be ruled peaceably is through the Emperor, but the Soviet view is that if Hirohito as Number One Japanese escapes punishment the entire trial will become a mockery.

Emperor Hirohito in an interview with three American newspaper executives today said: "I hope you will report on conditions in Japan as you find them, because I believe that will contribute to international understanding."

(Other members appointed to the tribunal whose names were announced by General MacArthur, were: Lord Patrick, Senior Judge for the United Kingdom; Mr. Macdougall Stuart, Canada; Mai Ju Ao, China; M. Henri Bernbaysaz, Procureur-General France, "and Bernard Victor A. Roling, Judge of the Court of Utrecht, Holland; Judge Pro-ç Harvey Northcroft, Judge of the Supreme Court of New Zealand; M. I. M. Zaryanov, Russia and Mr. John P. Higgins, Chief Justice of the Superior Court of Massachusetts, United States.

Emperor Hirohito in his interview with the newspaper executives, including the Robert Nielson, President of the "Associated Press" also asked for American co-operation to speed Japan's commercial and industrial reconstruction.

Tokio's Metropolitan Police have asked the United States Military Police to help maintain a 24-hour guard at all the banks and post offices during the period between February 25 and March 7 when it is estimated that 20,000,000,000 yen (about £1,000,000,000) will be exchanged as a result of new currency conversion measures announced on Saturday.

They also called on the American military police to provide armoured cars to escort vehicles carrying large issues of new notes from the mint to financial houses in the outlying districts.

Russia is not at present placed to send occupation troops to Japan, Gen. Derevyanko, the Russian representative, told General MacArthur, says the 'Globe'.

SOUTH-EAST ASIA'S FOOD PROBLEM

Lord Killearn's New Post

LONDON, February 18. Lord Killearn former British Ambassador in Cairo has been appointed special Commissioner in South-East Asia. He will have the special task of urgent investigation of the food situation in South-East Asia and of taking prompt action.

Lord Killearn will leave for Singapore within a week or ten days with special authority from the Cabinet to deal with the food situation. Anyway those who will consult as soon as possible the Admiral Mountbatten, Supreme Commander SEAC. Lord Wavell, Viceroy of India, and the Government of Burma.

Lord Killearn who saw Mr. Ernest Bevin today, will be responsible in the Foreign Secretary and have his headquarters at Singapore. Normally he will be mainly concerned with problems in South-East Asia affecting foreign affairs, but with the local situation requiring such grave proportions the British Cabinet has decided that he should hurry out and to the part plus deal primarily with the problem.

Sir Ronald Ian Campbell, a present deputy to the secretary of state for the Council of Foreign Ministers, has from a special British Ambassador at Cairo in succession to Lord Killearn. —Reuter.

BRITISH FORCES FOR JAPAN

First Troops Land In Kure

From A Noyes Thomas, "The Times of India" War Correspondent.

KURE, February 18.

The first troops of the British Commonwealth Forces of occupation came ashore amidst the rubble of this wrecked port last week.

They were astonished to see of the extent of the damage throughout the British occupation area, in which the only two towns are Kure and Hiroshima.

Although each officer and man is a volunteer for service in Japan no one has been given an accurate idea of the conditions in this desolate corner of the country or of the enormous acreage of countryside.

The force which arrived last Wednesday consists approximately of 1,000 Australians, mostly drivers, electricians and other tradesmen. As they sailed into the harbour, they received a noisy welcome from the warships at anchor in the port, including the R.I.N. sloop "Cauvery." The vanguard of the British Indian occupation force is expected to arrive here on March 1, but I learn that the arrival of the main body of British and Indian troops has been further postponed until the end of March.

Zemindar's Sentence Commuted

KARACHI, February 18. The order of the Sind Government to commute into transportation for life, the death sentence passed on a zemindar of the Dadu district a the subject matter of a motion expressing lack of confidence in the Sind Ministry sent by Mr. B. K. Bidwai, M.L.A. (Congress) today.

Another Congress member, Mr. Sreomal Vishindas, from Larkana, has given notice of an adjournment motion to censure the Government for the same.

Allah Khan Fakir Buksh Khan Kachi, the zemindar, had been charged with having turned a police chowkey, burning a post office and firing at a marriage procession resulting in four persons being killed and five others wounded in the village of Manjhand in March 1945.

The death sentence passed on Allah Khan which had been confirmed by the Chief Court in Sind has been commuted by the Sind Government under section 402 of the Criminal Procedure Code

---

Indian Ratings On Strike In Bombay

BETTER CONDITIONS DEMANDED

Indian Ratings On Strike In Bombay

BETTER CONDITIONS DEMANDED

About 1,000 ratings in H. M. I. S. "Talwar," the signal training ship in Bombay, went on a sit-down and hunger strike on Monday morning with a view to seeking immediate redress of their grievances.

The strike was precipitated after the alleged insult to a rating by an officer on his attention being drawn to some of their problems.

One of the ratings told a representative of The Times of India that unless a categorical assurance from the authorities, backed by any well-known leader, to look into their demands was forthcoming, the strike would not be given up, whatever the consequences. He referred to the detention at Arthur Road Prison of a telegraphist attached to the ship as the turning point in the relations between the ratings and the officers.

RATINGS DEMANDS

He also said that there was ground for complaint with regard to the food served to them. The demands listed by him included speedy demobilisation of R. I. N. personnel, with reasonable provisions for re-settlement in peace-time employment, revision of scales of pay, allowances and other facilities, including travelling, as in the Royal Navy, no return of kit at the time of discharge and provision of the best type of Indian food.

An A.P.I. report says: Rear-Admiral A. R. Rattray, Flag Officer Commanding Bombay, stated on Monday: "Indian naval ratings of H. M. I. S. Talwar have since this morning refused to take their food. Menus have been prepared at regular times, but no one has entered the mess to eat. The men have been asked to state their grievances, but so far no one has come forward and no statement has been made. Immediately it is known what their grievances are a full inquiry will be put up in hand and every effort made to redress their grievances."

New Delhi: Rear Admiral Rattray, says a communique issued by Naval Headquarters, visited the establishment, but was unable to ascertain the nature of the grievances which have led to this collective indiscipline. Investigations are proceeding. —A.P.I.

Indian Ratings On Strike In Bombay

BETTER CONDITIONS DEMANDED

About 1,000 ratings in H. M. I. S. "Talwar," the signal training ship in Bombay, went on a sit-down and hunger strike on Monday morning with a view to seeking immediate redress of their grievances.

The strike was precipitated after the alleged insult to a rating by an officer on his attention being drawn to some of their problems.

One of the ratings told a representative of The Times of India that unless a categorical assurance from the authorities, backed by any well-known leader, to look into their demands was forthcoming, the strike would not be given up, whatever the consequences. He referred to the detention at Arthur Road Prison of a telegraphist attached to the ship as the turning point in the relations between the ratings and the officers.

RATINGS DEMANDS

He also said that there was ground for complaint with regard to the food served to them. The demands listed by him included speedy demobilisation of R. I. N. personnel, with reasonable provisions for re-settlement in peace-time employment, revision of scales of pay, allowances and other facilities, including travelling, as in the Royal Navy, no return of kit at the time of discharge and provision of the best type of Indian food.

An A.P.I. report says: Rear-Admiral A. R. Rattray, Flag Officer Commanding Bombay, stated on Monday...

U. S. Steel Strike Off

NEW YORK, February 18. Steel production was resumed in the United States today. 7500 trucks in a day since the start of the great strike by 750,000 Congress of Industrial Organisations United Steel Workers. —A.P.

MOBS SET FIRE TO TRAINS

Disturbances Between Dacca & Narayanganj

DACCA, February 18. Two trains running between Dacca and Narayanganj on the Bengal Assam Railway were set on fire by mobs today after they had made the passengers get down. The train service between the two stations was disorganised for three hours owing to disturbances at different points.

While hartal was being observed in Narayanganj town as a protest against the recent firing incidents in Calcutta, mobs squatted on the railway line staging demonstrations. A passenger train which was returning to Dacca in the forenoon was stopped near Digubahar Bazar by pulling the alarm chain. The mob then forced passengers to get down and set fire to the train.

Another train was also set on fire at Chasara station after similar demonstrations by a mob.

Armed police was then drafted leaving the situation under control. The normal train service was resumed three hours later with armed pickets posted in running trains at different railway points.

It was later learnt that damages caused to the two trains at Digubahar Bazar and Chasara, respectively, were not serious.

The Calcutta Mail which runs between Dacca and Narayanganj stations left here 40 minutes late owing to the disturbances. —A.P.I.

Trouble In Delhi

NEW DELHI, February 18. The police quelled a disturbance in Delhi today after the Provincial Muslim League had called a one-day "hartal" to protest against the imprisonment of Mr. Rashid. A European courier was assaulted and his car damaged with brickbats and stones. The police appeared on the scene and broke up the crowd with a lathi charge. —A.P.I.

British Cabinet Changes Likely

LONDON, February 17. Speculation credits the British Prime Minister Mr. Clement Attlee, with the intention of making some early changes in his Government before Reuter's political correspondent.

It may well be that after six months of power the labour administration has found its feet sufficiently to review portfolios all of which Mr. Attlee wants his Ministers when he took office would be subject to a change as and when needs dictated.

Political quarters believe that if Mr. Attlee decides upon a Government reshuffle, it will entail a lower level. The Labour Cabinet hierarchy, it is expected, will be maintained in the rank, even if there are one or two switches. —Reuter.

"GOVT. OF COUNTRY DID NOT SERVE INDIA"

Mr. Gandhi's Suggestions To Avert Food Famine

BRITISH and American troops had come to India to fight Japan and Germany. What he had told Government in 1942, what he would repeat again was that they should have rendered service to India as their prime consideration. But fortunately, India had been looted. Whether that looting was deliberate or merely incidental he could not say. It was part of a Government's duty to exercise greater care than had been exercised in India, said Mr. Gandhi, who arrived in Bombay on Monday, in a speech after evening prayers.

"If the Government was of India and for the service of the Indian people, the story might have been different," added Mr. Gandhi.

The Calcutta Mail, in which Mr. Gandhi travelled from Wardha, was three-and-a-half hours behind schedule. Hundreds of people had gathered at a level crossing between Kurla and Sion stations, where Mr. Gandhi alighted from the train. On his way to Birla House, by car, Mr. Gandhi called on Mr. Bhulabhai Desai, who is ill.

A huge gathering was present in the compound of Birla House, where Mr. Gandhi said his prayers. Addressing the gathering, Mr. Gandhi said that difficult times were ahead for India. If anyone wished to blame Government, they could do so as much as they liked. He would join them in criticising Government. If the Government was of India, and for the service of the Indian people, the story might have been different.

But, Mr. Gandhi continued, he did not take to dwell too long on the past. The present position was that there was not enough food and there was also a shortage of cloth. It was strange that that should have happened in India, a land of gold, whose natural resources were very great. If it had huge mountains and vast rivers, but the waters of the rivers were running waste and emptying into the sea. It was part of human duty to harness the water resources of the country for the welfare of the people.

The fact of the shortage, Mr. Gandhi observed, was there. Government had said so. He himself had travelled through Assam, Madras and Andhra. He had heard the same story everywhere. He had seen starvation in the eyes of the people, and the question was what should be done to meet the situation.

"FIND WATER"

It was no use gazing at the sky and waiting for the rains to come, Mr. Gandhi said. There was water not only in the sky above but also down in the bowels of the earth. It was the duty of Government and its engineers to dig, dig deeper if necessary till water in abundant gushing forth—thousands of feet too find water. They should also make use of the manure.

Referring to cloth scarcity Mr. Gandhi enjoined strict economy and expressed the opinion that if a sufficient number of spinning wheels were distributed in the village India need never go naked. Every village home was a potential mill. It was no use looking up to the factories alone for the supplies. He wanted to impress that primarily on Government.

ON NON-VIOLENCE

Proceeding, Mr. Gandhi referred to the recent events in Bombay and Calcutta, and said he greatly regretted these. He asked the people not to divert from the path of peace. What was the good of throwing stones at the British? They could not remove Government by throwing stones. Freedom could only be achieved through truth and non-violence and any action...

MISHAP TO MR. GANDHI'S TRAIN

Engine Rod Breaks

There was a serious mishap to the engine of the Bombay Mail in which Mr. Gandhi and party were travelling from Wardha to Bombay, between Lahavita and Asvali at about 7 o'clock. The open connecting rod of engine attached to the bogies of engine would have fallen in which train was in motion, seriously injuring the other parts of the engine, thereby averting a mishap, which would involve engine behind the engine, dislodge the one in which Mr. Gandhi was travelling.

After about 30 minutes, another engine rushed to the spot, a neighbouring station on a line and then being drawn by the hind engine. Sure after, one more engine from Deolali and coupled to the rear of the train. After two hours' delay the whole train came back to Lahavita, again at Lahavita, the train halted for about an hour to detach the broken engine. The driver stopped the engine when the train was moving to avoid serious accident. Foreign engine of military personnel occupied Gandhi's compartment for his own and contributed for the Jaz First.

Finally the engine of the military special was attached to Bombay Mail. One military told the special representative United Press of India too with Mr. Gandhi "We respect Mahatma so much that we have our engine for his train."

GERMAN DISTRESS EXAGGERATED

LONDON, February 18. The stories of the starving people of India to represent much food in Germany, said Lord Vansittart British Ambassador to the British Government, in an view on Monday, cables Reuter correspondent.

Lord Vansittart emphasises point of view that India too was earmarked for famine by adding: "I see no fun in saying that India should prefer one over Germany." —Reuter.

Canada's Spy Hunt

OTTAWA, February 18. Five government spy hunt entered week today amid reports that functions's new "atmosphere of suspicion" was threatening public relations just of the new engine be linked with the propaganda new radio stations, the stations which was disclosed night, were set up during the measure the height of "under and predict the best frequent communications between two parties.

Authorities across the country suspect of inquiry or a convert eight result from premature on in Washington of the Canadian investigation.

Fighting On South Of Mukden In China

COMMUNISTS' CHARGE AGAINST KOUMINTANG ARMIES

CHUNGKING, February 18.

FIGHTING between Kuomintang (Chinese Central Government) forces and Communist troops in Manchuria is spreading, stated a Communist spokesman on Monday. He reported fighting on a 45-mile front from the west of Liaoyang (south of Mukden).

The spokesman added that Kuomintang forces under the command of General Tu Yuming, commanding at least two American-trained and equipped armies "continued to push against popular local forces."

The new Chinese Sixth Army, he added had seized the towns of Tehui and Panshan, south-west of Mukden, and also the country town of Liaochang.

In Eastern Jehol, on the Outer Mongolia Province bordering on Liaoning, the Chinese Thirteenth Army stationed at Pishi had stabbed northwards to seize from Liaoyuan to the local forces, the spokesman stated.

Earlier the Communist spokesman said that Chinese Communists and Government troops had been involved in "sporadic" clashes but through out China proper the truce was being observed.

Several Chinese newspapers today described the situation in Manchuria as "critical." The independent newspaper "Ta Kung Pao" demanded that rest of "secret diplomacy" and open black-out on the situation in Manchuria.

Lieut-General Albert Wedemeyer the United States Commander-in-Chief of China, said on Saturday being transported to Manchuria in response to a request from the Chinese Government that additional troops should be sent there.

(General Wedemeyer left Chungking for Nanking today with Lieut.-General Alvin Gillem, former Commander of the Eighteenth United States Corps in France, who is reported to be advising on reorganisation of the Chinese armed forces, divided in committee by the People's Consultative Conference. Reuter.

BELGIAN CABINET RESIGNS

Catholic Party Tops Elections

BRUSSELS, February 18. The Belgian Prime Minister, M. Achille van Acker, today tendered the resignation of his Cabinet, after election results so far had shown that the Christian-Socialist (Catholic) Party would be the strongest in the new Chamber. The Prince Regent has asked the Belgian Premier to continue to discharge current business.

It is expected that the next move of the Regent will be to invite M. Auguste de Schrijver, leader of the pre-war old Catholic Party—which is outside the present Government coalition—to form a new Government.

The latest position of the parties returned: Christian Socialist (Catholic) 90; a gain of 17; Socialists 68, a gain of four; Communists 24 (a gain of 15); Liberals 18 (a loss of 16); Belgian Democratic Union, two (a new party).

On Other Pages

Russian reports are being hailed out by the anti-Communist in Press goal in forget who favour on in to by revolution, says the Poe dat recognition of the dividing Union a British newspaper.

KILLICK, NIXON & CO

(IMPORT & AGENCY DEPT.)

"SNOWCRETE," "COLORCRETE," "SNOWCEM" CEMENT
ROAD MAKING & OTHER CONCRETE PRODUCTS MACHINERY
WRITING, PRINTING & DUPLICATING PAPERS
"MASONITE," HARD-WOODS AND INSULATION
SILICA & OTHER FIRE-BRICKS & FIRE-CLAY
STEEL CASTINGS AND BRIDGE BEARINGS
PAPER SACKS AND PACKING PAPERS
PLYWOOD, CHAIR SEATS, TEABOXES, ETC.
LUBRICATING OILS AND GREASES
ARC WELDING ELECTRODES
AIR CONDITIONING MACHINES
CEMENT BAGS AND HESSIANS
CANVAS, TWINE & HOSE
CLEARING & FORWARDING

HOME STREET,   BOMBAY

6

THE REVOLT BEGINS

MONDAY, 18 FEBRUARY 1946

7.30 A.M.

Eighteenth February began as a normal day. The ratings at the HMIS *Talwar* were woken at 5 a.m. The men who had slept hungry the night before gathered in the mess hall. But at 7.30 a.m., anger grew among the men as they found the same dal they had rejected the night before was being served at breakfast. At 8.45, when the call for the assembly was sounded, no rating showed up at the parade ground. Angry murmurs began and then someone gave voice to the slogan: 'No food. No work.'

These four words were a battle cry. The men stood up as one, shoved aside their chairs and repeated loudly, 'No food. No work.' Elation and jubilation spread among the Azad Hindis and their ringleaders. 'They had crossed the line! They had done it.' Is how B.C. Dutt described the moment. It was now do or die and the ratings had made their choice – Freedom. The ratings left the mess shouting slogans.

Dutt was technically under arrest but he had been offered the option of waiting in the barracks for his 'demote and discharge papers,' which were expected to arrive on the 18th itself. He described his cathartic emotions as follows:

'I went berserk for a while… I embraced everyone in sight. Some friends told me later that I was like a man possessed and that I was screaming. "You have done it, man! You have done it, man!" "You have done it man!"'

Never in the history of the RIN had such an event taken place – mass open revolt. An entire establishment of Indian ratings challenging the might and authority of the British Navy was both unprecedented and epochal. By that one act of insurgence, the ratings had hit the British where it hurt them the most: mutiny in the armed forces!

The British were stunned and Indian officers serving the British were hated, perhaps even more than the British. Two Indian officers, lieutenants A. Batra and S.N. Sachdev, the officers-on-watch (OOW) on the 17th night and 18th morning, reported for work but were jeered and hooted away.

The ratings gathered and the leaders told the men this was not just a riot over the quality of food. This was to be a total takeover of the HMIS *Talwar*. They were no longer prepared to be 'hired assassins of the Empire' as they had been described.

8.45–10.45 a.m.

No ratings proceeded to the parade ground despite the sound of the pipes calling them to fall in line. Royal Navy ratings and WRINS, however, did so. The RIN men marched out of the mess shouting 'Inquilab Zindabad', and other nationalistic slogans despite officers individually trying to reason with them. The ratings refused to pay any heed.

Hearing the commotion, Commander King arrived at the *Talwar* at 9.05 a.m. but looking at the situation, left without giving any instructions or speaking to anyone. However, he returned at 9.45 a.m. only to find that none of the ratings had fallen into parade. King then ordered all WRINS to leave the *Talwar*. At 10.15, King called a conference of all officers and they huddled together. Despite the tension in the air, the officers again tried to reason with the ratings but without any success.

11.30 a.m.
At the conference it was decided that all small arms and ammunition should be removed to the Castle Barracks.

12 p.m.
Cries of 'Inquilab Zindabad' and 'Quit India' echoed across the *Talwar*. Commander King's authority no longer held sway. The ratings were now in charge. At noon, Flag Officer Commanding Bombay (FOB) Rear-Admiral Rattray rushed to the *Talwar* with Captain Inigo-Jones to try and retrieve what was fast turning into an open revolt. He promised to remove King temporarily and replace him with Captain Inigo-Jones. Rattray also gave an assurance of better rations. He said he would look into setting up an inquiry committee to examine their grievances. The angry crowd shouted him down. Finding he was making no headway, Rattray left the *Talwar* 20 minutes later.

3 p.m.
Meanwhile, King tried a desperate salvage operation. Summoning Dutt at 3 p.m. to his office, he pleaded. 'I want you to help me. If you help me, I promise to give you another chance in the navy.' His inherent arrogance, however, ensured he remained blind to the situation. Even if Dutt had wanted to help him, he could not. The men had surrounded King's office, suspecting Dutt's re-arrest. Pleading with Dutt to get the men to allow him safe passage, he hastily left the *Talwar* never to be seen inside its gates again. King had taken over what used to be an efficient, disciplined establishment and run it into the ground during his short tenure.

Talwar was now entirely under the control of the striking ratings with officers generally restricted to the area of the gateway and the CPOs and POs (Chief Petty Officers and Petty Officers) to their barracks. Only the ratings had a free exit from the establishment, which was now completely under their control. The 'ship' was, literally, no longer in the hands of British officers.

5 p.m.

Events now moved at a breakneck pace. Rear-Admiral Rattray returned at 5 p.m. with a stern message: a non-negotiable and immediate return to duty. The men could appoint representatives who could present their demands at 9.30 a.m. the next day, 19 February. Meanwhile, King was removed and the new CO, Inigo-Jones took over.

Rattray's ultimatum added fuel to an already raging fire. Inigo-Jones had ruthlessly suppressed a strike at the MT Barracks, next to the Bombay Dockyard, in 1944, an incident for which the ratings dubbed him the 'Butcher'. The unanimous rejection of Rattray's offer ensured that Inigo-Jones would not set foot on the *Talwar* as CO.

The mutual trust had completely broken, and the men feared that their representatives would be punished in order to make an example of them. They demanded that a 'national leader' negotiate on their behalf, preferably Aruna Asaf Ali, who not only sympathized with the striking naval ratings, but had also assisted a section of the ratings when the uprising was in its initial planning stage. This demand was something the naval establishment could not possibly allow.

6 p.m.

The speed at which the mutiny spread was amazing, even by modern standards of communication and technology. The *Talwar* ratings first rang the Central Communication Office (CCO) but could not get through. Then, they contacted the Receiving Station in Colaba, where the first news of the 'Talwar Strike' had already reached.

In support, the men there also struck work. Now, over 2,000 ratings were on strike. In quick succession after that, ratings at the WT Station Mahul, northeast Bombay, struck work, and the signalmen at the Dockyard Signal Station also refused to report for duty. Officers in charge at the Dockyard Signal Station removed some of the equipment and abandoned the station. POs kept watch on the telephones. Royal Navy ratings manned the signal tower in the CCO. The Bombay naval establishment had descended into chaos.

At 6 p.m., when AIR put out a news broadcast, the entire country knew the astonishing facts. By then, '11 shore establishments, 45 ships, 11 miscellaneous ships and 4 flotilla ships,' were ready and willing to do anything to support the brave men on the *Talwar*. The nearby Castle Barracks and Fort Barracks were agog with rumours and excitement.

Subrata Banerjee in his book *The RIN Strike* writes: 'There was excitement everywhere at Castle Barracks, Fort Barracks and other shore establishments – the ratings gathered in small groups and discussed the situation. It was something new, something unheard of... This seemed to be the beginning of the big battle. The humiliation, the discrimination, the suffering must be put to an end for all the time... something had to be done to support the *Talwar* ratings. Secret meetings, conferences of the leading ratings, long discussions... the whole night. Nobody could sleep. Tomorrow they would join the battle... They too would refuse to bear the insults and sufferings.'

This band of angry young men had shaken the British Naval authorities to the core – a feat that was apparently impossible. Fed up of injustice, racism and the denial of fundamental rights, the young men had crippled the one thing Britain had always been sure about – the navy. Now the eyes of an uneasy empire and the rest of India were on them. The first round of the rebellion had begun.

THE MEDIA PERSPECTIVE

The ratings wanted to stand as one with the nation, but they had another enemy to fight – the press or at least, those parts of it sympathetic to the British.

The Indian news reports were divided neatly into two groups. There were pro-establishment newspapers such as the *Times of India, Statesman,* etc., and there was the nationalist press, represented by the *Free Press Journal* and the *Bombay Chronicle.*

The one paper that stood steadfastly for the mutineers throughout was the *Free Press Journal.* The fiercely nationalist editor, S. Natarajan told Dutt that the paper would devote generous columns daily to the ratings' views. The result was that everyone read the *Free Press Journal* for the duration of the mutiny.

Monday, 18 February 1946 was summed up as follows the next morning, Tuesday, 19 February.

The *Free Press Journal* ran a front-page, four-deck headline: 'INDIAN NAVAL MEN IN CITY ON HUNGER STRIKE… Insulting Behaviour of C.O. Infuriates the Ratings, AUTHORITIES GET PANICKY, Communication Between India and Abroad Dislocated… ALL CABLE COMMUNICATIONS BETWEEN INDIA AND ENGLAND AND COLOMBO HAVE BEEN DISLOCATED AS A RESULT OF THE STRIKE.'

The body text read 'Jai Hind, Quit India, and Down with the British slogans resound throughout the establishment (HMIS *Talwar*).' Photographs of B.C. Dutt and R.K. Singh were printed on the front page alongside the lead story. Another story below the lead item carried the headline 'MRS ARUNA ASAF ALI ASKED TO INTERVENE… INSULTING BEHAVIOUR.'

In contrast, the British-owned *Times of India* published a single column, small story on its front page with the headline 'INDIAN RATINGS ON STRIKE—Better Conditions Demanded'… It quoted Rear-Admiral Rattray, Flag Officer Commanding Bombay: 'Indian Ratings of HMIS *Talwar* have since this morning refused to take their food. Meals have been prepared at regular times but no one has entered the mess to eat. The men have been asked to state their grievances, but so far no one has come forward and no statement has been made... which have led to this collective indiscipline...'

POLITICAL RESPONSES

The revolt had its impact on the political leadership. Mahatma Gandhi had arrived in Bombay from Wardha. He was met by Sardar Patel and S.K. Patil, the general secretary BPCC. It has been speculated that Gandhi was briefed about the situation by Sardar Patel, who was to play a significant role in the subsequent stages of the rebellion.

REFERENCES

Ajeet Jawed, 'The Unsung Heroes of 1946', 1 October 2008, *Mainstream*.

B.C. Dutt, *Mutiny of the Innocents*. Bombay: Sindhu Publications, 1971.

Dilip Kumar Das, *Revisiting Talwar: A Study in the Royal Indian Navy Uprising of February 1946*. Delhi: Ajanta Publications, 1993.

Hyper War: The Royal Indian Navy (Chapter 1), https://www.ibiblio.org/hyperwar/UN/India/RIN/RIN-1.html.

Kusum Nair, *The Army of Occupation*. Delhi: Padma Publications, 1946.

Lt. Cdr G.D. Sharma, VSM (Retd), *The Untold Story of Naval Mutiny: Last War of Independence*. Delhi: Vij Books, 2015.

Ratnakar Sadasyula, 'The Forgotten Naval Mutiny of 1946 and India's Independence', 19 February 2016, *Swarajya Magazine*.

Rear Admiral Satyindra Singh AVSM (Retd), *Under Two Ensigns: The Indian Navy 1945–1950*. New Delhi: Oxford and IBH Publishing Co., 1986.

Subrata Banerjee, *The RIN Strike*. Bombay: People's Publishing House, 1981.

The Indian Annual Register (January–June 1946), Vol. 1., pp. 235, 289–98, 301–07.

RIN, GoI, pp. 326–30: Resettlement/ Demobalisatoin (https://www.ibiblio.org/hyperwar/UN/India/RIN/RIN-15.html)

Evening News
OF INDIA

R.I.N. Ratings In Open Mutiny

R.I.N. Ratings at Castle Barracks, Bombay, today who after making an attempt to break out of the Barracks are believed to troops and armed police, and the outside city round the premises of the Barracks and maintained a constant fortified to keep its things out. Pictures show Army troops close to iron railings in the "lanes of Castle Barracks this morning RIGHT: Military pickets in one of the Barracks entrances.

Seize Armoury In Bombay Barracks

MACHINE-GUNS, BREN-GUNS AND RIFLES WERE BROUGHT INTO ACTION TODAY IN CASTLE BARRACKS BEHIND THE TOWN HALL, BOMBAY, BY R.I.N. RATINGS WHO ARE NOW IN OPEN MUTINY FOLLOWING THE OVERNIGHT ROUND-UP BY THE MILITARY OF RATINGS WHO HAD FAILED TO RETURN TO THEIR ESTABLISHMENTS BY 3-30 P.M. YESTERDAY AS DIRECTED BY THE NAVAL AUTHORITIES.

The ratings barricaded themselves inside the barracks, and taking up positions on roofs and ramparts kept up firing continuously into the air from ten onwards this morning. So far there have been no casualties of any kind.

The barracks are surrounded by British and Indian troops whose strength was increased from hour to hour till the time of reporting, which is noon today.

Brigadier C. Southgate, Officer Commanding Bombay Sub Area, was in conference with the naval authorities at the Town Hall which has been turned temporarily into an "operational" headquarters to deal with the extraordinary situation.

FLAG OFFICER COMMANDING ON SITUATION

The following communiqué has been issued by the Flag Officer Commanding in connection with the situation in Castle Barracks.

Warning To Public

Owing to the disturbances and the danger of casualties from stray shots, the public are advised not to move about the port area unnecessarily.

Officers Leave

M. Mahster Sees Iran Premier

Soviet Scientists' Atom Claim

7

HURRICANE SPREADS
BRITISH ENSIGN DOWNED
INDIAN FLAGS UNFURLED

19 FEBRUARY

5.30 a.m.

When the morning bugle sounded in HMIS *Talwar*, the ratings did not stir out of their barracks. They were defiant. They did get up but only to discuss their plans for the day and not to fall in for assembly.

6.30 a.m.

The bugle sounded again. Usually, by the second bugle the ratings would fall in for 'clean ship' duty. Instead, they gathered to discuss the tyranny they had been subjected to by their officers and the racist insults ranging from 'Sons of bitches' to 'Black bastards'. Laughing at the helplessness of the British officers, they got ready to face whatever the day would bring. By now, all the ratings across the Bombay establishments had downed tools.

News of the strike spread like wildfire to all the eleven shore establishments in Bombay and the suburbs, leaving the proud Royal Indian Navy – a mighty arm of the British Empire helpless. Without a leader, without any political backing and in full knowledge that they were risking their careers and lives – 20,000 ratings in over 60 ships struck in solidarity for their brothers in HMIS *Talwar*. But there was an even more significant cause – the country.

8 a.m.

By now, the die was clearly cast. To loud yells and cheers, the Union Jack was pulled down in *Talwar* and the three flags of the Congress Party, the Communist Party of India and the Muslim League were hoisted as all the men gathered and saluted on deck. The crowd outside clapped and cheered in a frenzy while the officers watched helplessly. They could do nothing.

8.15 a.m.

Captain Inigo-Jones, the man who had taken over as CO from Commander King, had been apprised of the situation by Rear-Admiral Rattray. He reached the *Talwar* to be greeted with loud slogans. A volley of stones was hurled in his direction by a few hot-headed ratings. Inigo-Jones wisely decided retreat was the best course of action.

8.30 a.m.

Tensions escalated at the Castle Barracks. False rumours that fellow ratings from the *Talwar* were being 'bayoneted' roused the others to frenzy. An angry mob of 300 ratings marched grimly towards the *Talwar*, leaving the authorities looking both foolish and helpless. The Castle Barracks CO, Commander Streatfield James, came across them but wisely, sensing their mood, slunk past them at the gate. The sentries at the main gate of Castle Barracks unbuckled their belts and joined the procession.

The sentiments of freedom, defiance and brotherhood united the ratings as they chanted slogans such as 'Inquilab Zindabad',

'Hindu Muslim Ek Ho'. The flags of the Congress Party, Communist Party and the Muslim League were held aloft and paraded proudly by the leaders of the procession.

The *Talwar* ratings joined their fellow ratings waiting at the gates. Class and social barriers were breached as men hugged and backslapped one another with tears in their eyes. They had struck the first blows, but there was still much work to be done.

Over 10,000 ratings from all across Bombay marched towards the harbour. They divided up their tasks and boarded each RIN ship: the *Berar, Moti, Neelum, Jumna, Kumaon* and *Oudh*, among others. On each ship, the hated symbols of British domination – the White Ensign of the Royal Navy and the Union Jack – were pulled down only to be replaced proudly by the three Indian flags. Very soon, ratings posted on other ships like the *Madras, Sind Mahratta, Teer, Dhanaush* and *Assam* followed suit and soon the British flag was nowhere to be seen.

As the ratings took over, the officers huddled together, mute and frightened. On one ship, an unnamed British officer tried to resist when the White Ensign was being removed but the ratings eagerly pounced on him to give him a sound thrashing. After that there was no more trouble. Rebellion and revenge was in the air and the British began fast losing control.

9.30 a.m.

Rear-Admiral Rattray arrived in *Talwar* with his other officers to meet with the ratings on strike and hear their demands. The ratings drew up a list of demands to be presented to Rattray. Their demands included:

1. No victimization of strikers;
2. Immediate release of R.K. Singh from Arthur Road Prison;
3. Speedy demobilization in accordance with age and service group with reasonable chance of peace-time employment;
4. Immediate action against Commander King for inhuman behaviour and using foul language;

5. Best quality of rations and Indian food;
6. RN – Royal Navy – scale of pay, family allowance, travelling facilities and use of NAAFI stores;
7. No kit return at time of release;
8. Immediate grant of more gratuity and treasury pay to men on demobilization and release from the Service;
9. Good behaviour of officers towards lower-deck personnel;
10. Quick and regular promotion of lower-deck personnel to officers;
11. A new Commanding Officer of the Signal School to be appointed.

10 a.m.

These demands were presented as grievances before the FOB and an accompanying group of officers. Rattray assured them that he would give due consideration to their demands and grievances. The demands beyond his power to grant would be forwarded to the Navy Headquarters in Delhi.

The ratings insisted that these demands should be decided by naval authorities and a national leader by 5 p.m. The ratings also made the following political demands which they insisted should be sent to the Government of India.

1. Immediate release of political leaders as well as all personnel of the INA;
2. Immediate and impartial inquiry into public firing all over India;
3. Immediate withdrawal of Indian troops from Indonesia and the Middle East.

By now, an increasing number of protestors were marching together. Ratings from other establishments had begun to arrive in *Talwar* via the Fort Barracks, shouting nationalist slogans. By the time they reached the parade ground in *Talwar*, they were nearly 10,000 in number.

As news of the strike spread to other naval establishments, daring ratings started to gather at the parade ground in HMIS Talwar, *the second-largest signal school in the British Empire, located in Colaba, South Bombay. A line map of areas affected by the naval mutiny, published in the* People's Age *in February 1946.*

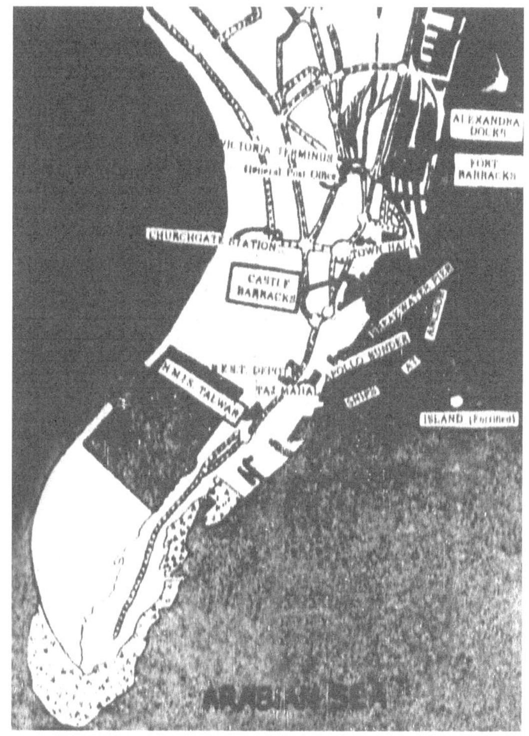

10.30 a.m.

After spending over two hours trying to pacify the striking men, Rattray left *Talwar*.

The ratings who had gathered to discuss the plan of action ended the meeting by shouting slogans loud enough to reach their officers. As they reached the main road towards Fort Barracks, some ratings unfurled Congress and Muslim League flags. Someone called, 'We are working class and we must put Red Flag with hammer and sickle symbol of the Left.' The flags fluttered wildly, throwing their defiance in the faces of the British.

They got hold of units' trucks and mounted them. The procession merged with a waiting group of ratings at Fort Barracks, who greeted them with loud cheers. More trucks arrived, carrying more flags and banners.

All along the route to *Talwar*, residents peered out of their windows, some lined the streets, and gazed at this amazing spectacle of protesting sailors marching down the streets. En route, on Hornby Road, they asked shopkeepers to down their shutters. The Indian shopkeepers did, but the British retailers refused. Furious, the ratings smashed their shop windows. It was carnage.

In the frenzy, everything foreign became a target. Stopping in front of the United States Information Library, they hauled down the US flag and set fire to it [an act the ratings would express deep regret for later]. A mail van with the British Royal insignia was also vandalized.

Even as the hatred for the British burned, the sense of brotherhood remained strong. Jokes and loud laughter filled the air. The mob marched ahead with a mix of anger, zeal, and happiness.

One rating was overheard saying he had heard the rating who was supposed to sound the morning bugle on the *Talwar* had himself joined the strike.

11.45 a.m.

It was an army of 10,000 strong! The naval establishments were bustling with activity. Ratings from all the nearby establishments and supporting civilians were pouring in. While the ratings were asked to assemble in the parade ground, civilians gathered outside. Cracking jokes, they narrated stories of individual protests.

There were two main anchorages for RIN ships in Bombay. At the first one *Berar*, *Moti*, *Neelum*, *Jumna*, *Kumaon* and *Oudh* were anchored and the other was where *Narbada*, *Heera*, *Khyber*, *Clive*, *Lawrence* were anchored.

The ratings posted onboard, had already taken over all these ships and had raised their combination of three flags on the *Berar*, *Moti*, *Neelum*, *Jumna*, *Kumaon* and *Oudh* earlier in the morning. The ratings onshore now launched boats to reach the *Narbada*, *Heera*, *Khyber*, *Clive*, *Lawrence* and a few others as messages flashed from the

Deck Signal stations. Having accomplished the job of replacing the flags on these, they returned ashore.

An announcement said that a request had been made to Aruna Asaf Ali who had promised to come and address the strikers at 4 p.m. The ratings also vented their frustration and anger about the ill treatment meted out to them.

The meetings continued up to 1 in the afternoon in *Talwar* where there was no official administration visible. The ratings were even directing traffic to preserve order in and around the area. Each new arrival of groups of ratings from other ships and establishments was greeted with loud cheers.

12.30 p.m.

By noon, things began to calm down and the ratings gathered at the *Talwar* conferred to decide what the next course of action would be. It was a moving act of solidarity. A crowd of 10,000 ratings gathered at the parade ground of the *Talwa*r, where a few of the leaders of the different ships and establishments spoke.

Pride and patriotism were running high as an unnamed strike leader spoke emotionally about how they all had come together for themselves, but especially for Mother India! 'When we started the strike, we never thought that we would get such enthusiastic support from our fellow ratings. We have received the news that practically all the ratings have joined the struggle. We are proud of our unity.'

The strike leaders concurred that there was an immediate need to form a Central Strike Committee (CSC) where representatives would be selected from each ship or establishment. The FOB wanted to meet these representatives and hear their demands. Over a dozen members were selected. Though B.C. Dutt, R.K. Singh and Salil Shyam were still in prison, they too figured in the list.

Another issue of profound symbolic significance that emerged from the meeting was that the Royal Indian Navy needed to be called the Indian National Navy. This done, the biggest question loomed.

Who would take overall charge of managing the strike? The ratings discussed it at length and finally, Leading Signalman M.S. Khan was elected president and, PO and Telegraphist, Madan Singh, a clean-shaven Sikh, was elected vice president. The duo were fluent in English, Hindi and Punjabi and considered politically suave – a quality the ratings thought would serve them well. Both members were younger than twenty-five and it was thought that they would also make a good impression on political leaders and the public at large. Apart from negotiating with the authorities, their main function would be to coordinate action and activities of the units outside the *Talwar*. Prominent members of the Strike Committee made speeches at each shore establishment.

Who were these two men? Though Khan was mild-mannered, he had often made his objections regarding bad food and other issues known to British officers in the past. He was described by those who knew him as quiet but someone who hated foreign rule. What also made him stand out from other ratings was that he had gone through regular navy training.

As for Madan Singh, he was considered a tough and competent seaman. Anglicized, with his hair cut, he was a sailor par excellence, who had kept his cool while serving on ships that had faced several crises. From sinking ships to handling cyclones in the North Sea, or the Atlantic – Madan's professionalism and competence had won the hearts of his colleagues as they greeted his appointment with loud cheers.

1.30 p.m.

Some journalists who were informed of the unrest visited *Talwar* to try and get first-hand accounts of what was happening. Sentries tried to block their entry through the main gate. A rating then took them inside the Royal Gate, which they had now renamed 'Azad Gate'. Some journalists were brought in through makeshift ladders that ratings lowered from the walls of *Talwar* to get them to witness the scene first-hand. If journalists expected to hear the usual complaints about poor food and amenities, they were in for a shock.

They were welcomed with cries of 'Jai Hind' and 'Quit India' and able to witness first-hand the patriotic fervour that gripped these men onboard. Inside, they saw further proof of the nationalistic fervour with the same slogans painted across all the walls.

It was nothing like they had ever seen or expected. Indian seamen working for the British had been considered part of the Raj for so long that it was hard to take these scenes in.

In small groups, the ratings used loudspeakers to address the gathering, standing on top of desks or tables. They answered the questions in detail.

Asked why they needed a national leader to function as an intermediary between themselves and the government, the reply was immediate. Replied one rating, 'We have learnt the art of how to defend our freedom unfortunately so far of other lands... We are now ready to offer our services to the nation and that is why we want our national leaders to lead us in this strike and link our demands with our national demand for freedom.'

The journalists present explained to the ratings that newspapers were divided on the issue of this revolt. While the *Bombay Chronicle* and the *Free Press Journal* were accurately reporting the strike and the demands, the pro-British papers like the *Evening News*, the *Times of India* and the *Statesman* were reporting the British version of events.

The strike was now a national affair, with unrest spreading to other RIN stations like Calcutta, Karachi, Vizag, and Madras.

2.30 p.m.

In the meantime, the British naval authorities had started to plan for the trouble they anticipated. They were strengthening security. The area commander apprised the army police of the building tension and asked for two companies of 18 Mahrattas to be ready at very short notice.

It was also decided to remove the arsenals to safer places and secure the arms. The administration also arranged mobile patrols to round up RIN ratings found on the streets. A reinforcement troop of 18 Mahrattas were ordered to stand by at one hour notice.

Rear-Admiral Rattray received information that a large disorderly crowd of ratings and civilians had gathered outside Fort Barracks. They were threatening to break in and release prisoners in Castle Barracks. The report turned out to be exaggerated. Only one policeman had been hurt so far by a missile thrown from a civilian building.

3 p.m.

The meeting at *Talwar* resumed. Representatives who had gone to meet some political leaders relayed their account of the meeting. They also reported that negotiations had begun and Rattray had been persuaded to give them a hearing. Rattray arrived to take stock of the situation. He was given the charter of demands.

He promised nothing but said he would send the demands to the Naval Headquarters in Delhi. He only agreed to their demand for better food. He left and many British officers were allowed to leave with him. Many Indian officers left as well. The ratings were disgusted but not surprised. They saw the Indian officers as lackeys of the British.

Given the impasse, how much would the authorities relent? Rattray had promised to give the men a sympathetic hearing and set up a committee to hear their demands. Instead, all around him, he saw the men charged up with patriotism, a new experience for him and the other British officers.

There had been strikes before, from 1942 onwards – often over bad food – but this one was turning out to be different. These men were no longer content with being servants of the British Empire; they wanted to be treated as equals. Every bit of anger and bitterness against the British, every call for revolution, every link of their cause to the broader freedom struggle was being shouted out and loudly applauded.

The fury and hatred took Rattray and his committee members by surprise. Until then, they had been unable to grasp the seriousness of the situation.

4 p.m.

Meanwhile, the NCSC meeting continued even after Rattray's departure as the ratings waited eagerly for the one political leader who had stood by them all this time – Aruna Asaf Ali. She was expected to come at 4 p.m. The emotional speeches of Aruna and the other national leaders had stirred a fire in them, and they were confident she would not abandon them now. But to the ratings' great surprise she did not come. Not only that, she advised the delegation who had come to meet her to advise the men to 'remain calm'. What sort of advice was this? But it would not be the first time they were disappointed by their national leaders.

Despite her absence, these valiant men decided that the strike would be conducted in accordance with the Gandhian principle of non-violence. Everything they did, they would now do per the tenets of the freedom struggle as followed by their national leaders.

This was accepted even if the concept of non-violence was difficult for many of them to comprehend. Their entire working lives had been spent fighting, and subduing enemies with arms. What sort of fight was this? How could they ever possibly hope to win this way?

6 p.m.

There was no effort by the administration to enforce discipline, indeed there was no sign of the authorities. Swiftly getting to work, the NCSC issued orders. Each man's role was made completely clear. The first and most important objective was getting the public on their side. A group of ratings hired three trucks and, carrying loudspeakers with the three flags displayed prominently on each truck, went on a procession covering important places in Bombay before returning to *Talwar* along the Backbay. En route, they asked people to discard anything English, even asking them to remove English caps.

It was not just the politicians who would let these men down; a large section of the media was also biased against them and the Anglophile newspapers continued to portray these ratings as 'unruly monsters'. They faced these canards even as they returned to their respective ships and establishments, planning and plotting the next course of action.

This was a study in contradictions. While the men were laughing, singing and cracking jokes – at Castle Barracks as they sat on *charpais* around roaring fires, the Anglocentric media was busy sharpening their pencils and deciding how best to attack them. This was something the ratings had never expected.

7 p.m.

It was around this time the first sign of discontent with the media coverage emerged. Carrying a copy of the *Evening News,* an angry rating stormed into the *Talwar* demanding an explanation. 'Ratings Run Amuck' was the headline boldly splattered across the front page. 'What is the meaning of this,' he asked the journalists who had been sitting with the ratings.

The journalists were taken by surprise. Some of them tried to explain the difference between the Anglophile papers and the nationalist press and that they were in no way responsible for the headlines, but the ratings were in no mood to listen. The journalists were immediately asked to leave and exited the *Talwar* in silence.

As the media wondered what the future would hold, the ratings asked themselves the same questions. They had already come far but this was uncharted territory. Still, optimism prevailed.

The headlines had hurt but it was the view of a minority who were still confused. After all, weren't they all a little confused by what had happened? But very soon, everything would be all right.

The people were with them, the country was with them, and they would triumph.

It was on this note the night ended. Jubilation and optimism ruled. Whatever happened, they would face it together as brothers, and their leaders would guide them. They waited, full of hope for freedom and liberty for their beloved country.

Little did they know then how cruelly they would be betrayed.

REFERENCES

Admiral Godfrey's letters, NAI.

Andrew Davis, *Identity and Assemblage of Protest.*

B.C. Dutt, *Mutiny of the Innocents.* Bombay: Sindhu Publications, 1971, pp. 151–85.

Biswanath Bose, *Royal Indian Navy.* New Delhi: Northern Book Centre, 1988, pp. 10-38, 41–47, 77–79, 87, 92–111, 134, 167–69, 180, 182, 197–99, 202–03, 207–08.

Dilip Kumar Das, *Revisiting Talwar: A Study in the Royal Indian Navy Uprising of February 1946.* Delhi: Ajanta Publications, 1993, pp. 90–158.

Kusum Nair, *The Army of Occupation.* Delhi: Padma Publications, 1946, pp. 40–48.

Legislative Assembly proceedings (Strike at Bombay and Karachi, RIN), NAI.

Lockhart-RIN Mutiny; Hour by hour event description, 1946, NAI.

Note on incidents connected with RIN Mutiny, NAI.

Opinion of Board of Enquiry Held to Investigate the Cause & Circumstances of the Mutiny on HMIS SIND and MAHARASHTRA, 1946, NAI.

Report on Royal Indian Navy, NAI.

The Indian Annual Register (January–June 1946), Vol.1., pp. 235, 289–98, 301–07.

'The Unsung Heroes of 1946', *Mainstream Weekly.*

Top Secret Cypher Telegram, NAI, 1946.

The Hindustan Times

LARGEST CIRCULATION IN NORTHERN, NORTH-WESTERN & CENTRAL INDIA.

Regd. No L. 1733 — DELHI EDITION

VOL. XXIII. NO. 50 — NEW DELHI: WEDNESDAY, FEBRUARY 20, 1946 — PRICE 1½ ANNAS

3 BRITISH CABINET MINISTERS FOR INDIA

PETHICK-LAWRENCE, CRIPPS & ALEXANDER IN MISSION

NEGOTIATIONS WITH POLITICAL LEADERS TO BEGIN BY END OF MARCH

DELEGATION GIVEN FREE HAND EXCEPT ON MATTERS OF MAJOR POLICY

LONDON, FEB. 19—THREE BRITISH CABINET MINISTERS ARE GOING TO INDIA TO DISCUSS WITH LEADERS OF INDIAN OPINION THE FRAMING OF AN INDIAN CONSTITUTION. THEY ARE LORD PETHICK-LAWRENCE, SECRETARY FOR INDIA, SIR STAFFORD CRIPPS, PRESIDENT OF THE BOARD OF TRADE, AND MR ALBERT ALEXANDER, FIRST LORD OF THE ADMIRALTY. THIS WAS OFFICIALLY ANNOUNCED IN THE HOUSE OF LORDS TODAY BY LORD PETHICK-LAWRENCE.

The Prime Minister, Mr Clement Attlee, in making a similar statement in the House of Commons added that the mission would go to India towards the end of March.

Lord Pethick-Lawrence

Sind Premier Denies Plan To Arrest Or Intern Mr Syed

KARACHI, Feb. 19.

MUNSHI REJOINS CONGRESS

BOMBAY, Feb. 19.

LATE NEWS

Sir Stafford Cripps

NEED FOR DEFINITE PURPOSE

Sorensen On Cabinet Mission's Task

DUTCH ATROCITIES IN JAVA

Indian Troops Threaten Direct Action

LONDON, Feb. 19. British and Indian troops in Batavia have informed their officers that they intend to take direct action against Dutch troops unless British Army authorities act to prevent Dutch atrocities against Indonesians, according to a despatch in the Melbourne Herald today by the paper's correspondent in Batavia.

JAI PRAKASH MAY BE RELEASED IN MARCH

AZAD TO MEET VICEROY ON THURSDAY

CALCUTTA, Feb. 19.

GANDHIJI IN POONA

POONA, Feb. 19.

R.I.N. RATINGS' REVOLT SPREADS: 7,000 NOW ON STRIKE

Wild Demonstrations In Bombay: U.S. Protest Against Insult To Flag

BOMBAY, Feb 19.

VITAL ATOM BOMB SECRETS ALREADY LOST BY U.S.

LONDON, Feb. 19.

PROCLAMATION OF INDEPENDENCE MUST COME FIRST

NEHRU OUTLINES COUNTRY'S DEMAND AFTER ELECTIONS

ALLAHABAD, Feb 19.

No Vendettas

Attitude To Pakistan

No Compulsion

BRITAIN & RUSSIA DRIFTING APART

Divergent Policies May Lead To Catastrophe

LONDON, Feb 19.

Suspicions Revived

Tikka Ram Loses To Congressman

(From Our Correspondent)

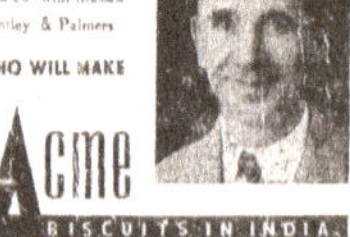

8

EYEBALL TO EYEBALL: FOCRIN FLIES IN

DAY 3, WEDNESDAY, 20 FEBRUARY 1946

Wednesday dawned with screaming headlines across global media. 'CITY NAVAL STRIKE SPREADS… Noisy Demonstration in Fort Area… National Flag on RIN Vessels' featured on the front page of the *Free Press Journal*.

The body text carried a detailed description which read in part: 'The second day of the Indian naval men's strike saw some 20,000 men involved… Practically all men of all shore establishments in Bombay area came out in sympathy with "Talwar" Strikers and they were further augmented by the ratings manning some 20 odd RIN vessels in the Harbour… It is reported that India's tricolour was flown on… RIN vessels in the harbour in place of Union Jack…'

'…thousands of Indian ratings from *Akbar, Feroz, Machlimar, Humla,* and the wireless stations at Colaba and Marol and different vessels of the RIN came out on the streets in sympathy with the *Talwar* strikers… they congregated at Azad Maidan. A procession of several thousand strong, some carrying hockey sticks, started along Hornby Street towards the museum, raising slogans of Jai Hind,

Inquilab Zindabad.' It further reported: 'Europeans were chased and the USA Flag at the US Information Library was hauled down and burnt. A military mail-van was attacked and letters were littered on the street.'

The *Times of India* relegated the story to page 8 and called it a 'REIGN OF TERROR BY RATINGS ON "STRIKE". Indiscriminate Attack on Pedestrian & Traffic… RIN Demonstrators Run Wild In Bombay… Brutality Against Loyal Troops – Council of State Rejects plea to Withdraw INA Cases.'

The body text said: 'Britons in the Fighting Services were singled out for attack by groups of "Strikers" who were armed with steel hammers, crowbars, hockey sticks, bludgeons and a variety of weapons. Three British servicemen, three police officers and two constables were injured.'

News of the strike was reported by mainstream newspapers in Britain, the US and elsewhere. The *New York Times* said, 'Indian Navy Strike Spurs Bombay Riot,' while the jingoistic *Daily Mail* lamented, 'Indian Navy Mutiny: Haul Down our Ensign.'

In terms of hard news, rather than opinion, it was widely reported that the FOCRIN (Flag Officer Commanding Royal Indian Navy), Admiral J.H. Godfrey would fly to Bombay on Wednesday, 20 February.

The rapidly developing events of 19 February meant that everyone had endured a tense night. Thus far, the ratings' actions had been successful, and this had given them hope and they had received popular support. But they still lacked basics like food supplies which had depleted in the last two days. They were also still seeking leadership and direction from the Indian political elite.

But this was their first big day in command, free from their hated British seniors. The British were equally tense, given the speed and intensity with which the events were unfolding and the way in which they had been taken by surprise.

★ ★ ★

1 a.m.

It was a night full of anxiety and trepidation for the British officers. A minute after midnight, the CO of HMIS *Hamla* at Marve rang up the sub-area commandant stating that most of his ship's boys had broken out and were moving towards Bombay in commandeered transport. This led to all-night tense parleys and phone calls.

2.15 a.m.

Rear-Admiral Rattray had earned a reputation as a masterful tactician during the Second World War, and he lived up to it when it came to dealing with the mutineers. He realized that the existing naval strength would not be enough to tackle thousands of angry ratings.

So shortly after 2 a.m., he rang up the sub-area commander, 18 Mahrattas and also the deputy commissioner of police, briefing them on the critical situation for which, he said, he required immediate assistance.

2.45 a.m.

The area commander collected the sub-area commander of 18 Mahrattas and proceeded immediately to Castle Barracks. It was reported that a party of over 100 ratings were believed to have entered Bombay, travelling by commandeered lorries from establishments outside the city and forced their way into the communication centre and tried to intimidate naval ratings and WRINS on night duty. Some damage was done too.

3.15–4.30 a.m.

A conference was held at Rear-Admiral Rattray's residence where the area commander, sub-area commander and deputy commissioner of police were present. It was decided
1. To safeguard signal and communication stations;
2. Outside ratings should be prevented from entering Bombay;

Appeal To All R.I.N. Personnel From Central Naval Strike Committee

The Central Naval Strike Committee has reviewed the situation created by the all-in strike of the R.I.N. personnel in all establishments and ships. The Committee appeals to all R.I.N. personnel to compulsorily observe the following code of conduct in order to prosecute the strike to a successful conclusion:

1. Strike of work must be your first and last concern till success is fully attained. No injuries should be caused to persons or property in any circumstances or even under the gravest provocation. No such action can be part of the strike.

2. You should maintain complete solidarity and discipline in your ranks.

3. You must immediately form establishment or ship committee of strike and formulate specific demands regarding service and other conditions.

4. You must also immediately elect a representative who will be the member from your establishment or ship on the Central Naval Strike Committee.

5. No personnel shall communicate or negotiate with any officials. Every matter for individual representation or grievance must be conveyed by personnel ONLY to the elected spokesman.

6. A Central Naval Strike Committee will soon be established composing of representatives of all establishments and ships.

7. Invite the mediation of trusted public leaders.

8. All personnel should keep within their ships or establishments, except when they go out for food and in all circumstances they should maintain the highest discipline.

IF THE ABOVE CODE OF CONDUCT IS STRICTLY OBSERVED AND IF THE PERSONNEL STAND SOLIDLY BEHIND THE CENTRAL

The Naval Central Strike Committee issued a code of conduct to ratings on all naval ships and establishments to take the strike to a 'successful conclusion'.

3. Not to issue a 'Confinement to Barracks' order at this juncture as it might prejudice C-in-C's policy.

It was also decided that additional forces would be sent to

Signal Centre, Castle Barracks, Mahul Wireless Station, and Colaba Signal Station. One *paltan* each was to be sent to Mahim and Sion Causeways to prevent ratings from pouring into Bombay.

The entire police *bandobast* was discussed in detail.

One unit each of the 18 Mahrattas and the police was to be dispatched to Castle Barracks to provide relief and support to the Royal Navy. A unit to be sent to the Colaba Signal Station and a larger unit to the Mahul Wireless Station.

Finally, all naval establishments in Bombay were to stay on high alert and attempts should be made to seal and secure them.

6 a.m.

At the *Talwar* and Castle Barracks, very few ratings had got any sleep the previous night. The scene was surreal. There was no bugle, no siren to wake them up as would have been the case normally.

The ratings were interested in the morning headlines relating to the *Talwar* strike and Commander King's now infamous abuse.

The Associated Press correspondent in Bombay had filed a detailed report. Touring the harbour at nightfall on 19 February, he reported that he found almost all the 20-odd RIN ships practically unmanned. 'The Orange, Green and White Congress flag flew from most of the ships… Colaba and the surrounding Naval area was agog with all kinds of rumours…'

The *Daily News* of Perth, Western Australia, quoted the *Daily Mail* Bombay correspondent and wrote: 'A false message was radioed from a shore station that two strikers had been shot. Warships picked up the message and pandemonium broke out as sirens morsed it around the harbour… boatloads of ratings poured ashore while bewildered officers stood passively. Demonstrations followed all day until word spread that the report was false…'

Alarmed by the mutiny, Westminster also hastily announced the visit of a high-powered Cabinet Mission, with three members of the British Cabinet, to India. They did not want to risk a repeat of the 1857 Mutiny.

The *Free Press Journal* reported this in a story datelined London: 'BRITISH BIG GUNS FOR INDIA… Lord Pethick-Lawrence to fly in towards end of March, Constitutional Making Mission, Sir Stafford Cripps and Alexander to accompany.'

The visit, the paper wrote, was triggered by the rebellions and uprisings of all three arms of the armed forces in the recent past, 'the current Naval Mutiny being the immediate trigger'.

Lord Pethick-Lawrence, the secretary of state for India, in a statement in the House of Lords, said: 'In view of the paramount importance not only to India and to the British Commonwealth but to the peace of the world of a successful outcome of discussions with the leaders of Indian opinion, the British government has decided with the approval of His Majesty the King to send out to India a special mission of cabinet ministers consisting of the Secretary of State for India (Lord Pethick-Lawrence), the President of the Board of Trade (Sir Stafford Cripps) and the First Lord of the Admiralty (A.V. Alexander) to act in association with the Viceroy in this matter. This decision has the full concurrence of Lord Wavell.'

On the same day, Prime Minister Clement Attlee had made a similar statement in the House of Commons stating the Cabinet Mission will go to India towards end of March and remain there with the objective of 'promoting in conjunction with leaders of Indian opinion early realisation of full self-government in India.'

The *Times of India* termed this 'Setting Up Machinery To Help Indians Decide Their Own Destinies,' while the *Hindustan Times* elaborated three major areas of discussions as objectives of the mission: 'Firstly preparatory discussions with elected representatives of British India and with Indian states in order to secure the widest measure of agreement as to the method of framing a constitution. Second, setting up of a constitution-making body and, third, bringing into being of an executive council having the support of the main Indian Parties.'

6.30 a.m.

For the ratings, food remained a big concern at the centre of the discussions in *Talwar*. Food stores were running out. Given their meagre pay, the ratings could not afford to eat out and there weren't enough arrangements to cook in the mess. Besides, the cooks were on strike themselves. It was decided to request the cooks to prepare food in the mess with whatever was available.

The cooks agreed on one condition: '*Hum ek shart par razi honge, ki agar waqt aye to hame bhi tum hathiyar doge aur ladne se nahin rokoge.*' (When the time comes, we would be given arms to fight alongside the ratings.) At Castle Barracks, it was a different story. Due to no food being available, the ratings went on a rampage.

Napoleon has been quoted as saying that an army marches on its stomach, underlying the importance of forces being well-provisioned. That was a crucial issue facing the ratings.

None of them had eaten anything the previous night, nor was breakfast available, owing to the prevailing tensions. The military police that surrounded *Talwar*, refused to let them step out to buy food. Tensions rose. Desperate and hungry, they decided to break open the Family Canteen, and targeted fittings and fixtures while chanting anti-British slogans.

To stop them from going on a rampage, the military police opened fire. Meant as a warning, this had the opposite effect. The ratings then broke into the armoury, grabbed rifles, climbed on parapets and started to shoot back at the military police.

One report said that a hand grenade had been thrown at the guards and while this was proved false, things were fast getting out of hand. In anticipation of an assault, the ratings sent signals to all the ships in the harbour that they should open fire with their big guns if the military guards were not withdrawn.

8 a.m.

Once again, the ratings from Fort Barracks and Castle Barracks marched towards *Talwar* but not quite in the same spontaneous way as on the first day. This time they marched ceremonially in threes as if they were in an official parade, in full uniform. But instead of the Union Jack, the lead marchers were carrying the three flags of the Indian National Congress, Muslim League, and the Communist Party. They marched in step, shouting nationalist slogans while people lining the streets cheered them on.

The British officers at the gates looked on helplessly as the ratings could now move in and out of *Talwar* as they chose.

8.30 a.m.

The *Talwar* was getting crowded. Many new faces could be seen amidst the swelling numbers. The ratings from HMIS *Gondwana* were asked, why did they not join the strike earlier? They explained how, on 18 February, they had only heard whispers and rumours and it was only on 19 February that ratings from HMIS *Punjab* had come over and narrated the whole story.

On the way to the *Talwar*, ratings from other ships and shore establishments stopped and gathered at the Oval Maidan, soon adding up to a crowd numbering several thousand. While speeches were made and slogans were raised, patriotic songs rent the air. They even apologized for the previous day's act of indiscipline when a few ratings had burnt the American flag. From there, they proceeded to the *Talwar*.

HMIS *Akbar*, Thana
9 a.m.

About 2,000 ratings marched out and by the time they reached the parade ground, their numbers had swelled to 3,500. They demanded transport to go to Thana railway station. The authorities refused.

Defying orders, the ratings commandeered the parked lorries. They wanted to join their brethren on the *Talwar* as quickly as possible. Upon hearing that ratings on HMIS *Cheetah* at Trombay had also struck work and were surrounded by the military, they became all the more agitated with renewed courage to fight. In their belligerence, they broke into the Guard Room, released the prisoners and set the room on fire.

They walked in a procession, waving Congress, Muslim League and Communist flags, shouting nationalist slogans. The residents of Thana looked on in admiration and amazement; they had never seen something like this. 'Britishers are now doomed' was how they greeted the ratings.

At the station they divided themselves into two groups to catch the first available trains to Bombay, one lot going to Victoria Terminus, the other lot going to Churchgate. Fellow passengers stood up and offered them their seats. At the station, singing, shouting slogans, they were given right of way. It was a battle cry for freedom. They reached the *Talwar* at about 1 p.m.

HMIS *Talwar*
10 a.m.

The gathering at the *Talwar* had become massive, with each group shouting nationalistic slogans, their voices ringing louder as they reached the *Talwar* and embraced the fellow ratings. As if on cue, somebody started to sing Iqbal's song: '*Saare Jahan se accha Hindustan hamara, Hum bulbulen hain iske yeh gulsita hamara   ,*' and it soon became a chorus.

In the charged atmosphere created by that patriotic anthem, the president of the NCSC, M.S. Khan, delivered a stirring speech: 'We will carry on our fight till our demands are fulfilled. We must stand firm on our own legs and maintain our unity…'

Despite the bad food, abusive behaviour and ill treatment, the ratings had kept their focus on the larger picture. At various meetings, one major demand was the release of political prisoners, especially members of the INA.

As one member of the newly formed NCSC was quoted saying. 'Release of the INA prisoners is a very important demand. The British have no right to try them. We must stand behind our brothers. We must demand the withdrawal of all INA cases.'

Another speaker announced: 'During the last six years of the war, all the British officers have treated us like dogs, not like human beings. We have to not merely fight for our own demands but have also to join the bigger battle for the independence of our country. For this we must demand the release of all INA prisoners.'

One more militant member of the ratings said, 'We fight better than these white dogs… we must give our lives, if need be, in the cause of freedom, but not serve as British slaves. And we should never surrender.'

Most of the speeches ended with cries of 'Inquilab Zindabad'. A large number of journalists had arrived and they asked for permission to attend all the meetings. The ratings welcomed most of them but raised objections to the presence of the *Times of India* reporter because the paper had published reports that were not favourable to the strikers. The reporter was allowed to attend only after he apologized and promised not to report negative stories.

11 a.m.

A historic meeting of the NCSC was attended by all the members. M.S. Khan was reconfirmed as president. Four members were elected to form a negotiating committee. The job of this committee was to carry on negotiations with naval authorities, and also to meet leaders of various political parties and elicit their support.

Thereafter, the Charter of Demands was discussed. Besides the ill treatment, bad food, racism, unfair terms of demobilization and low salaries, most of the crucial demands were political.

They included the release of INA prisoners and withdrawal of cases against them. One of the more striking demands was the complete withdrawal of Indian forces from Indonesia, where Indian soldiers were being used to fight Indonesians to help the Dutch colonizers to recapture the islands which had been occupied by the Japanese during the Second World War. Indian forces stationed in Egypt were similarly to be withdrawn.

It was then announced that FOCRIN Admiral Godfrey had

Admiral John Henry Godfrey had an impressive career before coming to India. Starting as a cadet in 1903, he became the youngest commander in the Royal Navy. He was the chief of RIN when the mutiny took place in 1946. Ian Fleming, creator of James Bond, was once his assistant and created the character of 'M' based on him.

flown into Bombay from Delhi to have direct talks with the ratings.

Admiral John Henry Godfrey (10 July 1888–29 August 1971) was appointed Field Officer Commanding Royal Indian Navy (FOCRIN) in 1943. He was the chief of the RIN when the mutiny took place.

Admiral Godfrey had an impressive career before coming to India. Starting as a cadet in 1903, he became the youngest commander in the Royal Navy, aged thirty-two. He was promoted to director of Naval Intelligence in 1939, one of the most sensitive positions during the Second World War.

He worked closely with Winston Churchill, though not always agreeing with him. In a 90-minute meeting with American President Franklin D. Roosevelt, he was instrumental in setting up a joint intelligence group.

As director of Naval Intelligence, he appointed Ian Fleming, the creator of James Bond, in May 1939, as his assistant. Together, they made a formidable team. Godfrey treated Fleming as the son he never had, and was so fond of him that he once remarked, 'Ian should have been the Director of National Intelligence, and I, his Naval adviser.' Fleming on his part immortalized Godfrey, based the character of James Bond's boss 'M' on him.

Godfrey arrived in India in March 1943 for a three-year term. He made significant contributions to naval reforms in India but stumbled at the difficult task of demobilization. There were over 27,000 ratings in the RIN when he took over. He was instructed to reduce this to a peace-time force of 11,000, by demobilizing 500 every week.

This process was carried out in a slipshod, hasty and unfair manner, with the demobilized men receiving less than their dues, and were unhappy due to the fact that they had been promised permanent careers and promotions. This inevitably led to an acute sense of discontentment and was, in fact, one of the important reasons for the mutiny.

Godfrey was at Udaipur airport when he was informed about the rebellion. He writes in his memoir: 'As we drew into Udaipur, I noticed an RAF plane on the airfield. This looked a bit ominous… I saw Kirkbride, the Resident, standing on the platform with a sealed envelope. The letter informed me a mutiny had broken out in Bombay… I flew to Delhi that afternoon, and on to Bombay on 20 February.'

Ignoring his chief, Field Marshal Claude Auchinleck's suggestion, Godfrey asked Rattray to continue a dialogue with the leaders of the strike committee while at the same time, preparing to crush the rebellion with an iron fist, if needed. He made this clear in an infamous broadcast on the afternoon of 21 February.

11.15 a.m.

In a dramatic development, an Indian officer entered the room where the meeting of the NCSC was being conducted. Everyone looked up in disbelief. He was initially greeted with hostility. The four-member negotiating team did not want any Indian officer to be present, knowing where their loyalties lay. To their great surprise, the officer tore off his badges and every official symbol on his uniform. 'I have come to join you,' he told the ratings. There was stunned silence and disbelief. The officer continued: 'I know you don't believe me… you think I have come to spy on you… I have come here to join your freedom struggle… to assure you and as a mark of my honesty, I remove my badges of rank.'

This was Lt Ishaq Sobhani, the only RIN officer who joined the revolt. He was welcomed into the committee meeting. After this dramatic interruption, an announcement was made that workers and students of Bombay, many associated with the Communist Party, had decided to organize a sympathetic strike – a *hartal* – across the city.

12 noon

The first meeting of the NCSC ended with a resolution that barring an emergency, they would meet the next day again at 10 a.m.

From adjoining buildings, rooftops, windows and balconies overlooking the meeting bungalow, thousands of citizens, including women and children, shouted slogans and cheered the strikers, expressing their solidarity.

The most critical aspect of the negotiations was to be the meeting between the newly formed negotiating committee of the ratings, the NCSC, and Rear-Admiral Rattray The NCSC had been authorized to place their demands before FOCRIN Admiral Godfrey.

Even before they entered the meeting, the ratings had one key demand: They would under no circumstances be considered 'Ringleaders' in the mutiny. The ratings were immediately put on the back foot when FOCRIN Godfrey made no attempt to come inside the *Talwar* to meet the strike committee. Instead, the leaders of the committee were expected to meet him.

It was too much to expect the young ratings to sit across the table from a fine military tactician, and return victorious from the negotiations. Instead, the committee returned with a 'request' from the FOCRIN that 'all ratings should return to their respective ships and establishments by 3.30 p.m… The FOCRIN "request" came to us as the first sign of the gathering clouds,' writes B.C. Dutt.

The ratings were furious upon hearing the terms but the NCSC representatives persuaded them to go back to their own ships and establishments. One prominent representative of the NCSC announced, 'On behalf of the Naval Central Strike Committee, I appeal to you to go back. Do not give the authorities a chance to put us in the wrong. Leave the whole matter in the hands of the leaders you have elected. Remain calm, disciplined, united and non-violent.'

Not all the ratings agreed. In fact, a majority were furious. 'They talk of negotiations and threaten us at the same time. This is a trick… we should give them a time limit and then take up arms,' said one rating. Another rating reportedly added, 'Why should we go back. We should fight back…'

Despite such disagreements, the majority decided to abide by the decision of their leaders. This round had gone to the British, who were quick to use the option of placing military guards around all the RIN establishments, including the *Talwar*, Castle Barracks, and Dockyards.

The ratings were to be informed of the deployments only after these were complete and they were told anyone found outside their establishments and ships would be forcefully sent back. Patrolling on the streets had already begun, leaving the ratings at a distinct disadvantage.

Shortly after 1 p.m.

A special meeting was held to welcome around 3,500 ratings from HMIS *Akbar*, a training establishment in Thana, a Bombay suburb. The *Akbar* had a tradition of rebellion. Only two years earlier, in 1944, Hindus and Muslims had joined together and struck work because Muslims were not being allowed to say their prayers. The men on *Akbar* had received the news of rebellion late, on 19th afternoon. They struck work immediately.

In response, naval authorities warned the *Akbar* strikers that they would be severely dealt with if they joined the *Talwar* strikers. The threat added fuel to the fire and made them furious, but to avoid putting obstacles in the way of NCSC negotiations, they went back to work that day only to march to Bombay on the next day, 20 February.

The British were taking no chances. Anger and resentment were visibly building among the thousands of ratings. Castle Barracks alone had between 6,000 and 8,000 men on the strength of the establishment.

As a preventive measure, the FOCRIN had already issued a press release at 2.30 p.m. which said, 'Owing to the many incidents of violence and hooliganism that took place on Tuesday, 19 February, it became necessary for the safety, not only of the general public but also of the RIN ratings themselves to return to their ships and establishments today.'

To drive the point home, vans fitted with loud hailers were sent round the city repeating the message and also threatening arrests as well as summary treatment to anyone disobeying the orders. Pickets were put up at the gates of the establishments where large cages with guards were set up to catch erring ratings and keep them confined on display like animals.

Additional guards were posted at railway stations to prevent ratings from coming into the city from suburban establishments. The basic strategy was to use military guards at choke points to cut the ratings off from the outside world.

The retaliation to this was swift and inevitable. At the Castle Barracks, even unarmed ratings collected stones and whatever objects they could find, to attack the military guards. They had at their disposal empty cannon shells, iron balls, flower pots, etc., to throw at the guards below. The British then brought in artillery and established machine-gun posts covering all the exits and entrance to Castle Barracks.

At the Fort Barracks, some ratings started to attack the Mahratta guards but cooled down when they learnt the guards were sympathetic to their cause. The Mahratta troops had been told their services were needed to bring order to a Hindu–Muslim clash. Upon realizing that they were brought to fight against the ratings, their attitude changed.

3 p.m.

As the deadline approached, most ratings decided to go along with their elected leaders and re-boarded their ships by 3 p.m. Those who remained outside after 3.30 p.m. were picked up by the military police and brought back to the *Talwar*, though they were not officially arrested. Tension was rising across the city and military guards could be seen everywhere.

So tense was the atmosphere that the NCSC issued a press statement reading: 'It has been brought to the notice of the committee that the ratings on strike are perturbed and annoyed over the action of the authorities in calling armed police to guard and surround the barracks and ships. This is provocative and unwarranted.' The statement was signalled to all the ships and shore establishments.

Angered by the presence of military guards on the streets and at the shore establishments, the ratings decided that they should prepare to fight back, determined never to give in. They started to prepare an inventory of arms and ammunition to retaliate if the need arose. The ships in the Bombay harbour were well armed with 4-inch guns, machine guns, grenades, and small arms. Being in control of these ships meant the ratings had access to a deadly arsenal.

However, the committee again gave assurances and appealed to the ratings to remain peaceful and non-violent. Later in the day, members of the NCSC, led by M.S. Khan met FOCRIN Admiral Godfrey, and FOB Rear-Admiral Rattray to demand the withdrawal of the guards, which was flatly refused. Godfrey insisted that he could not recommend withdrawal of the guards unless a guarantee of surrender was given. 'I cannot remove the guards. It is up to GHQ [General Head Quarter]. I cannot recommend it. Now, of course, if you give me an undertaking to surrender and go back to work unconditionally, we might remove the military guards.'

According to Subrata Banerjee, Godfrey also promised to restore water and food if the strike was called off. This was a ploy to break the unity of the strikers. British authorities were aware that many ratings were without food for two days and an offer to restore food supply might work well. This would also project the cause of mutiny to be food rather than political issues.

Significantly, the FOCRIN and FOB refused to discuss any political demand, which was a clear indication that they were aware of the indifference of the Indian political leadership.

The stalemate continued along with strong possibilities of violence. To cool things down, the NCSC issued another statement: 'False rumours are being made by the naval authorities to break our organization through some ratings. Do not listen to any propaganda. Mind well that you are under NCSC. Please keep complete calm, peace, and non-violence until further orders.'

Upon their return to the *Talwar* after the failed talks, members of the NCSC briefed the ratings who were so enraged that they started to discuss an armed struggle.

Members of the negotiating committee then met all the members of the NCSC. It was a delicate moment. On one side was the British might with all its resources. But on the plus side, there was their grit, determination and tremendous public support they were getting.

The news of the strike had spread all over India, including to ships sailing on the high seas. They were getting encouraging feedback of support. Even as food and water was running short, the NCSC was banking on the fact that the political leaders would intervene and armed conflict would be avoided.

Writes B.C. Dutt: 'We were not totally helpless. All the ships' guns were ours and by then, we had also received some reassuring news of the reaction of the men in Royal Indian Air Force and the

Ratings on strike in Bombay, who failed to return to their ships and establishments by 3.30 p.m. on Wednesday, 20 February, were rounded up by the military police.

Indian Army… There were rumours that some of the men of RIAF in Bombay had gone on strike. It was quite likely that they would join us if it came to shooting it out.'

Outside the Castle Barracks, the situation was tense when the ratings started to return. There were demonstrations outside the gate demanding the withdrawal of the guards and allowing those ratings inside the barracks to go out and purchase food. The military guards took positions at the entrance and the tension escalated. A British commander came and threatened the ratings that they would start firing if the ratings did not return to the barracks.

The president of the NCSC, M.S. Khan, hearing of the tension, arrived at the gate and addressed the agitating ratings. There was a massive surge towards the entrance. In the melee, Khan who had not eaten for forty-eight hours, fainted. He had to be given first aid to be revived.

The NCSC decided to send urgent signals to all the ships and establishments regarding the plan of action for the next day, 21

February. The signal said:

1. Wait for information from *Talwar* if the military guards were withdrawn.
2. If you do not get desired news, go out on a lying down hunger strike from 7.30 in the morning.
3. No violence in words or deeds to be committed.
4. The hunger strike will go on until the military is withdrawn.
5. No rumours to be believed until confirmed by NCSC.

After a prolonged discussion, the meeting of the NCSC ended at 10 p.m.

At the *Talwar*, the ratings moved in and out as they willed. The Mahratta guards, who were brought in on false pretexts, had become reluctant to carry on their duty. Their sympathies clearly lay with their fellow Indians and comrades-in-arms.

Says B.C. Dutt, 'As soon as the guards appeared at the gates of *Talwar*, ladders were placed against the back wall and it was renamed with the legendary name "Azad Hind Gate", which was painted flamboyantly on it. The guards at the main gate knew of it. But they did not object.'

Soon, doubting their integrity, the authorities replaced the Mahrattas with British military guards. Everyone felt Thursday, 21 February, was going to be decisive, one way or another. Night fell on the 20th but no one slept. Indeed, the tension exploded the next day.

REFERENCES

B.C. Dutt, *Mutiny of the Innocents*. Bombay: Sindhu Publications, 1971.

General RMM Lockhart report on Indian Navy Mutiny, National Army Museum London, accession number 8310-154.

Subrata Banerjee, *The RIN Strike*. Bombay: People's Publishing House, 1981.

Talwar Commission of Enquiry report, NAI.

EARLY MORNING EDITION

NATIONAL HERALD

VOL. X NO. 51   REG. NO. X 327   LUCKNOW, FRIDAY, FEBRUARY 22, 1946   PRICE TWO ANNAS

R. I. N. RATINGS MUTINY

REGULAR WARFARE IN BOMBAY

STRIKERS CAPTURE ARMOURY AND HOLD TWENTY SHIPS

ONE KILLED AND NINE INJURED AT KARACHI

THE STRIKE OF INDIAN RATINGS OF THE ROYAL INDIAN NAVY, WHICH BEGAN ON FEBRUARY 18 IN BOMBAY AND THEN SPREAD TO CALCUTTA, KARACHI AND DELHI, TOOK A NEW TURN ON THURSDAY WHEN THE STRIKERS MUTINEED IN BOMBAY AND KARACHI.

A kind of regular warfare was in progress in Bombay from 10 a.m. when Indian ratings took possession of the armoury in the Castle Barracks containing a large quantity of ammunition.

There were repeated exchanges of fire between the mutineers and British troops, who have been considerably reinforced. It is understood that twenty ships in the possession of the ratings have given an ultimatum that unless firing British squads are withdrawn immediately they will open fire.

The situation in Karachi deteriorated when military police opened fire on the strikers of H.M.I.S. Hindustan, who retaliated with naval guns and other weapons at their disposal. Nine persons were injured and one killed. The strikers have given an ultimatum that they will open fire on the military if their demands are not conceded by 6 p.m.

As a precautionary measure a Royal Naval vessel berthed near H.M.I.S. Hindustan has also mounted its guns.

Strong naval, military and air detachments are on their way to Bombay from Fort and Karachi as announced by the General Headquarters.

LATHI CHARGE ON R.I.A.F. MEN

CANTEENS CAPTURED

(Continued on page 8)

INDIA SECRETARY CONFIDENT

Cabinet Mission Is Bound to Succeed

CAVEESHAR TO BE RELEASED

NEW DELHI, Feb. 21.—
Sardar Sardul Singh Caveeshar, who is to be released at Ferozepore.—API

MAULANA AZAD IN DELHI

NEW DELHI, Feb. 21.—
Maulana Azad arrived here this afternoon.—API

BIHAR GOVERNOR LEAVES DELHI

NEW DELHI, Feb. 21.—The
Governor of Bihar left here today.—API

PURPOSE OF THE MISSION

THE ONLY POSSIBLE START

Latest

WAR SECRETARY REFUSES QUESTION ON WAVELL SCANDAL

NEW DELHI, Feb. 21.—

LEAGUE AND COMMUNIST WORKERS RELEASED

NEW DELHI, Feb. 21.—
—API

WARNING TO RATINGS

GOVT. WON'T GIVE IN TO VIOLENCE

STRONG STEPS

R. I. N. STRIKERS' DEMANDS

The central committee of the RIN strikers in Bombay have formulated the following demands which have been forwarded through their flag officer to the flag officer of the Royal Indian Navy Vice-Admiral Godfrey:

First, suspension of INA trials;

Secondly, withdrawal of all production prosecutions against INA men;

Thirdly, withdrawal of Indian troops from Indonesia;

Fourthly, better facilities for Indian establishments of Royal Indian Navy;

Fifthly, dismissal of the officer commanding HMIS Talwar;

Sixthly, release of naval rating B. K. Singh arrested in connection with the first day's demonstrations.

JAIPRAKASH'S CASE STILL UNDER REVIEW

NEW DELHI, Feb. 21.—
During question hour in the Central Assembly today the Home Member informed Mr. Satyanarain Sinha that the case of Mr. Jaiprakash Narayan was still under review. There had been no decision to reinstate him on his Forward Bloc. He had no information about removal of ban on the Congress Socialist Party; their removal was a matter for provincial Governments which imposed them.—API

(See page 3)

ELECTIONS TO DISTRICT BOARDS LIKELY

RIOTS AND CLASHES ALL OVER CAIRO

British Barracks Attacked: Pitched Battle Rages

SOVIET DISCOVERY

DISINTEGRATION OF URANIUM

MOSCOW, Feb. 21.—

TELEGRAPH STRIKE ON MARCH 11

DELHI, Feb. 21.—Mr. P. C.
Chatterjea, general secretary of the All-India Telegraph Union, in a statement says that he has served a notice of strike on the Director-General of Posts and Telegraphs to be launched on or after March 11.—API

PANT TO MEET GOVERNOR TODAY

HURRICANE ELECTION TOUR

28 PUNJAB SEATS GO TO CONGRESS

LAHORE, Feb. 21.—

9

BLOOD AND BETRAYAL

THURSDAY, 21 FEBRUARY

The mutiny was no longer confined to Bombay, nor was it purely a naval affair. The RIN establishments across India were at a standstill. There were widespread public demonstrations of support and violent confrontations in several places such as in Karachi, and also Calcutta, Madras, Delhi, etc.

Elements of the Royal Indian Air Force (RIAF) also went on strike in sympathy. The more defiant members of the army also began to show their sympathies with the strikers. Indian army units consisting of battle-hardened veterans who had fought on behalf of the British in multiple theatres in the Second World War turned out to be unwilling to fire at their *fauji* brothers in the navy.

From the initial flashpoint in Bombay, by now the mutiny spread to involve 78 ships, 20 shore establishments, and 20,000 sailors. It was, in many respects, the tipping point in the long battle for freedom from British rule. Tragically, the heroism and sacrifice the ratings showed would be reduced to a footnote in history.

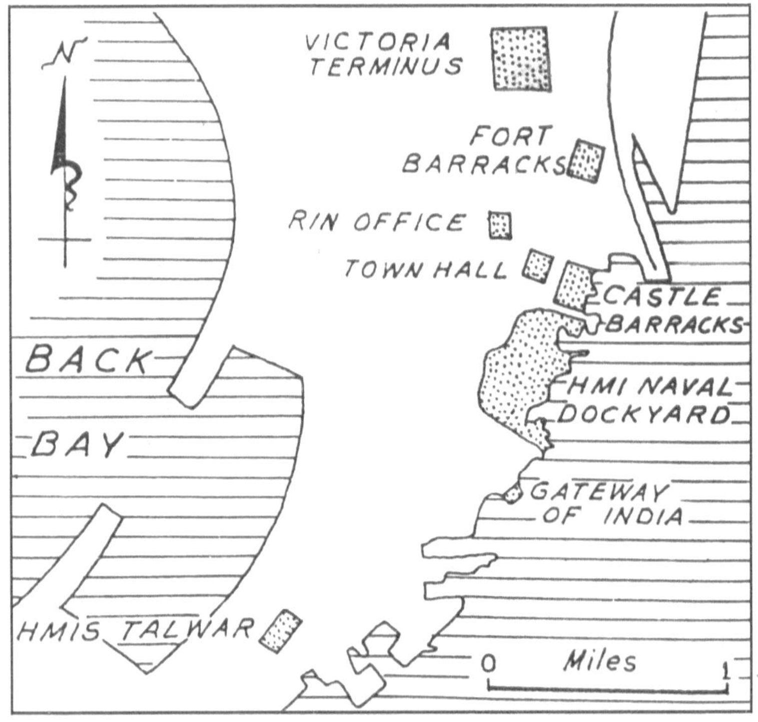

An old line map of Bombay harbour showing storm centres of the mutiny, 1946.

Newspapers in India and all over the world splashed news about these events across their front pages, many carrying multiple stories.

The *Amrita Bazar Patrika* summed up 21 February thus, in its banner headlines and straps: 'Ratings Seize 20 Ships & Armoury—Brisk Exchange of Shots with British Military in Bombay—Air & Naval Reinforcements Being Rushed to Areas of Unrest—British Prime Minister Announced Royal Navy vessels Proceeding to Bombay. Sympathetic Strike by R.I.A.F. Naval Rating Strike Spreads to Delhi—Firing in Karachi—Indian Ratings Retaliate with Naval Guns Situation Tense—Paratroops Stationed All Over Area—Bombay and Karachi Happenings.'

The *Dawn*, then published from Delhi, also devoted its entire front page to the naval strike. Its eight-column headline read:

'R.I.N. REBELS' GUN DUELS WITH TROOPS… Truce at Bombay Follows Admiral's Ultimatum. Karachi Sailors Shell British Soldiers: One Killed… Sympathetic Strike in Calcutta and Delhi.'

Fort Barracks, Bombay
7.30 a.m.

Thursday morning saw the ratings refreshed and rejuvenated. They were up against formidable odds, but their burning desire to give their all for freedom kept their morale high. Revolutionary slogans and patriotic songs had replaced the morning bugle that had governed most of their working lives.

They sat down to breakfast, prepared with the help of sympathetic cooks. After breakfast, the chatter gave way to serious discussions of the plans for the day, ideas to confront the adversary, and suggestions and speeches to motivate fellow ratings. Violence or non-violence, this was a war they intended to win.

8 a.m.

They had barely finished their tea when a rating barged in shouting: 'They are shooting down our brothers at Castle Barracks. We must rush to their help.' It was so sudden that it took a few minutes to absorb the news. Once the enormity sank in, they all felt the time for discussion was over. It was time to act.

Some wanted to rush to Castle Barracks with whatever arms they had collected, while other, more mature heads tried to reason with them. Castle Barracks was some distance away. The issue was, how would they reach there with arms? They had fewer arms and were likely to be shot at by the guards posted outside the *Talwar* gates if they attempted to leave.

After some discussion, a consensus was reached. They would appeal to the common man. The morning newspapers had been full of news about the sympathy strikes by student unions and mill workers and it was logical to reach out to them for help.

Bombay had seen widespread disturbances the previous night.

The *Free Press Journal* described it: 'DISTURBANCE IN THE CITY… Later in the night disturbance took place in the Dhobi Talao and Girgaum areas where three BEST buses were smashed… a tram and post office set on fire in the same area. Some of the airmen of the RIAF in Bombay area went on strike in sympathy with the RIN. Airmen from Andheri joined those in Marine Drive and marched through the streets in peaceful demonstration… it is reported when the police attempted to arrest, they were stoned and forced to withdraw…'

Mill hands, railway workers and other port workers, especially those with allegiance to the Communist party, struck work. They had taken out processions. Banks were attacked, shops looted. Disappointingly, the two main political parties, Congress and Muslim League, had not issued even a word of support.

After receiving news of the assault on Castle Barracks, two of the ratings were sent there to gauge first-hand what was happening. The rest changed into civvies, slipped past friendly sentries, and moved out to meet student leaders and heads of worker unions.

The sound of firing and gunshots in the distance lent urgency. The senior ratings knew that the arms and the numbers on their side were not sufficient to take on the British.

Bombay Dockyard
9 a.m.

Nearby, in the Dockyard, the sound of firing from rifles and machine guns could be heard. Across the water, the ratings could see the Town Hall and the cluster of houses in the background teeming with military activity. They could also see a signaller on the roof of Castle Barracks desperately sending a message. The message said British troops were attacking from all sides, and they were answering bullet for bullet.

The message was relayed to all the ships and shore establishments with the help of the Deck Signal Station (DSS). On every ship and establishment, ratings broke open magazines, collected whatever arms and ammunition they could, and took up action stations. In less than an hour, the ratings were ready for the next phase. Those in vantage positions could see a large force of British troops moving towards Castle Barracks.

Castle Barracks
9 a.m.

Castle Barracks, located in the Fort area opposite the Town Hall and Reserve Bank of India building, was overflowing with people that day. The ratings posted there had been joined by a large number of ratings who had come in from ships and shore establishments and spent the night at the barracks. There were close to 5,000 ratings in the Castle Barracks that morning.

The atmosphere was tense with large numbers of British troops taking positions all around the Castle Barracks. Civilians working in adjacent offices and at the Gun Gate were told to vacate the area, which was placed firmly under the control of British army units.

The British were obviously preparing for a massive offensive as the entire Fort area was flooded with troops. From the roof of the barracks, British soldiers were visible occupying the Town Hall.

The ratings realized they had no time left for discussing tactics or options of violence versus non-violence. The British were set for an armed assault and they had to be braced to give a suitable reply.

Earlier, the ratings had found that the sentries were refusing to let them through the gates to get breakfast and even the morning papers, something the more educated ratings relied on for the news.

Tempers frayed and the situation quickly slid out of control as the younger ratings clashed with the guards. They rushed to the Master-in-Arms office and yelled at the guards in Hindi: 'You are Indians and we are Indians. You must not fight against us. Know that we are not fighting just for ourselves but all of you as well.' Hearing this, the guards were silent until one spoke: 'We must carry out our orders. But rest assured, no harm will come to you from us. We are only carrying blank ammunition.'

The British had converted the Town Hall into a military headquarters. It was akin to a war room. From the roof of the barracks, the ratings could see British soldiers studying charts and maps as they prepared for a full-blown assault. The Indian troops of the Mahratta Brigade were posted a couple of hundred yards from the main gate of Castle Barracks.

Seeing the preparations for an offensive, the ratings rushed to the guardroom and collected arms stored there. Shortly after 9 a.m., Indian troops upon orders from their British officers, opened fire on the ratings. The Mahrattas pretended they were firing live ammo, but they mostly had loaded blanks.

According to Dilip Kumar Das in his book, *Revisiting Talwar*: 'Several ratings rushed towards Mahratta guards—they bared their stomachs and endeavoured to scratch them on the bayonets of the guards crying out "Spill our blood on India and let it fall on Indian soil."'

Around this time the ratings heard few gun shots coming from the side where Mahrattas were stationed. The Mahrattas were seen trying to enter the gate. It was as if a full battle was about to begin.

The ratings got into the battle stations. They next opened the prison cells and let all the prisoners out. The Mahratta guards under the British officers opened fire and the ratings answered bullets with bullets. They broke open another magazine, which contained medium machine guns (MMGs). These were placed in strategic positions, such as the captain's cabin facing the sea and another point near the barrack's infirmary, also facing the sea.

The British were doing much the same things, occupying the high ground and placing machine guns in strategic positions. Sensing the reluctance of the Mahratta soldiers to fire on the ratings, they were withdrawn and replaced with troops of the Leicestershire Regiment.

The British were receiving reports that the ratings were getting out of Castle Barracks over the back wall and one truckload had already left the barracks.

With both sides placing military assets in strategic locations, the battle began in earnest. Writes Subrata Banerjee, 'On the army side too there was a lot of activity... They wanted to attack the Barracks or at least neutralise some of its fire-power. Some of the military were reported concentrating in the area of the Draft Reserve Barracks, where the gun-mountings were. Four ratings were immediately despatched there, armed with rifles with fixed bayonets and a few hand grenades.'

A naval officer climbed to the balcony of the Reserve Bank of India building to act as an observer, directing operations. He was brought down by a single bullet, and so was another British soldier standing on top of the gate. By this time, a large number of British troops had gathered around Castle Barrack to launch attacks from all sides in order to force an entry.

The ratings responded by hurling hand grenades, clearing the area and dislodging soldiers who had climbed trees for a better vantage. The soldiers started to fire from the ramparts and the ratings' response with automatic weapons and hand grenades intensified the battle.

A short lull followed the first engagement, while the British regrouped outside, the ratings discussed logistics and organizational problems inside.

Depleting food and water was a matter of grave concern. The British had earlier offered food but the ratings had refused this. Fortunately, food did not turn out to be much of a problem. People from all over Bombay had gathered around the Gateway with food packets. Men, women and children of all classes and religions crowded the area, making it resemble a fair. Not just food packets, people had come with baskets of fruits, cake, milk, bread, and fresh vegetables. They were determined to aid their heroes and deny the British a chance to starve them.

Motorboats were sent from the ships to collect food. 'As the ratings stepped up on the shore, they were greeted and welcomed by the people with revolutionary slogans,' according to Dr V.M. Bhagwatkar in his dissertation on the RIN mutiny.

Hindus, Muslims, and the Parsi owners of the local Irani cafés, invited the ratings into their establishments and told them to take whatever they wanted. All of Bombay, it seemed, was behind the mutineers. The food was then distributed to various ships by those manning the motorboats. The Mahrattas who were supposed to police the area and prevent ratings from landing onto the shore did not stop people from handing over food packets.

According to B.C. Dutt, 'Restaurant keepers were seen requesting people to carry whatever food they could to the beleaguered ratings. Even a street beggar, it was reported in the press, was seen carrying a tiny food packet for the ratings. The harbour front presented a strange spectacle... The whole area was patrolled by armed Indian soldiers. The British force was kept ready at a distance. Indian soldiers with rifles slung across their backs helped to load the food packets brought by the public, sent on boats to the ships in the harbour. The British officers were helpless spectators...'

He further adds: 'On the *Talwar* itself, in a few minutes, we received so many food parcels sent over the wall that we had enough to eat for a few days. A lot of food reached us through the main gate of the *Talwar*, which was still guarded by Indian soldiers. There were 1,500 ratings in the *Talwar*. Thus the people of Bombay identified themselves with the ratings and not with the national leaders.'

HMIS *Kumaon*, Bombay
10 a.m.

The hostilities had spread by now from Castle Barracks to the ships. Khan had come to the breakwater at 10 a.m. News of his arrival spread and the ratings in their respective ships waited for instructions. Some had not yet heard of the battle of Castle Barracks.

Boarding the *Kumaon,* Khan used a loudhailer to inform them about the battle at the Castle. Addressing the ratings, he spoke in a voice charged with emotion: 'I call upon you to join us in this life and death struggle. It is our common battle against a common enemy. If, however, you are not prepared to cast your lot with us, you too had better follow your white masters and leave your ships.'

Not a single rating left. They listened intently as Khan told them to get ready for battle. 'Gather steam, load guns and be ready for orders to fire. If necessary, we will have to take positions around the whole of Bombay. We will defend our dockyard and our own ships at all cost.'

Khan left by 10.30 a.m. but his words stirred the men into action. Guns were loaded, boilers stoked and the ships hooted in unison, as if in encouragement. The ratings did everything they could to ensure they were battle-ready. Passions were running high as they trained their guns on any British target that might appear on the horizon. The battle on land had already begun. How long would it take for a battle on the sea to erupt?

Tensions mounted on the HMIS *Gondwana* as a Royal Navy ship sped towards them. The ratings got ready and guns were trained on the British ship watching its every move. Would it fire on them? The ship however, changed course and sped away into the distance. It was then that they turned their guns towards the shore and waited for the next move in this violent game of chess.

Enquiring into the causes of the mutiny, the RIN Commission of Enquiry found overwhelmingly that it was the British who had fired the first shots and initiated the violence at Castle Barracks.

'Despite persistent demands by the ratings for British forces to step back, not only did the British not do so but on the FOB' s orders fired the first shot. At 12.00 noon a signal had been sent by the British, warning the ratings at the Castle and those manning the ships on the breakwater that, unless they stood down the British troops would open fire.'

★ ★ ★

Being well-armed and capable of communication meant a lot for the ratings, who were ready to do or die. In an extensive interview to Reeta Sharma of the *Tribune* on 25 February 1999, Madan

Singh who was elected vice president of the NCSC said, 'We took possession of Butcher Island (where the entire ammunition of the Bombay Presidency was stocked) and telephone and wireless equipment, including transmitters at Kirki near Poona.'

In the same interview, Singh further said, 'You see, next to Castle Barracks there was an "iron gate" closer to the Town Hall of Bombay. It was cleverly wired to the system so that in the event of an enemy trying to capture Bombay, a press of the switch would blow up the whole of Greater Bombay.'

The 'enemy' referred to here would probably be Axis forces during the Second World War. But if we take this statement at face value, it indicates that the British were prepared to cause widespread death and destruction of property as a last resort.

The same interview continued, 'Fortunately for us this "iron gate" was heavily manned by Indians who obviously obeyed our command when General R.M.M "Rob" Lockhart, GOC-in-C, Southern Command, attempted to capture it. When he tried to advance towards the gate, NCSC ordered firing which led to many casualties among the British (which they would not admit to)… By the 21st, it (the Mutiny) had become such a big blown affair, where most of the ships and shore establishments had gone on strike that it was difficult to stop.'

The authorities were reworking and upgrading their strategies and action continuously. An order was issued by the C-in-C Gen. Sir Claude Auchinleck that, 'w.e.f. 6 pm on 21 February, Lieutenant-General RMM (Rob) Lockhart GOC-in-Chief Southern Command will take over joint command of all three services in Bombay at 1800 hrs on 21st February.' Godfrey was to report to him.

Writes Rob Lockhart in his special confidential report dated 5 March 1946 on the mutiny: 'During that time Admiral Godfrey accepted the position of serving under me, a soldier and his junior, with very good grace and cooperated most willingly.' As a result, Admiral Godfrey left the Bombay area on 25 February.

Castle Barracks
11 a.m.

The ratings took up defensive positions as British forces prepared to storm their defences. The first attack using the Mahrattas had failed. At exactly 11 a.m., the British launched their second attack and the battle began in right earnest.

The *Bombay Chronicle* reported the scene: 'Outside on the road a large crowd of people waited and watched. A few shots hit two of the buildings situated on the road. The crowd swayed forward as the danger seemed to recede, and rushed back and stampeded as rifle fire increased. Apart from these incidents, nothing could be seen from the wall side, as Castle Barracks was completely shut off from the view by a cluster of intervening buildings. A number of people, however, watched the day's developments from the terraces of the buildings adjoining the Elphinstone Circle.'

The ships then joined the battle. The HMIS *Punjab* was short of ammunition. It raided a Royal Navy ship anchored next to it and carried across all the arms from there. Then *Punjab* opened with the 12-pounder mounted on deck and followed it up with concentrated fire from the Oerlikon anti-aircraft guns targeting British positions around the barracks. Some 120 rounds were fired from the ship.

The other ships also trained their guns on the same area. HMIS *Oudh* also opened up with her 12-pounder. The area was cleared of soldiers although stray sniping and firing continued for a long time. The main offensive was thus countered by a combined action from the ships, and from within the barracks, and this neutralized the enemy. The firing stopped for a while.

The British then launched yet another assault. They first opened fire at the men guarding the gates. The ratings fired back. By midday, more troops swarmed into the area. There were at least seven trucks and armoured cars packed with troops, armed with machine gun, rifles and other weapons held ready.

General Rob Lockhart in his report, submitted post-mutiny, writes that at 12 noon 'It was reported that HMIS *Jumna* had trained guns on Castle Barracks with a view to opening fire as soon as barracks were empty of ratings.' According to him, 'Ratings were reported to be firing at police on Mint Road. Police fire party had to open fire in self-defence.'

Lockhart stated reinforcements consisting of four platoons of 34 Royal Marine Amphibian Regiment, five platoons and one company of 2 Leicesters and one platoon and two company of 13 Mahrattas, were sent to guard the Lion Gate to prevent the exit of RIN ratings. Military guards got in position at Gateway of India, Yacht Club, Flora Fountain area, Shandy Tavern, Town Hall area, Elphinstone Circle, Ballard Pier, and at the junction of Fort Street and Frere Road.

A company each was kept in reserve at the Prince of Wales Museum and at Colaba. The 13 Mahrattas cordoned off Sion and Duncan Causeways, M/T Station Colaba and HMIS *Talwar* to prevent ratings getting out of, or coming into Fort area, from outlying establishments.

Castle Barracks
12 noon
The British simply could not prevail and take this well-fortified position held by determined men. Swarming all around the barracks, the British desperately tried to find any weak spot from where they could force an entry. But the ratings hurled hand grenades and shot at the soldiers, forcing the British to regroup.

Around this time, the ratings called all the cooks together and hurriedly told them their roles. Their jobs were to keep feeding the ratings and to feed those who were fighting first. The rations offered by Godfrey, which had been refused earlier, would now be used to feed them all. This was war and all available resources would be utilized by them.

Battle was now joined again with intense firing from both sides. Though the ratings knew of the superior firepower of the enemy, they were ready to fight to the end 'in the glorious traditions of the Indian Navy' and sacrifice their lives for the freedom of their country. There was no officer, no one to guide them. Their experience during the recently concluded war and the determination to free their motherland from the clutches of the British held the enemy at bay.

According to General Lockhart's report, at 12.55, a conference of the officers led by the area commander was held where he informed those present that Royal Air Force (RAF) Mosquitoes as planned, had arrived and 3 Coast Battery guns were manned at Oyster Rock and Middle Ground, (small islands measuring less than an acre in the harbour), directed on RIN ships.

It was also planned that batteries will be placed in position to round up any stragglers. Platoons of the 34 Royal Marine Amphibian Regiments were to occupy Dockyard, Castle Barracks and the *Talwar*. The Royal Marine Amphibian Regiment placed pickets on the Versova Ferry and on Causeway Marve and Malad.

HMIS *Talwar*
10 a.m.

The situation inside the *Talwar* was also tense but most of the action was happening in and around Castle Barracks. Inigo-Jones left the *Talwar* for Castle Barracks with NCSC President M.S. Khan and two other members of the NCSC to try and bring peace and stop firing between the two sides. Though Inigo-Jones made several trips between the *Talwar* and Castle Barracks, Khan was brought back to the *Talwar* by Inigo-Jones only towards the evening.

The ratings were freely using R/T and W/T equipment to communicate with other ships and establishments. The British authorities were fully aware of this, having intercepted the communications but allowed it to continue without trying to jam the radios, in order to monitor the communications.

HMIS *Narbada*

12 noon

Members of the NCSC were coordinating their resources and making battle plans. At noon, a war council meeting took place on the HMIS *Narbada,* a RIN sloop, which would become a hub of activity.

Narbada was the flagship of FOCRIN Godfrey and it was a major achievement for the ratings to take control, pull down the British ensign and hoist the flags of the Congress, the League and the Communist party.

Narbada served as the ratings' war room. The deliberations centred round the British offensive at Castle Barracks. The logistics of food supply and other preparations to resist an increasingly intense British offensive were discussed.

Even as these discussions were taking place, an urgent signal was received from the *Talwar*. British troops were massed around the Gateway of India. The NCSC guessed a sea-based attack on their ships could be launched shortly.

There was no time to be lost and no time to manoeuvre any new ships into action. The offensive had to be resisted with whatever arms were available and whatever ships were in the vicinity. The NCSC issued precise instructions.

A signal was relayed to the ratings at Castle Barracks not to surrender even if they ran out of ammunition. The ships would come to their aid. The HMIS *Narbada* used her loud hailer to connect publicly to the other ships, 'All guns loaded. Do the same and if any shots were fired from ashore, open fire.'

Every hour, the ships sent messages to Castle Barracks enquiring about the ammunition situation and assuring them of all support. The War Council meeting by the ratings ended at about 12.30 after discussing the logistics of water and food supply, and battle strategies.

Reassured by the messages, the ratings at Castle Barracks resisted every attempt by the British guards to enter the Dockyard and Castle Barracks. Despite the provocation, the ratings had shown great restraint in not using the ships' guns indiscriminately. If they had, they would have killed many British troops for sure. But they also knew shelling would cause widespread damage, and civilian deaths.

The British too seemed to be unsure about how far they could go. Any increase in firepower from their side would mean heavier retaliatory fire from the ratings. It was thus that the battle continued sporadically as each side played a waiting game.

As B.C. Dutt wrote: 'We did not use the ship guns. We could not without killing our own people. In the situation, as it stood then, the use of the ship guns could have meant senseless carnage of the civil population and destruction of private properties. The British too did not make a determined effort to rush the ships and the shore establishments. They seemed to be waiting. Yet unwilling to retreat. The hesitant attitude of the British could be attributed to the fact that they were not yet ready to swing into action. Perhaps they were not sure as to how far we would go. After all, we had all the ship guns at our disposal and any action on their part might precipitate the activation of our gun decks.'

However, the ratings needed to be ready and prepared for any offensive. The NCSC relayed orders. Three ships – *Clive*, *Khyber* and *Lawrence*, moored near the Gateway of India, could resist any offensive from that end, while the *Narbada, Jumna* and *Kumaon*, near the Dockyard, could cover the Ballard Estate area.

A signal was sent to *Jumna* to be relayed to all ships and the DSS. Any hostile movement around these ships should be fired on. The *Narbada* was kept ready to supply extra ammunition, wherever it was needed and also to relay messages between ships by semaphore.

In their excitement and the heat of the moment, the ratings had forgotten to use the communication code they had developed. They sent messages in plain English and these were easily intercepted.

Having intercepted the signals, the FOCRIN's publicity machinery got to work and very soon India's political leaders received news that the 'mutinous' and violent ratings were planning to blow up the iconic sea front of Bombay in order to give a bad name to the British. The truth lay somewhere in-between.

The ratings had indeed trained their guns from the ships towards Gateway of India and Yacht Club mainly to target the British troops being amassed in that area. But this was purely a defensive tactic.

Reacting with anger as they believed the British version of events, national leaders blasted the ratings, not caring that these young men were risking their lives for them and for the country.

Godfrey's threat to destroy RIN
2.30 p.m.

The 'take no prisoners attitude' of the British was exemplified by the FOCRIN Admiral Godfrey's address at 2.30 p.m. over All India Radio where he warned the ratings that they would suffer 'dire consequences' if they did not surrender. For this, the FOCRIN said, he had authorized 'overwhelming force at the disposal of the government' to crush the ratings even if it meant the 'destruction of the Navy'.

Claiming a 'state of open mutiny' prevailed in Bombay with the ratings having 'completely lost leave of their senses,' the FOCRIN tried to convey the message that despite the British investigating 'reasonable complaints' the ratings were continuing to hold them to ransom.

He went on to threaten the ratings with naked force if they did not surrender unconditionally. 'To continue the struggle is the height of folly when you take into account the overwhelming forces at the disposal of the Government and will be used to the utmost even if it means the destruction of the navy of which we have been so proud,' he announced.

This broadcast turned out to be highly controversial. It was an exercise in brinkmanship and since it didn't work, the fallout included Godfrey's premature retirement.

The British understood that the address would have widely

disparate repercussions. The address was drafted by the top defence brass and revised as many as five times.

Instead of being cowed by the threats, the ratings reacted with anger. But the address caused much anxiety to the Indian political leadership. Common citizens also responded with trepidation to the hectoring tone of the address, as the British displayed their arrogance and sense of superiority.

The FOCRIN's speech reflected attitudes at the higher levels of the British military establishment, where the C-in-C of the Indian Army, Sir Claude Auchinleck, and Lt Gen. R.M.M. Lockhart, C-in-C of Southern Command were united in desiring to 'restore order in the RIN' by persuasion, or force. If force was to be used, the justification would be the 'Mutiny' of the ratings.

General Lockhart visited Castle Barracks and the *Talwar* that afternoon and then conferred with Godfrey, indicating various arms of the British establishment were now on the same page on the strategy to deal with the ratings.

By 2 p.m., all naval control of the British counter-measures had ceased, and the army had completely taken over. The *Times of India*, then owned by a British company, front-paged five stories the next day related to the uprising.

The lead story's body-text read: 'Bombay lay under the threat of the guns of its own Royal Indian Navy for the greater part of Thursday when thousands of naval ratings broke into open revolt to take undisputed possession of every shore establishment and ship anchored on the shore.'

'(There were)… four-inch guns trained on the Taj Mahal Hotel, the Yacht Club, and buildings along the shoreline from morning till evening when the mutineers finally hoisted a "cease fire" signal.'

In reference to the movement of naval reinforcements by the British, the story continued: 'A cruise squadron and a destroyer flotilla of the East Indies squadron (of the Royal Navy) have been summoned by radio to aid the authorities in their task of putting down the mutiny… Emissaries under the protection of a large

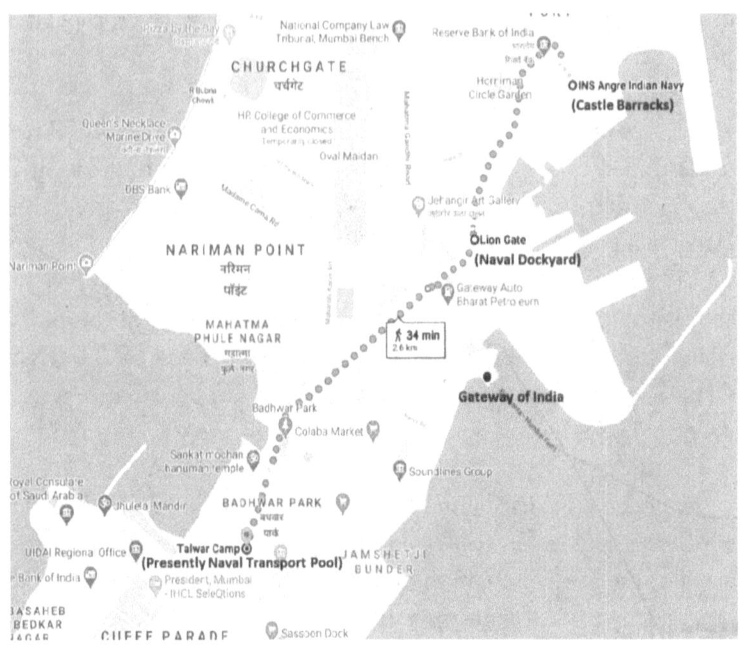

A present-day map of Bombay showing the distance between HMIS Talwar *(presently Naval Transport Pool) and Castle Barracks (INS* Angre*).*

white flag entered the barricaded barracks. The Naval authorities, it is understood, made unconditional surrender a condition of any peace move.'

★ ★ ★

4 p.m.

The historic British expertise in the art of double-dealing, was evidenced in the combination of the threat of using force, followed by an offer of dialogue. M.S. Khan sent a message at 4 p.m:

> To Establishments
> All Ships
> I hope you will be non-violent. I am meeting FOB and

FOCRIN in Castle Barracks. I shall let you know last decision afterwards. Up to that time you should keep complete peace.

Khan's message was reinforced by a British messenger who came to Castle Barracks and announced that the FOCRIN was personally coming and that an agreement would be reached and signed. The ratings were still suspicious and worried that they might be walking into a trap.

Hurried discussions ensued and, finally, the messenger was sent back conveying a pledge from the ratings that three of their representatives would come out of Castle Barracks holding white flags. The FOCRIN should be prepared to do the same. Only then, the message said, could they be assured of his good faith.

5.30 p.m.

At 5.30 p.m., three representatives from the ratings stepped out of Castle Barracks carrying white flags as agreed. The firing had stopped completely but there was no sign of the FOCRIN or any other British official. The ratings waited for 45 minutes after which a British team comprising two Indian officers, Lt Inder Singh and Sub Lt S.S. Chaudhari, and a civilian, Hatim Darbari, came to meet the NCSC team.

The FOCRIN, it seemed, had opted to negotiate. Though there was a complete ceasefire, the ratings had also made it clear that there was no question of surrendering. There were ceasefire flags flying over most ships and establishments. However, the FOCRIN's threat of using 'overwhelming force' had ensured that the ratings were not prepared to surrender their arms.

Three British officers had been detained by the ratings a day earlier. Arguments also flew back and forth over their release. After over an hour, the ratings agreed to release Lt Commander Martin and Lt K.C. Dewan but they decided to hold on to Lt William.

Escorted by one of the NCSC leaders, Lt Inder Singh and Sub Lt Chaudhari were allowed to examine the ammunition room. Despite these measures, the suspicion and mistrust regarding British intentions remained. A Pro Tem (temporary agreement) ceasefire was signed but it was still an uneasy truce.

The British also let the NCSC know that Lt Gen. Lockhart will take over the operations as joint commander of all three services in Bombay, with full authority from the C-in-C to restore order in the RIN. This was a signal that the authorities were prepared to escalate the use of force.

The FOB, Rattray, went on to conduct an inspection of the Deck Signal Station DSS. He was met by the captain of the guards appointed by the ratings and greeted with patriotic slogans. What made it more humiliating for him, was the open defiance.

The FOB and his party were ordered by the captain of the guards to remove their caps, a clear insult. Shepherded by six armed men, Rattray could feel the hatred of the men against the British. 'Inquilab Zindabad', 'Go back FOB,' 'Fulfil our demands' yelled the men, unleashing pent-up sentiments. The reception was too hot to handle. Rattray and his men beat a hasty retreat.

The standoff would continue.

By now, news of armed actions by *Hindustan* and other ships based in Karachi had been received in Bombay and the ratings had also learnt that elements of the RIAF were sympathetic.

They were also aware that 'strong naval and military reinforcements are on their way to Bombay, Karachi and Poona' as announced from Delhi. In London, Attlee said seven naval ships, including HMS *Glasgow*, anchored at Trincomalee, were heading full steam to Bombay.

HMS *Glasgow* was a battle cruiser, fitted with 8 Bofors guns of 40 mm, 16 anti-aircraft guns of various calibres, 6 deck-mounted torpedo tubes and 20 MK Naval guns of various capabilities. It was among the deadliest ships available in the theatre.

After being assigned to the East Indies Fleet, her stint in the

Indian Ocean had been inauspicious. At midnight on 9 December 1941, she accidentally sank a RIN patrol vessel HMIS *Prabhavati*, mistaking it for a surfaced Japanese submarine. There were considerable casualties, including the brother of an RIN rating, who took an active part in the uprising of February 1946.

Hearing about the imminent arrival of reinforcements, the mood at the *Talwar* was grim. How should they respond? The NCSC met to review the situation, discuss future plans, and issue a press statement.

News about the strike by the RIAF and some army units in sympathy, brought some cheer. An API report quoted by B.C. Dutt said, 'An RIAF Squadron, which had been ordered to proceed to Bombay, was grounded at Jodhpur. Every aircraft had mysteriously developed engine trouble…'

The support from common citizens and the news of sympathetic action by other branches of the forces, meant the ratings' morale was high. A statement was issued by the NCSC, addressing political leaders and the public at large. It read as follows:

'News from Talwar.

'Yesterday night Indian military pickets went over to the Castle Barrack Strikers. So this morning about nine, the pickets were made up of British Other Ranks (BORs) and Pathans.

'At nine firing started at Castle Barracks and it was thus isolated from the Dockyards. Approximately ten ratings were killed and fifteen BORs. The firing continued now and again till evening…'

The statement further said: 'In the afternoon, 1200 RIAF men went in a procession in support of the strike… In the Dockyard… there was no firing. The ships are standing ready to act… pending further decisions of the committee and the talks of M.S. Khan, the President, with the FOCRIN… In general, the spirit and determination of the ratings to fight on is high.'

The *Free Press Journal* carried another statement from the ratings, alongside a story headlined 'ADMIRAL THREATENS TO DESTROY THE NAVY'.

This was a direct appeal to the people and political parties: It read 'The NCSC of the strikers in the Indian Navy makes this earnest appeal to the leaders of the political parties and Indian People… we have undergone hardships, low pay, bad food, and most outrageous racial discrimination… The authorities, however, have refused to listen to us.

'Instead, they have called up the military, particularly British troops, since naturally (they) could not trust Indian Army brothers. They opened fire on us in Castle Barracks and forced us to take to arms to defend ourselves… Now, the flag officer is threatening us with total destruction, using the overwhelming armed forces of the empire… We shall not surrender to threats, though we are always prepared to negotiate our demands… But we know FOB will carry out his threat unless you, our brothers, our people and our respected leaders come to our aid.

'You do not want your Indian brothers to be destroyed by British Bullets. You know our demands are just. You must support us… We appeal to you all, particularly to the leaders of the Congress, League and the Communist Parties. Use all your might to prevent a bloodbath in Bombay. Force the naval authorities to stop shooting and… negotiate with us. Rally our people to support us, we appeal to you, our brothers and sisters, to respond. We await your reply.'

Despite this fervent appeal, the Congress and the Muslim League did not offer support. News of parleys between Maulana Azad and the British war secretary were also not encouraging.

When night fell, the main thing lifting the ratings' spirits was that ordinary people had come out in huge numbers to support them, with no thought for their own safety.

It was an uneasy night, with the ratings standing at action stations throughout.

REFERENCES

B.C. Dutt, *Mutiny of the Innocents*. Bombay: Sindhu Publications, 1971.

Biswanath Bose, *RIN Mutiny: 1946*. New Delhi: Northern Book Centre, 1988.

Court Martial of Mutineers at Karachi, NAI.

Dilip Kumar Das, *Revisiting Talwar: A Study in the Royal Indian Navy Uprising of February 1946*. Delhi: Ajanta Publications, 1993.

Dr V.M. Bhagwatkar, *The Role of RIN Mutiny of Feb. 1946, (Royal Indian Navy Uprising), in the Indian Freedom Struggle*, 1989.

HMIS CHAMAK (events & statements), Karachi, NAI.

HMIS TALWAR, NAI.

Kusum Nair, *The Army of Occupation*. Delhi: Padma Publications, 1946.

Legislative Assembly proceedings (Strike at Bombay and Karachi, RIN), NAI.

Lockhart-RIN Mutiny; Hour by hour event description, NAI.

Navy Day Celebration, NAI.

National Archives of India, Karachi Statements (97 pages).

Ratnakar Sadasyula, 'The Forgotten Naval Mutiny of 1946 and India's Independence', 19 February 2016, *Swarajya Magazine*.

Rear Admiral Satyindra Singh AVSM (Retd), *Under Two Ensigns: The Indian Navy 1945–1950*. New Delhi: Oxford and IBH Publishing Co., 1986.

Subrata Banerjee, *The RIN Strike*. Bombay: People's Publishing House, 1981.

The Indian Annual Register (January–June 1946), Vol. 1, pp. 235, 289–98, 301–07.

'The Unsung Heroes of 1946', *Mainstream Weekly*.

The Times  of India

ESTABLISHED 1838

NO. 46. VOL. CVIII. BOMBAY: FRIDAY, FEBRUARY 22, 1946 PRICE TWO ANNAS

R. I. N. MUTINEERS' REPORTED SURRENDER OF ARMS

Vice-Admiral Godfrey's Stern Warning

STRIKERS TRAIN GUNS ON CITY

BOMBAY lay under the threat of the guns of its own Royal Indian Navy for the greater part of Thursday when thousands of naval ratings broke into open revolt to take undisputed possession of every shore establishment and ship anchored in the port.

Indian Naval sloops and minesweepers in the hands of rebellious crews had their four-inch guns and lesser armament trained on the Taj Mahal Hotel, the Yacht Club and buildings along the shore line from morning till evening when the mutineers finally hoisted a "cease fire" signal.

A cruiser squadron and a destroyer flotilla of the East Indies Squadron, it is learnt, has been summoned by radio to the aid of the authorities in their task of putting down the mutiny. These ships are making at full speed for the port.

In a radio warning to the mutineers, Vice-Admiral J. H Godfrey, Flag-Officer Commanding the Royal Indian Navy, warned the men that Government would use the utmost force to suppress the uprising, even if it involved the destruction of the navy of which India has been so proud.

Emissaries under the protection of a large white flag entered the barricaded barracks. The Naval authorities, it is understood, made unconditional surrender a condition of any peace move.

At 1 a.m., it was reported that following talks with the Flag Officer Commanding Bombay, which began at 10.30 p.m., the men in Castle Barracks had decided to call off the "strike" and hand their arms over to the military authorities. Surrender of the weapons is believed to have begun in the early hours of the morning.

GEN. LOCKHART IN CITY

Lt.-General R. M. M. Lockhart, G. O. C-in-Chief, Southern Army, arrived in Bombay by air on Thursday afternoon and after a brief visit to Castle Barracks and some naval establishments spent the evening conferring with His Excellency the Governor and Major-General Beard. He also met and discussed the situation with Vice-Admiral Godfrey and Rear-Admiral Rattray. Gen. Lockhart has been charged with the task of restoring order in the R.I.N. as rapidly as possible by Sir Claude Auchinleck who is Commander-in-Chief of the Army, Navy and the Air Forces.

Mr. Vallabhbhai Patel, it is understood, has been approached by a number of people to intervene in the dispute and bring about a peaceful settlement. He is in touch with the Governor of Bombay and the Commander-in-Chief through Mr. Asaf Ali.

Three British troops and five Indian naval ratings were wounded in the "battle of Castle Barracks", which raged throughout the day. The crackle of rifle fire and the dull roar of hand grenades echoed through the Fort area from 10 a.m. to 4.30 p.m. when 700 mutinous ratings, who had sheltered in the walls of the establishment on what was the ancient Bombay Castle repeatedly fired short sharp bursts as a warning to British and Indian troops outside, crouched ready to attack.

The demonstrating naval men had been driven into the barracks at bayonet point by military pickets, who had guarded the buildings overnight and whose presence they deeply resented. The ratings retreated to complete possession of the centre. They tore down the doors of the two armouries to equip themselves with service rifles, light machine-guns, revolvers, grenades and ammunition.

Laden with the weapons, the men posted themselves behind the battlements along the walls and in a high watch tower on the eastern extremity of the barracks close behind the Town Hall. Others took up strategic positions on points overlooking the sea and the entrances.

From these positions, the mutineers fired occasional salvoes creating widespread panic and chaos over the whole area from Ballard Pier to the Museum on one side and Crawford Market on the other. Lorry-loads of troops belonging to the Leicester shires and to Maratha Regiments of the Bombay Garrison were rushed to

(Continued on Page 5.)

NO "HARTAL" IN CITY TODAY

Mr. V. Patel's Appeal

PANIC CAUSED BY FORT CLASH

An appeal to the Royal Indian Naval ratings to be patient and peaceful and to the people to maintain strict discipline and to do nothing to disturb the peace in the city in the present state of high tension, is made by Mr. Vallabhbhai Patel in a statement on Thursday night.

Mr. Patel says: "The unfortunate clash between the naval ratings and the military and military police has resulted in creating an atmosphere of tension in the city. The tension has been further accentuated by reports of the pitched battle between the naval ratings and the British naval and military police which were spread throughout the city. The immediate cause of the firing is not known; nor is it possible to ascertain the actual loss of life which it is feared may be very large. Without knowing all the facts it is not possible to say whether all this regrettable loss could not have been avoided.

"The Congress was making all possible efforts to bring about a peaceful settlement of the long-standing legitimate grievances of the naval ratings. Until Wednesday there was good hope for restoring harmony and goodwill between them. Who was responsible for the unfortunate turn of events which led to these disastrous consequences and what was the actual provocation which led to them is not known, but this is not a proper moment to apportion the relative responsibilities or to apportion blame between the parties concerned.

PREVENTING PANIC

"The primary and immediate duty of every responsible man is to see that peace is restored between the parties so also to see that the city is not plunged into trouble and the resultant atmosphere not disturbed. Every effort should be made to prevent panic and to control the unruly elements which always are on the look-out to take advantage of such a situation. The best thing for the people to do is to go about their normal business as usual.

"There should be no attempt to call for a 'hartal' or stoppage or rattle or closing of schools and colleges.

"Such a thing is not likely to help the unfortunate naval ratings in their efforts to get redress of their legitimate grievances or in the great difficulty in which they find themselves. All possible efforts are being made by the Congress to help them out of their difficulty and to see that their genuine grievances are immediately redressed. The Congress has a big party in the Central Assembly and is doing its best to help them. I would, therefore, earnestly appeal to them to be patient and peaceful and allow the people to maintain strict discipline and to do nothing in disturbance of the public order in the present state of high tension."

(Mr. S. K. Patil's appeal on page 5.)

The Bombay Municipal Corporation adjourned without transacting any business on Thursday as an expression of its sympathy with the R.I.N. ratings. Mr. Baloobhoy A. Medar moved an adjournment motion which was seconded by Mr. Minoo Putekhan. A. D'Souza, the Mayor, presided.

REINFORCEMENTS TO CURE MUTINY

Royal Navy Units For Bombay

NEW DELHI, February 21. Strong naval, military and air reinforcements are on their way to Bombay, Poona and Karachi, it is announced by the General Headquarters.—A.P.I.

Premier's Statement

LONDON, February 21. Certain vessels of the Royal Navy are proceeding towards Bombay, said the Prime Minister, Mr. Clement Attlee, in the House of Commons today after the Liberal National Secretary, Mr. Henderson Stewart, had moved an adjournment of the House on a matter of urgent public importance namely, the grave extension of mutiny among a section of the Royal Indian Navy.

Mr. Attlee said he had no more information but had telegraphed urgently to India and hoped to make as full a statement as possible on Friday.—Reuter.

reinforce the small military guards of Indian troops at the barracks when the ratings first rebelled.

Between 500 and 600 troops were drawn up in battle order and in battle array round the establishment within an hour. Many wore steel helmets and crouched with bayonets fixed and Bren and tommy-guns at the ready at every exit from the barracks. Stretcher-bearers lay amidst the ranks, and the Red Cross Headquarters were emptied to be prepared as a casualty clearing station.

There was a grim realistic feeling of battle over the scene. Despatch-riders poured in and out of the Town Hall compound. Boxes of ammunition were brought and dumped alongside the troops. Machine-gun posts were established and logs and boulders moved up as protective screens.

As Major-General E. C. Beard, Area Commander, Brigadier C. Southgate, Sub-Area Commander, Company Commanders and Naval Officers were closeted in conference appraising the situation, there was a sharp exchange of shots between the troops and the ratings. Casualties were sustained on either side.

The barracks lay under siege throughout the day and night and military vigilance was not lessened even when peace talks were initiated and continued.

While action was being taken to confine mutinous men to Castle Barracks, a signal was intercepted by our historic investigation of the nation's prosperity and independence.—Reuter.

(Continued on Page 5.)

WIDESPREAD HOOLIGANISM IN BOMBAY

Demonstration To Sympathise With R. I. N. Mutineers

MOB rule held sway over large sections of Bombay late on Thursday evening when demonstrations in sympathy and support of the Royal Indian Naval mutineers were staged.

The demonstrations stemmed from a procession which began at the Museum and circulated through the Fort area shouting Congress slogans. The procession broke up, after stoning and breaking the plate-glass windows of the Metro Cinema at Dhobi Talao, into a series of disorderly groups. These drifted along Girgaum, Kalbadevi, Bhuleshwar and Mohomedanali Roads and buses were attacked and burnt, a post office at Bazaargate Street was looted and tyres punctured and laid across the road and set on fire. Several lavatory sheds in several bazaars and a powerhouse near Charni were ransacked and business establishments at the time of going to press

POLICE OPEN FIRE TWICE

The police fired twice before midnight first near the Metro Cinema and later at Kamwadi. On both occasions police parties were summoned to prevent looting. One man was killed and seven were wounded.

Two British soldiers were singled out for attack at Bori Mode Street. They were beaten and rushed to hospital. Lights along Girgaum and Kalbadevi Roads were smashed plunging entire localities into darkness. In the early hours the localities near Charni Road were free from blazing trams and buses and the dying flames showed the havoc.

(Serially on page 5)

The Port Technical Committee of the Government of India at its meeting met at New Delhi last week has before it a number of important questions bearing on working, housing, etc., of labour in major ports—Bombay, Calcutta, Madras, Mysore and Rajkisnes.

ABOUT 1,600 MEN of the R.I.A.F. camped at Marine Drive, Bombay, and Andheri, struck work on Thursday in sympathy with the mutineers of the R.I.N. The picture shows R.I.A.F. units marching in procession through the streets of Bombay on Thursday afternoon.

R.I.A.F. Men's Sympathy With Mutineers

Raising Of Railway Fares & Rates

DEBATE IN UPPER HOUSE

From Our Special Representative

NEW DELHI, February 21.

An indication that Congress representatives are likely to join the defence Consultative Committee was given by Mr. Asaf Ali speaking on a motion moved by the War Secretary, Mr. Philip Mason, in the Assembly today.

The motion recommended the addition of six non-official members to the committee. Welcoming the motion, Mr. Asaf Ali suggested that it would be useful for non-official members of the House to co-operate in this matter, particularly in view of the impending constitutional changes. The Congress Deputy Leader, was of known to have had more than one interview with the Commander-in-Chief on the post-war days and though the function of the committee would be mainly consultative, it after all scope for useful information on a wide variety of strategic subjects. Such an association, he felt, would not be without utility in the near future.

An amendment moved by Mr. B. Sinha to increase the number of non-official members from six to ten was accepted.

Bombay representatives figured prominently in the general debate on the railway budget in the Council of State. The speakers, including Mr. Shantidas Askuran, deploring the likelihood of an increase in rates and fares, observed that it would be unwise and shortsighted policy for the railways to increase imposts without regard to their effect on the agricultural and industrial economy of the country. At this juncture, said the Bombay Knight, when the agriculture should be encouraged to increase production, it was regrettable that the railways could not see their way to reduce freights. He commended the examples of the Bombay Government, which was subsidising the transport of dry cattle to the attention of other provincial Governments.

PRIORITY FOR FOODSTUFFS

Mr. Dalal, urged that the utmost priority should be given to the movement of foodstuffs, while Mr. Mathai suggested various improvements in accounting.

Surveying the debate, Mr. Arthur Griffin, the Chief Commissioner of Railways observed that neither he nor the War Transport Member had suggested an increase in rates and fares. All they had done was to point to the stern reality of the budget figures and leave the Honble members to draw their own conclusions. The threatened gap in expenditure and revenue, he said, could be covered only in one of two ways: the railways could decrease their expenditure, but that was not practicable in the present circumstances. Alternatively, they could increase their revenue, but this was only possible by raising the rates and fares. We wish to have systematic planning, declared Sir Arthur Griffin. "We do not want to return to the troubles of the thirties."

In the Assembly the main item in the day's proceedings was a discussion on the Bill amending the Factories Act. Explaining its purpose of these amendments the Labour Member Dr. Ambedkar who made an extremely effective speech, said that Government intended bringing the Factories Act in line with the Washington Convention of 1919. The Bill also provided for a regulated standard of overtime payments and for maximum working hours a day.

After some discussion on the Hindu Mahajan's motion referring the Bill to a select committee which should report by March 1, The Assembly concluded its consideration of the Insurance Amendment Bill with the exception of Clause 28, discussion of this clause was postponed to February 25.

EGYPTIAN MOBS RAID BRITISH BARRACKS

Pandemonium In Cairo

CAIRO, February 21.

PANDEMONIUM was let loose in Cairo this morning with machine guns crackling through the smoke of fired buildings, when Egyptian mobs, rioting in a general strike called by Egyptian and labour union leaders to press the evacuation of British troops from the Nile Valley, surged violently against the biggest British military barracks in the city.

Riots and clashes spread all over the city, and casualties were this afternoon—in the first, semi-official estimate—given as 10 killed and over 50 injured.

Twelfth Egyptian troops with armoured cars had cordoned off all streets leading to the Kasr el Nil (Palace of the Nile) Barracks where an almost pitched battle raged throughout the morning and British soldiers inside the barracks were standing to arms in full battle order with more heavy armoured vehicles drawn up ready for action.

Earlier British troops had opened fire when a huge crowd of demonstrators tried to force their way in. At Lady Tedder raf club, an armoured car urgently summoned reinforcements while 12 airmen fought off rioters who snatched curtains from windows and flung them into the building, attempting to set it on fire. Egyptian troops were sent and they took up positions near-by.

Continued losses Army Hostel was set on fire, and mobs stoned the fire brigade to keep them away. Later, R.A.F. men were attacked at the desert purchasing organisation opposite Shepheards Hotel.

"Reuter" correspondent who was an eye-witness of the clash at Kasr el Nil Barracks, where several thousand demonstrators formed Midan Ismalia Square outside the barracks into a smoke-filled battleground and set fire to British ammunition lorries.

"The trouble began when three three-ton lorries came over a bridge on their way to the barracks. A crowd tried to stop them. The first driver reversed his vehicle and got away, but the second lorry was stopped by a crowd by men using sticks, many of them six feet in length with which they tried to break the windscreen.

"The crowd dragged out the driver. I do not know if he is dead or not, but I can see him lying in front of the barracks.

TROOPS OPEN FIRE

"It was immediately after this that British troops in the barracks opened fire as the crowds by then were throwing every kind of missile at the barracks.

"Two of the lorries are now on fire. I cannot see what has happened to the driver of one of them. Every car that passes through Midan Ismalia Square is being attacked. The Midan is one mass of swaying bodies.

"Now the crowd is trying to break into the barracks gates. They have forced the gates, but British troops managed to close them.

"The whole Midan is filled with smoke from one of the burning lorries. One of them contains rifle ammunition, which explodes and drives back the crowds from the gates.

"The Egyptian ambulance drives at full speed, but it is not allowed by the mob to stop to pick up any casualties. Stones and anything that hand can be laid upon continue to be thrown at the barracks.

"Just before the attempt to fire the barracks police reinforcements had arrived, but the crowd waving huge sticks show no sign that they will disperse. They have been seen at military mien in the square.

PROTECTIVE SCREEN

British troops have again opened fire, machine-guns are rattling. Egyptian troops are now arriving to form an arc and are being deployed as a protective screen covering the barracks.

The crowd has got hold of an Armenian staff car and is smashing it with sticks and big branches of trees. Some demonstrators are carrying every heavy gun apparently that is how. More persons are being set on fire.

"The situation at Kasr el Nil barracks did not improve until 2 p.m. Extra time when the crowds began to melt away obeying Egyptian troops who had by then arrived in the strength of a whole battalion.

A number of police were also barred off the road leading to the British Embassy, where huge crowds

had demonstrated earlier in the morning.

British armoured cars were patrolling the Midan.

Other clashes in the city occurred when a mob looted the Bishop's house and set fire to the Anglican Cathedral hall smashing the windows of the Cathedral.

In Alexandria, where the strike appears to be complete, students and workers marched through the streets shouting anti-British slogans following up the mutiny in India. The city is out of bounds for Allied troops. Crowds beat up Europeans in streets wounding some. Others surrounded a British military post and asked the soldiers to leave their quarters. Two Union Jacks were torn down.—Reuter

---

Indian Troops In Iraq

LONDON, February 21. Withdrawal of Indian battalions from the Persia and Iraq force is being actively discussed between the Indian and Middle East commands, said Mr. Arthur Henderson, Under-Secretary for India, in reply to a question in the House of Commons today. He added that their behaviour had been exemplary.

Reforming Viceroy's Council

BILL IN LORDS

LONDON, February 21. The House of Lords today passed through the committee stage the India (Central Government and Legislature) Bill which removes the limitations on the membership of the Viceroy's Executive Council which might be an obstacle to the Viceroy in reforming that Council in accordance with Indian opinion. It also gives the Legislature temporary powers to make laws, continuing the legislation which would lapse when the emergency was declared over including that enabling food distribution to be made on an all-India basis.

Lord Pethick-Lawrence, Secretary of State for India, moved an amendment which was accepted dealing with the clause on requisitioned land. As provided in the Bill, it covered only land and buildings requisitioned by the Government of India and still held by the Government of India on the expiry of the Defence of India Act 1939.

Lord Pethick-Lawrence said it was desirable that the clause should also cover land and buildings requisitioned by the provincial Governments and held by the provincial Government or held on behalf of the Government of India by other authorities.

The Bill has two further stages to go in the Lords (the report stage and the third reading) before being passed to the Commons.—Reuter.

PERSIAN MAJLIS UPROAR

Members Call Each Other "Thieves"

TEHERAN, February 21. The Persian Majlis (Parliament) broke up in disorder today, with Right and Left wing deputies calling each other "Thieves."

Persian newspapers joined the quarrel.

The cause of the uproar was deputy Yamin Isfandiary who referred to tables received recently from the north Persian Mazanderan province and said "People rolling themselves from among the leftwing factory owners and car owners in pay the mutiny in india. He they it any. More persons are being set

Newspaper reports said that 16 democrats were killed in a clash between democrats and patriots in Banjan, in north Persia. The number of patriot casualties was not mentioned.—Reuter.

On Other Pages

Principal Place In London Press

LONDON, February 21. The Indian Navy strikes take the premier place in London evening newspapers today and the Evening Standard editorially states: "There stands revealed the depth and turbulence of the waters upon which the special corps of Cabinet Ministers is now preparing to embark."

With the pot so nearly boiling it is natural for Government to resort to extraordinary measures. The new move will in effect constitute transference of power of the Cabinet to Indian control.

It concludes: "It is to be hoped that Indian parties will for their part display the high qualities of statesmanship which the occasion demands and which the empty politics of eloquence and this wasting opportunity for the historic foundation of their nation's prosperity and independence."—Reuter.

10

ROYAL INDIAN AIRFORCE AND ARMY JOINS THE NAVAL MUTINY

The discontent with poor food, racist officers, bad terms of service, etc., were not confined to the navy. Discontent in the army and the air force was equally pervasive. Post Second World War, there had been a series of mutinies in different cities such as Bangalore, Cawnpore (Kanpur), Lahore, Karachi and Delhi by these two arms of the armed forces. Radical soldiers and airmen willingly backed the demands and were keen to support the RIN ratings.

It is not widely known but there had been a strike in the RIAF immediately preceding the RIN strike. Six hundred airmen struck work on 7 February 1946 against racial discrimination and demanded the same treatment as the Royal Air Force. Additionally, 400 airmen had also struck in Andheri Airbase, demanding better facilities and pay. This had not, however, attracted much attention because it had been tactfully handled before it spread.

The RIN strike captured the headlines. The first indications that it would resonate with Indians in the other defence services came from the reluctant responses of Indian soldiers ordered to guard the *Talwar*, and then to fire on the Castle Barracks. Even in Karachi and elsewhere, Indian troops – Mahrattas, Garhwalis, Gurkhas, Punjabis, Baluchis – refused to fire on their fellow Indians.

The brave actions of the ratings also triggered sympathy strikes in other arms. Many stories of actions by Indian soldiers and airmen in support of the RIN strike lie hidden in the information circulars at GHQ marked 'Top Secret'.

One of the earliest units to come out in support of their naval brethren in Bombay consisted of airmen from the RIAF camps at Marine Drive and Andheri. On 21 February, while fierce fighting raged in Bombay Harbour and Castle Barracks, the airmen came out on strike to express sympathy and solidarity. Waving a bloodstained white flag, they marched through the streets of Bombay, shouting nationalistic slogans and support for the RIN strike. This spontaneous demonstration received enthusiastic support from civilians.

On the same day, at Kurla, an RIASC unit struck work and marched to the nearest naval barracks at HMIS A*kbar* in solidarity. That night 200 airmen protested against the firing at their sea brethren at Castle Barracks. Demonstrating their sympathies, they went on a hunger strike the next day. Around 1,500 RIAF men continued their strike in Andheri, Marine Drive and Sewri for the next two days. The *Free Press Journal* carried their appeal: 'As a mark of solidarity with our brave and patriotic RIN ratings, we, the RIAF airmen of Andheri, Marine Drive Camps and other units in Bombay have gone on a sympathetic strike since 21st... We congratulate the RIN ratings, students and citizens of Bombay for their united support... facing British bullets in the fight for national self-respect and freedom.'

The authorities clamped down on them, armed guards were posted to keep them in their stations, communication stopped and newspapers were not allowed to be brought in.

In Calcutta, an army unit, the 1386 Indian Pioneer Company struck work shortly after the RIN ratings had surrendered at Bombay. This company was stationed at Majerhat, near the suburb of Behala. Their living conditions were pathetic. They got rations of rotten wheat and rice full of stones and husk. Their pay was niggardly and they also had to pay levies in the name of 'Company Funds'. The money was to be spent for their own welfare but they never received a paisa.

Discontent had been brewing for some time. Then came the RIN strike. The ratings close to their camp also struck work. This was followed by the men of the 1519 Pioneer Company. Most of them were boys from lower-middle-class families. Their lives had always been a struggle and they were not afraid of fighting.

On 24 February, the company fell in for the morning parade. Then the usual daily routine would start. That afternoon was different. As soon as the CO came on parade, the men declared: 'We refuse to carry on this parade until our grievances are redressed. We declare a strike.'

Captain Griffiths, the CO, was astounded. 'This is mutiny, you idiots!' The sepoys responded: 'Mutiny then.' Captain Griffiths tried to pacify them, even threatened them, but it was all in vain. Their patience had worn thin and now, inspired by the naval ratings, they were ready to do or die.

Finally, Captain Griffiths asked, 'Who is your leader? A young man stepped forward. His name was Naik Budhan Sahab and he was one of the best non-commissioned officers in the unit, liked by officers and men. Captain Griffiths hesitated but then issued his orders: 'Return your Files, ammunition and kit to the Quarter Guard.'

'We refuse,' was the spontaneous response from the sepoys. Budhan was standing in front of the CO. A furious Captain Griffiths slapped Budhan across the face. Budhan slapped him back. The white officer was shocked. The incident created a furore in army circles. An Indian daring to hit a white officer!

The Captain promptly ordered Punjabi and Garhwali troops to suppress the strike. They refused to fight against brother Indians… At 1.30 a.m., the area commander arrived at the camp accompanied by tanks, armoured cars and British infantry. Indian sepoys had no option but to surrender. Budhan was court-martialled and sent to jail for life. Budhan's story became folklore and is described in great detail by Subrata Banerjee in his book *The RIN Strike*.

'The RIAF in Bengal were also inspired to action by the RIN strike. As soon as they heard of the RIN strike, they passed a resolution expressing their solidarity with their naval comrades.

'They issued a statement: "The strike of the RIN ratings is a direct result of the foolish actions of the Naval authorities and we are firmly of the opinion that an armed resistance to the ill-treatment meted out to our countrymen by the British forces was absolutely necessary. Accordingly, we express our deepest sympathy towards the RIN ratings and demand an immediate and impartial enquiry. In order to improve our relations with the British troops, we must be given the same rights and privileges and pay. Our problems must be solved through discussions with our elected representatives."'

By evening, however, they heard that British troops were coming to arrest them. They armed themselves, ready to fight. British troops surrounded their camp. The sepoys got ready to respond but the CO of the British troops did not give the order to fire. Instead, a small tank crawled up towards the gate. Havildar Krishnan gave the order to his men: 'Ready!' Immediately, the officer said: 'We do not intend to shoot. Let us come in. We want to speak to you.'

After hurried consultations, seven senior officers were allowed to enter the camp. In the meantime, sounds of firing came from the neighbouring camp. The officers were ordered to point their rifles to the ground when entering the camp. Reluctantly they obeyed the orders of the sepoys. The company commander of the unit asked the sepoys to give the authorities more time to consider their demands. They agreed. They were requested to remain peaceful in the meantime.

For the next two days, nothing happened. The 1,500 men of the unit waited anxiously for something to happen. They did not realize that they were being stalled. On 27 February, news came in that the RIN ratings had surrendered. The CO ordered two platoons to move to Panagarh and the third to Kanchrapara. They were assured that their demands would be considered at their new stations. Thus, they were tricked into dispersing and being isolated from each other.

As soon as they had been dispersed, the leading sepoys were taken to Group Headquarters. Forty-five of them were disarmed and placed under arrest. For 48 days they remained in jail without trial. Finally, on 16 April, they were brought before their CO. A farcical trial followed, where the accused were given varying sentences.

History has largely ignored these incidents, but the bravery shown by the other services in support of their naval colleagues deserves recognition. These incidents influenced the British decision to start pulling out. They recognized they could no longer rely on the same troops who had fought valiantly for them through the Second World War.

REFERENCES

B.C. Dutt, *Mutiny of the Innocents*. Bombay: Sindhu Publications, 1971, pp. 186–193.

Biswanath Bose, *RIN Mutiny: 1946*. New Delhi: Northern Book Centre, 1988, pp. 39, 110, 170, 181, 224.

Dilip Kumar Das, *Revisiting Talwar: A Study in the Royal Indian Navy Uprising of February 1946*. Delhi: Ajanta Publications, 1993, pp. 159–88.

Kusum Nair, *The Army of Occupation*. Delhi: Padma Publications, 1946, pp. 40–48, 49–56.

Legislative Assembly proceedings (Strike at Bombay and Karachi, RIN), NAI.

Lt. Cdr G.D. Sharma, VSM (Retd), *The Untold Story of Naval Mutiny; Last War of Independence*. Delhi: Vij Books, 2015, p. 86.

Subrata Banerjee, *The RIN Strike*. Bombay: People's Publishing House, 1981.

Hindusthan Standard

VOL. IX, NO. 145   CALCUTTA : TUESDAY, FEBRUARY 26, 1946. FALGOON 14, 1352 B. S.   *PRICE TWO ANNAS*

QUIET IN BOMBAY AFTER THREE DAYS OF UNREST

STEEL RING PLACED AROUND THE CITY

BRITISH CRUISER LYING OFF THE HARBOUR

TOMMIES WITH DRAWN BAYONETS PATROLLING AFFECTED AREAS

BOMBAY, FEB. 24.—After three days of rioting, looting, arson and destruction of property leading to repeated shootings by the police and military Bombay had a comparatively quieter day today. Except for three or four minor incidents there were no acts of mass violence.

A virtual steel ring has been placed around Bombay since morning. Large contingents of troops, both British and Indian, have arrived in the city from outside and have taken up positions all over the city.

The six-inch gun cruiser of the Royal Navy 'Glasgow' arrived in Bombay today and is standing off the Bombay Harbour. Other units of the British fleet are expected today.

Two destroyers of the Royal Navy have also arrived in the Bombay Harbour. Heavier units are reported to be near Bombay and will be brought to Bombay, if required.

KARACHI NORMAL

Firing Casualties Mounting

KARACHI, FEB. 24.—The situation is completely normal here today. The military has been withdrawn.

Matunga Rly. Station Destroyed

BOMBAY, FEB. 24.—The Station Master's office, the railway booking office and the public shelter at the Matunga railway station on the B. B. and C. I. railway line have ceased to exist as a result of yesterday's organised attack by infuriated mobs on the railways.

Shooting At Tollygunge

NEHRU LEAVES FOR BOMBAY

ALLAHABAD, FEB. 24.—Pandit Jawaharlal Nehru has left for Bombay from Allahabad.

MAHATMA ON HYPNOTISM OF I.N.A.

NO HARTAL BY STUDENTS

PATEL'S APPEAL

PEOPLE WARNED AGAINST INTERESTED PARTIES

BOMBAY, FEB. 24.—Strong disapproval of any hartal by students tomorrow is expressed by Sardar Vallabhai Patel in an appeal issued tonight.

Gandhiji is crossing an overbridge at Wardha Railway Station to entrain for Poona.

NO FORMATION OF BRITISH TROOPS IN INDIA?

WAR OFFICE DECLINES TO DISCLOSE STRENGTH

50 P.C. OF WAR-TIME FORCES IN MIDDLE EAST

LONDON, FEB. 23.—Both the War Office and the India Office today refused to discuss British and Indian army strengths in the British Empire's storm centres of India, Palestine and Egypt.

However, according to the best information, at least 50 per cent of war-time forces are being maintained in the Middle East area—about six to seven divisions, some Indian.

In India itself it was admitted there are not likely to be any organised formations of British troops. The job of maintaining internal security, therefore, falls on the Indian Army which at the war's end had a strength of 3,000,000 and is now estimated at least half—about fifteen war-time divisions are believed available.

B. A. Railway

NORMAL TRAIN SERVICE RESUMES

No Incidents In Calcutta : Shops Remain Closed

COMPOSITE CABINET IN PUNJAB

Azad To Explore Possibilities

LAHORE, FEB. 24.—That Maulana Azad on his arrival here on Feb. 21 will make the leaders of the various parties and explore the possibilities of forming a composite ministry in Punjab.

HOW TO CANALISE HATRED

ADVICE TO IMPATIENT LOVERS OF COUNTRY

STRESS ON POLICY OF TRUTH AND NON-VIOLENCE

AHMEDABAD, FEB. 23.—"The hypnotism of the I. N. A. has cast its spell upon us. Netaji's name is one to conjure with. His patriotism is second to none. (I use the present tense intentionally.) . . . My praise and admiration can go no further. For I know that his action was doomed to failure," writes Mahatma Gandhi under the caption "How To Canalise Hatred" in today's 'Harijan'.

He says, hatred is in the air and impatient lovers of country will gladly take advantage of it; it they can, through violence to further the cause of independence. "But it is more wrong and unbecoming in a country where fighters for freedom have declared to the world that their policy is truth and non-violence.

POLICE USE TEAR GAS ON WORKERS OF DHAKESWARI MILLS

STRIKE IN NARAINGANJ FACTORY CONTINUES : SEVERAL ARRESTS MADE

NARAINGANJ, FEB. 24.—Tear gas was used by the police at the Dhakeswari Mills No. 2 on workers who are on strike since Feb. 18.

PANTHIC PARTY'S POLICY

Azad-Wavell Meeting

PESHAWAR, FEB. 24.—A Wavell-Azad meeting is scheduled to take place in Delhi on Monday afternoon.

As an 'advice to impatient lovers of country', Mahatma Gandhi stressed that the 'hypnotism of the INA has cast a spell upon us'. Published in Harijan in February 1946, he wrote that 'it is unbecoming in a country where fighters for freedom have declared to the world that their policy is truth and non-violence.'

11

THE POLITICAL DIVIDE

As the Inquiry Commission reported, the FOCRIN offered to talk directly with the NCSC. But before that, the FOCRIN reached out to Sardar Patel to act as an 'intermediary' in bringing about a peaceful settlement.

The *Free Press Journal* reported, 'SARDAR IN COMMUNICATION WITH DELHI… Sardar Vallabhbhai Patel was in consultation with the Governor of Bombay and with Mr Asaf Ali at Delhi and the latter is reported to have had talks with the Commander-in-Chief, who gave the assurance that there would be no victimisation of the personnel involved in the present strike.'

This attempt to use the Sardar as a via media was, in itself, an indication that the British were not acting in good faith. They knew quite well, from IB reports, and the public utterances of political leaders, that all the national leaders, with the exception of Aruna Asaf Ali, were opposed to the strike. Sardar Patel had publicly condemned the ratings' actions as 'acts of goondaism and anarchy'.

Another *FPJ* story read: 'Aruna Offers Services as Peace-Maker'. But she was considered too sympathetic to the ratings' cause and her offer was ignored by both Congress and the British.

The mutiny presented a dilemma for the leaders of the three

main parties. The national sentiment was strongly in favour of the mutineers and they realized it would not benefit them politically to publicly go against the tide. So, at one level, they had to show solidarity in spirit with the movement. But at another level, it did not suit them to support a rebellion when the peaceful transfer of power seemed in their grasp.

The Communists were open and aggressive in their support, inciting students, trade unions and ordinary citizens to revolt and calling on the naval ratings to avoid surrender. On the other hand, the Muslim League focused on its own constituency with statements and appeals directed to Muslims.

Sensing a transfer of power and imminent independence, the Congrees did not want to rock the boat at this crucial juncture. So the Congress leaders were bent on persuading the ratings to remain peaceful and surrender unconditionally, giving them assurances that were well beyond Congress' capability to deliver.

Only one leader displayed the gumption to stand up for what she believed in. That was Aruna Asaf Ali. She was the sole dissenter who refused to join the conspiracy of silence or indulge in condemnation of violence, which was not of the ratings' making.

Aruna, a firebrand socialist member of the Congress, is most famously remembered for her activities during the Quit India movement in 1942. She raised the flag at Gowalia Tank Maidan during the Quit India movement and then went underground, running a clandestine operation that included releasing a periodical magazine and radio broadcast station.

A friend of Jayaprakash Narayan, she was ideologically closer to Nehru than Sardar Patel. For her, the achievement of Independence took precedence over the method. As mentioned earlier, she was a friend and mentor of the Nairs and had been engaged with the ratings and activists from the Ex-Services Association for weeks, if not months, before the mutiny.

She knew exactly when the strike would begin. In fact, it had been announced by the striking ratings that she would address them on 18 February at 4 p.m. at HMIS *Talwar*, the day the strike began. However, for reasons still unknown, she did not show up that day, and her absence left the ratings hugely disappointed.

However, she had taken a stand. On 19 February, she urged the naval strikers not to permit uncoordinated and spontaneous actions to mar the disciplined movement they had crafted.

In a press statement, she said: 'Almost 15,000 naval ratings of the RIN units in Bombay have struck work and refused to eat canteen food since Sunday (17 February) evening. Their demands are essentially legitimate… At last young Indians in the services are no longer prepared to submit sheepishly to the hectoring and swearing of their British rulers. Unity and discipline are first essentials of all collective actions of this nature. They must formulate their demands precisely and conduct their struggle with dignity. Naval ratings must conduct their negotiations through the Central Naval Strike Committee.'

To British authorities, her advice was: 'The Naval authorities should note that at the instance of the representatives of the strikers, I am giving them this advice. I am sure the Congress and the labour and student organizations of Bombay will extend their moral support to their legitimate demands.'

She travelled to Poona on 20 February, and met Gandhi. It was a long meeting that lasted almost two hours. She also sent a telegram to Nehru. It said: 'Naval strike, tense, situation serious, climaxing to close. You alone can control and avoid tragedy. Request your immediate presence in Bombay.'

The telegram angered Sardar Patel, who wrote to Gandhi about it. In his letter, Patel expressed shock that she had persuaded Nehru to come to Bombay to meet the sailors. He wrote: 'She sent a telegram to Jawaharlal and gave out to the Press that under such circumstances, Jawahar was the only leader who could lead them. This she did as she could not find my support. Jawahar wired me asking if his presence was necessary; and in that case, he would come, setting aside all his preoccupations. I advised him not to come. Yet he is reaching here. He has wired back to me telling that he was feeling out of sorts and that he would come. He will come here at 3 p.m. Well! Let him. But the fact that he comes here on account of Aruna's telegram is sorrowful indeed! This was how she is encouraged and if we would not resist their rashness, things will go from bad to worse.'

Nehru had taken the first train to Bombay but he was persuaded by Sardar Patel not to meet the striking ratings. He returned to Allahabad the same night. That was the beginning of the end. From then on, far from receiving any support from the Congress high command, the ratings were under their continuous pressure to surrender.

Moreover, the nation's moral compass, Mahatma Gandhi, was wedded to a non-violent approach to achieving freedom. By sheer coincidence, he had arrived in Bombay, travelling from Wardha by the Calcutta Mail on 18 February.

The *Hindustan Times* carried a front-page report on 19 February, which said: 'Sardar Patel stepped up the ladder, got into the compartment in which Mahatma Gandhi was travelling and received him. A large gathering, which had collected at the level crossing, had to wait for a long time as the train was late by more than three hours... On his way to Birla House, Mahatma Gandhi accompanied by Sardar Patel called on Mr Bhulabhai Desai who is lying ill.'

The *Times of India* edition reported: 'A huge gathering was present in the compound of Rungta House where Mr Gandhi said his prayer. Though Gandhiji may not have been fully apprised of the naval disturbance that day in HMIS *Talwar* he did refer to recent disturbances and violence in Calcutta and Bombay. He asked the people not to "divert from the path of peace. What was the good of throwing stones at the British? They could not move the government by throwing stones. Freedom can only be achieved through truth and non-violence..."'

Gandhi had a packed schedule on 18 and 19 February when he

met several prominent congressmen like B.G. Kher, K.M. Munshi and Lilavati Munshi at Birla House. Sardar Patel was with Gandhi practically the entire time he was in Bombay. The two could not have failed to discuss the disturbances in *Talwar* and Castle Barracks. Gandhi left for Poona on the evening of 19 February without commenting on the naval uprising. But it was evident that he would not deviate from his principled stand on non-violence.

Meanwhile, while the strike was ongoing, the Congress president, Maulana Azad, issued a statement saying: 'India is not in a mood to tolerate any action that may even have the semblance of the suppression of the national spirit in any quarters,' while adding, 'The unexpected RIN strike has led to a sequel which has assumed distressing proportions… I am in contact with the authorities and I am seeking a prompt and practical termination of the strike.'

There were several internal discussions and parleys within the Congress. The mutiny had upset political calculations. Nehru and Patel had been focused on a smooth transfer of power. Freedom, they believed, would not have to be wrested by a bloody confrontation. There was also the apprehension that the mutiny would delay what was being considered inevitable – the peaceful handover of power to Indian leaders.

In his book, *Revisiting Talwar,* Dilip Kumar Das writes: 'The Congress leaders had been in touch with the British authorities in Delhi and Bombay since the beginning of the strike. While they had conveyed their disapproval of the strike, in public their stance till February 21st was neutral, and one of non-intervention. The Governor of Bombay was kept abreast of various steps Congress was taking to neutralise the situation. On the 22nd evening, Patel intervened to induce the ratings to lay down arms on the same terms as demanded by the British authorities.'

The statements of leaders are quite revealing. Most supported what they claimed was a just cause – the treatment meted out to the ratings by their British superiors. However, once the confrontation intensified, political leaders soft-pedalled.

In the early stages of the uprising, Congress had taken a backseat to the Communist Party of India in mutiny-related political gamesmanship. On 19 February, the day after the ratings went on strike, D.S. Vaidya, secretary of the Bombay Committee of the Communist Party of India issued a leaflet which said: 'Yesterday 5,000 men in the Indian Navy went on strike. Among them are Hindus, Muslims, Christians, men from all provinces of our great country, speaking all languages. They all stand united behind their demands. We appeal to the leaders of all political parties in Bombay to support these demands.'

G. Adhikari, who edited the party newspaper, the *People's Age*, issued a call to the citizens of Bombay, students and transport and mill workers on 21 February: 'Every Indian will resent the arrogant "submit or perish" threat given by the FOCRIN... I appeal to all parties and all our people to refuse to allow this brutal suppression... and to observe tomorrow (Friday, 22 February) a complete Hartal in all shops, schools, colleges and mills.'

The next day, he issued another statement: 'British soldiers paraded through the streets in armed cars and shot indiscriminately at crowds when they were thickest... they have thus murdered several innocent workers... the days when Bren guns, tanks and bombers could terrify India are gone forever. If the Imperialists think that they retain their rule by staging a "Jallianwala Week" in our fair cities, they are sadly mistaken. The bloodbaths will enable us to cement our unity and determination to end the regime of terror.'

The *People's Age* declared in an editorial: 'Everybody from Gandhi ji downwards seem to believe that the cabinet ministers are coming to India to achieve a final settlement with the Congress as the basis of "Quit India" and independence. They expect freedom as a gift from the British. That is why they wanted the ratings to desist from the strike and why they did not want the people of Bombay to support the strike by hartal.'

Criticizing the Congress and Sardar Patel, the editorial

continued: 'He (Patel) shed tears over those who died and condemned "hooliganism". But he had, however, no single word to say in condemnation of the British military "hooliganism" who had fired indiscriminately and killed hundreds of innocent lives.'

The editorial was also critical of Gandhi. 'Gandhi ji said that the Hindu Muslim unity achieved in joint violence at the barricades must lead to mutual violence… in saying so he deprecates the glorious Hindu Muslim unity in resisting the police and the military repression… the fact is that Congress leaders are not thinking in terms of joint struggles and not even in terms of struggle.'

On Nehru, he had this to say: 'To say that a slave people shall never take to arms because its guns are not as big as those of the handful of oppressors, would not be a counsel of wisdom but of cowardice.'

S.A. Dange speaking on behalf of the Communist Party of India also appealed to all political parties to join hands to help the ratings as quoted by Dr V.M. Bhagwatkar in his brilliant dissertation.

On 21 February, the Congress issued a series of statements, first by S.K. Patil, general secretary Bombay Province Congress Committee (BPCC), saying that BPCC has been following the situation arising out of tension between Indian ratings and British naval authorities with 'anxious concern and deepest sorrow. Congress feels that the situation has become extremely dangerous and consequences are bound to be much more disastrous and the tension in the Dock area no longer remains confined to that area alone. It is fast spreading far and wide and the city of Bombay has completely gone into its grip.'

He also mentioned that a section of naval ratings had been in touch with the Congress party and 'We have passed a resolution urging naval authorities to redress the just grievances of the naval ratings.' The Congress also felt, he said, that some interested persons and parties, mainly communists, are trying to take advantage and asking mills to close; affiliated student bodies are going around schools and colleges to shut down on 22 February. Some of the commercial associations are also likely to be closed but they are going to shut not because of *hartal* but 'in honour of Kasturba's death anniversary' (Gandhi's wife had died on 22 February 1944).

The BPCC appealed for peace and order and asked the citizens of Bombay to 'go about their normal business and give up the idea of Hartal. We are in complete sympathy with our naval brethren but we will not serve their purpose by adding to the tension.'

That evening, Congress issued another statement, this time by Sardar Patel, which was circulated to the media. Patel had been in consultation with the governor of Bombay, John Colville, and with Asaf Ali in Delhi, who was in close touch with the C-in-C, Sir Auchinleck.

Sardar Patel was now articulating the official Congress position on the naval uprising situation. His statement advised the ratings to be patient and peaceful and urged citizens to maintain strict discipline. He talked about grave tension in the city because of clashes between naval ratings and British Naval and Military police and said that the Congress was making all 'possible efforts to bring about a peaceful settlement of the long-standing legitimate grievances of the ratings.'

On 21 February, Aruna Asaf Ali felt the need to intervene again as the tension escalated. She issued a statement offering her services as a peacemaker. In a special message to the ratings, she said: 'The strike of the Indian naval ratings is now four days old. There has been some firing yesterday although there is no authoritative statement yet.

'Vice Admiral John Henry Godfrey's broadcast seems to threaten further bloodshed lest the behaviour of the ratings be deemed not to provide for further repression. I should like to state emphatically that I am prepared to address the ratings ship by ship and barrack by barrack to ensure that their indiscipline does not give ground for further violence. This should remove any later pleading by the Admiral that force was used as there was a danger to public peace.'

On 22 February, all major newspapers gave prominent coverage to an appeal by the Communist Party as well as the NCSC to carry on the struggle. In response to this, Sardar Patel issued a statement asking naval ratings to lay down their arms and surrender.

Congress President Maulana Azad also pressed the ratings to call off the strike. His statement said: 'The unexpected RIN strike has led to a sequel which has assumed distressing proportion… I am in contact with the authorities and I am seeking a prompt and practical termination of the strike.'

Later, in an interview after the surrender, he admitted that 'It is quite obvious from the facts we have been reported that Indian ratings of the RIN went on strike as the result of what they considered was gratuitous insult to national self-respect.'

Aruna also called a press conference at which she said: 'Only the unconditional withdrawal of military patrols and the immediate lifting of bans on civil liberties fulfil the formality of surrender and bring normal conditions in the city of Bombay.'

She continued with the revelation that 'uniformed men' had approached her on various occasions and sought her advice. She had asked them to maintain solidarity and discipline and form a central committee to direct their actions. She had also directed them to Sardar Patel, the highest Congress functionary in the city.

Referring to the seven-hour battle in Castle Barracks and shooting on the streets of Bombay, she stressed the fact that the military authorities resented the political feelings of the men and in order to curb this tendency they wilfully resorted to wholesale arrests 'thereby rousing up their pent up fury,' adding, 'It was a welcome sign that Indian people had plucked up enough courage to face bullets from machine guns… there was a time when our people shuddered at lathi blows but those days were of the past.'

Later that day the members of the strike committee, led by M.S. Khan, met Sardar Patel who asked them to surrender unconditionally. It was widely believed that the British authorities assured Patel that if he persuaded the ratings to surrender unconditionally, he could ensure the ratings that there would be no victimization.

When Khan asked Sardar Patel to give this in writing, the Sardar lost his temper according to Dilip Kumar Das, who wrote in his book: 'The worthy Sardar flew into a rage and thumping the table said "when you don't trust my words, how can you trust my writing… I assure you on behalf of Congress that not a single one of you will be victimized."'

Finally on 23 February, Khan, president of the NCSC, made the announcement: 'In the present unfortunate circumstances that has developed, the advice of the Congress to the RIN ratings is to lay down arms and go through the formalities of surrender.'

In March 1946, a month after the mutiny ended, Patel wrote an article in the *FPJ* in which he said: 'It was not without the greatest difficulty that I persuaded the Ratings to surrender unconditionally, giving them the assurance that whatever their just cause, would be championed by the Congress.' He seemed worried that the acts of violence which he condemned should not delay the process of granting India's Independence.

★ ★ ★

On its part, the Muslim League's stance was clearly aimed at its own constituency. Nawabzada Liaquat Ali Khan, general secretary of the All-India Muslim League, had held a long discussion with Auchinleck who assured him that there would be no victimization of the men involved.

The Nawabzada asked Muslims to 'follow the advice of Quaid-e-Azam Jinnah and help restore normal conditions.' He went on to state: 'Mr Jinnah in a statement issued from Calcutta has already assured the RIN men that he will do his best to see that their legitimate grievances are redressed… Quaid-e-Azam has made an appeal to the Muslims in particular not to create any trouble and not to play into the hands of those who want to exploit the situation for their own ends.'

Jinnah clearly did not equate the RIN uprising with the

freedom struggle. Ibrahim Chundrigar, president Bombay Provincial Muslim League, termed the episode an 'unfortunate situation'. The *Bombay Chronicle* reported Chundrigar had a meeting with Liaquat Ali Khan after which he assured the ratings that the Muslim League will extend all possible help to get their legitimate grievances resolved.

The Pakistani Rear-Admiral (retd) Mian Zahir Shah, in his book *Bubbles of Water*, relates an interesting anecdote that offers an insight into Jinnah's mindset. 'The mutineers who were in Calcutta located Quaid-e-Azam and expected to get his sympathy and support. One of the Navy persons, PO Yeoman of Signals, Sulaiman, had arranged the meeting by calling on Mr Jinnah at the residence of Mr MAH Isphahani, where the Quaid was staying. Mr Jinnah had met him and given the mutineers a one-hour slot

Naval ratings with Muslim League leader M.A. Jinnah in Calcutta, where they met him for 'sympathy and support'.

for meeting the following morning. He instructed his secretary, Mr KH Khurshid, "Please make sure there are no press photographers." Unlike Congress leaders, Mr Jinnah wanted to keep it out of the papers.

'On 21 February, when the mutiny was in its third day, eight CPOs, POs and ratings, mostly of the communication branch, met with the Quaid-e-Azam. During the meeting – before which the mutineers were made to leave their small arms outside – the Quaid-e-Azam asked them to tell him about their grievances. He had the day's newspapers in front of him, all of which carried headlines on the mutiny.

'They started telling him about their grievances, which mainly concerned welfare matters and discrimination. But after a bit of cross-questioning by the Quaid, they soon ran out of steam. What was more, the Quaid-e-Azam made it clear that he was not in favour of them going on with the mutiny. He said that civil disobedience and political agitation are matters for the politicians, and not for the people in the armed forces, nor for students for that matter.

'With the wind effectively taken out of their sails, the mutineers were now feeling uncomfortable. They asked him, "What shall we do?" The Quaid replied, "Retreat with grace. You have achieved your objective. You have obtained publicity and sympathy." He pointed at the newspapers. "I can assure you that even His Majesty King George the Sixth, is not sleeping in peace these days."

'Soon, his visitors were feeling fidgety and were ready to bolt at the slightest hint being given. But the Quaid looked at his watch and said that they still had a lot of time left… and invited questions to clarify any issue they may have. So they sat and discussed a number of things as he smoked his Craven A cigarette. They talked about the Quaid's political life, the emerging political situation in India, and about Pakistan.

'Towards the end of the discussions, Quaid-e-Azam asked, "By the way, what are you all wearing?" One rating replied, eagerly,

"Uniform, sir." "No," said the Quaid-e-Azam, "This is not uniform. Uniform means *ek jaisa!*" Like one! He pronounced the words *ek jaisa* three times for emphasis, his forefinger raised. He continued, "You call this uniform? Some are wearing *khakis*, some whites; some shorts, some longs; some shoes, some boots. Remember, uniform is a sense of discipline; and without discipline there can be no welfare."'

'The men looked at each other uncomfortably. The Quaid was worse than their CO! Then Quaid-e-Azam added, with a far-away look, "I would want *uniform,* and *discipline,* in the Pakistan Navy."'

★ ★ ★

On 24 February, the day after the surrender, Aruna Asaf Ali again felt the need to clear the air about her involvement and her disagreement with other Congress stalwarts.

She issued a public statement: 'There has been considerable speculation about my part in origin of RIN strike… in the public meetings I was addressing everywhere, particularly in Bombay I noticed members of the forces attending them… on Saturday (16 February) ratings of the RIN apprised me of the tension in the navy and their grievances. On Monday 18 February I was informed that they have struck work.'

According to her, the ratings had asked her for guidance and she found that they had mixed up their political demands with their grievances of food, racial discrimination, etc., and asked them to separate the two.

She added: 'They called upon me to intervene on their behalf and to address a meeting of the ratings. They even wanted me to be their spokesman to Flag Officer Bombay… I also gave an account to Sardar Patel.'

She then said she had given RIN ratings a 'clear cut' plan and asked them to 'maintain complete solidarity'. She added: 'The situation was very grave as the navy held out a threat of bombardment within 12 hours. I was therefore compelled to wire Pandit Nehru to come and save the situation.'

On his part, it was clear that Mahatma Gandhi, would not compromise on non-violence. On 23 February, after getting news of firing by British troops in Bombay and the resultant deaths of hundreds, he issued an appeal to stop the 'thoughtless orgy of violence', adding, 'Let it not be said that India of the Congress spoke to the world of winning Swaraj through non-violent actions and belied her word in action and that too at the critical period of her life.'

His statement added: 'I have followed the events now with painful interest... in as much as a single person is compelled to shout "Jai Hind" or any popular slogan; a nail is driven into the coffin of Swaraj in terms of the millions of India. Destruction of churches and the like is not the way to Swaraj as defined by the Congress. Looting and burning of tramcars, insulting and injuring Europeans is not non-violence of the Congress type, much less mine. Let the known and the unknown leaders of this thoughtless orgy of violence know what they are doing... what I see happening now is not thoughtful. Why should they (naval ratings on strike) continue to serve if service is humiliating for them or India? Action like this I have called non-violent, non-non-cooperation... a combination between Hindus and Muslims and others for the purpose of violent action is unholy and will lead to and probably is a preparation for mutual violence – bad for India and the world.'

Gandhi also said, 'In resorting to mutiny they were badly advised. If it was for grievances, fancied or real, they should have waited for the guidance and intervention of political leaders of their choice. ...if they mutinied for freedom of India they were doubly wrong. They should not do so without a call from the prepared revolutionary. They were thoughtless and ignorant if they believed that by their might they would deliver India from foreign domination.'

It was here that Aruna publicly disagreed with Gandhi. She

said she was unable to understand Gandhiji calling upon the RIN ratings to resign if their condition was humiliating.

'If they did that they will have to give up their only means of livelihood. Moreover they were fighting for principles… it simply does not lie in the mouth of Congressmen who were themselves going to the legislatures to ask the ratings to give up their jobs… Gandhiji further says that the rulers have declared their intention to quit in favour of Indian rule. This statement is not borne out of facts. If the INA, Navy Day, and the present RIN disturbances are a prelude to their quitting, then it is really a grim way of giving up their rule. The way of renunciation is the way of the Sanyasi and not of the Bren gun and the bullet. I do not think therefore that Gandhiji is justified in his belief. The people are no more interested in ethics of violence and non-violence. They just want to resist repression. They are no more cowards… they have adopted a certain amount of recklessness in their resistance. They are dying but do not complain…'

She regretted that Gandhi should have called the combination of Hindus and Muslims for the purpose of violence unholy. She declared that she 'would rather unite the Hindus and the Muslims at the barricade than on the constitutional front. The anti-British front is the only front on which Hindu Muslim unity, if it is to be genuine and lasting and not patched up, can be achieved.'

She also revealed at a press conference on the same day, 24 February, that a radical section opposed to the surrender had approached her after the central committee accepted Sardar Patel's advice to surrender.

'I told them to avoid a split and since the majority had accepted the award to surrender and as Sardar Patel had guaranteed that their demands will be met, they should follow suit.' She also advised them that if the authorities went back on their words, the ratings could go on strike again.

On 26 February, Gandhi issued another long statement from Poona advising that India should bank upon the arrival of the

Cabinet Mission in March. 'Nothing will be lost by waiting… it betrays want of foresight to disbelieve British declaration and precipitate a quarrel… is the official deputation coming to deceive a great Nation? It is neither manly nor womanly to think so.'

The spat between Gandhi and Aruna Asaf Ali was on full public display. He was critical of her statement that people are not interested in the ethics of violence or non-violence. He said, 'People were very much interested in knowing the way which would give freedom to the masses. Aruna and her comrades have to ask themselves whether the non-violent way had or had not raised India from her slumber of ages and created in them a yearning… I congratulate her on her courageous refutation of my statement on the happening in Bombay. Except for the fact that she represents not only herself but also a large number of underground workers, I would not have noticed her refutation, if only because she is a daughter of mine – not less so because not born to me or because she is a rebel… I admired her bravery, her resourcefulness and burning love for the country. But my admiration stopped there, I did not like her being underground… Aruna would rather unite Hindus and Muslims at the barricade than on the constitutional front… even in terms of violence this is a misleading proposition. If the union at the barricade is honest there must be union also at the constitutional front. Fighters do not always live at the barricades. They are too wise to commit suicide. The barricade life has always to be followed by the constitutional. I appeal to Aruna and her friends to make wise use of the power their bravery and sacrifice has given them.'

The political divide over the naval uprising was beneficial to the British, aiding them in their crackdown on the strike and its leaders. Sir Claude Auchinleck issued a statement where he spoke out against politics in the armed force, clearly referring to the Indian naval uprising. 'It matters not what form collective disobedience takes – whether negative – such as refusal to work or refusal to eat – or positive such as demonstrations, mark an act of violence. The milder forms of insubordination are infectious and can easily lead to violence,' he wrote.

On 24 February, M. Asaf Ali met C-in-C Auchinleck and also met War Secretary Philip Mason several times. While these meetings were ostensibly regarding the functions of the Defence Consultative Committee which had been debated earlier in the Central Assembly, the conversation was also to do with the fact that the C-in-C was very keen to have the cooperation of the Congress party. In turn, the Congress, in anticipation of an early assumption of power at the Centre, expressed its willingness to join the committee. The Muslim League, however, showed little interest and only two members were present when the nominations of ten new non-official members were discussed.

Whatever the method and motive of political reaction to the naval strike, in terms of public opinion and sympathy, the Communists scored over the League and Congress. Realizing this, Congress gave a call for a public meeting on Tuesday, 26 February at 6 in the evening on Chowpatty Beach.

Pandit Nehru had cancelled his election tour of Bihar and United Provinces and arrived in Bombay on Monday, 25 February. A huge crowd was waiting for him at Victoria Terminus. Instead, on the advice of Sardar Patel who had sent a special messenger to meet him en route, he alighted at Byculla station. Authoritative accounts of the time say that Patel spoke in strong words to Nehru and advised him against the folly of helping the rioters. Nehru persuaded himself to be converted to Patel's point of view.

According to Kanji Dwarakadass in his book *Ten Years of Freedom:* 'From Byculla he [Nehru] drove straight to Sardar Patel's residence in Marine Drive. Meeting between Sardar and him went on for close to two hours. He was briefed on the tense situation in Bombay by Sardar. Before addressing the public meeting, Pandit Nehru met members of the media. At the press conference, he admitted that there was great sympathy for the Naval ratings in the city but condemned the violence instigated by Communists.

Referring to the exchange of gunfire in Castle Barracks on 21 February, he said a great deal of excitement had been caused by the firing of guns which made people think that a pitched battle was being fought in Bombay Harbour.

'"When there is excitement, it is very easy to put spark to that excitement." When asked, "Should not the city of Bombay observe a *hartal* in response to Royal Indian Navy Ratings appeal?" Nehru flew into a temper. "RIN Central Committee had no business to issue such an appeal. I will not tolerate this kind of thing."'

This was not the only time he lost his composure. He had meetings with several groups of ratings, naval officers, and delegation of politicians.

One such delegation, as mentioned in Admiral Satyendra Singh's book *Under Two Ensigns*, met Pandit Nehru at his sister Krishna Hutheesing's residence at Carmichael Road. The group consisted of Commander S.G. Karmarkar who had taken over as CO of *Talwar*, his businessman friend Venkatrao Ogale, politicians Rao Saheb Patwardhan and his brother Janardan Patwardhan, Appa Pant, and Lt S.N. Kohli (a future chief of naval staff).

Commander Karmarkar described the meeting: 'It was an interesting meeting. Salient features regarding the mutiny were communicated to Mr Nehru. Mr Nehru went off track and started talking about youth, enthusiasm, aspirations, etc. When asked would he support the youth if they went haywire while ruining a very fine, extremely well-regulated service, this upset the old man and he got angry. As a result, the meeting was cut short.'

Narrating the same meeting, S.N. Kohli is quoted as saying: 'After arrival at Mrs Hutheesingh's house, we waited for our turn. When we went in, Panditji said: "What can I do for you?" I was taken aback because I thought he had sent for us… I piped up. "At no point has the Congress given the armed forces clear guidelines or a clear directive how to conduct themselves in the present politically disturbed condition of the country." Panditji went red in the face and retorted, "Thank you for teaching me my job." They had to quickly change the discussion to the origins of the mutiny.

All of India was in anticipation of 26 February when the public meeting at Chowpatty beach in Bombay, presided over by Sardar Patel and held under the auspices of BPCC, was scheduled. Nehru was also to address the meeting.

It was agreed that the subject matter of the public meeting would be 'The tragedy from which the city has just emerged.' Citizens were requested to maintain peace and discipline at the meeting.

Both Sardar Patel and Nehru gave stirring speeches. Presiding over a mammoth rally of over two lakh people, Patel started the proceedings by asking the gathering not to be misled by 'those who attempt to exploit the anti-imperialist feelings and political awakening of the masses and direct them into wrong channels. Such a step will lead to complete anarchy and chaos. After three days of complete anarchy followed by the military shooting of innocent people, it was time for all to do heart searching over the tragic happenings… over 300 people have lost lives and over a 1000 injured… what was all this suffering and of human life for? …I cannot understand why people think of an uprising when the Congress had not given a call for revolt but was engaged in normal peaceful constructive activities… I ask the people of India not to listen to those who calling themselves Congressmen are determined to create anarchy and disorder… if you think the Congress leadership is wrong it is up to you to replace the Congress leadership.'

The Communist Party, Sardar Patel said, was giving the wrong lead to the people and trying to exploit their patriotism. 'It was merely a feeble attempt on their part to revive their rapidly losing influence among the people of India.'

The Sardar also condemned the steps taken by the ratings calling it 'nothing but hooliganism'. He reiterated: 'Ship of freedom was coming close to the shore of India, people should not go out and sink it.' Repeating his assurance that there would be no victimization, he emphasized that, 'Technically such collective action might be described as an offence but there could be no punishment for such offences especially when racial discrimination in regard to status, pay and conditions of living were involved.'

Pandit Nehru was even more forthcoming when he declared at the meeting: 'If politics meant the love of freedom, I am 100 per cent with politics in the army.' In India, he pointed out, there was a conflict between the duty of a man as a soldier and as a citizen. But in such a conflict, he was of the view that 'it would be fit if the duty of fighting for freedom prevailed over the duty of obedience for his superiors. Our armed forces have every right to revolt against the foreign ruler in order to achieve the freedom of our country.'

'Our boys,' said Nehru, 'cannot divorce politics and work as mere mercenary automations of the foreign government. Our army should be fully politically conscious because besides being soldiers they had to be citizens and must know that as citizens of the country they have to discharge certain responsibilities to their people... The conflict that has been going on is to find a way out to serve their country in a fitting manner rather than remain as mere tools of a foreign government to repressing their own countrymen or work as an army of occupation for India. They are lost between their duty to their country and their soldierly discipline.'

Referring to the riots and the killings, he said, 'My heart bled when I read reports of the mounting death toll. I could not resist coming to Bombay. The RIN episode has opened an altogether new chapter in the history of the armed forces... it has been my special conviction that our armed forces should be closely connected with civilian population... So far the armed forces have worked as the army of occupation and have been freely used as instruments of repression by our foreign rulers... The present RIN strike was one of a series of demonstrations of vehement protest against the humiliation and discrimination between the whites and Indians.'

Speaking forcefully, he continued: 'The INA episode, the recent RIAF and RIN strikes have rendered the country a very great service. The gulf that separated the people from the armed forces had once for all been bridged. The "Janata" and the soldier have come together and realized that they both have one common aim – the freeing of their country from foreign yoke.'

He then publicly admitted that Sardar Patel and Maulana Azad had given a guarantee that there would not be any victimization. He said neither the Sardar nor Maulana Azad are now in a position to deliver upon that guarantee in the present state of our slavery.

This was the first admission that Congress was going back on its word barely four days after the ratings had been persuaded by the Sardar to surrender by giving guarantees that he would make sure there would not be any victimization.

Touching on the disturbances in the city, Nehru expressed great resentment about the 'reckless and wanton' firing resulting in the loss of innocent lives. Taking a swipe at the communists, he said: 'Obviously there was tremendous sympathy in the city for the naval ratings… When there is excitement it is very easy to put spark to that excitement. There are all manners of groups who rush in to exploit such a situation to their advantage. Some groups call themselves revolutionary, who cannot function normally in the public, because their revolution is of eighteenth-century variety.'

He also condemned the 'irresponsible way in which the rowdy elements had behaved towards some foreigners and gave vent to their racial discrimination by burning their ties and hats. India has no need for violence in her struggle for freedom: If I am satisfied that violence is needed, I shall be the first to give the call.'

★ ★ ★

There is an interesting extract from a letter that Governor Colville wrote to Viceroy Wavell on 27 February, which reads: 'Since dictating this [letter] have seen S.K. Patil (General Secretary, Bombay Provincial Congress Party) who asked for an interview to convey a message from Vallabhbhai Patel. This was to express a hope that there would be no victimisation following the RIN mutiny, and that leniency would be observed.'

Colville went on to say that Nehru had come to Bombay on the invitation of the more fiery members of Congress, and against the advice of Patel. He had, however, been restrained from inflaming the situation, as on arriving here he had been impressed by the necessity of curbing the wild outburst of violence which had taken place. Now that the city was quiet again, there were many elements anxious to exploit the RIN case and represent the leaders as martyrs.

'Vallabhbhai admitted that indiscipline must be punished, but he hoped not heavily, and hinted that the main punishment should not be immediate discharge. I told Patil that this was not a matter

"The other lesson which is evident is that it is essential that at least one British battalion should be stationed in Bombay.

"Since dictating this Have seen S. K. Patil, who asked for an interview to convey a message from Vallabhbhai Patel. This was to express a hope that there would be no victimisation following the R.I.N. mutiny, and that leniency would be observed. He went on to say that Nehru had come to Bombay on the invitation of the more fiery members of Congress, and against the advice of Vallabhbhai Patel. He had, however, been restrained from inflaming the situation, as on arriving here he had been impressed by the necessity for curbing the wild outburst of violence which had taken place. Now that the city was quiet again, there were many elements who were anxious to exploit the R.I.N. case, and represent the ring-leaders as martyrs. Vallabhbhai admitted that indiscipline must be punished, but he hoped not heavily, and hinted that the main punishment should be immediate discharge. I told Patil that this was not a matter in which I could in any way intervene, as it was entirely for the Commander-in-Chief, and that I could not accept the view that no victimisation meant no punishment for any one. On this he appeared to agree with me, and went on to talk of other things. I pass this on for what it is worth. It is clear to me that local Congress leaders here are distinctly anxious about the position, and are convinced that the Communists are intent on working up a state of chaos. Whatever Congress plans may be for concerted movement later, I believe they do not want trouble just now, and feel that they are in danger of losing grip of their Left Wing."

Governor of Bombay, John Colville's letter to Viceroy Lord Wavell sent on 27 February, had a message of 'request' from Sardar Patel and the Congress, carried by S.K. Patil, regarding victimization of the naval ratings.

in which I could in any way intervene, as it was entirely for the commander in chief to decide, and I could not accept the view that no victimisation meant any punishment for anyone. On this he appeared to agree with me, and went on to talk of other things… It is clear to me that local Congress leaders here are distinctly anxious about the position and are convinced that the communists are intent on working up a state of chaos. Whatever Congress plans may be for the concerted movement later, I believe they do not want trouble just now, and feel that they are in danger of losing grip of their Left Wing.'

The conflict between the naïve patriotism of the young ratings, and the political ambitions of various leaders would cast a lengthening shadow over the naval mutiny. As a result, it would, sadly, be relegated to obscurity once Independence became a reality.

REFERENCES

B.C. Dutt, *Mutiny of the Innocents.* Bombay: Sindhu Publications, 1971; pp. 151–85.

Dilip Kumar Das, *Revisiting Talwar: A Study in the Royal Indian Navy Uprising of February 1946.* Delhi: Ajanta Publications, 1993, pp. 234–370.

Kanji Dwarkadas, *Ten Years of Freedom.* Delhi: Popular Prakashan, 1968.

Kusum Nair, *The Army of Occupation.* Delhi: Padma Publications, 1946.

Lockhart-RIN Mutiny; Hour by hour event description, NAI.

Lt. Cdr. G.D. Sharma, VSM (Retd), *The Untold Story of Naval Mutiny: Last War of Independence.* Delhi: Vij Books, 2015.

Memoranda for Board of Enquiry Commission by Sub. Lieut. M.M. Qasin, RINVR. National Archives of India (NAI).

Mian Zahir Shah, *Bubbles of Water.* Islamabad: PN Book Club, 2001.

Rear Admiral Satyindra Singh AVSM (Retd), *Under Two Ensigns: The Indian Navy 1945–1950.* New Delhi: Oxford and IBH Publishing Co., 1986.

The Indian Annual Register (January–June 1946), Vol. 1, pp. 235, 289–98, 301–07.

The Hindustan Times

LARGEST CIRCULATION IN NORTHERN, NORTH-WESTERN & CENTRAL INDIA

Regd. No. L. 1733

DELHI EDITION

VOL. XXIII. NO. 53 — NEW DELHI: SATURDAY, FEBRUARY 23, 1946. — PRICE 1½ ANNAS

BOMBAY IN REVOLT : CITY A BATTLEFIELD

CONTINUOUS FIRING BY POLICE AND MILITARY

CASUALTIES UNOFFICIALLY LISTED AT 60 KILLED, 600 INJURED

MOBS LOOT BANKS AND POST OFFICES BURN POLICE POSTS

Bombay witnessed for 12 hours on Friday the fiercest mob fury in its history leading to repeated clashes between the police and military armed with rifles, machine-guns and armoured cars on the one side and angry mobs on the other. The police and military resorted to repeated firing at frequent intervals.

All the city's workers were on the streets and the disturbance became more and more widespread as the day wore on till it enveloped the entire city from the Fort to Dadar and Mahim, a distance of 10 miles.

Naval ratings going out in a truck on the first day of their strike.

BOMBAY RATINGS DECIDE ON SURRENDER

STRIKE CALLED OFF ON SARDAR PATEL'S ADVICE

BOMBAY, Feb. 22.—Indian Naval ratings have informed Sardar Patel that they have decided to accept his advice to surrender un-

THE SURRENDER OF 'HINDUSTAN'

6 RATINGS KILLED IN GUN BATTLE WITH TROOPS

ENTIRE SHIP'S COMPANY ARRESTED: ALL QUIET AT KARACHI

IT IS OFFICIALLY ANNOUNCED AT NEW DELHI THAT ALL IS QUIET AT KARACHI. H.M.I.S. 'HINDUSTAN,' WHICH HAS SURRENDERED, HAS BEEN EVACUATED.

H.M.I.S. 'Bahadur,' H.M.I.S. 'Chamak' and H.M.I.S. 'Himalaya' are under military guard which will remain until such time as the authorities are satisfied that they have been brought 100 per cent under control. It is hoped normal routine will start tomorrow.

As a result of the action to bring H.M.I.S. 'Hindustan' under control, R.I.N. casualties number 6 dead and 33 wounded.

Approximately 300 ratings from H.M.I.S. 'Hindustan' are under arrest. Of these approximately 75 are H.M.I.S. 'Hindustan's' own ship's company, the remainder from shore establishments. A number withdrew before the ultimatum expired.

H.M.I.S. 'Tijasar' is quiet.

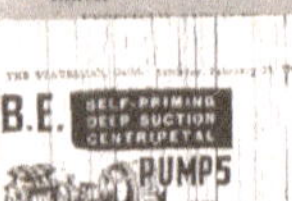

NORTHERN INDIA EDITION

The Statesman.

(THE STATESMAN AND FRIEND OF INDIA & INCORPORATED)

PUBLISHED SIMULTANEOUSLY FROM CALCUTTA AND DELHI

DELHI, SATURDAY, FEBRUARY 23, 1946

TWO ANNAS

VOL. CXII. NO. 25633

RIOTERS MACHINE-GUNNED IN BOMBAY

MOBS ATTACK POLICE AND MILITARY

60 KILLED, 600 WOUNDED IN ALL-DAY FIRING

CURFEW IMPOSED IN

R.I.N. STRIKERS AT BOMBAY TO SURRENDER

R.I.N. MUTINEERS IN BOMBAY

WORLD STATESMEN PLEAD FOR ENDURING PEACE

"NOBODY IS INTRIGUING AGAINST RUSSIA"

MR. WILLIAM HUGHES

STRONG U.N.O & BIG THREE ACCORD ESSENTIAL

LONDON, Feb. 21.—The paramount need for a strong United Nations Organisation and for co-operation between the big three as pillars of enduring peace was stressed today in different parts of the world, by leading statesmen following the British Foreign Secretary, Mr. Ernest Bevin, declaring on the floor of the House yesterday that Britain desired cordial friendship for all time with the Soviet Union.

CITY EDITION

Dawn

Founded by MOHAMMAD ALI JINNAH

Edited by ALTAF HUSAIN

VOL. V NO. 54 — DELHI: SUN. FEB. 24, 1946, 21 RABI-UL-AWWAL, 1365 A.H. — PRICE 1½ ANS.

NIGHTMARE GRIPS BOMBAY

FRESH TROUBLE BREAKS OUT IN MANY PARTS OF THE CITY

Two Trains Set On Fire At Dadar Station

MILL AREA MOST AFFECTED: REPEATED FIRING ON CROWDS

TOTAL CASUALTIES ESTIMATED AT 250 KILLED 1300 INJURED

SATURDAY morning's quiet was short-lived in Bombay. Trouble broke out at different points in a widespread area in the heart of the city. Several cases of stone-throwing and attempt to loot banks and shops and set fire to buildings occurred in a number of localities along Sandhurst Road, Ripon Road, Northbrooke Gardens, Abdur Rehman Street and Kalbadevi Road.

UP TO 10.30 A.M. EVERYTHING WAS QUIET BUT BETWEEN 10.30 AND

Unconditional Surrender of RIN Ratings

IT was officially stated in New Delhi on Saturday that the ratings in Bombay have surrendered unconditionally. The surrender has been accepted.

A signal from the Strike Committee that the ships are ready to surrender was received at Naval Headquarters at Bombay at 6.11 a.m. on Saturday after which the ships surrendered one by one in accordance with the terms laid down by the Flag Officer Commanding the Royal Indian Navy.

The Indian Naval ratings who had barricaded themselves inside Castle Barracks also surrendered simultaneously.

The naval ratings strike has been called off.

Control Measures

Soon after the surrender signal was hoisted by the Royal Indian Navy ships under the control of the strikers, Rear-Admiral Rattray, Flag Officer, Bombay, and Lt. Commander went on board the ships and addressed the ratings.

The flag of Vice-Admiral Godfrey was hoisted on the 'Narbada', the flagship of the Vice-Admiral.

Arrangements were made for the

CENTRAL ASSEMBLY

GOVERNMENT CENSURED ON RIN RISING

RACIAL DISCRIMINATION, THE ROOT CAUSE

By 'Dawn' Gallery Correspondent

THE Central Assembly censured the Government on Friday by 74 votes to 40 for "the grave situation that had arisen as a result of the mishandling of the R.I.N. situation in Bombay."

The Assembly met in a tense atmosphere and in view of the gravity of the occasion, the Deputy Leaders of the League and Congress parties adopted a self-imposed restraint in their utterances.

Prior to the discussion on Mr Asaf Ali's adjournment motion, Mr Mason, the War Secretary announced the policy of the Government about the so-called "mutiny" of the RIN ratings and told the House that the situation in Bombay and Karachi had returned to normal.

Mr Asaf Ali prefaced his speech on the motion by saying that he was capable of subjecting the treasury benches to withering fire but the delicate nature of the subject compelled him to observe restraint. He said that he was proud of Indian army, navy and air force.

Auchinleck's Assurance to Nawabzada

NAWABZADA Liaquat Ali Khan, General Secretary of the All-India Muslim League, who had discussions with the Commander-in-Chief on Saturday in Delhi on the RIN strike, in the course of a statement said that His Excellency has assured him that there would be no victimisation of the men involved in the strike.

12

BLOOD, TEARS AND HEARTBREAK

Bombay woke to what became the bloodiest day of the mutiny. On Friday, even as the political leadership turned their backs on the ratings, ordinary citizens took to the barricades to bravely face tanks and bullets in support of the strikers.

Newspaper reports estimated that several hundred, somewhere between 350 to 700 people were killed and between 1,000 to 1,500 people were injured, some gravely.

This day of martyrdom belonged to the workers and students of Bombay. The civilian death toll was comparable to the massacre at Jallianwala Bagh on Baisakhi Day, 13 April 1919. The difference was, in Bombay, civilians – mill-workers and students – fought pitched battles against British troops and policemen. And, in contrast to Jallianwala Bagh, 22 February 1946 is not commemorated by any memorial or ceremonies, and it has been edited out of the 'approved' history of the Independence Movement.

The British press covered this in detail with their stories reflecting the breadth of opinion in the UK. The *Daily Telegraph* headlined: 'Indian Ratings Defy Order to Surrender, Crowds fight Police.' The *Manchester Guardian* said: 'Mutineers Loot Bombay Shops – Bombay Mobs Out of Hand'.

While the *Lancashire Daily Post*'s front page was alarmist, it had a box highlighting an incongruity. The front page said: 'Wild Bombay Scenes: Mobs Riot, Loot… Troops Rushed to City as Tension Grows.' The box was headlined: 'Cricketers Carry On' with body text: 'In the midst of troubled Bombay there was one haven of peace and quiet – the Cricket Club of India, whose ground is in the Fort area. The play in the Zonal cricket tournament continued uninterrupted.'

The *Citizen*, published from Gloucester, came up with a somewhat balanced editorial, 'The Government have done well to order prompt measures for the suppression of the mutiny in the Indian navy… Reinforcements are converging upon Bombay by land, sea, and air. The mutineers, proclaims Vice Admiral Godfrey, will be dealt with by overwhelming force.'

The *Citizen* added: 'While we commend this… we also deplore the necessity for it. It is tragic that British and Indians, so lately joined against a common foe, should be firing upon one another… The British people will never forget India's mighty contribution to victory or the gallantry of her fighting men. They have the fullest sympathy with India's political aspirations and have pledged themselves to assist her towards self-Government…'

By this time, the ratings had gauged that the national leaders were not on their side. Two major political parties, the Congress and the Muslim League, had been uncaring and unequivocal in their disapproval and were both discouraging the ratings from continuing their protest. Only the Communists had stood solidly behind these brave young men.

The Communist Party's statement read: 'Every Indian will condemn the brutal attempt of the alien government to suppress with blood and iron the attempts of the men of the RIN establishments in Bombay to obtain redress of their just and urgent grievances. Every

Indian will resent the arrogant "Submit or perish" threat given by the FOCRIN to these brave men… On behalf of the Communist Party of India, I (Secretary Bombay Committee Communist Party of India) appeal to all parties to observe tomorrow [Friday, 23] as a complete *hartal* in all shops, schools, colleges, and mills as a mark of their disapproval of government repression and to demand immediate cessation of repression, the opening of negotiation and the satisfaction of the just demand of the strikers.'

The CPI's demand faced opposition from Congress. Fearful that the Communists and ratings were gaining public sympathy, Sardar Patel stated that Congress was fully qualified to resolve their grievances.

Whether by design or accident, Patel undermined the ratings' cause by publicly speaking out against the strike. Congress clearly wanted a negotiated settlement with the British.

One theory is that Congress simply did not want to share the glory of gaining freedom with these young men who had become the new poster boys for the freedom movement. Another possibility was that they wanted the British on their side, even after Independence. Whatever the underlying reasons, Patel undermined the ratings' cause by opposing any strike, knowing full well the effect his words would have.

On the morning of 22 February, the *Free Press Journal* and other newspapers carried a statement by Sardar Patel, 'There should be no attempt to call for a *hartal* or stoppage of mills or closing of schools and colleges. The Congress is a big party in the central assembly and it is doing its best to help them (ratings)… Such a thing is not likely to help the unfortunate naval ratings in their efforts to get redress… All the efforts are being made by the Congress to help them out of their difficulty and to see that their genuine grievances are immediately redressed. I would, therefore, earnestly appeal to them to be patient and peaceful and to the people to maintain strict discipline and do nothing to disturb the peace in the city in the present state of high tension.'

The Sardar was an elder statesman and his words carried a great deal of weight. His statement was a quintessential example of 'neutrality in a conflict'. It did what it was intended to – it left people confused.

But Sardar Patel and the British ignored one crucial factor: the FOCRIN's speech and its impact on public opinion. Carried in full in the morning papers and on All India Radio, this bullying belligerent statement was a harsh reality check for common citizens. The idea that 'overwhelming forces' would do their utmost to crush the ratings and destroy the navy triggered public fury and Patel's advice was ignored.

The FOCRIN, Admiral Godfrey's address was interpreted by civilians and ratings alike as arrogant as well as threatening.

'To start with, every one of you must realize that the government of India has no intention of allowing indiscipline to continue... They will take the most stringent measures to restore discipline using the vast forces at their disposal... As regards the requests made by those of you who waited on the Flag Officer, Bombay, on Tuesday the 19th February, you may be assured that all reasonable complaints or grievances will be fully investigated... The situation in Bombay this morning both afloat and ashore is deplorable. A state of open rioting prevails in which ratings appear to have completely lost control of their senses... in order to ensure that ratings are confined to barracks... it was necessary to place small guards of soldiers on the gates of *Talwar* and Castle Barracks last night... This morning ratings from Castle Barracks burst through the guard which was forced to open fire. This fire was replied to by the ratings inside the barracks... I want again to make it quite plain that the government of India will never give in to violence. To continue the struggle is the height of folly when you take into account the overwhelming forces at the disposal of the government at this time, and which will be used to the uttermost even if it means the destruction of the navy of which we have been so proud.'

His words and the condescension with which they were uttered had the opposite effect from what was intended, even after Sardar Patel's equivocal statements. Let down by the political leaders who claimed to be fighting for Independence and threatened with overwhelming force by the British, the ratings saw their best option as a direct plea to the people.

They issued an appeal to citizens to support them by conducting a sympathy strike. People poured out into the streets in response.

Although people were confused at the contradictory positions taken by two major political parties, their sympathies lay with the ratings. The FOCRIN's statement led to a hardening of attitudes. Many people spontaneously committed to supporting the ratings, and citizens responded with open defiance.

Shouting patriotic slogans and plastering posters urging Indian soldiers in the British Army not to fight their fellow Indians, crowds thronged the Gateway of India. By now, the authorities had replaced Indian troops with British ones, preventing ratings from coming ashore. This created more anger as people made their feelings known to the forces who tried to beat them back.

*Bombay Students'
Union called for
a protest strike on
22 February to
offer support and
solidarity with their
brothers in the RIN.*

The *Bombay Chronicle,* the *Free Press Journal,* and other nationalist papers played up the patriotic feelings by carrying the NCSC's appeal. 'Force the naval authorities to stop their shooting and their threats, and make them negotiate' was the message from the media.

Carried away by the shouts and slogans of the people demonstrating on their behalf, many of the ratings on ships dressed up in civilian clothes took boats to the Gateway of India only to encounter British troops vainly trying to beat back the people.

The troops trained their guns on the ratings, preventing them from landing. The shouting and sloganeering reached fever pitch. The British troops sensed the dangerous mood of the crowd and hesitated to attempt a crackdown which could backfire badly.

While ratings on the ships could not come ashore, those in the barracks had no problems moving around. Dressed in civilian clothes, the ratings at the Fort Barracks moved out into the city early in the morning. Roused by cries from the baying crowd, they came close to attacking patrolling soldiers.

They had endured much injustice and countless insults, and longed to take the British on in no-holds-barred street fights! It was only with great difficulty that they restrained themselves as the negotiations were ongoing, and the cooler heads among them understood that violence would have been used to justify actions against them.

Instead, they met up with fellow ratings from the *Talwar* and walked through the streets to see the impact of the *hartal.* While moving about they could sense the heightened tensions between striking citizens and the police.

While the ratings were scouring the streets of Bombay, M.S. Khan was running from pillar to post. Khan visited the homes of Sardar Patel and Ibrahim Chundrigar of the Muslim League, desperately urging them to intervene and prevent imminent bloodshed. 'Please get the British to act on our demands quickly, or there will be violence,' Khan urged, and he was right. Bombay was a tinderbox. At any moment, it could explode.

Nerves already stretched tight by the situation snapped when the FOCRIN issued another message at 11 a.m. through FOB Rattray. Relayed by loudhailers, the tone was even more aggressive.

Addressing the ratings, it said, 'I told you yesterday that ample forces are available to restore order. The GOC, Southern Command, has been ordered by his Excellency the C-in-C to assume supreme control in Bombay. To show you that ample forces are available, he has ordered a formation of RAF aircraft to fly over the harbour today. These aircraft will not fly over the ships nor take any offensive action, provided no action is taken against them. Should you now have decided in accordance with my warning to surrender unconditionally, you are to hoist a Black Flag, or a Blue Flag and muster all hands on deck on the side facing Bombay city and await further orders.' To reinforce the message, a formation of Royal Air Force Mosquitoes flew over the city and harbour at 2.20 p.m., to put psychological pressure on the ratings.

Even before the speech was broadcast, Godfrey had arrived at the gates of *Talwar* at 10.30 a.m. After some discussion with Inigo-Jones, he announced Inigo-Jones was being replaced with Commander Karmarkar as CO of the *Talwar*. Karmarkar was known for his pro British attitude, and for reporting on the ratings from the balcony of his flat in Riviera. This did not make him very popular and his emergency appointment enraged the ratings even further.

The common people of Bombay were also in no mood for reconciliation. Following a conference between the Chief Presidency Magistrate and police authorities, steel-helmeted British troops with fixed bayonets were placed all over the Fort area. The first shot was fired shortly after 1.30 p.m. near the JJ Hospital junction to disperse a stone-throwing riotous mob.

At around 2.30 p.m., the city exploded and pitched battles began in several locations. Police opened fire multiple times in

British troops getting ready on the streets of Bombay.

several areas, including Kalbadevi, Girgaum, and Bhuleshwar. The angry mob looted almost forty cloth, grain and jewellery shops, especially targeting those that belonged to Britishers and Europeans.

The May & Baker store on Sandhurst Bridge was stoned and totally damaged. Phirozeshah Mehta Road and Hornby Road became war zones. The glass showroom of the Whiteaway Laidlaw Department Store was completely smashed. Wine shops were looted and set on fire. The Mumbadevi Post Office was also set ablaze. Police patrols were heavily stoned.

By 3.30 p.m., the official count was 18 dead and over 250 severely injured, most of these being bullet injuries. 'The three main city hospitals were overwhelmed with a continuous flow of casualties, and doctors and nurses were hardly able to cope. More doctors and nurses were summoned,' records the Annual Register.

Barricades were thrown up in various parts of the city by the

People of Bombay, armed with stones and nothing else, were up against well-armed and well-trained British forces in armoured cars and tanks.

locals, and behind them, the flags of the Congress, Muslim League and the Communist Party fluttered proudly. The people were ready to defend these flags and, by extension, Mother India at any cost.

The police opened fire over twenty times in the Fort area when police lorries were stopped at roadblocks and set on fire. The BEST bus drivers who had joined the protest attacked English and European civilians and soldiers. Those in European attire were marked out, and their ties and hats were snatched. All transport along Hornby Road and adjoining areas was suspended. The offices and shops in Fort area closed, and the Government of Bombay declared a half-day bank-holiday to avoid banks being looted.

The revolutionary zeal of the ratings had infected them and the military might of the British was impotent against the common man. Much blood was spilt in these pitched battles. Bombay witnessed unprecedented mayhem and pandemonium in

Bombay burned for three days, with no end to the mob fury. As per official figures, over 400 were dead and 1,500 injured in Bombay.

confrontations between the public and police. Though the people ignored the potential threat of an aerial attack, their fury was met with rifles, machine guns, and armoured cars.

The battle between the British and common citizens intensified with each passing hour. It spread beyond the Fort area to Dadar, Mahim and beyond. The Muslims in Bhendy Bazaar barricaded Ibrahim Rahimtoola Road that connected Bhendy Bazaar with Pydhonie.

Trains and buses were stoned near the Parel workshop. Many people were injured as a result. A prominent local worker of the Communist Party, Kamal Donne was killed, and Kusum Ranadive was injured when British guards opened firing on Elphinstone Bridge. Curfew was imposed from 9 p.m. to 6 a.m. prohibiting movement.

Starting 22 February, Bombay burnt for three days. There

was no end to the mob fury. Battles between British troops with machine guns and stone-throwing mobs took place all over the city.

Looting, arson, and stone-throwing was especially severe in Sandhurst Road, Ripon Road, Northbrooke Gardens, Abdur Rehman Street, Kalbadevi, as the unrest spread all over the city. The Imperial Bank on Abdur Rehman Street was looted; military lorries were torched at Shivaji Park, and the Kohinoor Mill in the same Dadar area was set on fire. Tram tracks in Crawford Market, Ibrahim Rahimtoola Street, Girgaum, Dhobi Talao, Sankli Street were obstructed by empty drums, stones, and barricades.

Indiscriminate firing in all of Bombay, particularly Fort area to Dadar, led to bodies piling up. But the fights continued as defiant citizens huddled behind barricades and hurled stones. Well-armed and well-trained British forces were unable to control civilians armed with stones. Common citizens, sick of years of brutal suppression, refused to back down.

The casualties incurred during those 72 hours of mob frenzy and military madness have never been precisely counted. The unofficial estimates range anywhere between 250 to 700 and over 1,500 wounded and nobody was spared. One account mentions: 'Of the 31 dead bodies at the morgue, there was a body of a young woman and a boy ten year old.'

It was brave but foolhardy. As thousands of people vented their pent-up wrath, the battered and bruised British administration resorted to deploying armoured cars and tanks in desperation to control unarmed, leaderless mobs. This led to them becoming a laughing stock.

The media descriptions make it amply clear how deeply the city descended into anarchy. The *Bombay Chronicle* of 23 February reported: 'The tension which characterised the water fronts and docks yesterday, had, since this morning passed on to the city… Traffic is completely disorganised, business houses, shops have put down their shutters… The city police armed with lathis and revolvers and the armed police with rifles and British troops patrolled the streets and chased the crowd hither and thither amidst a hail of bullets… Every time a stone came hurling, the police and the military rushed to the spot and opened fire… Trouble started when a European military lorry driver lost his nerves on Phirozshah Road, an excited crowd jeered and rushed at him. In panic he accelerated the vehicle and blindly ran over some persons, who were crossing the road… (three people were killed on the spot). The first shots were fired by the police near the British Library at 10.20 a.m.… Due to burning of vehicles, the Fort area and Ballard Estate areas were enveloped in a thick pall of smoke.… Eleven Lorries including an RAF staff car were seen smouldering in the Fort area alone… In all these areas the people moved around with the tricolour and Muslim League flags. Crowds moved about carrying these flags irrespective of bullets whizzing past…'

Local newspapers reported that of the sixteen cloth mills in the city, only five worked to their full strength on 23 February, while in the other eleven, workers either abstained from coming to work or only did token work. Tempers were at boiling point. Bombay remained on edge, and it seemed only a matter of time before violence would erupt again.

The police were taking no chances, entering middle-class localities and chawls to track down protest leaders. Beatings and mass arrests took place, with even women and children not being spared. The government issued a shoot-on-sight warning against building barricades.

In Girgaum, Lamington Road, and north Bombay, small urchins and boys were intercepting every vehicle. Occupants were allowed to pass if they gave the password 'Jai Hind' and often warned of the dangers ahead.

The *Free Press Journal* also described the grim scenario of those three days 'BRITISH BULLETS CLAIM OVER 100 BOMBAY LIVES. DEMONSTRATORS MACHINE GUNNED… Military vehicles burnt, Post offices reduced to ashes, Bank furniture on fire…'

The *FPJ* reported that: 'KEM Hospital presented a very grim picture with ambulances rushing in at regular intervals and anxious relatives of the injured awaiting their fate… Dr Jivraj Mehta… (said) all the seven operation theatres were working at full swing… 50 people were brought… in a dying condition while a hundred others had sustained serious injuries… At nightfall, fires were smouldering in the centre of roads and numerous traffic blocks had been built… A large number of police chowkies and tram sheds were ablaze.'

The *Bharat Jyoti* reported: 'Concentrated firing… in Mahim Post Office area near the Kohinoor Mills… Looting of grain shops continued unabated… police and military… open fire at several places between Dhobi Talao and Parel… Barricades on the roads… authority to shoot at sight those who attempted to erect barricades… The largest number of casualties today came from the Shivaji Park and Lady Jamshedji Road areas. The Lady Jamshedji Road was filled with rubble, drums and dustbins, wire fencing and heaps of smouldering paper. A grain shop… looted…'

The *Bombay Chronicle* reported in a similar vein. 'The casualties had reached such a peak… the hospitals could not accommodate any more. As for the dead… families stood outside crematoriums waiting to cremate their loved ones.'

Much later, the British admitted how bloody and ruthless the battles had been. A report by the Home Department confirmed over 236 civilians were placed in various morgues. The dead included women, children, students, and workers. In addition, there were nearly 100 casualties among policemen, including officers.

On 26 February, Prime Minister Attlee announced in the House of Commons that 'Damage in Bombay last week included the looting or destruction of 9 banks, 32 government grain and cloth shops, 30 other shops, 10 post offices, 10 police stations, and 1,200 street lamps. The number of vehicles destroyed had not yet been estimated.'

The street battles occurred despite the Congress and Muslim

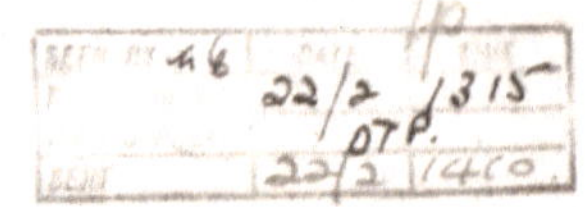

Facsimile of Prime Minister Attlee's desperate telegram to Viceroy Wavell, where he mentions, 'I am now about to make a statement in the House of Commons...' and have no latest information.

League workers trying to dissuade people from participating in the *hartal*. In spite of this shameful display of obeisance to the British, civilians across India risked their lives to come out in support of the naval ratings.

PUBLIC DEMONSTRATIONS ACROSS INDIA

The ratings' rebellion lasted just four days. But it inspired common people, who took to the streets in solidarity. While Bombay was the epicentre, and suffered the most, there was unrest in Karachi, Vizagapatam, Madras, Calcutta, Ahmedabad, Trichinopoly, Madurai, Kanpur, and elsewhere. Inspired by the RIN mutiny, people risked their lives to fight for freedom.

The British struggled to control the crowds that poured out onto the streets. The protesters were undeterred by indiscriminate firing. The courage of the ratings had infected ordinary people.

In Vizagapatam, the Communist Party organized a procession of workers and other citizens carrying posters, which said 'Release Arrested Navy Boys,' and 'Down with Imperialism.' The authorities retaliated with the imposition of Section 144 and banning all mass gatherings for one month.

In Calcutta an unprecedented strike led by Calcutta Tramway workers resulted in a complete paralysis of all forms of transport – trams, buses, taxis, and even trains. Almost one lakh students and workers took to the streets. The demonstrators carrying the flags of the Communist Party, Congress and Muslim League went around the city shouting slogans and urging the three parties to unite and help the naval ratings. They congregated at Wellington Square, where they were addressed by the leaders of all three parties.

On 24 and 25 February, Ahmedabad also saw massive demonstrations. Some 6,000 communist workers rallied at Kamdar Maidan and called for a *hartal*. Taking a cue from the Communists, over 10,000 mill workers, mostly owing allegiance to Congress and Muslim League, struck work and eighteen mills were wholly shut.

In Trichinopoly, almost 10,000 mill and office workers took out a mile-and-a-half long procession to demonstrate solidarity with the ratings. There was a complete *hartal* in Madras where students, workers, shopkeepers staged another massive rally in Tilak Ghat. There were bloody clashes with the police at Elliot Road and Royapuram. In Madurai on 27 February, a day-long bandh culminated in a meeting of over 50,000 people pledging support to the naval ratings.

Karachi also witnessed widespread protests and violence. The surrender of the HMIS *Hindustan* after a pitched battle led to people pouring out onto the streets. On 22 February, the city came to a standstill as a public meeting held by the CPI asked people to support the ratings. An estimated 5,000 people were in attendance.

Another 30,000 – Hindus and Muslims, mill workers and students – poured into the famous Idgah Maidan on 23 February in another protest march led by the CPI, which the Congress and the Muslim League noticeably avoided. A panicky district magistrate (DM) issued Section 144, but people refused to stay at home.

By 12.30, authorities had fired tear gas shells repeatedly but their efforts were thwarted by brave women who used buckets of water to drench the protestors and ensure the tear gas had little effect. At 2.00 p.m., young men and women started to throw stones at their oppressors, who retaliated with machine gun fire. Four protesters were killed on the spot but the battle continued as more men ferried in from Manora Island and joined the protest. The police opened fire several times. Official figures mention eight deaths and twenty-six seriously injured. The injured were ferried to the city by public vehicles, with owners/drivers refusing payment.

Reporting the unrest in Karachi, *Dawn*'s front page declared: 'Karachi Police Open Fire.' The body text read: 'The Police opened fire in Karachi on Friday (22 February) on a crowd near

Idgah Maidan that advanced on the police three times at about 2.30 p.m... Two rounds were fired each time... An authoritative version of Saturday (23 February) incident so far was given by an official spokesman at a press conference in Sind secretariat. He said that the district magistrate has issued orders under Section 144 CrPC banning processions and public meetings since 6 a.m. on Saturday for an indefinite period on the ground that provocative speeches are likely to be made in regard to RIN Mutiny... Three Communist leaders were arrested on Saturday morning, who were addressing a meeting calling upon the public to observe *hartal*. Later six school boys and milk vendors were arrested... for attempting to take possession of the municipal office... and for stoning the police...'

The spontaneous and widespread demonstrations by common civilians, including women and children, was yet another factor that accelerated the British decision to quit India. They could no longer rely on their overwhelming advantage in weaponry to cow the common people and there had been multiple incidents where Indian policemen and soldiers refused to shoot at their countrymen.

National Herald
AVAILABLE IN MADRAS
c/o MR. V. R. PEETHAMBARAM
The Hindustan General News Agency, CHINTADRIPET, MADRAS

EARLY MORNING EDITION

NATIONAL HERALD

VOL. V N. 83   REG. NO. A.327   LUCKNOW, TUESDAY, FEBRUARY 26, 1946   PRICE TWO ANNAS

R. I. N. MUTINY LEADERS TO BE TRIED

NO COLLECTIVE PUNISHMENT

Commander-in-Chief's Broadcast

"POLITICAL INTRIGUES IN ARMY CAN'T BE COUNTENANCED"

NEW DELHI, Feb. 25—General Sir Claude Auchinleck, Commander-in-Chief, in a broadcast tonight on the RIN mutiny, said that there would be no collective punishment, no vindictive action or indiscriminate retribution but ringleaders and others would be individually tried and those found guilty would be punished.

To refrain from awarding punishment, where such is due, would put a premium on insubordination, he said.

"Legitimate grievances can be and are being rectified continually and as quickly as possible," added the C-in-C, but he made it clear that some of the men's wishes could not be met.

DR. KHAN SAHIB ASKED TO FORM NEW GOVT.

PESHAWAR, Feb. 25.—During press conversation here arranged from Abbottabad Press, Peshawar.

His Excellency the Governor received the hon'ble Doctor Khan Sahib this morning. Doctor Khan Sahib, on behalf of himself and his colleague, offered their resignation as leader of the Congress Party in NWFP which was unanimously accepted by his electorate.

WELL DONE, PATHANS

AZAD CONGRATULATES FRONTIER PEOPLE

PESHAWAR, Feb. 24. Giving darshan to the devout, crowd Maulana Azad and congratulating the Frontier people on their success in the recent elections said.

"The brilliant success you have achieved has brought the cherished goal nearer." God willing, you will soon reap the fruits of your...

ALL QUIET IN BOMBAY

NEHRU'S TALKS WITH CONGRESS LEADERS

TOMMIES QUITTING THE SCENE

BOMBAY, Feb. 25. "Bombay is completely quiet, and public confidence is returning, a commander issued by Joint Advance H.Q. southern command at 4.30 p.m. today.

The latest official figures of civilian casualties admitted to hospitals since the beginning of the disturbances are:—

Killed 229, Injured 1243

RIN ratings are getting ready to quit their ships and the RN is the ratings to report.

"Every case of enquiry have been ordered, of which four are to be held immediately."

Pandit Jawaharlal Nehru arrived here today. He drive round at a wayside station and immediately afterwards got himself in touch with Sardar Vallabhbhai Patel.

The conference between Sardar Patel and Pt. Nehru lasted one hour during which it is understood the Sardar explained to Pandit Nehru all facts relating to the Bombay situation.

After the meeting Pandit Nehru drove to his visitor's residence at Gamadia Hill.

The Bombay Provincial Congress Committee is making arrangements to hold a public meeting at Chowpatty.

RIAF STRIKE IN BOMBAY SPREADS

BOMBAY, Feb. 25. One hundred and fifty men of the R.I.A.F. wing at Sion, Bombay went on a one-day-strike this afternoon in sympathy with the strikers of other R.I.A.F. camps in Bombay and other parts of the country.

The strikers have formulated a list of grievances and asked the authorities to consider them. The demands of the strikers include the formation of pay for all service personnel after demobilisation, early release of disgruntled men to the basis of age and service, prompt payment of allowances and grant of leave and increase in scales of pay and inquiry into the ill-treatment by the R.I.A.F. personnel on February 11 made by Maruti Drive camp.

The strikers stated that it was inevitable that the warrant-officers and relations resorted to lathi charge as recently in Bombay, did not contact any members of the R.I.A.F. corps but only set officers.

LAHORE STRIKE

LAHORE, Feb. 22 (delayed) Nearly 400 Indian airmen stationed at Lahore Cantonment, have gone on strike. The striking airmen who come from different parts of India, in also come from Ceylon, comprise Hindus, Muslims, Sikhs and Christians. They have met a lengthy note to the air authorities demanding prompt and practical steps within a fortnight, so as to assure better...

GENERAL STRIKE IN MADRAS

Crowd Lathi-Charged Twice

MADRAS, Feb. 25.— There is a general strike of workers and students in the city today as a protest against military firing at Bombay and to express their sympathy with the RIN ratings.

The tramway and motor transport workers, printing press workers and labourers in various workshops abstained from work this morning with the result that tram and bus services are completely at a standstill.

Hotels, restaurants and shops in most of the localities remain closed. Processions of workers and students, organised by their respective organisations, went through important thoroughfares.

Three military officers returned minor injuries as result of stones thrown by demonstrators. One private car passing along North Beach Road was damaged and occupant sustained minor injury to his forehead. Stray cases of looting of petty shops in fringe of city limits are reported.

SEVEN DEAD AND 33 INJURED IN KARACHI FIRING

KARACHI, Feb. 24.—Total casualties in Friday's police firing here were seven dead and 33 injured according to figures now available here late...

CITY EDITION

Dawn

Founded by MOHAMMAD ALI JINNAH

Edited by ALTAF HUSAIN

VOL. V NO. 56   DELHI: TUES, FEB. 26, 1946, 23 RABI-UL-AWWAL, 1365 A.H.   PRICE 1½ ANS.

CHERISHED LETTER OF REFERENCE

Mr. James Dewar, former Hall keeper at the Melbourne Town Hall who has died at the age of 64 always cherished a letter of reference which helped in his appointment in 1912 says he was from Melbourne.

It was signed by his office to the death with Lieutenant A. P. Wavell—now Lord Wavell, Viceroy of India.

RIN RINGLEADERS TO BE PUNISHED

AUCHINLECK'S HINT IN BROADCAST TALK

NO PREMIUM TO BE PAID ON INDISCIPLINE

C-IN-C will not Tolerate Political Intrigue in Army

THE C-in-C, General Sir Claude Auchinleck in a broadcast on Monday night, on the RIN strike said that there would be no collective punishment, no vindictive action or indiscriminate retribution, but ringleaders and others would be individually tried and those found guilty would be punished. "To refrain from awarding punishment where such is due would put a premium on insubordination" he said.

"Legitimate grievances can be and are being rectified continually and as quickly as possible," he went on. But, he made it clear that some of the men's wishes could not be met.

"If we cannot find police have not something to give with recent grievances subornations in the workers," General Auchinleck said. "As to problem to my own I the C-in-C, I have nothing whatever to do with police..."

INDONESIAN PAPER ON BOMBAY RIOT

THE leading Indonesian National newspaper "Merdeka" expressed joy at the reports of riots in India and analysed the cause across, replies Reuter from Batavia.

The Merdeka said "The Indian people are beginning to understand that the policy of non-violence cannot procure what they desire," and added that the trouble which began in Bombay and Calcutta, would soon throw over the whole of India. Mr. Gandhi and Pandit Nehru ought to use the cause and are not prepared, read the Merdeka. The entire Indonesian people sympathise with their own revolution in which failures by time will win spread over India, Burma and other countries. The Merdeka concludes "Not such declaration can we throw out the burden of the white coat, but only by fighting as we the Indonesians have already proved."

THE FRENCH DISMISS 20 GENERALS

THE retirement of 20 French generals and many other high ranking officers was officially announced in Paris on Monday, Reuter states.

It is widely believed that the stage indicates elimination of de Gaullist elements, although the retirements are officially described as due to new army laws retiring officers over...

The retirements are due and received in circles where army officers extravagance is a shocked reputation experience. Among the most shortly criticised on the move is General Juin on Lattre de Tassigny.

Most authorities say senior General de Tassigny of working 1,300,000 francs on setting up new headquarters in Boulevard les Invalides in Paris.

General de Tassigny who is not among the generals whose retirement is abandoned knows to be sharing the most determined opponents of de Gaulle's drastic reductions in military credits.

Paris Talks on Troops Withdrawal from Levant

BRITAIN is to be Represented at the conference of France and Britain began here shortly which are likely have handed a Minister on Tuesday in next officially stated on Friday.

It is understood, quotes Reuter's diplomatic correspondent that the parties of the Paris Talks, will be to reach a new military convention replacing the existing one, for Arab levant.

The British Government considers that Mr. Anglo-French Agreement on the Levant of September 1944, has gone unrealised by reality. It regards the agreement as a relic of the past when it was essentially in the name of the 1920 quadruple now signed by Mr. Edward Harrison of the United States.

Britain has not yet reached official views for Government of Syria and the Lebanon whether long are willing to take part in the Paris Talks, but the British correspondent here understands it to be associate either to the party of a four-party conversation according to the correspondent—Reuter.

NAWABZADA LEAVES FOR LAHORE

Nawabzada Liaquat Ali Khan left Delhi on Monday night for Lahore.

YENAN FORCES MERGE WITH CHUNGKING ARMY

CHIANG TO BE C-IN-C: 15 YEARS' RIVALRY ENDS

CHINESE Communist forces were formally merged with the Chinese National Army on Monday afternoon in an agreement signed by General Chang 'Chin Chung, Head of the Political Affairs Department of the National Military Council, General Chou En-Lai the Communist Leader and General George Marshall, the United States Ambassador.

The official fusion of the Kuomintang and Communist armies into a single right-left force which took place with the signature of a bulky document covering terms of agreement put an end to the 15-year period of rivalry and divided the Chinese Military Command.

Under the agreement reached the end old divisions scattered throughout the country will be formed into 20 armies within 12 months. These will be organised along Western lines since in operation in both Chungking forces.

Calcutta Ratings See Mr. Jinnah

THREE representatives of the Ratings Artillery Reserve branch of Calcutta branch on Monday gave their grievances two short accounts to the President of the All India Muslim League. This story was in one of the representatives put in, as the representatives that really had been played by the grievances of the other National leaders, who begged that their rightful demands should be met with the authorities suppressed.

No Hope of Soviet Withdrawal from Manchuria Soon

There are no definite but persistent reports in Chungking that the Russians who were scheduled to withdraw from a decision of troops out into North China soon begin Priest.

Thus far there is no unofficial report on the part of Russian authorities for to any sort proper withdrawal soon and appears from Chinese groups says far late.—APA.

Central Assembly

LEAGUE MEMBER CRITICISES DECLINE IN PERCENTAGE OF MUSLIMS IN RAILWAYS

By "Dawn" Gallery Correspondent

THE Central Assembly passed a number of cuts in grants to the Railway Board after a dull discussion in which Government's policy with regard to railways was subjected to severe criticism from League and Congress benches.

Bombay Situation Improves: Life in the City Steadily Returning to Normal

CITY life in riot-torn Bombay is slowly returning to normal after a week of naval uprising and civilian rioting.

The situation on Monday was completely normal. The curfew period was revised and military pickets were gradually wound up. Most of the shops were open and others opening.

2 LEAGUERS RETURNED UNOPPOSED IN C.P.

Two Congress candidates were declared elected unopposed from two seats of the Central Provincial Assembly.

JINNAH DEMANDS DISCIPLINE

MAMDOT LIKELY TO LEAD LEAGUE PARTY IN PUNJAB ASSEMBLY

NAWAB OF MAMDOT, President of the Punjab Muslim League, is expected to be unanimously elected League party...

Punjab League To Observe V-Day on March 1

NAWAB OF MAMDOT, President of the Punjab Muslim League has directed the provincial and District branches of the Muslim League in the Punjab to observe...

13

SURRENDER: BETRAYAL
AND BROKEN PROMISES

The NCSC met at the *Talwar* on 22 February at 3 p.m. By then, the ratings had seen the sacrifices the people of Bombay had made. They were overwhelmed by both pride and anger. They yelled and screamed at each other.

The people's heroism they had witnessed reduced many of these tough men to tears. 'They are not sailors, they are not soldiers, and they are not trained fighters,' said one speaker emotionally. 'They are just the ordinary sons of our people. But they have shown us today that they can fight and that too without arms. Now there can be no surrender. Blood has been spilled. They have sacrificed their precious lives for us. The debt has to be paid back a hundredfold. We can never surrender now. If we do we shall never be able to show our face to the people. We must continue the fight. The whole country is behind us. Our victory is assured.'

The fighting spirit of the ratings echoed across all the ships and shore establishments. But the politicians making cold calculations were unmoved by the display of courage and sacrifice. Indifferent to the high death toll among civilians, these leaders continued to persuade M.S. Khan and Co. to surrender.

Khan sent out a message hinting at possible surrender, but this did not dampen the fighting spirit. 'Do not surrender unconditionally. Be peaceful and carry on the strike. Come what may...'

The ratings interpreted Khan's missive as defiance. Many thought the struggle would continue. They greeted the message with 'Inquilab Zindabad' and 'Jai Hind', determined that, with the common people behind them, they would continue the struggle.

But this hope was soon dashed. At about 6 p.m., Khan came to the breakwater with other NCSC members. The ratings gathered around expectantly but quietened when they saw his sombre face.

In a voice that was almost breaking, he read out the message from Sardar Patel.

In the present unfortunate circumstances that have developed, the advice of the Congress to the RIN ratings is to lay down arms and go through the formality of the surrender, which has been asked for. The Congress will do its level best to see that there is no victimization and the legitimate demands of the naval ratings are accepted as soon as possible.

There is considerable tension all over the city and there has been heavy loss of life and property. There is also considerable strain both on the naval ratings as well as on the authorities.

While fully appreciating the spirit and courage and also having full sympathy in their present difficulties, the best advice the Congress can give them in the present circumstances is to end the tension immediately. The advice is in the interests of all concerned.

The letter was a death blow to the ratings' hopes. The dagger had been wielded not by the British, but by the Congress. One can only imagine the feelings of these young men as they listened to Khan reading out those words. Their national leaders had just thrown them to the wolves.

Patel's words created a storm and sparked a new flurry of arguments. How could they surrender? If they did, how would they ever show their faces to the common people of India?

'We don't want to fight, but we won't give up the strike,' shouted one rating.

But the die was cast. Many of these brave young men who had stood unflinching against British assaults broke down and sobbed uncontrollably when they heard Khan's words. 'I am of the opinion that, having received this assurance, we should now surrender and lay down our arms. We can rely on our leaders to see that justice is done. Do not think we are surrendering to the British. We are surrendering to the people, because the whole nation is with us.'

Khan was being generous in terming the national leaders 'our people'. As far as the ratings were concerned, the leaders had betrayed them. It meant their fates and futures would lie in the hands of the British. There was nowhere to go, not even an inkling as to whether they could continue to serve in the navy.

For the first time since the uprising, Muslim ratings asked Khan what guarantees the Muslim League had given, to which he could only reply there had been none. Jinnah was in Calcutta at the time and his directives, if any, would only be learnt in a few days. Khan told them that he had met Ibrahim Chundrigar, who could not give any assurance unless he got one himself from the League High Command.

'We don't want to put ourselves in the hands of one party,' chorused the Muslim ratings, 'We at least want an assurance from the Muslim League before we give up.'

Khan's message travelled like wildfire through the ships. Shattered, weary men broke down. All their struggles, all their efforts to fight for Mother India, had been for nothing? This was resonating in their minds as Khan asked for representatives from the various ships and establishments to thrash things out at the *Talwar*. The NCSC met for the final time at 11.30 p.m. in an atmosphere of anger, bitterness, and utter dejection.

A statement was issued to the press. It said:

'Brothers and sisters of Bombay. We congratulate you, dear citizens of Bombay, workers, students, and all, for the great expression of solidarity with us today. We mourn with you the deaths of many due to the indiscriminate firing of the British military forces and condemn the wanton murder by the imperialists of so many of our people. Here among us our strike continues and it will continue so long as you help us. Here we are solid and sure. We are doing our best, with the added strength that you by your stand have given us, to bring victory to our cause, a victory that will be yours and ours together.'

The message added: 'We are negotiating and we hope to achieve success. But for success your help, your disciplined protests and strikes must continue. This alone will show the brutal military and bureaucratic authorities that they must reckon not only with us but also with you, dear brethren and sister of Bombay if they try to drown us in blood.'

That last meeting of the NCSC carried on through the night and into the morning, almost until the deadline for surrender at 6.30 a.m. on 23 February. A messenger went from ship to ship, asking NCSC representatives to proceed to the *Talwar*. There were thirty-six active ratings in the NCSC by that time, and due to the British doing their best to deny them free movement, they trickled in at 1.30 a.m. and 2 a.m.

Many of the men – Khan included – had not slept for over four days and could barely stand due to complete exhaustion and hunger. Nevertheless, the meeting carried on with many ratings emphasizing that they wanted to fight on.

Khan and Madan Singh sat with their heads bowed in utter dejection until finally, Khan spoke, his voice choked as he struggled to hold back his tears. Briefing the ratings who had not heard of his talks with Sardar Patel and FOB Rear-Admiral Rattray, he once again advised surrender. If the ratings did not do so by 6.30 a.m., the British threatened to use all the forces at their command to massacre them. Whatever they decided, whether it was truce or war, they had to reach FOB Rattray by 6.30 a.m.

Though Khan advocated surrender, the fiercely patriotic Madan Singh was otherwise inclined. The difference of opinions led to an uproar. The majority of the NCSC was against surrender.

Someone shouted angrily: 'What face will we show to the boys if we agree to this?'

There was pandemonium as others joined in, saying surrender was not and never could be, an option. Giving up would snatch defeat from the jaws of victory. Plus, they had a duty, a duty to the people of India.

One rating burst out angrily. 'We cannot surrender now. We are about to win our demands. The people are behind us. Our struggle has become a part of the struggle of our people to be free. If we surrender now, we shall be betraying them. We called upon them to come to our aid and they came and sacrificed their lives. The British military brutally mowed down men, women and children with machine guns. The people's spirit of resistance has risen. They are going to continue the fight. How can we back out now?'

Another rating spoke out. 'If we surrender, we give the command of the ship to the officers. The strike must continue. We cannot give it up till our demands are fulfilled. Such an action will help everyone. You know that our national leaders are moving an Adjournment Motion in the Central Assembly. We must strengthen their hands by continuing the strike.'

The discussion went on, but without the support of the national political leaders, and in the face of overwhelming military force, and in the absence of any practical course of action, hope was slipping away.

The last hope of political support evaporated early next

morning. Jinnah had issued a statement on the evening of 22 February in Calcutta. It reached the *Talwar* as the NCSC met.

Subrata Banerjee writes, 'It was at this moment (around 2.30 a.m.) that a rating came in with a message. The *Free Press Journal* had rung up to say that Mr Jinnah, in a statement issued at Calcutta, had expressed his sympathy with the ratings.'

Acknowledging the RIN men have 'some very just grievances' the statement read that Jinnah was willing to offer his services 'unreservedly for the cause of the RIN men to see that justice is done to them'. They, however, had to promise that they would adopt 'constitutional, lawful and peaceful means'. If they were willing to do so, he would do his best to ensure that their 'grievances were redressed'.

Jinnah stated they must call off the strike immediately.

'I'm appealing to all RIN men not to play in the hands of those who want to create trouble and exploit those on strike for their own ends. I urge upon them to restore normal conditions and let us handle the situation, which will surely result in their welfare and will be in their best interest.

'I, therefore appeal to the men of the RIN and to the ratings to call off the strike and to the public in general not to add to the difficulties of the situation. Particularly I call upon the Muslims to stop and to create no further trouble until we are in a position to handle this very serious situation. If we fail to make the authorities understand and meet the just demands, then it will be time for us all with perfect unity amongst ourselves to force the hands of the government if they are not reasonable.'

Initially, the ratings greeted the statement with a loud cheer. Some shouted that now there was no question of surrender... both the League and the Communists have pledged support. Was this not what they wanted?

But the celebration was short-lived as the full import of what Jinnah had said, sank in. Jinnah had categorically asked them to 'Call off the strike'. 'Now there can no question of not surrendering,' said Khan.

Khan and Madan Singh sat through the unending arguments demoralized and exhausted. At last, Khan rose again: 'Brothers, stop being children, please stop. You are talking like children. It is too late for us to do anything more. Now hurry up and make up your minds. There is very little time left.'

Khan said, as far as the *Talwar* group was concerned, their minds were made up. The *Talwar* ratings had decided to call off the strike and surrender unconditionally. 'If any of you want to continue to fight, you can do so,' Khan said.

The emotional pendulum had swung by now, all the way from exhilaration and ecstasy, to agony. This sounded like a 'betrayal' by the very man who had led them. But as Khan continued, they realized that he was speaking blunt if unpleasant truths.

The ratings had held the British army and navy at bay, an act unwanted by their national leaders. They had sworn to act in accordance with, and abide by, the wishes of the national leaders. If they continued, would not the leaders accuse them of breach of faith and even accuse them of seeking appropriate political power for themselves?

Such bullheadedness would not only harm their cause but the freedom movement as a whole. Khan's voice shook and he was on the verge of tears, but his argument carried weight. None of the ratings had an answer. The fact that their actions could hurt their leaders and harm the freedom movement was something that had never occurred to them. Khan was right. If this bitter pill had to be swallowed, then it would be. They would brave the taunts of the nation and even their fellow ratings before splitting the movement.

Freedom came first, and so the ratings resigned themselves to an uncertain fate. The only thing that remained was the terms of surrender. Could some sort of compromise be reached with the British?

With the deadline approaching, the ratings gathered to vote on the surrender. In the end, only six members of the NCSC opposed surrender. Besides *Assam, Khyber, Jumna, MMS 129,* and

Castle Barracks was against any surrender. Castle Barrack had two representatives. Their vote was split. It was nearly 6 a.m. by the time the decision to surrender was made. There was barely half an hour left before the FOB's deadline expired.

Khan left to convey the decision to the FOB. At the same time, a statement was sent to the press. It was decided a fuller statement would be drafted but the members had to rush to their respective ships to inform the rank and file.

Writes B.C. Dutt, 'With a heavy heart, the members embraced each other and hurried to their ships and barracks. So it was all over. I had a feeling of vast emptiness. Painfully, I dragged myself to my feet to attend to what I felt was my last important task. I collected all the records, every scrap of paper which had been used by the members of the NCSC and, with tears blinding my eyes, consigned them to the flames. The papers appeared to me as records of a grand futility. Our hopes had been smashed. Our dreams lay in the dust; the flames at the time appeared to be the right place for the records of our futile endeavour. I just wanted to destroy all the evidence of our miserable failure. To me, it was a colossal failure.'

Informing the ratings in the various establishments was not an easy task emotionally, especially so for the representatives who had opposed surrender.

'I don't have the heart to inform the boys,' said one, but the decision had to be conveyed. At first, it was met with shock and disbelief. Some ratings shouted in anger, some wept, others simply walked away in despair. But as disciplined members of the armed forces, the ratings respected the decision taken by their representatives.

Finally, a signal was sent… 'To the General RIN. All ships hoist black flag. Remain quiet on board. Will endeavour to send rations.' At 6.13 a.m., the three flags of Congress, Muslim League and the Communist Party started to come down from the masts. It was over. All across the ships and establishments, the ratings read the last message from the NCSC. It was an inspiring document that should find a place in the history of the freedom movement.

It said:

The Naval Central Strike Committee wishes to inform the people of India, particularly the people of Bombay, that it has decided to call off the strike. It has come to this decision after discussion with Sardar Vallabhbhai Patel, who has assured them that the Congress would see that there was absolutely no victimization of any of the strikers and that their just demands would be taken up with the authorities. Confident that the Congress would stand by them and sure of the support of Muslim League after the sympathetic statement of Mr Jinnah, the committee decided to call off the strike.

The committee, however, reminds the naval and government authorities and tells the people and leaders of all political parties, particularly Sardar Vallabhbhai Patel and Mr Jinnah, that the ratings in the navy will not hesitate one moment to come out and strike again if the authorities make any attempt to victimize a single striker.

The Naval Strike Committee once more congratulates the people of Bombay, particularly the workers, students and citizens, for their sympathetic strike during the past two days. These actions have inspired the men in the navy with the consciousness that all India believed their cause to be just and right.

Together with the people, the committee mourns the loss of hundreds of lives due to brutal and absolutely unjustified firing by the British military forces on innocent men and women. It condemns with all the forces at its command this action of the Military and the Government which has resulted in a bloodbath in Bombay, worse than India has yet seen.

And a last word to our people:

You have stood by us. We are glad, proud, and grateful for that. We mourn the loss of life. Had you not stood by us and demonstrated in your thousands, our cause and our strike would have been drowned in blood. The authorities may yet try to victimize us and punish us. We shall fight that – we ask you also to be ready to fight that and redeem the solemn promise of Sardar Vallabhbhai Patel and Mr Jinnah.

Our strike has been a historic event in the life of our nation. For the first time the blood of the men in the services and the people flowed together in a common cause. We in the services will never forget this. We also know that you, our brothers and sisters, will not forget. Long live our great people. Jai Hind.

Newsmen who had covered the mutiny for five days had been updating their copy desks on a minute-to-minute basis of the dramatic scenes unfolding at the NCSC meeting. They knew one way or another, this was crunch time, and major newspapers held back their front pages to cover the 'Breaking News'.

The late city editions of the *Free Press Journal* flashed the news of surrender prominently on the front page, reading, 'NAVAL RATINGS AGREE TO SURRENDER ARMS, Submission to Sardar's Advice, Sit Down Strike to Continue.' The *Hindustan Times*, published from Delhi, carried a two-column front page report: 'BOMBAY RATINGS DECIDE TO SURRENDER'. In a single column front-page report, the *Dawn*, also published from Delhi, headlined, 'Unconditional Surrender of RIN Ratings'. The *Hindustan Standard*, published from Calcutta, squeezed in a single column front-page report saying, 'THE BATTLE ENDS'. The *Times of India* printed a single column right in the middle of front page: 'RIN MUTINY ENDS, Ratings Decision, Mr V Patel's Advice Accepted'.

SATURDAY, 23 FEBRUARY 1946

At 8 a.m., the FOB began to tour the ships and establishments. The surrender ceremony over, arms were collected and the strikers moved out from their positions to be replaced by British troops. The men stood helpless, as if under open arrest, while their ships and establishments had all their weapons removed and inventories checked.

Out in the streets, newsboys were shouting headlines at the top of their voices, repeating the depressing news. People could hardly believe what they were reading and hearing. The resolution of the NCSC, which they had sent out earlier, was also splashed prominently on the front pages.

History would record the naval uprising of February 1946 as the beginning of the end for the British Raj. The epic struggle for freedom would finally bear fruit eighteen months later, and undoubtedly, the heroic efforts of the ratings made a significant contribution.

For four days and nights, the ratings took on the military might of the British and they almost succeeded. They had nearly pulled off the incredible feat of taking over the Royal Indian Navy and delivering it to the national political leaders. They might well have succeeded but for the lack of support from the political leadership.

The death toll, primarily recorded in the street battles across Bombay was already among the highest ever recorded at that time. The street clashes would continue with citizens battling the police for several more days.

For the ratings, the surrender was a poignant, heart-breaking moment. The failed uprising and the punishment subsequently meted out to the ringleaders and others was even more heart-rending

Within forty-eight hours, the authorities had launched mass arrests picking up every rating who had taken part in the uprising. Khan, Madan Singh, and other key members of the NCSC, were taken into custody and transported to detention camps.

In a broadcast on 23 February, Field Marshal Auchinleck said there would be no collective punishment, but individuals would be punished. He said, 'To refrain from awarding punishment where such is due would put a premium on insubordination.'

According to Kusum Nair in *The Army of Occupation*: 'Everything was found in perfect order. There was Rs 80,000 in cash in Castle Barracks alone. Not a pie was missing. Everywhere there was much that could have been damaged or destroyed. Nothing had been touched.'

Meanwhile the street battles continued, and the newspapers reported the continuing bloodshed with varying degrees of editorial independence: The *National Herald* of 24 February had banner headlines on its front page: 'ARMOURED CARS IN BOMBAY STREETS, 210 Killed And Over 1,200 Injured, 3,00,000 MILL-HANDS DOWN TOOLS.' A two-column front page prominently displayed news item that read: 'BOMBAY MUTINEERS SURRENDER, SARDAR PATEL'S ADVICE ACCEPTED. C-IN-C ASSURES NO VICTIMIZATION.'

The *Dawn* also carried banner headlines on the front page: 'NIGHTMARE GRIPS BOMBAY, Two Trains Set On Fire At Dadar Station, MILL AREA MOST AFFECTED: REPEATED FIRING ON CROWDS.' The body text read: 'It was officially stated in New Delhi on Saturday (23 February) that the ratings in Bombay have surrendered unconditionally. The surrender has been accepted. A signal from the strike committee that the ships are ready to surrender was received at Naval Headquarters at Bombay at 6.13 a.m. on Saturday after which the ships surrendered one by one in accordance with the terms laid down by the Flag Officer Commanding the Royal Indian Navy. Soon after the surrender, signal was hoisted by the Royal Indian Navy ships under the control of the strikers. Rear-Admiral Rattray and Lt Choudhury went on board the ships and addressed the ratings. The flag of Vice Admiral Godfrey was hoisted on the *Narbada*, the flag ship of the Vice-Admiral.'

The *Times of India* on 25 February carried a front-page lead story with an extended description of the surrender: It was headlined 'Bombay Returning to Normal… Big Roundup of Bad Characters… Latest Casualty list – 270 Dead: 1260 Hurt'. The second lead read: 'RIN Ratings' Surrender Accepted: Men Resume Duty… Royal Navy Cruiser Steams Into Bombay Harbour.'

The story further read: 'The White ensign flutters again over the flotilla of sloops and minesweepers of the Royal Indian Navy lying close inshore in Bombay Harbour. It was run up and the large black flags signifying unconditional surrender of the crews were lowered on Sunday afternoon as senior officers boarded the ships to assume official charge. Shore establishments were entered and the unconditional surrender of the ratings was accepted. Small parties of armed British troops accompanied the officers up ships' gangways to mount guard over vessels of the fleet, immobilise their guns, and take charge of all small arms and ammunition in their magazines. Vice Admiral Godfrey FOCRIN was piped aboard his flagship HMIS *Narbada* later in the day as the Royal Navy light cruiser *Glasgow* mounting 12 six-inch guns steamed into the harbour in a smother of foam, stripped for action and with her guns trained on the port to drop anchor… Vice-Admiral's flag was temporarily hoisted as he mounted the deck of his flagship.

'The men were called up and clustered around him as he addressed them in the following words: "Now that order has been restored, it is your duty to return quietly to work without delay. No passive resistance to duty will be tolerated… There will be a full and impartial inquiry into the complaints and grievances."'

The *Free Press Journal* said: 'India Betrayed by the C-in-C, Auchinleck goes back on his assurance… RIN Strike Committee Members to be whisked away.'

Back in the Castle Barracks, the ratings stood on parade before their officers on Saturday. Rations were issued to men and they set about 'Clean Ship', clearing the litter and tidying up the establishment. The damage caused to the interior of the barracks was negligible and the important naval records were untouched. The authorities allowed for the removal of the body of Sub-Lt Krishnan who died in the battle.

Bharat Jyoti, published from Bombay, reported: 'Ratings were justified in their revolt. CENTRAL ASSEMBLY CENSURES GOVT. BUNGLING…' the body text read: 'The assembly at a special sitting this afternoon passed by 74 votes to 40, Asaf Ali's adjournment motion to discuss "the grave situation that has arisen in respect of the Indian Navy, affecting practically the whole of it, as a result of mishandling by the immediate authorities concerned."' Minoo Masani, who also spoke on the motion asked a rhetorical question, as reported by *Bharat Jyoti*: 'Why do the people of Bombay unanimously support the mutineers? It is because Indian and British conceptions of discipline differ. We do not accept the moral basis of your authority. Your law is not law to us, because it has not got the consent of the people behind it.'

The *Free Press Journal* on Monday, 25 February, carried as many as twelve stories relating to the naval strike on the front page. The headline of the lead story read: 'CONDITIONS RETURNING TO NORMAL… Leaders Urge Withdrawal of The Military… Sporadic Firing in Bombay North…' Other major headlines were: 'OFFICIAL POST MORTEM OF RATINGS' STRIKE… NAVY MEN RESENT ARMY INTRUSION. Armed Guards On RIN Ships…'

After a tense and bloodstained week, Bombay and the naval ships and establishments slowly limped back to normalcy. A very significant chapter in the history of the freedom struggle ended in tears.

The full extent of the political betrayal would not become apparent for years. But it soon became clear that the Congress and Muslim League were washing their hands off the whole affair and leaving the ratings entirely to the mercy of the British state.

In all good faith, the ratings had trusted assurances from Sardar Patel and Jinnah along with others, who then conveniently forgot them as they were arrested and victimized in precisely the fashion that the Congress and the League, and the C-in-C had promised they would not be. They were betrayed by the very leaders in whose name and cause they fought.

M.S. Khan's words, as the British soldiers moved into the HMIS *Talwar* to take the ratings prisoner, was a bold and patriotic realization they were on their own, but even then, he proudly stated that they would not falter.

'We surrendered to India and not to the British. I don't know where they are taking us… we shall never give in. Goodbye and good luck,' were Khan's last words before he was detained, according to Subrata Banerjee.

While no official figures have ever been released, Dutt estimates that over 2,000 ratings may have been rounded up across various centres in mass arrests. They disappeared from the pages of history. This is a fairly credible assessment since roughly 400 ratings were arrested in Bombay alone during the first wave of detentions and at least another 500 were held in Karachi.

The arrests were certainly sweeping. Within ten hours of the surrender, 396 ratings were arrested in Bombay. Of them, about 80 were from the shore establishments, like *Talwar*, Castle Barracks, Fort Barracks and another 180 ratings from ships in the stream, and about 130 more from the wireless station in Mahul and the smaller ships in the Bombay docks.

Khan's subsequent ordeal would be painful. Alongside Madan Singh and other ringleaders, he faced the full might and vindictive fury of the British.

At first, they were packed into detention centres with cooks and other helpers who could scarcely believe what was happening. For the cooks, and even for some ratings, there was the faint hope they would be transferred to other shore or ship establishments. But this was belied.

Khan and Singh both knew very well the British would show them no mercy and they were in the first batch of 396 ratings who were moved in secrecy to the Mulund camp, located in the northeast of Bombay. High barbed-wire fences greeted them every morning and there was no news of fellow ratings, or of the outside world. The British wanted to break these men and snuff out any possibility of future resistance.

At the Mulund camp, caged in all sides by barbed wire, they were herded into groups and housed in the most inhuman conditions in Nissen huts. They were beaten and kicked and even denied food, water, and medicines. Many broke down and had to be hospitalized with guards keeping a watch on these men as they lay emaciated and unconscious on unsanitary bug-infested beds.

Those of their colleagues who had been lucky enough not to have been arrested kept up a semblance of resistance by smuggling nationalist papers past sympathetic Mahratta guards. These newspapers carried stories of their valour, which helped to keep their spirits and morale high. They still hoped that nationalist political leaders, who had promised to protect them against victimization, would come to their aid. But this hope turned out to be naive.

The subsequent fates of many of these brave young men remain unknown. They did time in jail or in detention camps; they were then dishonourably discharged. Many disappeared and have never been found, or traced till date, and their stories remain lost to us. This is a gap in the historical record, which is simply unforgivable.

Eventually, depression set in as most of the incarcerated ratings realized their fates were sealed. The *Free Press Journal*, *Blitz* and *People's Age* were read avidly by both British and Indian officers. It would certainly have pleased the ratings, had they known, that FOCRIN suffered a humiliating dressing down as a direct result of mishandling the mutiny.

Admiral Godfrey's broadcast had upset London, and a naval public relations officer would monitor his utterances henceforth.

However, even that was not enough to salvage his career. The *Free Press* headline stated quite bluntly, 'Godfrey Must Go', a remark many Indian and British officers privately agreed with. The FOCRIN had failed.

Meanwhile, unbroken and unbowed, the ringleaders maintained secret contacts with fellow ratings who were still at large through the good offices of sympathetic guards. The imprisoned ringleaders heard the ratings who were free were planning to strike again to protest against the arrest of the ratings put in these 'Concentration camps'.

Though elated at the spirit of the courage of those still at large, the imprisoned leaders were unhappy with the plan. They thought that this was not the opportune time and another strike might be counter-productive.

They opposed another strike and, in huddled consultations, the ringleaders drafted a letter addressing their comrades:

Dear Mates,

While you may be lacking the details of our life here in the camp, we, on the other hand, are aware of the things you are fated to put up with… We also realise the present restlessness in all place from where we come. We fully appreciate the spirit of solidarity – the great support of which you never failed us in the past, and the present moral support of which we feel mighty proud.

We further think it necessary at the present moment to remind you of the danger of premature steps to launch a further struggle. We call upon you to hold on with any further initiative until the courts martial or other psychologically current moment when the whole issue will be up in the forefront of the nation's mind and it will be easiest to rouse the nation.

Until then your job, plus those of the others who are

spirited like you in our cause, should be to organise, to keep up the spirit-read literature and prepare for the next struggle [not to be initiated until given a call from here].

The best you can do is this. The copies of the letter should be circulated to all ships and establishments telling them not to be provoked into any senseless, isolated action, which will result in defeat.

Let us know at the earliest if you fail to carry this message to all concerned. And indicate the names and establishments where you have not sent typed copies of this letter.

Anything you may think fit to pass to us, you may do so as we have done.

Your grateful Comrades Behind the Bars
N.S.C.

Despite the urging by the detenues to watch and wait, another crisis point was triggered by the same proximate cause – bad food. For the prisoners who were beaten and malnourished, the tipping point came when a rating was thrashed because he dared to ask for adequate rations for himself and fellow ratings.

The furious ratings burst into nationalistic slogans and Khan who had till then counselled restraint, called for a hunger strike on 12 March. Fed up and disunited, some ratings turned against Khan's call, grumbling that such a hunger strike served little use if the outside world did not hear of it. But they were soldiers first and Khan's order were carried out and the already emaciated ratings decided they would starve themselves in protest.

The most authentic account of the hunger strike in the camp featured in a front-page story in *Free Press Journal*, on 14 March. The headlines read: 'OVER 300 RIN RATINGS ON HUNGER STRIKE IN MULUND CAMP.'

The story read:

Since Tuesday (12 March) morning the 390 Naval Ratings who have been segregated in the Mulund camp have been on hunger strike.

Early on Tuesday morning the ratings had their breakfast as usual. Later in the morning, messengers from each barrack went to the canteen to fetch the mid-day meal. When they reached there and were given the food to take away, the messenger from H block said that the amount of food given to him was not enough for the 50 men in his block. He was told to go to the officer-in-charge of the canteen.

When the messenger from the H block approached the officer-in-charge, one Lt Singh from the Punjab, the latter took hold of him by the ear and dragged him four or five yards, telling him to get out. When the messenger returned to the block and reported this to his comrades they decided not to take any food unless the officer apologised and they were given more food.

All 396 ratings in the camp joined in the strike and refused to take any food. Thus they were without food for last 48 hours. The authorities have been sending in the food but the ratings have one and all refused to touch it. On Wednesday morning at 10 a.m. the FOB, Rear-Admiral Rattray, and an army brigadier visited the strikers.

They talked with leaders of the strike and were told that the hunger strike would only be called off if the following two demands were accepted: 1. Lt Singh should apologise to the men for his action in insulting and maltreating a rating and; 2. The food must be improved so that the ratings inside the camp get as good food as the ratings outside the camp.

Instead of considering the demands the authorities

tried to break the strike. Since the flag officer left the camp two Indian lieutenants Lt Singh and Lt Syed have been making every attempt to break the strike. They have been taking ratings out in batches and tempting them with sweets and fruits. But till now not a single rating has been taken in by the flattery and the strikers are still solidly united behind the strike committee.

Hunger strikes always alarmed the British in India because of the powerful political significance. Nor did they want news of possible deaths spreading to other ratings and to a nation, which was still boiling over with patriotic fervour. They placed spies within the camps to induce disunity and break the strike.

On 13 March, a day later, the CO of the camp, Captain Knott and a brigadier, met with the ringleaders to ask them for a list of their demands. They did not address these with any seriousness. They were confident the strike would soon be broken.

But once again, the British officers had misjudged the resolve of the ratings. Offering of better food to some ratings was turned down and the showing of a popular film was ill-advised. Some ratings went against the advice of others, causing a mini-riot and one brave, infuriated young man, Aslam, tore down the screen itself.

Aslam a bold teenaged rating from *Narbada* had shown his courage during cross-questioning earlier at the *Narbada* board of enquiry proceedings conducted immediately after the mutiny. (Every ship and establishment faced a board of enquiry.)

Upon being asked by an officer in a raised, angry voice to make a statement about the mutiny, he replied, 'My statement is that as an Indian, I participated in the strike which was shared by all Indian Navy men. It was my moral as well as national duty to join the strike.' The officer, raising his voice, further growled, 'I want a detailed statement.'

Aslam replied with a straight face, 'I participated in the strike like all other Indian Navy men. The entire country and the whole world know that we Indian soldiers have made up our minds not to rest as long as this distinction of Black and White is maintained and as long as we are treated as inferiors. The fire of hatred and enmity will go on burning in our hearts and you will know of it when the time comes. Are there any more details to give?'

Tearing of the screen and causing serious commotion was the limit, the British decided. The ringleaders must be moved to another camp and so they were, in the dead of night.

Khan cut a brave solitary figure by refusing to move and he was pushed into a lorry at bayonet point. Aslam was so infuriated seeing his president treated like this that he charged towards Captain Knott in rage threatening to hit him, and was pulled back with great difficulty.

The Mahratta guards posted to protect the detention centre refused to fire upon them and the charged-up ratings attempted to force open the gates. The British fired upon them and after that it was an easy fight as ratings, weak from hunger, collapsed on the ground and were taken to hospital, where now-panicked officers fearing large-scale deaths tried to force-feed them.

But this was the last act of collective defiance. The brave resistance put up by the ratings would soon collapse. Some weak from the hunger strike accepted food and water, while others refused.

The thirty main ringleaders were now locked up in another camp in Kalyan and, very soon, the British began their policy of 'divide and rule' at this camp too. The camp was further subdivided so only six to eight ratings could be together at one time; the guards were replaced and the camp was tightly sealed off from the outside world.

It was then that the morale of the majority broke in Mulund. Starved and depressed with no hope, many gave way, with only twenty or so prisoners continuing the hunger strike.

Their hunger strike was so extreme that two of these twenty

ratings fainted from lack of food. Death seemed to be imminent for them. Three days after the men began their fast around 9 p.m. on 15 March, the CO finally asked the men what they wanted to which they replied, an immediate audience with their leaders.

So, at 10 p.m., two ratings were taken to Kalyan camp. They returned past midnight carrying a message from their leaders to give up the hunger strike. On 16 March, after four days of starvation, the last of the ratings finally gave up the strike and took breakfast. The British, seeing their resolve, decided that some of the demands would be met, and the food and living conditions did see some improvement.

The British were embarrassed by this incident and the resulting outcry in the press. There was extensive coverage of the hunger strike and the conditions in the camps, from the *Free Press Journal* and the *Evening Standard, Bombay Chronicle, Morning Standard, Bharat Jyoti*, and the *Times of India*.

Clearly rattled by the reports, the secretary to the governor of Bombay wrote a letter to J.G. Simms ICS, secretary to the government, Home Department, asking him to speak with the editors. The home secretary (political) wrote to S. Sadanand, editor *Free Press Journal*, R.K. Karanjia, editor *Blitz*, and K. Srinivasan, editor *Morning Standard*, asking them to see him individually in connection with their respective coverage. In the meeting, the editors were cautioned against reporting false and unsubstantiated news. According to an internal report, the editors were warned to exercise more caution. One story mentioned in the meeting had appeared in *Blitz*, led by its fearless editor, the legendary Russi Karanjia. Published on 2 March, it carried the provocative headline: 'A BULLET FOR A STONE, A SHOT FOR A SHOUT… Full Story of Bombay Riots.' Another headline had read: 'Will Congress Make of RIN Another "INA" Cause?'

But while things improved at the Mulund camp, they remained as bad as ever in Kalyan camp, where Khan and his fellow ringleaders faced daily kicks, abuses and were shoved into stinking cells smelling of urine. According to some accounts, British soldiers called them 'Jai Hind Bastards'.

Despite having partaken in the hunger strike and having eaten nothing for over 72 hours they were forced at bayonet point to run and given food that was inadequate and unhygienic. They were subversive, dangerous individuals according to the British and they were treated as badly as the British dared. It was many days before they were allowed to see the sun again.

The board of enquiry convened to investigate the cause of riots remained unconcerned about the plight of the men who had instigated the revolt in the first place. As a result, it was only a matter of time before the axe fell.

On 5 April, the first batch of ratings was transported out of the Mulund camp to face an uncertain future. The ratings, some of whom were just teenagers, wept like children. Hindu, Muslim, Sikh, it did not matter. All of them had become brothers thanks to the common struggle they had waged. Led out of the camps at bayonet point and marked 'Unsuitable' they knew that they would probably not see each other again.

Even so, the desire for freedom still burned bright within them. This was something the British could not control. Cries of 'Inquilab Zindabad' and 'Jai Hind' sounded as the ratings were stuffed into the trucks. It was clear though, despite these cries of hope, their part in the freedom movement was over. Betrayed by the political leaders they had trusted, and crushed by a brutal, uncaring system, most were discharged dishonourably.

They had to fill up forms and face trumped-up charges. Essentially, the ratings had to hand over everything. Kits issued to them six years ago had to be returned; the accounts office told them there was nothing in their balance when it came to their dues. No room for appeal or any hearing was possible.

These men were not even issued a simple discharge certificate by which they could prove to future employers that they had indeed served in the RIN. The famed British sense of justice did not exist as far as they were concerned. All they could do was stand in line as the CO of the camp read out their names one by one and they were dragged off to the railway station where they were given a third-class, one-way ticket home. They were issued a form letter that said, 'The CO of your ship has charged you with taking a leading part in the Mutiny and has recommended for your discharge and this has been confirmed.' These men who had spent years fighting in wars that had nothing to do with them were now left penniless, without clothes or food.

It is thus that most of them became lost to history.

What happened in Bombay was more or less replicated in Karachi. There, the ratings were taken to Malir camp, which was more of a cage than a camp. Barbed wire surrounded the walls and British soldiers placed on guard did their best to divide the ratings on religious lines.

Intense torture was inflicted on the 500 ratings held there. Some of them, when testifying before the Commission of Enquiry, described their conditions as no less than that of a 'concentration camp'. Beatings and kickings were a matter of daily life and under intense physical and mental torture, men broke down like their counterparts in Bombay.

Around 350 of them were finally released as 'unsuitable' though they pleaded for leniency, while the remaining 150 were also court-martialled, tried and punished like their fellow ratings in Bombay. They too, were never heard of again.

REFERENCES

B.C. Dutt, *Mutiny of the Innocents*. Bombay: Sindhu Publications, 1971.

Dilip Kumar Das, *Revisiting Talwar: A study in the Royal Indian Navy Uprising of February 1946*. Delhi: Ajanta Publications, 1993, pp. 234–370.

Kusum Nair, *The Army of Occupation*. Delhi: Padma Publications, 1946.

Lockhart-RIN Mutiny; Hour by hour event description, NAI.

Lt. Cdr G.D. Sharma, VSM (Retd), *The Untold Story of Naval Mutiny: Last War of Independence*. Delhi: Vij Books, 2015.

Ratnakar Sadasyula, 'The Forgotten Naval Mutiny of 1946 and India's Independence', 19 February 2016, *Swarajya Magazine*.

Role of RIN Mutiny (Thesis), Role of political parties and their leaders towards RIN uprising, pp. 212–16.

Subrata Banerjee, *The RIN Strike*. Bombay: People's Publishing House, 1981.

Sub. Lieut. M.M. Qasin, Memoranda for Board of Enquiry Commission by RIN. National Archives of India (NAI).

The Indian Annual Register (January–June 1946), Vol. 1, pp. 301–07.

https://www.indiannavy.nic.in/sites/default/themes/indiannavy/images/pdf/chapter1.pdf

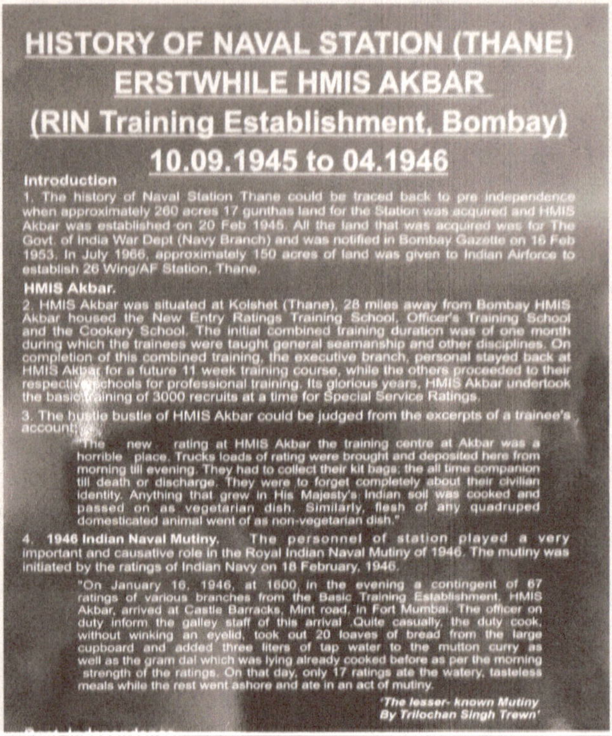

HISTORY OF NAVAL STATION (THANE)
ERSTWHILE HMIS AKBAR
(RIN Training Establishment, Bombay)
10.09.1945 to 04.1946

Introduction

1. The history of Naval Station Thane could be traced back to pre independence when approximately 260 acres 17 gunthas land for the Station was acquired and HMIS Akbar was established on 20 Feb 1945. All the land that was acquired was for The Govt. of India War Dept (Navy Branch) and was notified in Bombay Gazette on 16 Feb 1953. In July 1966, approximately 150 acres of land was given to Indian Airforce to establish 26 Wing/AF Station, Thane.

HMIS Akbar.

2. HMIS Akbar was situated at Kolshet (Thane), 28 miles away from Bombay HMIS Akbar housed the New Entry Ratings Training School, Officer's Training School and the Cookery School. The initial combined training duration was of one month during which the trainees were taught general seamanship and other disciplines. On completion of this combined training, the executive branch, personal stayed back at HMIS Akbar for a future 11 week training course, while the others proceeded to their respective schools for professional training. Its glorious years, HMIS Akbar undertook the basic training of 3000 recruits at a time for Special Service Ratings.

3. The hustle bustle of HMIS Akbar could be judged from the excerpts of a trainee's account:

> "The new rating at HMIS Akbar the training centre at Akbar was a horrible place. Trucks loads of rating were brought and deposited here from morning till evening. They had to collect their kit bags; the all time companion till death or discharge. They were to forget completely about their civilian identity. Anything that grew in His Majesty's Indian soil was cooked and passed on as vegetarian dish. Similarly, flesh of any quadruped domesticated animal went of as non-vegetarian dish."

4. **1946 Indian Naval Mutiny.** The personnel of station played a very important and causative role in the Royal Indian Naval Mutiny of 1946. The mutiny was initiated by the ratings of Indian Navy on 18 February, 1946.

> "On January 16, 1946, at 1600 in the evening a contingent of 67 ratings of various branches from the Basic Training Establishment, HMIS Akbar, arrived at Castle Barracks, Mint road, in Fort Mumbai. The officer on duty inform the galley staff of this arrival .Quite casually, the duty cook, without winking an eyelid, took out 20 loaves of bread from the large cupboard and added three liters of tap water to the mutton curry as well as the gram dal which was lying already cooked before as per the morning strength of the ratings. On that day, only 17 ratings ate the watery, tasteless meals while the rest went ashore and ate in an act of mutiny.
>
> *'The lesser- known Mutiny*
> *By Trilochan Singh Trewn'*

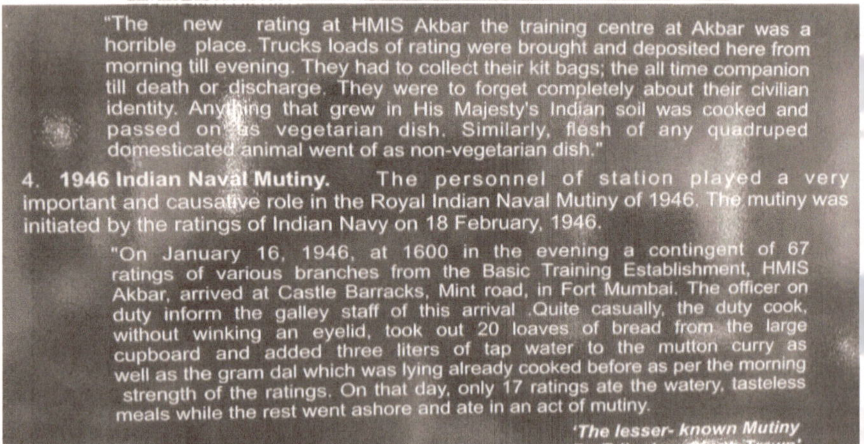

"The new rating at HMIS Akbar the training centre at Akbar was a horrible place. Trucks loads of rating were brought and deposited here from morning till evening. They had to collect their kit bags; the all time companion till death or discharge. They were to forget completely about their civilian identity. Anything that grew in His Majesty's Indian soil was cooked and passed on as vegetarian dish. Similarly, flesh of any quadruped domesticated animal went of as non-vegetarian dish."

4. **1946 Indian Naval Mutiny.** The personnel of station played a very important and causative role in the Royal Indian Naval Mutiny of 1946. The mutiny was initiated by the ratings of Indian Navy on 18 February, 1946.

"On January 16, 1946, at 1600 in the evening a contingent of 67 ratings of various branches from the Basic Training Establishment, HMIS Akbar, arrived at Castle Barracks, Mint road, in Fort Mumbai. The officer on duty inform the galley staff of this arrival .Quite casually, the duty cook, without winking an eyelid, took out 20 loaves of bread from the large cupboard and added three liters of tap water to the mutton curry as well as the gram dal which was lying already cooked before as per the morning strength of the ratings. On that day, only 17 ratings ate the watery, tasteless meals while the rest went ashore and ate in an act of mutiny.

'The lesser- known Mutiny
By Trilochan Singh Trewn'

A plaque inside Receiving Station, Thane, erstwhile HMIS Akbar *reads: The personnel of station played a very important and causative role in the Royal Indian Naval Mutiny of 1946. The mutiny was initiated by the ratings of Indian Navy on 18 February 1946.*

14

THE LONE WARRIORS
AKBAR AND *KATHIAWAR*

The *Talwar* strike sparked off revolts across different arms of the services, and across locations as far-flung as Indonesia and Bahrain.

According to the Commission of Enquiry, the mutiny affected 54 ships and 22 shore establishments. However, the commission may have been using a narrow legalistic definition of 'Mutiny' versus 'Strike' versus 'unrest' since Vol. 1 of the Enquiry Report states that only twelve ships and shore establishments did *not* experience unrest during that fateful week in February 1946. B.C. Dutt claims that 20,000 ratings, 78 ships including 4 flotillas and 24 shore establishments, experienced mutinies.

Every RIN rebellion had its own story. At HMIS *Hamla*, a shore establishment 20 miles from Bombay, a cinema show was disrupted when ratings from Castle Barracks arrived on the evening of 19 February. They shouted political slogans and threw stones to damage the guard room. The armoury was taken over.

Lt Sobhani, the only officer to rebel, led hundreds of ratings to join the rebels in the *Talwar*. In HMIS *Machlimar*, an anti-submarine school located in Versova, about 12 miles from Bombay, the ratings joined by their brethren from HMIS *Kakauri* pulled down the White Ensign, tore it up and hoisted a 'Jai Hind' flag, broke windowpanes, pulled down the notice board and smashed windscreens of parked vehicles.

There were similar scenes elsewhere. At the shore establishments, HMIS *Feroze, Sind, Mahratta, Assam, Shivaji,* and *Cheetah,* there were hunger strikes, rebels hoisting Congress, League and Communist flags, ratings breaking into the armoury, the shouting of nationalistic slogans and patriotic and provocative speeches.

The situation on the ships was not significantly different. The FOCRIN's flagship *Narbada* was converted into a control room by the ratings. HMIS *Clive, Punjab, Kumaon, Jumna, Dhanush, Khyber, Gondwana, Kistna,* were some of the other ships, of the 78 ships in all that saw rebellion. The ratings took control of motorboats and made trips to the shore and back at their will.

The *Punjab* saw ratings rushing to shore with guns and sticks; at the *Kumaon,* officers were ordered to leave the ship, and the ratings armed themselves with small arms and loaded the Oerlikon 20 mm cannons. In Bombay harbour, many of the RIN ships trained their guns towards the shore, threatening to blow up some of the iconic buildings of the Raj.

Two of the most heart-wrenching incidents involved the HMIS *Akbar,* a shore establishment in Thana, and the HMIS *Kathiawar,* a ship docked in Morvi in Gujarat. In both instances, the ratings were isolated from their fellow seamen but opted to join them in solidarity anyway. In both cases, the resistance continued after the surrender at the *Talwar.* These events showed how outgunned forces with determination can stun the mighty.

HMIS *AKBAR*

HMIS *Akbar* was a training ship permanently berthed in the Thane Creek (now Receiving Station [RS] Thane) with a complement of around 3,500 ratings. It would live up to its illustrious name.

The ratings took control of *Akbar* on the morning of 21 February. They had received news of the strike only on the morning of 19 February. That whole day, they spent discussing what their response should be.

Late on the evening of 19 February, some ratings from *Talwar* came to *Akbar* to brief the ratings about the strike. However, the CO refused permission for them to enter. This infuriated the *Akbar* ratings, and they spent a tense night discussing their next plan of action.

The following morning, Wednesday the 20th, some of the ratings of the *Akbar* decided to go to Bombay in full strength. They met their fellow ratings there, and were apprised of the situation. But they had to return to Thane by 3.30 because of the stern warning issued by Admiral Godfrey.

The following morning (21 February), sensing the ratings were angry and defiant, the officers on *Akbar* made themselves scarce. As a result, the entire establishment came under the control of the ratings. They communicated with their fellows from *Talwar* following which they sent a group of representatives in a commandeered truck to central Bombay. They were stopped at a picket in Kurla.

The ratings argued with the officers, explaining that they had to join an urgent and important meeting. They were flatly told they could go no further and were ordered back to Thane. A heated argument followed but the ratings were unarmed, and confronted by heavily armed soldiers, were forced to go back. They were now totally cut off from Bombay.

The news of the gun battle on 21 February in Castle Barrack only reached them at 11 a.m. the following day. They were angry and frustrated since they had no weapons. A little after midnight, in anticipation of an attack by the British, they broke open the armoury but were shocked to find it empty. Sensing the rebellious mood, the British had removed all the arms and ammunition on 19 February itself. Determined to do something, they declared a hunger strike. This seemed the best way to stand in solidarity with their fellow ratings and the resolution was duly put forth and followed.

But they were soldiers after all, not civilians, and they were itching to be in the thick of battle. Finally, by evening, it seemed that their wish would be granted.

The next development will go down in the pages of history, whenever the naval mutiny is mentioned. Around 300 sepoys of the RIASC (Royal Indian Army Supply Corps) camp at Kurla marched to the *Akbar*. The officers were missing, and the ratings were the masters of the shore establishment. The sepoys entered the establishment with no resistance from anyone and uttered these fighting words: 'We have gone on strike. We are joining you.'

Their arrival uplifted the mood. It turned out that the RIASC sepoys had raided the armoury when they decided to break out of their camps. They were armed with rifles and other small arms.

They embraced the ratings and shouted 'Inquilab Zindabad' and 'Jai Hind'. The *Akbar* was now under the absolute control of the ratings and sepoys. Filled with joy and optimism, the ratings treated the sepoys to food and drinks at their canteen. Their leaders climbed onto chairs and delivered a welcome address, declaring that now they were together and nobody could defeat them. They asked their army brethren to go around to other units and persuade them to join the fight for freedom.

In return, the leaders of the sepoys thanked the ratings saying, 'You must not surrender. The fight must be fought to the finish. We shall send our messengers to other units to ask them to revolt. We will join you to launch the final battle to liberate our country.'

The meeting ended at 9 p.m. after which the ratings arranged for trucks, now under their control, to take the sepoys back. All along the journey home, the sepoys were heard shouting the revolutionary slogans they had adopted as their battle cry – 'Inquilab Zindabad' and 'Jai Hind'.

The plan of action was simple. The leaders of the sepoys would go and spread the word amongst their other army colleagues while in the meantime, the ratings would fight on, till death, if necessary.

As mentioned by Subrata Banerjee in *The RIN Strike*, emotions overwhelmed them all as one rating rose to speak, to loud cheers. Addressing the sepoys, he declared: 'Today we have to show the world that Indian soldiers not only know how to smash fascists and liberate other countries, but also to fight against their own oppressors and liberate their own country.'

The sepoys were charged up hearing talk of fighting and one of them responded: 'We assure you that we will stand by you to the last, whatever happens. You must not surrender. The fight must be fought to the finish.'

By then, the British crack-down had suppressed the revolt in Bombay and, aided by persuasion from the Congress and the Muslim League, induced the ratings in Bombay to surrender. But it was a different story in Thane and Karachi.

The ratings at *Akbar* proudly fought on alone. Having joined the strike late, they could not voice their opinion when it mattered. Perhaps it would not have made much difference, but while Bombay had surrendered, Thane had not. They were outnumbered and outgunned, and the ratings knew they would probably die. But as they all pledged solemnly – they would die fighting to the end.

But what were they to do?

Cut off from Bombay and the *Talwar,* the ratings of the *Akbar* had no idea of what was transpiring there and elsewhere. Ironically, as the mood and morale of the ratings in Bombay was deteriorating, in the *Akbar* it was on the rise.

The next morning brought a bigger shock than they could have foreseen. Their widely-detested CO returned to inform them that their efforts were useless, and their struggle was over. Showing them a signal, he told them that counterparts in Bombay had thrown down their arms, and now they had no choice but to also surrender.

The stunned ratings refused to believe him. The momentum was with them; their brothers could not have done this. This man, they believed, was lying. 'Bring back a member of the CSC. If he confirms what you say only then can we talk.'

The CO was taken aback. He had hoped to bully the ratings into compliance. But it had not worked. The *Akbar* ratings were unafraid of threats and despite the overwhelming odds against them, they remained defiant. Nevertheless, the thought that their brother ratings had given up was a bitter pill to swallow. Anger and disgust dominated their emotions, and the day passed with much bickering and tension. What had happened? Was the CO really telling the truth? By morning, they had worked themselves up into a blind fury. They would fight on, even if it meant fighting alone.

On Sunday, 24 February, well after the surrender in Bombay, the ratings of the *Akbar* were warned in no uncertain terms that if they did not come out for parade by 4 p.m., British military police would be called and force would be used to get them to the parade ground. Sullen and saddened at the news of the surrender, they still stood unified in defiance. They decided to defy orders and locked themselves into the barracks.

Shortly after the 4 p.m. deadline expired, the CO took a round of the barracks, peeping through the windows. He saw angry, determined faces. Seeing the mood of defiance, the CO, reluctant to move on his own, asked the British troops waiting some distance away to move in.

At 5 p.m. the troops made their move. Armed with rifles with fixed bayonets and light machine guns, they surrounded the barracks and asked the ratings to come out and surrender. Again, not a single rating moved. The guards loudly repeated the orders, but there was still no movement.

The British then entered the barracks and what followed was a cowardly, brutal, one-sided fight. Attacking unarmed ratings with bayonets, the British displayed the same brutality as on the streets of Bombay, when they had used tanks against unarmed civilians. The ratings at the HMIS *Akbar* showed the same level of heroic resistance. They were beaten but not broken.

Dragged to the parade ground by force, rebellion still remained on their minds. 'Do with us what you will but we will not yield,' was the silent but defiant message as each man sat on the ground and refused to march. The message was clear – they were not going to get up.

They heard the bugle being blown to signal the surrender ceremony, still not one rating moved. They also saw the guards carrying black flags of surrender to be handed to them. The ratings sensed their struggle was over but they were not going to give in easily. They knew by now that the NCSC had announced that they were surrendering to the people of India and not to British forces. For that reason, they were determined not to take the black surrender flags into their hands.

Again, the bugle was sounded but the ratings remained seated. Exasperated, the CO shouted orders, yet again, they ignored him. The CO then ordered the British soldiers to prepare to open fire. Even this threat made no dent in the defiance on display. The ratings made it clear they were ready to sacrifice their lives for the larger national cause.

The CO then gave the call for a bayonet charge. This time the ratings stood up but did not move an inch. The CO shouted, 'Fall in by the Division.' Again, there was complete silence and no movement from the ratings. He repeated the order three times in a thunderous voice, but to no avail.

Finally, the soldiers rushed in with bayonets fixed and… succeeded in separating the ratings by Division. A roll call was taken. Nearly 500 ratings stayed stubbornly silent. They were arrested on the spot and released the next morning. The strike was broken at the point of bayonets but the ratings refused to return to work.

The ratings were moved to the point of tears, many so overcome that they did not even talk. Their hearts were heavy and the atmosphere was one of gloom. The heroic struggle was over.

The CO tactfully declared the next day, 25 February, a holiday. But these brave men now knew it was just a matter of time before they were punished. They were alone, unarmed and helpless and they had failed. The euphoria of the last few days was forgotten as the men carried out their tasks mechanically, refusing to greet or even stop to talk to fellow ratings, something unheard of in naval life. Desperation and gloom pervaded the atmosphere. It was better not to think, better not to talk.

As the black flags fluttered over the *Akbar*, British War Secretary Philip Mason informed the Central Legislative Assembly that normal work had resumed. He deliberately omitted the fact that almost 400 ratings had been arrested.

On 24 February, twenty-two of the ringleaders of the *Akbar* were rounded up and taken to undisclosed locations. It was after these arrests that the resistance of the *Akbar* was finally broken.

HMIS *KATHIAWAR*: VOYAGE INTO HISTORY

In every conflict, many stories of heroes and heroism remain untold. The HMIS *Kathiawar* is one of those tales. *Kathiawar*, a minesweeper with a crew of about sixty, claimed the distinction of being the first RIN ship to be commanded by an Indian.

She embarked on a mission to come to the aid of her colleagues during the mutiny. The *Kathiawar* was docked in Morvi port, in Kathiawar on 22 February, when the ratings first heard of the RIN strike in Bombay.

Once all ratings were back on board after shore leave, they conducted discreet group meetings so as not to arouse suspicion, and decided a plan of action. While going about their normal work, they were receiving messages at regular intervals from HMIS *Narbada* and other ships.

At 10 a.m. on 22 February, the *Kathiawar* was ordered to set sail for Bombay. After receiving a flurry of signals from the ships in Bombay, the ratings aboard *Kathiawar* launched a lightning strike.

They were encouraged by a signal from HMIS *Hindustan* docked in Karachi saying she had received an ultimatum to surrender but she was going to fight. Another signal followed saying that fighting had broken out and that they were experiencing great difficulties, being isolated in Karachi harbour.

The *Kathiawar* strikers decided to rush to her aid. Anti-British slogans were painted on the bulkheads, along with photographs of national leaders while the captain of the ship, was called from the bridge by the ratings.

Facing angry, defiant faces, he asked what the ratings expected him to do. 'You must take the ship to Karachi!' shouted one. The captain kept his cool. 'I cannot accept your demands. Never in my entire career in the service have I disobeyed the orders of my superior officers. My orders are to proceed to Bombay and that is exactly what I am going to do.'

The ratings were undeterred. Their demand was clear: 'We want to go to Karachi! Our brothers are dying there. Do what you are told!' The captain quietly walked away.

In anger, the ratings pulled down the White Ensign, tore it up and threw it into the sea. Some rushed to the magazine to collect arms and ammunition. Others were shouting: 'Inquilab Zindabad!' and 'Jai Hind!' They went to the bridge and gave the captain an ultimatum, at gunpoint. 'Take us to Karachi or we take over complete control of the ship.'

The captain sensing the danger to his ship and personal life, said: 'It seems that you will go to Karachi in spite of what I might say. You are even determined to use physical force. Do what you like. But you shall have to face the consequences.' The ratings ignored the warning. Instead, they bluntly informed him: 'We now command HMIS *Kathiawar.*'

The captain ordered all the officers to join him in the wardroom. Once the captain departed, the ship's course was changed, and it headed for Karachi. The problem was at the current speed, it would take them at least 26 hours to reach Karachi. The ratings in the engine room were consulted and they decided to operate both engines at full power. The ship gathered speed. At her top speed of 16 knots per hour, they calculated that it would still take 16 to 17 hours to get to Karachi.

There was only one rating who knew navigation and he would have to be on the job for 16 hours at a stretch, given rough seas where the ship was pitching and rolling. Some ratings asked the captain to let them have the services of one of the officers to help with navigation. He agreed.

That officer, Lt Pal, addressed the ratings in Hindi, trying to convince that their decision was fruitless. He said, once they reached Karachi, they would be isolated and outgunned and asked them to return command of the ship to the captain. The ratings refused his help, and the rating who was navigating promised to get them to Karachi 'even if it means that I have to give my life for it'.

Then disaster struck. At 1 o'clock, they picked up the wireless signal sent by the *Hindustan to FOCRIN*, saying they had surrendered after a battle lasting 25 minutes. With British troops now in control of the ship, the situation had drastically changed. Anger was now replaced by an understanding of the new reality. The ratings decided it was pointless going to Karachi. Instead, they decided to proceed to Bombay to join their fellow ratings.

Since they were heading for their original destination, they felt there was no harm in returning the command to the captain for navigational purposes if he agreed to take the ship to Bombay. They approached the captain who agreed and the ship altered course and headed for Bombay.

On 23 February, as the *Kathiawar* neared Bombay, RN cruisers were patrolling the seas. No ships were being allowed to enter the harbour. The ratings collected weapons and ammunition and took up strategic positions. The gun-crews were asked to be ready for a battle. They were prepared to fight to join their comrades in Bombay.

The *Kathiawar* was ordered to anchor 15 nautical miles away from the lighthouse. The ratings told the captain to ignore the order. Seeing the armed ratings and their determination, he agreed to disobey the orders of his superiors.

As soon as *Kathiawar* moved towards Bombay harbour, the RIN cruiser, *Glasgow*, quickly closed in and turned her guns on her. The ratings of the *Kathiawar* trained their own guns on the *Glasgow*. This was audacity at its best. The *Kathiawar*, a Bangor-class minesweeper with one single 12-pounder, 3-inch anti-aircraft gun and one 2-pounder anti-aircraft gun was taking on a Town-class cruiser with sixteen 4-inch Bofors guns and sixteen powerful anti-aircraft guns.

The *Kathiawar* sped past the *Glasgow* and entered Bombay harbour at 10.30 a.m. *Glasgow* let her pass. 'On the bridge, along with the captain were a number of ratings. It was going to be a triumphant entry, the first India ship commanded by Indian ratings sailing into Bombay harbour,' wrote Subrata Banerjee in *The RIN Strike*.

Another account describes how the officers and the ratings of the *Glasgow* saluted as the minesweeper *Kathiawar* passed by. It was indeed a proud moment.

But this was when they saw the black flags of surrender and the White Ensigns on every ship. They realized they had reached too late. The surrender was complete. Some of them wanted to fight but it would have been suicidal. They reluctantly laid down their weapons and British troops boarded and took control. The strike was over and the *Kathiawar* had her place in history even if it was not the sort the ratings would have wanted.

REFERENCES

Admiral Godfrey's letters, NAI.

Andrew Davis, *Identity and Assemblage of Protest.*

B.C. Dutt, *Mutiny of the Innocents.* Bombay: Sindhu Publications, 1971, pp. 186–93.

Kusum Nair, *The Army of Occupation.* Delhi: Padma Publications, 1946, pp. 40–48, 49–56.

Lt. Cdr G.D. Sharma, VSM (Retd), *The Untold Story of Naval Mutiny: Last War of Independence.* Delhi: Vij Books, 2015.

Military and Aerospace, HMIS Hindustan - Disturbances Spreads.

The Indian Annual Register (January–June 1946), Vol. 1., pp. 235, 289–98, 301–07.

CITY EDITION

Dawn

Founded by MOHAMMAD ALI JINNAH

Edited by ALTAF HUSAIN

VOL. V NO. 53 — DELHI: FRI. FEB. 22, 1946. 19 RABI-UL-AWWAL, 1365 A.H. — PRICE 1½ ANS.

R.I.N 'REBELS' GUN DUELS WITH TROOPS

TRUCE AT BOMBAY FOLLOWS ADMIRAL'S ULTIMATUM

KARACHI SAILORS SHELL BRITISH SOLDIERS: ONE KILLED

SYMPATHETIC STRIKES IN CALCUTTA, MADRAS AND DELHI

DRAMATIC gun battles in which heavy artillery and tommy guns were used broke out on Thursday in Bombay and Karachi between "rebel" RIN ratings and British troops in which one British soldier was killed and many Indians and Britons were injured.

A broadcast warning from G.H.Q., New Delhi, late Thursday afternoon "that strong land, sea and air forces are on their way to Bombay, Poona and Karachi" was followed by the announcement of a truce in Bombay, but late last night the situation at Karachi, where the RIN ratings had fired 4" guns on British soldiers was stated to be serious.

At Madras, Calcutta and New Delhi RIN ratings came out in sympathetic strikes. Many were arrested.

The first indication of the grave turn the RIN strike had taken was an A.P.I. announcement at lunch time on Thursday that RIN "rebels" at Bombay are "returning the fire of British troops."

Later it was officially announced: "At 9 this morning the situation in Castle Barracks in Bombay and HMIS 'Talwar' was generally quiet. Men were on hunger-strike; inmates in Castle Barracks and HMIS 'Talwar' were broken into and most of the contents removed.

Sporadic Firing

"At 9:40 the situation deteriorated in the barracks. Ratings began to break out of the gate barricaded from inside and military guards on duty were compelled to open fire with single shots. The guards were stoned by the ratings and the guard commander was injured. Sporadic firing continued for about half an hour, which was returned by ratings who had obtained arms.

"At 10:30 military reinforcements had to be called in for assistance in Castle Barracks. At the same time a signal was intercepted from HMIS 'Narbada' stating that if any shots were fired by the military, all ships would open fire. She is also reported to have invited other ships on the local boiler boiling them by saying, 'all guns loaded. On the same boat if any, shots are fired from ashore open fire.'

"Men from the barracks are also reported to have gone abroad

Mutineers' Message

"A message was sent by mutineers to ships in stream directing all British officers to quit ships and asking Indian officers who wish to join the mutineers to do so.

By midnight the position according to A.P.I. was that while the "battle" had ended, the situation-down strike of the Indian naval ratings continued reading a declaration on the latest hours by the Naval authorities.

The gate of the Castle Barracks continues to be guarded by British troops.

Commanding Officer's Warning

MUSLIM LEAGUE WINS 53 PUNJAB SEATS

THIS MORNING'S NEWS FLASHES

THIS MORNING'S NEWS FLASHES

NEWS flashes early this morning from Bombay stated:

• The C-in-C has instructed Lt.-Gen. Lockhart to assume command of all forces in the Bombay area and to restore order in the RIN as rapidly as possible.

• Sardar Patel has issued an appeal to Bombay citizens not to observe a hartal today (Friday) but to get on with their normal business.

• A.P.I. reports that Sardar Patel has offered his services to the Governor of Bombay and the C-in-C to assist "in helping in a peaceful settlement of the dispute."

• Bombay police opened fire last night on a mob which was smashing windows in the Girgaum Road. Three people were hurt.

Unconfirmed reports put the casualties among the RIN and British troops at about 15 wounded. Three are British.

AT KARACHI

In Karachi, Mr. M. H. Gazdar, President of the Sind Provincial Muslim League went to the Keamari area, met the strikers and discussed their demands.

BENGAL ASSEMBLY

FOUR LEAGUERS RETURN UNOPPOSED

EIGHTEEN unopposed returns to the Bengal Legislative Assembly have been announced so far. Thursday evening according to an A.P.I. report.

These consist of seven Congress, four Muslim League, two Hindu Mahasabha and six European candidates.

INDIA OFFICE

BRITISH TROOPS FIRE ON CAIRO CROWDS

10 KILLED, 50 WOUNDED IN 'QUIT EGYPT' CLASHES

BRITISH troops at Kasr-El-Nil barracks in Cairo on Thursday afternoon fired on a huge crowd of demonstrators trying to force their way inside. Huge crowds swarmed Cairo streets blocking the traffic.

Outside Abdin, the King's residence, the demonstrators shouted expressions of loyalty to King Farouk and slogans such as "Out with the British."

Thousands also demonstrated outside the British Embassy demanding evacuation of British troops.

In Alexandria crowds beat up Europeans in the streets wounding some.

Demonstrators could be seen in Cairo on Thursday morning with suppressed ones stealing through the streets of huge buildings when Egyptian mobs raiding in a general strike called for student and labour union leaders to press the evacuation of British troops from the Nile Valley raised slogans against the largest British military barracks in the city.

Rifles and clashes spread all over the city and squadrons spray this afternoon on the first two seven-o'clock outbursts over 10 killed and over 50 injured.

Streets Cordoned off

On Thursday night Egyptian troops with armoured cars had cordoned off all streets leading to the Kasr-El-Nil (Prince of the Nile) barracks where an armed pitched battle raged throughout the morning and British soldiers inside the barracks were standing to arms in full battle order with more heavy armoured vehicles drawn up ready for action.

Earlier, British troops had opened fire when a huge crowd of demonstrators tried to force their way in.

Nawabzada Warns

CABINET MISSION WILL FAIL COMPLETELY UNLESS PAKISTAN IS CONCEDED

DELHI LEAGUE WORKERS RELEASED ON BAIL

All the 37 Muslim League and Conference workers arrested in connection with Rashid Ali Day observance have now been released on bail, says an A.P.I. report.

AZAD IN DELHI

The Congress President Maulana Abul Kalam Azad, arrived in Delhi on Thursday evening from Calcutta en route to Peshawar.

Maulana Azad is leaving for Peshawar on Saturday, February 23.—A.P.I.

The Hindustan Times

LARGEST CIRCULATION IN NORTHERN, NORTH-WESTERN & CENTRAL INDIA.

DELHI EDITION

VOL. XXIII. NO. 52 — NEW DELHI: FRIDAY, FEBRUARY 22, 1946 — PRICE 1½ ANNAS

INDIAN RATINGS MUTINY AT TWO CENTRES

HEAVY EXCHANGES OF FIRE WITH BRITISH TROOPS

ULTIMATUM BY KARACHI REBELS: "TRUCE" AT BOMBAY

STRIKERS STILL IN COMMAND OF SEVERAL SHIPS

C.-IN-C. RUSHES REINFORCEMENTS TO TROUBLE SPOTS

Mutinies by R.I.N. ratings in Bombay and Karachi assumed grave proportions on Thursday with the mutineers opening fire on military forces sent out to lay down under siege.

In Bombay a "cease fire" was called in the afternoon, but in Karachi ratings from H.M.I.S. Hindustan lying offshore sent out a signal at 3 p.m. giving the following ultimatum: "If our demands are not conceded by 6 p.m. today we will open fire on the military." Their chief demand was the withdrawal of the military.

Seven hours after the time of expiry of the ultimatum, there was still no news of any fresh developments in the situation. The "Hindustan" lies in the harbour with all her guns mounted.

In Bombay, beside the shore establishment at Castle Barracks, 20 R.I.N. ships, including Vice-Admiral flagship "Narbada" joined in the mutiny. In Karachi three ships and all the shore establishments with complements numbering over 1,500 men were involved.

Meanwhile, strong naval, military and air reinforcements are on their way to Bombay, Poona and Karachi, it is announced by the General Headquarters from New Delhi.

Karachi Situation Still Tense

KARACHI, Feb. 21.—Indian naval ratings of H.M.I.S. Chamak, Himalaya and Bahadur and all shore establishments numbering over 1,500 ...

6-Hour Battle In Bombay

BOMBAY, Feb. 21.—There was a 6-hour battle between mutinying ratings at the Castle Barracks and troops in the heart of Bombay ...

NAVAL C.-IN-C.'s WARNING

Govt. Will Not Brook Indiscipline

BOMBAY, Feb. 21.—The determination of the Government of India not to brook indiscipline in the ranks of the service and never to give in to violence was expressed in the ranks of the Royal Indian Navy by Vice-Admiral Godfrey, Flag Officer Commanding, Royal Indian Navy, in a broadcast to the ratings from the Bombay station today.

Vice-Admiral Godfrey warned the ratings: "It can never be stronger than the feeling of just, when you take it in to assume the overwhelming forces at the disposal of the Government at this time are being used to their utmost even if it means the restoration of the Navy of which we have been so proud.

"In the gravest charitable state of indiscipline in the service, I have adopted this means of addressing the R.I.N. as being the way in which I can speak to the greatest number of you at one time.

"No man, with everyone of you must realise that the Government of India has no intention of allowing indiscipline a continuance or time or right to be reinstated to such a discipline. The Government will take the most stringent methods to put the discipline, using the vast forces at its disposal if necessary. I ask and in time this is trained nucleus of realise the what ships which I have to ask in your crew.

Redress of Grievances

"As regards the requests made by those of you who walked the Service Officer, Bombay, on Tuesday, February 19, you may be assured that all reasonable complaints or grievances, if any, will be fully investigated. Demobilisation will proceed strictly in accord with the age and service grades, though you must realise that this will mean that the service will lose its trained nucleus of experienced ratings, especially in the Communication branch.

"As regards questions as to pay, travelling allowances, and family allowances a new being examined by an Inter-Service Committee. This Committee has just been asked in the effort and has been waiting establishments in Karachi, Vizagram and Bombay. The views submitted in Bombay this morning both afloat and ashore is determine a state of mind ..."

ATTLEE ORDERS WARSHIPS TO INDIAN PORTS

LONDON, Feb. 21.—Certain vessels of the Royal Navy are proceeding towards Bombay, said Mr. D. R. Attlee, Prime Minister, in the House of Commons today after Mr. Sorensen asked Stewart (Lab. Nat.) had moved adjournment of the House on a matter of urgent public importance namely, the grave extension of mutiny among a section of the Royal Indian Navy ...

RUSSIA ADMITS RECEIPT OF SECRET ATOM INFORMATION

'IN CAMERA' INVESTIGATION INTO LEAKAGES

LONDON, Feb. 21.—Russia acknowledged in an official statement broadcast by Moscow Radio last night that Canadian citizens had given "some information of a confidential character" to the Soviet Military Attache in Ottawa.

The information, the broadcast stated, "could be found in the published works concerning radio location, etc., and also in the well-known American pamphlet 'Atomic Energy.'

The Soviet Government was considered it necessary to make the statement because the Canadian Government had raised a question on February 15.

The statement said, however, that the information was "not required by the Soviet Government in view of higher technical achievements in the matter of the Soviet Republics."

The broadcast added that the Soviet Vice-Commander of Foreign Affairs had handed to the Canadian representative in Moscow, Mr. L. Wilgress, the official Soviet Government's answer.

Mr. Mackenzie King's declaration of February 18 on the leakage of secret information.

For Gusenko, a Russian formerly employee, who is today preventive custody were in the investigation opposed to the Press had asked to leak of his life since he gave information today.

A former reporter at the Morning Journal, Miss Kathleen Fraser, said yesterday two Russians with his wife and their agent was the office of the newspaper—a desperate—saying there were things going on that could lead to arrest and you get superior and pointed out that he disappeared. He said he saw that his disappearance and denied but the Russian Government denied and ignored his aspects.

CANADA CONSULTING BRITAIN

OTTAWA, Feb. 21.—The Prime Minister, Mr. MacKenzie King, said the dominion Foreign Minister was reported to be in steady consultation with the British remote question while some reports of the Russian declaration on the espionage incident had reached Canada.

Ministries Not To Brook Interference From Governors

—MAULANA

CALCUTTA, Feb. 21.—"If there are any differences between Ministers and the Governor, it will the Governor and not the Minister who will have to resign," said Maulana Abul Kalam Azad, the Congress President, defining the attitude towards any possible interference from Governors where Congress ministries are being formed.

Maulana Azad said: "Now Congress Ministry has taken over in Assam, and will soon do so in provinces. I have been giving an assurance of non-interference from Governors. Those who raise questions remember that such questions were considered and dropped in 1937, but they do not in 1946 and 1937. The interference ...

CAVEESHAR'S RELEASE ORDERED

The Government of India ordered the release of Sardar Sardul Singh Caveeshar, who is detained at Dharamsala.

CANADA...

15

KARACHI: UNITY NOT MUTINY

When the news of the Bombay naval mutiny reached Karachi on 19 February 1946, it spread like wildfire. Over the next four days, unrest engulfed the city. The ratings mutinied, taking over a warship in the port, and at least three shore establishments. There were also massive public demonstrations in support of the ratings.

Karachi was the first port of call for British warships coming from Suez and, after Bombay, it was the second-most important naval base for control of the Arabian Sea and the Indian Ocean. It was home to some 2,000 officers and ratings during those fateful five days. The loss of that base would have dealt a death blow to the British Empire's prestige.

Along with its strategic importance, the political importance of Karachi in the freedom movement could not be overestimated. It was a combustible situation. British colonial administrators were loath to run the risk of mutinous ratings and politically aware civilians led by the Communists joining hands, and giving new meaning and purpose to the movement.

The British played a clever game to corral the politicians of Karachi. The Congress Party and the Muslim League were prepping for Independence and it didn't take much to dissuade them from giving their full support to the naval mutiny. The Communists were lone fliers and isolated in Karachi, and their leadership was quickly neutralized.

But the leaderless ratings proved harder to contain. Their mutiny had to be put down at any cost. Their actions inspired a spontaneous series of demonstrations by civilians. Over the four tumultuous days of the Karachi mutiny, the action shifted from ship to shore, and shore to ship in a dynamic and constantly changing pattern.

The British naval authorities took pre-emptive action to prevent the ratings from marching out of the port and into the wider environs of the city. The Napier Road Bridge connecting the port's Keamari jetty with Karachi city and its teeming, politically aware population was sealed by the British army. This effectively penned the mutineers in the port.

The military action was thus limited to the harbour basin, with its mostly enclosed breakwater architecture, densely populated working-class neighbourhoods, and treacherous low tides. This enabled the British to contain the uprising, and ultimately, it proved the undoing of the ratings.

There was a single warship at the port, an ageing 1,200-tonne sloop called HMIS *Hindustan* with two 4-inch guns, possibly Bofors, and Oerlikon 20 mm anti-aircraft cannons. It was commanded by Lt D. Rosser and it had a crew of 120. The *Hindustan* was where the mutineers made their last stand, only to find themselves finally outmanoeuvred and outgunned in a fierce ship-to-shore engagement lasting all of twenty-five minutes. It was these twenty-five minutes, however, which led to serious tremors in the British Empire which had already been shaken by the widespread mutiny.

Hindustan's companion was a trawler, HMIS *Travancore*, commanded by an Indian, T/Lt S.M. Singh. However, while the ratings from the *Travancore* were involved in the battle for the *Hindustan*, the ship itself remained peripheral to the action.

The Karachi shore establishments played geographically scattered, but undeniably critical roles in the mutiny. Ratings from

The HMIS Hindustan, *docked in Karachi, had an intense exchange of artillery fire, which resulted in the heaviest casualties on any ship during the mutiny.*

the shore establishments also sacrificed their lives fighting on the *Hindustan.*

The RIN shore establishments were located in and around Karachi port and in Manora peninsula, south of the wharfs, across a 2.5 kilometre stretch of harbour water. Of these establishments, three are worthy of special mention. These are the HMIS *Bahadur* that trained senior boys, the gunnery school HMIS *Himalaya*, and the radar school HMIS *Chamak.*

Chamak was under the command of the popular Lt Adhar Kumar Chatterji who would become India's first full admiral; *Bahadur* had K.R.U. Todd as commanding officer; and Commander A.W. Gush headed *Himalaya.*

The spark was lit in Karachi when the news of the Bombay mutiny reached the *Chamak* radar school on 19 February. The rest is history. While actual numbers remain uncertain, twenty ratings officially died during the mutiny, while the rumoured toll is twice as high, with several scores injured. Their largely unsung story of heroism and sacrifice unfolded as follows:

TUESDAY, 19 FEBRUARY 1946
Chamak

The news of the Bombay mutiny arrived at *Chamak* on the forenoon, and it spread to the ships and shore establishments. On one of his three precautionary inspections, M.R.A. Rao, *Chamak*'s acting executive officer and radar control training officer, found Anil Kumar Roy O/Tel (SS) in a hushed and agitated conference with other ratings.

At lunch break, the *Chamak* chapter of the sailors' association, formed just two days before to raise funds for the INA, decided on an evening sea beach meeting of all mutiny supporters.

Here, there was a consensus for a march onto Karachi city at 10 a.m. the following morning, with requests for the participation of Congress and Muslim League politicians and dock workers; hunger strikes; and work abstention for the duration of the mutiny.

By evening, officers and ratings in every naval facility in Karachi were discussing the Bombay *Talwar* mutiny in animated groups. Meanwhile, the commander of the *Himalaya*, Gush, sent an alert to the Sind governor's office and one of his aides made direct contact with the police. This alert may have prompted the decision to seal off the port.

Following urgent consultations with Gush about the building tensions in *Chamak*, Chatterji was tasked to pacify the ratings on the morrow.

WEDNESDAY, 20 FEBRUARY 1946

Chamak

As agreed between Gush of the *Himalaya* and Chatterji, the *Chamak* commander summoned his ratings at 9 a.m. Calling the Bombay mutiny local and unrelated to Karachi, Chatterji argued that the demand for an Indian CO in view of Commander King's attitude scarcely applied here. Implicitly referring to himself as an Indian CO who was far from abusive, he reasoned the ratings had no grounds to mutiny and indeed should admire the RIN as a proud force with a tradition of discipline.

Leaving the meeting, the ratings were uniformly unimpressed. Contrary to the assumption, they *had* complaints. The Bombay action was severe and impossible to ignore. There was no dissent about supporting the mutiny among themselves, and many possible courses of action were discussed.

It was, however, a half confirmed news that hastened the mutiny. According to the report submitted by Chatterji: 'Towards the evening an alarming rumour was going around *Himalaya* and *Chamak* to the effect that about seventy ratings from *Hindustan* and all the ratings from *Monze* (a local naval defence base) had struck and that they were taking a procession through the city… It is sincerely felt that this rumour was the immediate cause of the mutiny next day.'

Hindustan

There was a growing dissonance between Captain D. Rosser and his mutinous crew. When the ratings arrived on the bridge of the *Hindustan* and presented their demands, Rosser irritably ordered them to 'Go back to work now.'

When they surrounded him instead, urging fair treatment and the removal of a lieutenant in the racist mould of King, he baulked and asked them to present their demands 'in a civilised fashion'.

Seeing a no-win situation, the ratings warned that the *Hindustan* would not sail on the morning as scheduled, if their conditions were not met. Armed British officers would have been impossible to deal with at sea. Taking over the ship in the harbour was their sole option.

Chamak

As the *Hindustan* battled with the threat of immobilization, ratings from the *Himalaya* and another shore establishment, *Bahadur*, reached *Chamak* for a 9 p.m. meeting. The consensus was for a peaceful strike with the date and time left open. These open-ended plans were swiftly finalized in a further clandestine conference near midnight, when it was decided to stage a morning strike at the docks to prevent the sailing of *Hindustan*. Local civilian support, possibly with political backing, was expected and anticipated.

Communists at Bunder Road

While the Congress and Muslim League vacillated, the Communists had the conviction and resolve to back the mutineers after hearing of the horrors of Bombay. Many luminaries gathered at the CPI party offices at Bunder Road, northwest of Karachi port.

Inder K. Gujral, a future prime minister of India, the veteran Hindi film actor, A.K. Hangal, and Sindhi idealogues such as Sobho Gianchandani, Ainshi Vidyarthi, Jamaluddin Bukhari and Asif Karvani decided on a rally to announce a general strike for the morrow, 21 February. A rally was addressed by Hangal, Karvani and Gianchandani with a closing by the veteran Qazi Mohammed Mujtaba from a stretcher.

But the Communist leadership was rounded up and arrested late at night and locked up at the Sadar Police Station. They couldn't have known until later, that there had been an electric reaction to their rally and subsequent arrests. The following morning, the city of Karachi responded with a complete *hartal*.

Travancore

The situation on the trawler, *Travancore*, was comparatively peaceful and it was surprisingly insulated from the ferment raging around it. Few on board favoured aggressive support for the mutiny and any protest there would be orderly.

Significantly, at 3.25 in the afternoon of 20 February, *Travancore* left the Karachi wharfs, and awaited *Hindustan,* which was also scheduled to steam out to sea. Since some ratings had ignored duty summons, *Travancore's* prudent captain, S.M. Singh, called them all to a meeting at 9 p.m., and directed them to file a peaceful registration of complaints.

Taking no chances, the likely troublemakers and ringleaders were ordered down to the engine room below deck and other guarded spaces, while officers took stations on the deck.

It was an anxious and largely sleepless night for the ratings stationed in various establishments across the seething expanse of Karachi port.

.

THURSDAY, 21 FEBRUARY 1946
Karachi city

In the city of Karachi, there was civil mobilization in support of the mutiny. Credit for this should go to the Communists. As fit retribution for locking up their leaders, Karachi city was shut down totally by Communist sympathizers. This *hartal* included all commercial establishments and transport. At the Eidgah Maidan protest headquarters set up by the Communist Party, the flags of the CPI, the Muslim League, and Congress were flown.

'At about 10 (in the morning),' writes Aslam Khwaja in *Mainstream*, 'workers of the west wharf… and (from) dockyards, trams, buses and different factories… began reaching Eidgah Maidan, where police and military failed to stop the people pouring from Saeed Manzil to Dow Medical College and D.J. College to Ranchore Lane.'

Mahmood Haroon of the Muslim League, and Dr Tarachand and Swami Krishna of the Congress pleaded on behalf of the authorities for people to leave. But people asked them to join the *hartal*. As the situation became more fraught, the respected founder of modern Karachi, Jamshed Mehta, broadcast the chief minister of Sindh, Sir Ghulam Hussain Hidayatullah's appeal for dispersal but he returned empty-handed. Buoyed by the successful *hartal*, the Communist Party held a public meeting in the evening where Relaram Lilaran, Sheikh Ayaz and other leaders recited revolutionary poetry.

Hindustan and *Travancore*

There were also the makings of half-victories on the warship *Hindustan,* and the companion *Travancore*. Just when the ships were preparing to sail at 5 p.m. on new orders from naval headquarters, eleven *Hindustan* ratings broke suddenly for shore, shouting slogans.

They were joined by others over the next two hours. Having heard their grievances beyond his rank to settle, Captain Rosser went ashore with two ratings to consult the naval officer in-charge but discovered him missing.

Hoping to consult his superior on the *Himalaya*, he said he had to return '…three hundred yards off the jetty (since) it was obvious that *Himalaya* was in a state of mutiny…' Back in *Hindustan* and giving immediate orders to steam out to sea, Rosser encountered a mob on the jetty, which asked the ship's company to join them.

'A boat was now seen to be approaching from *Himalaya* packed with mutineers,' says Rosser in his account of the mutiny. '…as the boat came closer to my starboard quarter, it was noticed that it was flanked by two boat loads of armed soldiers…'

To protect themselves, the *Himalaya* ratings sped to shore. 'At this point,' says Rosser, 'an army officer in the bows of the motor boat which was under *Hindustan* stern opened fire with a sten-gun over the heads of the crowd on the gangway…' Eventually on Rosser's order, the officer ceased firing, but the incident spurred ratings from *Bahadur* (missing in Rosser's account) and *Himalaya* to board *Hindustan*, smash the locks of the midship Oerlikon guns, and load them.

'By the time they opened fire,' says Rosser, 'both army boats had vanished and they had to content themselves by firing into the direction of BOAC aircraft parked nearby.'

Running out of options, Rosser ordered all Oerlikon magazines to be thrown overboard, boilers shut, officers disembarked and dispersed, and charged the first officer to inform naval authorities. But unfortunately, *Hindustan* was dead in the water.

Travancore awoke mutinous to the new sailing orders. At 6 a.m., most of the ratings failed to respond to the reveille pipe. 'After some time the strikers dressed and having equipped themselves with hockey sticks attempted to haul down the RIN Jack and the ensign, but were prevented from doing so,' says Commanding Officer S.M. Singh.

At about 9 a.m., thirty-four *Travancore* ratings left the ship without permission to join the struggle on the *Hindustan*. More resolved to leave ship the next day. The captain then ordered all ratings' lockers emptied and ammunitions secured in magazines. Peace returned, but it was tenuous.

Army Vs *Hindustan*

Intimated about Rosser's imminent loss of command of *Hindustan* and sensing trouble in general, the British ordered army intervention, only to be rudely surprised. In solidarity with the ratings, the first- and second-choice soldiers of the Baluch Regiment, and the Gurkha 2nd Battalion of the Indian Parachute Brigade, flatly refused to storm the vessel. Finally, two platoons of the Scots Black Watch Regiment moved to the jetty alongside the *Hindustan* to confront its mutinous crew of 600 ratings massed in the creaky warship anchored across from Karachi's naval establishments.

The platoons' action signal was to be a shot from Captain Rosser's sidearm fired into the air, which he duly carried out as he was forced down the gangplank, with loss of command and face. Most of the officers left – only the ship's doctor remained on board with the ratings. The platoons readied for action. But up went a banner in large letters on the deck reading, 'IF YOU WANT TO SAVE YOUR LIVES, DO NOT COME UP.'

Pausing just long enough to gauge the resistance, they opened fire on the ship with light machine guns, only to encounter return fire. From the roof of the Embarkation Headquarters nearby behind sand bags, a new assault killed two ratings, one a boy of sixteen. Drawn by the fire-fight, dock workers gathered, and they counted ten minutes of 4-inch ship–shore gun salvoes that shook the harbour. Seeing the British retire, the longshoremen cheered.

Bahadur

Some hours earlier, shortly after breakfast and about the same time as the Karachi *hartal* took effect, the *Bahadur* ratings heard of the strikes in *Himalaya* and *Chamak* and made their own demands. Shouting slogans at the parade ground, they sought the removal of the racist *Hindustan* lieutenant and mirrored the Bombay mutineers' complaints of inedible canteen food, including mouldy rotis.

Bringing down the White Ensign and burning it while repelling an executive officer's attempts to save it, they hoisted the flags of Congress, Muslim League and Communists in its place. Rushing to release prisoners, they destroyed punishment records.

As they marched towards *Chamak*, the British flag at the *High Angle School*, another establishment, was desecrated. The guards there joined them. They smashed shop windows, before police pickets halted their progress between *Chamak* and *Himalaya*. Flanking off towards the jetty, British patrols around Keamari barred anybody from the ships going ashore. From his vantage position in *Bahadur*'s signal tower, K.R.U. Todd, the commanding officer, knew the score. The *Hindustan* was under attack but giving back as good as she got.

Himalaya

At the *Himalaya*, there was a more muted repetition of *Bahadur*'s dissent. Some 400 ratings, who had been unable to convince Commander Gush, (post his 9 a.m. address), to sanction better-class rail travel, nicer uniforms and comparable pay-scales to the Royal Navy, went on a rampage smashing cells and glass windows and damaging vehicles. They lowered and destroyed a quarter-deck ensign, hoisted a 'Jai Hind' flag, and set off for *Chamak* with Gush in pursuit entreating their return. The grimness of the situation was suddenly brought home on all sides, when automatic fire was heard in Keamari coupled with the booming of 4-inch guns.

Chamak

Nor was there peace at *Chamak*. The ratings there had also refused to rise to reveille. A British officer's *Diary of Events of Mutiny* records their paper slogans on pillars and posts saying, '…This is not Mutiny but unity… Quit India… We are Indian National Navy… Jai Hind.'

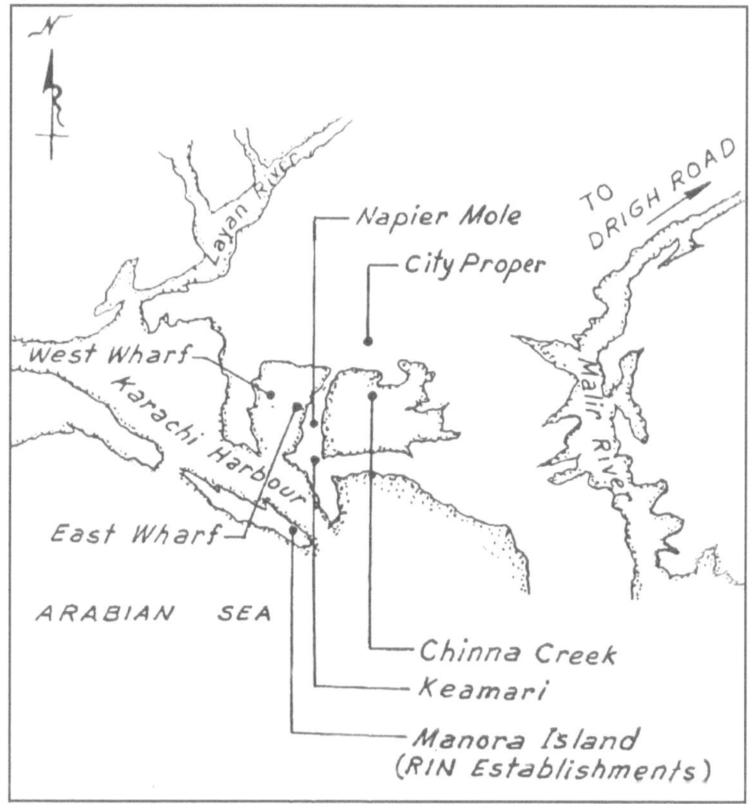

A line map of Karachi harbour and islands, 1946.

After an hour-long secret meeting with the *Himalaya* ratings, they marched to the parade ground with grievances. Encountering a party of *Bahadur* ratings armed with sticks who wanted to destroy the *Chamak* radars, establishment loyalties were suddenly aroused.

The mutineer-turned writer, Subrata Banerjee, recounts a plea from one of the *Chamak* ratings: 'Do not destroy this costly equipment. It is all ours, when we throw out these hated foreigners…This will be of use to us.'

Having safeguarded *Chamak's* interests in this way from their comrades, the ratings of *Chamak*, *Bahadur* and *Himalaya* decided to flood Karachi with peaceful protests and to simultaneously undertake the more hazardous mission of boosting the *Hindustan* defence with numbers. While the putative Karachi protesters took the circuitous causeway from Manora, 400 ratings set off for *Himalaya* and another 200 for *Bahadur* to attempt boat crossings to *Hindustan* for a last stand.

Stopped by police before Karachi city on the Bolton Market road, the first set of ratings returned to base and demanded the withdrawal of British troops. In reaching *Hindustan* by any means, including a sailboat and holding off the British army at least for the day, the second batch of ratings succeeded to a greater degree than anticipated.

ARMY AGAINST RATINGS

Having determined from *Hindustan*'s fiery resistance that the mutineers were no pushovers, the British authorities held midnight conferences involving local naval and army authorities. All arms potentially within reach of the mutineers was removed on instructions, except for the unmovable heavy guns. The men of the 23 and 159 regiments of the British Army and the Royal Artillery were called out and 25 pounders, 3-inch mortars and 75 mm guns were placed in strategic positions around the cordoned-off wharf.

Concurrently, paratroopers were deployed to guard Indian and British officer families; the High Angle School on Manora, which contained a variety of weapons in its armoury was occupied by soldiers; and closer to the hotspot of the *Hindustan*, the Embarkation Headquarters was sanitised for operations.

Neither side slept that night. As they had feared, a quick check by authorities showed that only a third of ratings were at their stations. Apart from taking heart from the defence of Bombay's Castle Barracks, the ratings had also received radio messages from their flagship *Narbada,* which had been seized by the Bombay mutineers, to resist if attacked, and not yield. They knew their backs were to the wall, having heard Admiral Godfrey's threats to destroy the navy if necessary, loud and clear.

FRIDAY, 22 FEBRUARY
Army Vs *Hindustan*

Clearly seeing *Hindustan* as the greatest threat in the Karachi mutiny, authorities isolated it in port and ring-fenced the shore establishments of *Chamak*, *Himalaya* and *Bahadur* with guards so their ratings couldn't make the boat runs from Manora to the warship's defence like they had on the previous day. Guards on establishments remained for eighteen days, well after the mutiny was quelled, in what amounted to a virtual arrest of all ratings.

With the Manora threat addressed and boarding *Hindustan* one last time at 8 a.m., Captain Rosser told mutineers that Karachi's naval in-charge, Commodore Curtis, would hear their grievances in half-an-hour, provided two representative ratings convinced him that these were just.

When they refused, Curtis arrived, and warned of army action, should the mutineers not surrender by 9 a.m. At the hour, two ratings gave up and Rosser's account suggests several others were either prevented from following suit, or persuaded to stay and fight.

Around 9.20 a.m., Rosser turned down the suggestion by Indian officers of seeking local Congress intervention for the mutineers' surrender since it was counter to army orders. As he handed a written ultimatum at the jetty to a rating and telegraphist from the ship, the mutineers took the high ground that they wouldn't be the first to fire.

Showing no such compunction, the officer commanding tasked to clear the *Hindustan* of mutineers, Brigade Major P.R.B. Mitchell, wired a brusque note to them warning of action five minutes after its receipt: 'You are hereby informed that unless you surrender unconditionally leave your weapons on board ship and march off under white flag, I shall shoot anybody who appears

A P P E N D I X 3B

To: HINDUSTAN

From: OC Troops.

You are hereby informed that unless you surrender unconditionally
leave your weapons on board ship and march off under white
flag, I shall shoot anybody who appears above deck unless he
has a white flag stop this order will come into effect
five minutes after receipt.

Certified true copy   Sd/ P. R. B. Mitchell
                                       Maj. B. M.
Malir Cantt. 22 Mar.46

Facsimile of Brigade Major P.R.B. Mitchell's curt and final warning to the mutineers aboard Hindustan *to surrender.*

above deck unless he has a white flag This order will come into effect five minutes after receipt.'

The die was cast. The action that followed was mercifully short but it would be brutal and bloody.

An ebb tide meant *Hindustan* was low in the water by 10.30 a.m., making it vulnerable to shooting from heights. Given this advantage, the British troops trained heavy machine guns and mortars on the exposed ratings, wounding five of them. The ships' guns could not be elevated sufficiently to retaliate because of the low tide. Also, if their shots went wide, there was a danger of causing death and destruction to the working-class neighbourhood of Keamari.

Even so, according to an official report, during the twenty-five minutes the *Hindustan* was under fire, it struck back by firing twenty-four rounds, sending a general and his staff scurrying to the nearest trenches, and forcing Captain Rosser to take refuge in the safety of a telephone booth.

More than this the mutineers couldn't do, showing the white flag at 11 a.m. This was after an exchange of fire left six ratings, all below twenty-four, dead and thirty wounded, according to the official account.

It was particularly heartbreaking when a teen with a white flag on a bridge was blown to pieces by a 75 mm shell. Full of guilt, remorse and shame and even tearful, British gunners were overheard saying, 'What a heroic resistance… dirty job we had. Why…blow up that little boy? …shameful.'

Taking control of *Hindustan,* finally the army arrested the leaders and removed them to prison cages in Malir camp that afternoon. By 9.30 p.m., all the ship's arms were secured in the captain's bungalow.

According to the official identification of the dead, two were *Bahadur* ratings, one each from *Hindustan, Travancore* and *Chamak,* and three belonged to the *Himalaya.* The unofficial toll was much higher, with the ratings claiming it was at least twice as high.

23 FEBRUARY

The trawler *Travancore,* which had escaped the fighting, steamed back into harbour at 8.30 a.m. Its crew had suffered losses, however, as quite a few of them had gone over to the *Hindustan,* they survived. One rating had died in the combat, three were injured, and twenty-four others were taken prisoners.

The warship at the centre of the Karachi mutiny, *Hindustan* itself, was virtually crippled. Inspections revealed significant damage to hull and main and auxiliary engines; two upper-deck fires; vandalization of cabins, living spaces and store rooms; and destruction of naval files, papers and objection statements.

Before going into oblivion for losing command of a ship,

Captain D. Rosser registered officially that sixty-six ratings were removed to the Malir prison cages that afternoon. As diehard patriots, they did not break under harsh incarceration. In torn paper notes that surfaced later, they said, '… the spirit of freedom cannot be suppressed by… prisons… If we die, we die for our country…'

Unlike the prisoners, the dead were denied the glory of precision, leaving some unaccounted for. Reconciling official and rumoured numbers, it is suggested twenty ratings were killed, and nearly a hundred wounded in those four days. Although the representatives of the Karachi mutineers were allowed to witness the last rites of martyred Hindu, Muslim and Sikh ratings, their faces, writes *Mainstream*'s Khwaja, 'were not shown to their comrades'.

After the surrender of Bombay and the storming of the *Hindustan* in Karachi, mutinous ratings elsewhere also surrendered. Despite lacking political support, they had braved the empire's military might, and shaken it. The public, at least those who read newspapers, knew of the sacrifices these brave young seamen had made.

Although the reporting was circumspect, the *Times of India* of 21 February admitted that '(*Hindustan*'s) departure had to be postponed as all… five wireless operators of the ship are among the strikers… (who) want immediate transfer of… officers who… insulted them…'

The *Statesman*'s front page of 22 February let the cat out of the bag with its headline, 'RIN Ratings Return Fire With Naval Guns…' The *Free Press Journal* spoke of 'Flags at Half Mast in Memory of Fallen Comrades'. And, the *Dawn* said of its founder that '(Mohammed Ali) Jinnah To Take Up RIN Case to Viceroy, He Will See To It That Justice Is Done to Ratings'. Britain's *Gloucestershire Echo* published 'Unconfirmed reports… that 30 Indian ratings were killed, and 64 injured in this action', which may have been closer to the truth.

So the mutiny was suppressed, and the lack of support from the two major political parties sapped the spread of information and its penetration to the masses. Nevertheless, in terms of open resistance to empire and the British military, it retains a salience alongside the exploits of freedom fighters like Bhagat Singh, Sukhdev, and Rajguru. In its way, it handsomely complements the non-violent independence movement of Mahatma Gandhi.

REFERENCES

Aslam Khwaja, 'Role of Karachi in the 1946 Naval Rebellion', 9 March 2016, *Mainstream*.

B.C. Dutt, *Mutiny of the Innocents*. Bombay: Sindhu Publications, 1971, pp. 151–85.

Dilip Kumar Das, *Revisiting Talwar; A study in the Royal Indian Navy Uprising of February 1946*. Delhi: Ajanta Publications, 1993, pp. 234–370.

Kusum Nair, *The Army of Occupation*. Delhi: Padma Publications, 1946.

Lockhart-RIN Mutiny; Hour by hour event description, NAI.

Lt. Cdr. G.D. Sharma, VSM (Retd), *The Untold Story of Naval Mutiny: Last War of Independence*. Delhi: Vij Books, 2015.

Memoranda for Board of Enquiry Commission by Sub. Lieut. M.M. Qasin, RINVR., NAI.

Ratnakar Sadasyula, 'The Forgotten Naval Mutiny of 1946 and India's Independence', 19 February 2016, *Swarajya Magazine*.

Report from the Commanding Officer, HMIS *Chamak* dated 1 March 1946, No RD/663, To The Naval Officer In-Charge, Karachi, NAI.

Report from the Commanding Officer, HMIS *Travancore* dated 2 March. 1946. No 5A46/EX To the Flag Officer, Bombay, NAI.

Report from Executive Officer HMIS *Bahadur* dated 23 February 1946. RIN/1/14 London. To The Commanding Officer *Bahadur*. London.

Subrata Banerjee, *The RIN Strike*. Bombay: People's Publishing House, 1981.

The Indian Annual Register (January–June 1946), Vol.1., pp. 235, 289–98, 301–07.

https://www.indiannavy.nic.in/sites/default/themes/indiannavy/images/pdf/chapter1.pdf

RIN. INQUIRY COMMISSION.

HELD FIRST SITTING IN NEW DELHI ON THURSDAY 18th APRIL 1946

CHAIRMAN. The Hon. Sir Saiyid Fazal Ali.
  CHIEF JUSTICE, PATNA HIGH COURT.

JUDICAL MEMBERS.
  Mr. Justice K. S. Krishnaswami Ayyangar,
  CHIEF JUSTICE COCHIN STATE.
  Mr. Justice Mahjan
    JUDGE LAHORE HIGH COURT.

SERVICE MEMBERS.
  Vice-Admiral W. R. Patterson. For. Cruisers
    EAST INDIES FLEET.
  Major-General T. W. Ress. Indian Army
    Commanding 4th Indian Div.

SECRETARY. — Lt. Col. Vishebhar Nauth Singh.
    INDIAN ARMY.

COMMISSION CONCLUDED SITTING IN DELHI — Sat 27th April 1946.
OPENED SITTINGS IN BOMBAY THURS. 2nd May 1946.

A Commission of Enquiry was appointed in March 1946 to look into the causes and origin of the mutiny. With Sir Sayyid Fazl Ali as chairman, other members of the commission were Justice K.S. Krishnaswami Iyengar, Justice Meher Chand Mahajan, Vice Admiral W.R. Patterson, and Major-General T.W. Rees.

16

THE COMMISSION OF ENQUIRY

Two months after the surrender, a Commission of Enquiry was announced. This turned out to be just a smokescreen for displaying the so-called British sense of fair play and an attempt to cool the political temperature. It served more as a political tool than a judicial enquiry.

The mutiny was discussed in the Central Legislative Assembly on 22 and 23 February and by the Defence Consultative Committee on 8 March 1946. The navy had already appointed boards of enquiry to study the events at every individual establishment and ship in detail.

At this 8 March meeting the C-in-C of Indian armed forces, Claude Auchinleck, announced that he would recommend that the Government of India appoint a commission to enquire into the causes and origin of the mutiny.

Following this, an announcement was made by the Government of India in early April. 'The Central government has been pleased to appoint a commission of enquiry to enquire into and report on the causes and origin of the recent mutinies in the Royal Indian Navy in February 1946.'

The Commission of Enquiry would have as chairman, the

Honourable Sir Sayyid Fazl Ali, chief justice of the Patna High Court (Judge, Supreme Court of India [1951–52], later Governor of Orissa [1952–56], and Assam [1956–59]). The judicial members were Justice K.S. Krishnaswami Iyengar (chief justice, Cochin State), and Justice Meher Chand Mahajan (Chief Justice, Supreme Court of India, January 1954 to December 1954; prime minister Jammu and Kashmir [1947–48]; judge, Lahore High Court). The service members were Vice Admiral W.R. Patterson, Flag Officer Commanding, Cruiser Squadron in the East Indies Fleet and Major-General T.W. Rees, Indian Army, commanding the 4th Indian Division.

The secretary to the commission was Lt Col Visheshar Nauth Singh. Sardar Patel and Aruna Asaf Ali asked the well-known Bombay lawyer, Purshottam Tricumdas, president of the Ex-Services Association, to appear on behalf of the Congress Defence Committee.

It was decided that the proceedings would be public, unless the chairman decided that it was in public interest to hold some part *in camera*. A total of 229 witnesses were examined, and a large number of official documents were studied.

At Bombay and Karachi, members of the commission visited a number of naval establishments and ships to see their galleys and mess decks. They even tasted the food served to the ratings.

The commission held its first sitting on 18 April 1946 in Delhi. Its first witness was Lt Col. Malik Haq Nawaz of the Morale Directorate at the General HQ. He deposed that he saw seeds of unrest in December 1945, when he enquired into the state of morale of the officers and ratings in Bombay and Karachi. Along with Col A.A. Rudra, security liaison officer, who was the second witness, Nawaz admitted that racial discrimination and political awakening were the primary causes.

The proceedings of the committee were, like the INA trials, open to the public, but it turned out to be a prosaic affair by comparison to the dramatic INA trials. The commission concluded its sitting in

Delhi on Saturday, 27 April. It moved to Bombay on the 2nd of May, where it sat on the third floor of the Bombay High Court.

The witnesses included the FOCRIN, Admiral J.H. Godfrey, who was examined on 22 April 1946. He was memorably pulled up by Justice Sayyid Fazl Ali when he contended, 'But in this country where there is nothing like public opinion, not one word has been raised against this (ratings' complaint of bad food)'. Hearing this, Justice Fazl Ali replied sharply, 'I consider the statement made by you ill advised. Aren't you prepared to revise your opinion?' The admiral apologized.

Speaking about the causes of the mutiny itself, Admiral Godfrey contended that left-wing Congressmen and Communists had considerable influence on the RIN ratings and this, along with the strong political spirit among many of the ratings, were the root causes which eventually led to the mutiny. The FOCRIN contended that media too had played its role with papers such as the *Free Press Journal* promoting anti–British feelings.

Questioned about his controversial broadcast that had enraged the ratings to boiling point, Admiral Godfrey said that the broadcast was directed mainly at the mutineers in Bombay who had their guns trained on barracks and other establishments, and not towards the other ratings. He contended that such actions warranted the use of force and it was for this reason that large military forces were deployed in Bombay, along with two squadrons of Mosquitoes.

The atmosphere within the courtroom was very tense as Admiral Godfrey's testimony continued through the day. He remained unapologetic about his actions, as he believed that force was the only means he had at his disposal to get the ratings to surrender unconditionally. At the same time, he expressed his regret that the RIN men had been made to return their kit when they were demobilized. This was not in the tradition of the British Navy, he admitted.

It was clear from Admiral Godfrey's tone that he and other British officers firmly believed that the mutiny was pre-planned.

How else could the ratings have had Congress, Muslim League and Communist Party flags at hand when they hoisted them on all the ships and shore establishments and lorries used by them? These flags were not on the ships, or readily available.

Admiral Godfrey also pointed that in Bombay there was a very good wireless organization between the shore establishments and ship-borne mutineers, which must have taken some time to work out. As a result, the HMIS *Chamak* in Karachi was ready for mutiny and only waiting for a signal from Bombay.

On their part, giving evidence few days later, the RIN ratings and others pointed out several fallacies in Admiral Godfrey's testimony. They continued to emphasize that it was not a mutiny, but a mass strike against brutal treatment by the British officers, who routinely called them 'bastards' and assaulted them if they complained. Often, they claimed, the officers got drunk and slapped and kicked ratings who could not hit back.

Kusum Nair had been part of the uprising, albeit clandestinely. On Saturday, 27 April 1946 the *Bombay Chronicle* published a syndicated column under her pseudonym 'Birbal', which ridiculed Admiral Godfrey for saying that terrible food was not one of the causes of the mutiny.

The column also questioned Colonel Malik Haq Nawaz's contentions that some of the most senior and outstanding leaders of the strike were Muslims, and said communal and provincial unity and harmony was one of the most marked features of the strike.

Condemning the summary trial and sentencing of the ratings it alleged that the British put pressure on the police to forcibly put them on trains under custody, and then put them in jails of the respective districts to which they belonged. This was to ensure that these ratings could not depose in front of the commission.

On a lighter note, some of the ratings complained that while British seamen of Royal Navy were allowed to smoke on work, and take girls on dates outside the barracks, Indian ratings were punished if they ever dared to do that.

One of the early witnesses in Bombay, when the commission started its hearing on 2 May, was Lt Surendra Nath Kohli, who later become chief of naval staff. Well-built and smart, Kohli had joined the RIN in 1936 where he began his initial training in England and joined *Talwar* on 4 February 1946, barely a fortnight before the strike began.

At the time of the mutiny, he was the chief instructional officer. Thus, he was well-positioned to give an assessment of the state of the ratings' minds before the mutiny. Cross examined on the first day, Kohli stated that he was one of the officers who had made reports about the mutiny to the CO.

Asked as to his opinions to the causes of the mutiny, he pointed to the officer and rating ratio. While there were 1,150 ratings in *Talwar*, there were just ten executive officers. These officers were technically qualified but lacked experience of sailing and administrative abilities to keep in proper touch with the ratings. More than double the number of officers was needed to maintain morale at the *Talwar*.

But this, he said, was a long-term problem and not the proximate cause. Kohli believed the immediate trigger points was the arrest of B.C. Dutt, Commander King's use of foul language, and the uncertainty caused by a poorly managed demobilization.

Some of the exchanges went like this:

Mr Justice Mahajan: We have been told that some of the British and Indian officers were having drinks and dances at the time these complaints (inedible food) were lodged. Is that correct?

Lt Surendra Nath Kohli: That is true. In the ratings' club, though the dances are completely prohibited.

Justice Mahajan: Would you regard the arrest of Dutt for shouting 'Jai Hind' justifiable?

Kohli: If 'Jai Hind' is said to mean 'Long Live India', I feel his arrest was unjustifiable.

Kohli also agreed with the commission member, Major General Rees, that the more educated ratings were highly motivated and influenced by politics.

On Friday, 3 May 1946, Chief Petty Officer Sher Alam, master of arms at Mulund and drafting master of arms at Castle Barracks was the first witness. He was asked frivolous questions like, 'I believe you are a chain smoker and that you spend as much as Rs 30 per month on smoking. How would you manage when you resign the service?' His simple reply was, 'Yes it will be difficult for me to maintain the same standard.'

Another leading telegraphist, E. D'Cullie narrated an incident when a telegraphist, fed up of constant abuse and ill treatment in *Talwar,* had committed suicide by hanging himself from a tree.

From Bombay the commission went to Poona and visited HMIS *Shivaji* at Lonavla, where 900 trainees had gone on strike in support of their brethren. On the way, they also inspected HMIS *Akbar* at Thana. After the weekend, the committee returned to Bombay where they interviewed more ratings.

Among them was nineteen-year-old P.G. Bokle, a Saraswat Brahmin who complained that when he joined the navy his sacred thread (*janeyu*) had been cut off as he was told that in the navy no rating could wear the thread. Bokle also claimed that he was called an 'Indian bastard' on many occasions by British officers.

In a startling statement on Thursday, 9 May 1946, Lt Mahendra Pal Singh of the HMIS *Clive*, a training ship in Bombay, contended that the COs of various ships on hearing the first rumbles of the mutiny became 'funky' and ran away from their posts 'to rest in peace and return after a couple of days.' The officers did not bother to show leadership but instead were content to hide themselves in the confines of the nearby Sea Green Hotel on Marine Drive.

Asked if the situation that first took place aboard the *Talwar* could have been averted, Singh said it could have been. 'The situation in the *Talwar* would have been averted if the authorities had sent officers who had the confidence of the ratings to handle the situation, such men as Lt Hassan or Lt Batra. But instead, they sent Lt Kohli and Lt Nanda, who were hooted out by the ratings.'

'It is my personal opinion that when officers became unpopular there is something definitely wrong with them.' He added: 'The allegation that the strike was pre-planned was totally untrue.'

He also denied that the Congress and League flags that were hoisted on the ships and establishments during the mutiny were purchased from the market. He deposed these were made on the ships itself, from parts of other flags. All the posters that were seen were put up only after the mutiny had started.

Another Indian officer, Lt Ghatak, speaking from his personal experience said: 'Although the Indian and British officers messed together, British always sat on one side.' Excessive drinking and disorderly behaviour under the influence of liquor brought the officers into contempt with their men. Dances and parties had often been the subject of derisive comments among the ratings.

Testifying in Bombay on Monday, 13 May 1946, a leading telegraphist bitterly complained about the medical officers who instead of taking care of the ratings ended up harming and even getting them killed through sheer callousness. Giving the example of a deceased rating, Gulam Hussein, he stated that Hussein had complained of acute abdominal pain to a doctor who instead of giving him medicine advised to take a swift run around the courtyard. Putting faith in the doctor's 'prescription', Hussein ran around once and then dropped dead. But his death did not change the attitude of the doctors.

The most startling testimony the commission heard was probably from Ahmed K. Brohi. A customs clerk before he joined the navy as a telegraphist, Brohi was arrested as soon as the mutiny ended and first put in Mulund camp before being transferred to the dreaded Kalyan camp.

Termed one of the kingpins in the RIN Mutiny as joint secretary of the NCSC, Brohi appeared before the commission in a dark brown jacket and white shorts, sporting a small unkempt beard. Calm and collected, Brohi spoke in a low determined voice, which made his testimony all the more compelling.

'Have you ever noticed why we like to read Russian literature or why communism is spreading in India at atomic speed? Why do we not read instead French literature? We are not revolutionary because we have fallen in love with the reds of Moscow but because we know they are the staunch enemies of your system of government, which has proved to be a second edition of Nazi rule. Our aim, ambition, and future policy is to revolt against British imperialism.'

Questioned by the committee as to the strike and his role in it, Brohi had this to say.

Q. Did you know that the strike was to begin on the 18th of February?

A. I knew only by intuition, it was only an accident that the strike occurred that day. In my mind, the 17th of February has got some association. On that date in 1942, 30,000 Indian soldiers were handed over to the Japanese in Singapore by their British colonel. That made me think it had something to do with INA. Yes, some INA literature was distributed among the ratings.

When asked why he did not report his misgivings to higher authorities, he replied, 'I am not a member of the CID.' During his testimony, Brohi read out a long statement to the commission, which was termed as a 'fine essay' by the chairman, Justice Fazl Ali.

In his written statement, Brohi said the main causes for the strike were: the INA trials, disappointing demobilization conditions, hatred of the British, the Indonesian issue where Indian ratings were reluctant to fight for the Dutch colonizers against the Indonesians, the RIAF strike, free availability of communist literature, and press propaganda regarding disturbances specially in Calcutta, loose discipline in HMIS *Talwar*, and the abusive language of Commander King.

Impressed by his statement, Justice Fazl Ali asked how long it took him to write the statement. Brohi's short reply was: 'Six hours.' Speaking during his cross-examination, Brohi said, 'Mischief-mongers among the RIN strikers in February last, signalled to ships in Bombay harbour to open fire, and if the men on the ships had done so thinking that the instructions had come from responsible persons, terrible havoc would have been caused.'

Purshottam Tricumdas then asked him for further elucidation of the statement to which Brohi replied that he was referring to some signals given from the Gateway of India and Ballard Pier to ships to open fire.

Confirming what others had said, Brohi also categorically stated that 99 per cent of the ratings were interested in politics, and bore deep hatred against the British. They also felt that like the INA personnel, they wanted to do something outstanding for the country.

Brohi went on to blame national leaders for misguiding the ratings by preaching non-violence to men who had been taught to fight. So, national leaders were responsible in a big way. 'Till the moment the ratings took up the arms, the national leaders were red hot in their speeches. But when the ratings actually took up the arms, what did they find? The leaders began to talk of non-violence. How could men trained in warfare think in terms of spinning wheels? How could men taught to kill take up the *charkha*?'

During cross-examination, Brohi contended that despite everything the strike would have remained peaceful if the British had not pushed the men into taking up arms.

He pointed out that the British had imprisoned B.C. Dutt and R.K. Singh – heroes to many of the ratings. He added, 'Government forced them to take up arms. They imprisoned their brothers. They stopped the water and food supply. The ratings therefore had no other way but to take up arms. Admiral Godfrey made his threat to sink the navy and this made the ratings adamant. I do not mind what will happen to me in the future, whether I live or whether I receive bullets in my chest, but the butchering of so many of my comrades will ever haunt my memory in days to come.'

On being asked by Justice Mahajan which newspapers incited the mutiny, he named the *Free Press Journal*, the *Bombay Chronicle*, and *Blitz*. 'The ratings were dead against imperialism. Indeed, British imperialism was a second edition of Nazi rule. Hence the ratings looked for a friend, everybody who was anti-imperialist. They know of the historic Mutiny of 1857.'

Basant Singh, one of the ratings transferred to and detained at the Kalyan camp, deposing in front of the commission on 14 May, stated: 'Some kind of matters and literature about INA, Subhas Bose's pictures and pamphlets such as "Blood and Thunder" were freely distributed among the ratings. The situation in India was peculiar. Political prisoners had been released, INA trial had started. In some respects, we became jealous of the INA deeds. They are being worshipped as heroes. But we are looked down upon as British stooges and despised. We too are patriots. We wanted to make clear to the public what we wanted to do and we struck work.'

The other notable witness after this was B.C. Dutt, the man who had started the mutiny by writing nationalist slogans on the walls of the *Talwar*. Testifying before the commission, Dutt described serving in the naval service in India as a 'living hell'.

Dutt claimed that he was disillusioned by his life in the navy and wrote of this in a letter to his brother, which was found and heavily censored and he himself was threatened with dismissal. A diary seized from Dutt's locker in the *Talwar* was produced in the court. It contained references to a 'boss', 'HQ' and to a 'Whisp Camp'. The last, Dutt explained, meant 'Whispering Campaign' and referred to his effort to educate other ratings.

Dismissing the charges of mutiny, Dutt claimed that he was charged with political affiliation solely because at the time of his arrest when his locker was searched, a communist book was found. British records reveal that when Dutt's locker was opened and searched, a number of articles and papers that included two diaries, a receipt for Rs 206 from Azad Hind Army Relief fund, a copy of INA pledge and a book on the Indian Mutiny of 1857 by Asoka Mehta, and a letter on a postcard from the secretary of the Indian

Ex-Services Association Y.K. Menon were found. Clearly, this was all much more than just a 'communist book'.

During his testimony, Dutt refused to answer questions on a few occasions saying he had already stated the answers before the Board of Enquiry, which had inquired into the *Talwar* incident. However, he was more forthcoming on his political beliefs. On being asked when he gained a liking for political activity, Dutt replied that after joining the navy he had the opportunity of visiting places, mixing with British soldiers and seeing how people lived in free countries. That is how his interest in politics began.

'When Indians are struggling for freedom, I think every Indian should join in the struggle… I would have joined the INA, if I was in Malaya.'

Questioned about his views on the 'Azad Hindis' and the fact that they were referred to as 'Dutt and his group', Dutt had little to say. The question was: This cadre (Azad Hindis) would join no political organization but would infiltrate into all services. Do you agree with this?

Answer: 'For the cause of freedom anything can be done.'

He did add, 'I would take the Azad Hind Fauj pledge as all Indians should,' and he pointed out that all the ratings had contributed to the INA fund. He was however, quick to emphasize that the mutiny started in spite of him, as he was under detention on 17 February.

While Dutt was most forthcoming about his interest in politics, he was understandably less so about the entries in his diary. When asked about his visits to 'N', and 'HQ', he purposely gave misleading answers stating N stood for Nambiar, who was not in Bombay, and not Lt Nayyar, and HQ stood for the Headquarter of Communist Party on Sandhurst Road (and not to any headquarters of any secret organization). In reality this was the Riviera, Marine Drive home of Kusum and P.N. Nair where all the planning for the mutiny was done.

Q. Do you remember that you gave a book called *March of Events* to Rishi Dev Puri?

A. I had some books at the signal school and sometimes he used to give me one or two books, but I can't remember what happened to this book. So many things have happened after that.

Q. On 3 January you entered in your diary: 'Went with Devu to HQ.' May I suggest that it was Lt Nair's flat?

A. No.

In this way, Dutt continued his bid to mislead and stonewall the commission. When asked about the 'Whisp Camp' reference in his diary, he said it meant 'whispering campaign' which was to educate some ratings about the history of the Indian National Congress and not to excite them. Asked about references in the diary to meetings with RIAF men, Dutt explained that these were made in connection with the formation of Ex-Services Association. In reality though, the British contended that Dutt was meeting them at the Nairs' home in a bid to get them to support and join the RIN Mutiny. The material seized from Dutt's locker was placed before the commission as exhibits.

As the cross-examinations continued, other interesting stories emerged. One of these was about Lieutenant J.A.G. Tottham who testified as one of the witnesses at Kalyan camp on 1 May 1946. In his evidence, Tottham related an incident, which highlighted the contempt and lack of trust the British held for Indians:

'In the Persian Gulf one of our leading signalmen reported one evening at 5.30 p.m. that he had sighted three suspected German U-Boats. This was subsequently reported to the senior officer commanding at Bandar Abbas, who asked for the name, ranking and the ability of the rating who had reported. He was told "RIN rating, signalman of very good ability." (On hearing that he was an Indian), we got back the reply, "Do not rely much upon RIN leading signalman's report." The same night, in that very area, three ships were sunk. The commander in the Persian Gulf stationed at Basra put an enquiry board on it and the officers in Bandar Abbas practically told us "to keep our mouths shut about the incident".'

By 16 May, almost 100 witnesses, Indian and British, had been cross-examined. Another interesting witness was Commander S.G. Karmarkar who was transferred from an establishment in Lonavla to HMIS *Talwar* on 19 February after the outbreak of the mutiny. This was the Indian officer who had kept an eye on the Riviera 'HQ' from his flat in the same building. He deposed that there was no serious ground for the mutiny. The grievances and discontent, he claimed, were not of a serious nature. He blamed political influence for the mutiny. He said he believed the prime cause was acute political tension in the country.

Karmarkar added that the other trigger was the effect of articles published in newspapers. He admitted that he had got threatening letters from the ratings stating that if he did not mend his ways of siding with British officers, they would 'make Commander King out of him'.

He admitted that when in Bombay, he stayed in a building at Marine Drive. 'Until recently Mr Nayyar, formerly a lieutenant in the navy, lived in the same building, and he noticed that ratings visited Nayyars.'

Despite his full support to the British and the navy, he said: 'Alleged abusive language of Commander King was another incentive for the Mutiny.' He also admitted that the effect of Admiral Godfrey's threat to destroy the navy was unfavourable.

There were some lighter moments when Karmarkar was cross examined.

Justice: You said that the WRINS (Women ratings of Royal India Navy) had preferential treatment.

A. Fortunately I had nothing to do with WRINS [laughter].

Tricumdas: Is it wrong on the part of the ratings to meet a politician?

A. It depends upon the type of political leaders he meets [laughter].

Q. You met Pandit Jawaharlal Nehru. Is Pandit Nehru a safe person? [Laughter]

Karmarkar did not reply.

Q. When you met Pandit Nehru, was a British intelligence officer with you?

A. You may ask Pandit Nehru himself [loud laughter].

Captain Inigo-Jones was the CO of the Castle Barracks until 18 February. On the 18th he was sent to the *Talwar* to take over from Commander King. He was described by a young rating before the commission as 'Butcher of the RIN'. His testimony added some colour to the proceedings. Inigo-Jones repeatedly wore a monocle to read extracts from his statement made before the Board of Enquiry at the HMIS *Talwar*. When asked if he had made those statements, he replied, 'I presume so.'

Lt Sachdev was a colleague of Lt Batra at the *Talwar* during the mutiny. Both of them were well-liked by the ratings as they were sympathetic to their grievances. Testifying before the commission he said, 'It was the frustration of the ratings' representation to the junior officers, and the frustration of the junior officers' representation to the authorities, which suddenly exploded into the Mutiny.'

★ ★ ★

The most striking testimony from the British officers' side was that of Commander Frederick William King, CO of the *Talwar* until 18 February. Giving his testimony on Monday, 20 May 1946, King denied his use of foul language was one of the reasons for the mutiny, and denied having used any foul language at all.

He asserted that there was not just the political but revolutionary movement behind the mutiny. 'Unfortunately, navy was not in a position to show them the other side of the picture.' King said the revolutionary fervour only grew especially when on a particular day the 'Quit India' slogan was found written on his motor car and the tyres deflated. He regarded this as a serious act of sabotage and consequently tried to get the number of ratings reduced.

Replying to a question if he knew any of those fourteen ratings who had complained against him, King replied that he did not remember having seen any of them. When asked if his administration had through being over-strict, created resentment,

King replied that the ratings themselves had his deepest sympathy, especially Dutt who was very clever and who would do credit to any navy.

'Most of the complaints against me were influenced by outsiders. I tried to call them to my office but it's very different when there are a large number of men involved and they are refusing to take orders from their immediate senior.'

Q. It has been stated in the evidence before us that when you came to know of the trouble, you gave no instructions to the officers.

A. All that is in the report of the *Talwar* enquiry. When I came to know of the trouble, I visited Vithal House. I saw the admiral there. He did not give me any instructions. He may have said, "Try to get hold of the representatives of the ratings" and that is what I have been trying to do.'

Q. You stated in the *Talwar* enquiry that some catcalls were made against the WRINS. What were they like?

A. I can't imitate the calls.

Q. What was the implication behind them?

A. It was embarrassing for the women – bad discipline and bad manners.

When Chairman Fazl Ali asked if the accusation that he was accustomed to using bad language was correct, King replied he sometimes used 'friendly language to his friends'.

Q. Which may not be parliamentary?

A. May not be.

Fazl Ali: You cannot categorically refute that you use language that may not be parliamentary, and may be misconstrued as bad language.

A: I use words occasionally which are not in the dictionary. Some words are more expressive.

Sayyid Fazl Ali then read out a statement by Lt Nanda before the *Talwar* board of enquiry which stated: 'Have had quite a lot of conclave (sic) with Commander King. I have heard him very often use bad language, which comes to him unintentionally. Commander King explained he sometimes expressed himself freely.'

Testifying next before the commission was Lt S.M. Nanda (then a divisional officer in the HMIS *Talwar*, and later the navy chief). Lt Nanda stated that he had gone to Vallabhbhai Patel during the mutiny and gathered from him that Lt Nayyar and Mrs Aruna Asaf Ali had approached Sardar Patel to get the support of the Congress for the mutineers and that they had been disappointed. He also stated that ratings wanted Mrs Asaf Ali to mediate between them and the authorities.

Speaking in support of Commander King, Lt Nanda categorically said 'No', when asked if Commander King's statement that 'ratings would not mind overcrowding if they got good food' was indeed true. On the actions of mutiny, he was more forthcoming.

Lt Nanda emphatically said that the writing of slogans in *Talwar* on the eve of Navy Day was not the work of certain disgruntled ratings. 'It was the work of some organized body which was trying to disrupt the discipline of the establishment in general, and to rouse feelings against the government and to magnify the service grievances.' He also emphasized that the presence of revolutionary elements in *Talwar* was well known.

'On the Navy Day the slogan writing was in full form and the officers were quite handicapped on how to put a check upon it. The indifferent attitude of the authorities towards the hunger strike at two messes added fuel to the fire. Lt Cole and myself volunteered to speak with the ratings. I asked the ratings that the authorities wanted to know their grievances. I also asked them to appoint representatives from amongst themselves, but they resented the idea and expressed a keen desire to have some national political leader represent them.'

Members of the Ex-Services Association, the organization accused of having political affiliations with the mutineers, also came forward to testify before the commission. It was here that Lt Commander Powar, a member of the commission, who was said to be a British sympathizer, began aggressively cross-questioning the witnesses.

Lt Powar asked Lt Nanda if a rating in the *Talwar* named Rishi Dev, was related to Lt Nayyar, an officer in *Talwar*. To that Justice Mahajan interrupted that Rishi Dev was a Puri, a Punjabi Brahmin (incidentally incorrect because Puris are Punjabi Khatri) and that Nayyars came from South India (also incorrect because this Nayyar was also a Punjabi). This remark led to some laughter in the court. Lt Cdr Powar sat down, protesting that every time he puts a question, he is ridiculed.

The next interesting witness was an officer of the Indian army, Lt Sachdev. The commission first asked whether he was a member of the Ex-Services Association and then read out a resolution passed by them on 20 February 1946 supporting the mutiny. Did he, they asked Lt Sachdev, know of this resolution? If so, did he condone it?

In reply Lt Sachdev said he was a member of the association but did not support this resolution. He was then asked.
Q. Who took you to the meeting?
A. I was told by Lt Commander Arland to go over there.
The commission then drew attention to the picture published in the *Blitz*. It was a picture of Jayaprakash Narayan with Lt Chandramani of the RIN, while contingents of the three Indian services gave the guard of honour.

Asked for his comments on the picture, Lt Sachdev simply replied, 'I want to keep aloof from the party politics.' Sachdev continued to play this game of cat and mouse until finally a question came up that ended all doubts about his loyalties.
Q. Do you realize under what government you are serving?
A. Yes, it is the British government of which we are all slaves… We are ruled by the Britishers as slaves and I do mean what I say.

Y.K. Menon, secretary of the Indian Ex-Services Association was the next important witness to be cross-examined. He described himself as author, journalist, correspondent of many foreign papers and contributor to the *Tribune* (which until recently had been associated with Sir Stafford Cripps). During his cross-examination, he mentioned that the association was mainly concerned with the resettlement of discharged servicemen and it would be wrong and libellous to say that one of its objects was to subvert the loyalty of people in the armed forces. There was no political tinge to the association.

Menon also pointed out that the association was formed on 20 February, which was after the mutiny had already broken out and that the resolution passed by the association to congratulate the strikers was not political but a humanitarian one. It should be viewed in that context.

He explained that the first meeting of fourteen persons was held on 17 December 1945 to consider a Draft Constitution. After four such provisional meetings, the association came into existence on 20 February 1946, when a resolution expressing sympathy towards the RIN strikers was also carried by the house. He said the association had almost 1,000 members in Bombay alone.

Both Tricumdas and Menon put up a strong effort before the commission to prove that the Ex-Services Association was not a political body and not responsible for the RIN Mutiny. They cited examples of other organizations such as the Indian Merchants Chamber, the Forward Bloc, British Portuguese Chamber of Commerce, and other important organizations, which were represented by well-known members of these bodies when they conducted a joint meeting.

Dr P.A. Wadia, a noted economist, was present as well in this 20 February meeting, where Mrs Lilavati Munshi was in the chair and a small committee was formed to collect funds. Some other prominent people who attended the meeting were Mr Gazdar representing the Tatas, Mrs Violet Alva of the Forum, well-known actor Prithviraj Kapoor, and Miss Lynette Solomon of the *Bombay Sentinel*.

It had been decided that Jayaprakash Narayan should be invited to inaugurate the fund and Tricumdas mentioned that it was recommended that the association should seek support from the government of Bombay and the collector of Bombay. He even suggested that it should work hand-in-hand with the district sailors, airmen and soldiers' association of which the collector was the chairman.

Menon denied that the association in any way was political in nature and that it had any hand in the mutiny though there were many members who had associations with the navy. Tricumdas added that the Ex-Services Association was moved by the pitiable condition of the demobbed soldiers and navy men. It was with the intention of doing some good for them that the association was formed.

Judge advocate Powar asked Menon: 'If non-violence were to fail would you believe in violent methods?' Without even a hint of hesitation, Menon answered, 'I would,' and emphatically added that he would adopt any means to get freedom. He, however, denied that he knew Dutt before the mutiny nor could he single him out in a crowd. Menon admitted, however, that he did know R.D. Puri.

The next witness was Prem Nath (P.N.) Nair, or Nayyar. Formerly a welfare officer in the HMIS *Talwar*, Nayyar stated that he joined the navy 'as he loved the sea' but left it when he found that conditions there were terrible.

'I have never seen more callous people who have utter disregard for human sentiments as in the navy,' he shared. However, he denied taking part in any subversive activities saying such accusations were baseless.

Nayyar, however, was quick to point out the follies and discriminatory practices carried out by the British. Talking about racial prejudice, he said that a young British officer, Lt Horabin, who was a favourite with everyone in the *Talwar*, fell into disfavour after he married an Indian girl whom he loved. His wife was never invited to any of the naval functions or parties just because he had married a 'black girl'.

By 23 May 1946 the commission had completed three weeks

in Bombay and, according to local newspaper reports, its hearings were humdrum affairs. It needed Mrs Nair, the only lady witness to be called, to inject some excitement into the proceedings.

Smartly dressed, Kusum Nair's answers delivered with quick confidence impressed everyone and she lent the commission an aura of glamour, which had hitherto been missing. One of the prominent visitors in the packed courtroom when she was examined, was Kamaladevi Chattopadhyay, former president of the All-India Women's Conference.

Describing herself formerly a member of the Women's Auxiliary Corps (India) [WAC (I)] Mrs Nair also stated that she was a journalist and the owner of a newspaper syndicate company in Bombay. Asked for her views on the mutiny, she said the mutiny was entirely an internal matter, and credit or discredit for it should go to the ratings.

Then asked to account for her movements, she admitted that she was seen near the HMIS *Talwar* on 22 February, and at Castle Barracks and other places in Bombay during the days of the mutiny. But she said she went there only to fulfil her journalistic duties.

Reiterating the objectives of Menon, Kusum Nair said the common man felt that the armed forces should participate in the freedom struggle and added daringly that she believed that it was the patriotic duty of every Indian to fight for freedom. Though she denied knowing B.C. Dutt, she admitted she knew R.D. Puri.

Kusum Nair's true sentiments came to the fore though when she stated that she felt sure that demobbed personnel would join the armed forces of free India at half their current salary. Questioned about a message attributed to her that the ratings should salute Azad Hind style, she denied it. She also admitted that an article 'Indian Mutiny' had been sent out through her syndicate.

No one could be in any doubt as to where her sympathies lay. Kusum Nair's statements were all the more impressive given the cross-examination that Lt Commander Powar the judge-advocate, and a supporter of the British, subjected her to.

He pointed towards her writings in an INA pamphlet, 'Even the armed forces are in a ferment.' She replied that she was referring to the RIAF strikes, the arrest of B.C. Dutt, and the statement to that effect by Auchinleck in the Assembly, concluding: 'I hadn't the faintest idea that there would be widespread trouble in RIN.'

Powar, however, was determined to drive her to admit that she had full knowledge about the strike from beforehand. However, she was unperturbed. Being asked by him about a quotation in a piece distributed under her pen-name Birbal, which said: 'Just wait for the next struggle. The fighting forces will walk over next time,' she replied with authority, 'This is an assurance to the Congress leaders that the armed forces are with the country... If there is a mass uprising, I think every Indian should participate in the struggle.'

However, Powar was not done yet. He then asked her, 'Were you in sympathy with the strikers?' a dangerous and leading question. Circumventing it with ease, she said, 'I tried to do my best to help the situation. I even went personally to Sardar Patel and persuaded him to use his good offices with the authorities and with the boys to stop it.'

Kusum Nair was a rock-solid witness on the stand. None of the commission's questions could shake her. On being asked accusingly by Vice Admiral Patterson that if she agreed, or was willing to concede that a reading of her political views in print would weaken the loyalty of the armed forces, and might have incited the mutiny, she replied firmly in the negative. She also said she believed that the mutiny was a spontaneous action by the ratings themselves.

'No political organization could have commanded the mutiny. If an organization like the Indian National Congress could not influence the Muslims during August 1942 (Quit India Movement), when there was a spontaneous action and mass upsurge all over the country and even the army remained aloof from the struggle, how could outside political influence have any affect during February 1946, when the international situation was far more favourable to the government than in 1942?'

★ ★ ★

Everyone was most interested to hear the testimonies of the mutineers themselves. The commission cross-examined Lt Sobhani, the only officer to be arrested and punished for 'making seditious speeches' and 'inciting other fellow officers'. Facing court martial on twelve charges, he was brought from a naval prison to appear before the commission under guard. Asked about the causes for the RIN mutiny, Subhani said that strike was due to long frustration among the ratings.

The newspapers gave wide coverage to the Commission of Enquiry proceedings and revealed some interesting sidelights. The column 'Twilight Twitters' (*Bombay Sentinel*, 17 May), was ironical. 'You will hardly believe – That Ahmed Brohi told RIN Court that politics was a vast and confusing subject. Who said it was also the last refuge of a scoundrel?

'That Telegraphist Brohi told the commission that as it was accustomed to deal with criminal cases, it suspected everything under the sun. Another way of saying a man is known by the company he keeps?

'That the witness informed the judges if he had good memory, he would have been the premier of some province. Brohi should know that Premiers have short memories, as they forget their election promises.'

The commission concluded its last hearing on Saturday, 1 June 1946 in Karachi after five consecutive days of sitting in Muslim Hostel. It examined over forty witnesses there, including two COs, and three other officers. Commander A.K. Chatterji, CO of *Chamak* was the first witness on the last day, and the last to be examined was Jaswant Singh, a rating who was discharged and had recently emerged from jail after serving a term of imprisonment.

After concluding the cross-examination in Karachi, the commission left for Simla on Tuesday, 4 June 1946, to draft the report. It was expected that the report would be submitted to the government within a month. The report was duly submitted in October but it was not made public until the third week of January 1947. Even now, it's not entirely clear if the full report has been placed in the public domain, although 598 pages of it are available.

The *Times of India* and other newspapers carried excerpts from the report on 21 January 1947. Wrote the *TOI*: 'The lessons of the mutiny, the government say are, first, that officers must consider the welfare of their men before their own comfort or safety and that grievances must not be explained away but redressed and, secondly, too rapid an expansion without proper provision for the training of officers is unwise, and the aim for the services in peace must be to prepare for expansion in war.

'The government mentioned that the inquiry commission is unanimous that the basic cause of the mutiny was widespread discontent arising mainly from a number of service grievances which had remained un-redressed for some time and were aggravated by the political situation.

'With references to politics, the Government of India expresses their belief that healthy interest in the affairs of the country is to be encouraged but that the use of politics as a lever to get the grievances redressed is highly dangerous and must be discouraged in the interest of the service.

'Officers and men are being instructed that although every man is entitled to his personal views, participation in party politics is not admissible to members of such a service.'

The report stated as follows:

Nine ratings, one officer, killed (34 were missing and reported as deserter), 41 ratings and one officer wounded. [Looking at the scale of mayhem this appeared to be highly understated data.]

It further concluded

1. Mutiny was not organized by outside agency. It was not pre-planned.
2. Politics and political influence had great effect in unsettling the

men's loyalty and in preparing the ground for the mutiny and its prolongation.

3. The glorification of the INA had undoubtedly the most unsettling effect on the morale of the men of the services.
4. The mutiny never assumed the shape of a political revolt.
5. Naval authorities did not take more active steps before the mutiny.
6. FOB Rear-Admiral Rattray did not step in over Commander King's head on hearing of the complaint about his conduct.
7. The duty officer in *Talwar* did not take active steps on 17/18 February over food and did not bring the grievances to the attention of Flag Officer Bombay.
8. There was indecision and inaction on the part of Commander King.
9. There was delay in taking action on 18 February by FOB, CO and other officers.
10. FOB Rattray failed to isolate *Talwar* and prevent rumours, which often becomes news and did not prevent news from travelling.

'It seems to us,' the commission said, 'that but for these mistakes this great catastrophe which caused so much damage, suffering and bloodshed, which has ruined so many young lives and careers which have left so much unhappiness and bitterness in the services would not have occurred.'

The naval authorities, as a result of the report issued the following instructions:

1. European officers will be encouraged by all means to acquire a full knowledge of their men not only in the services but in their homes too.
2. Everything possible is being done to eliminate any suspicion of racial discrimination and Indian officers are being posted to the command of the ships or to posts of executive officer in ships, and to higher staff appointments, as they acquire sufficient seniority and experience.

The *Free Press Journal* of 21 January 1947 carried the headline 'ALL STEPS TO REDRESS GRIEVANCES of RIN, Government Assurance. FORGET THE PAST NOW AND LOOK TO THE FUTURE…'

The *FPJ* further added that only Indians should be selected for permanent commission and the present naval canteens should be improved in India. It also deplored the fact that the report ignored the victimized men.

'The Report may have generally satisfied the Navy but has been severely criticized by the officers for recommending nationalization of the navy. The ratings, and ex-ratings are unhappy and despondent over non-references to the "victimized young men called as mutineers" and that they are not in general viewed favourably by the men of the navy.'

Aruna Asaf Ali criticized the report, 'The interim government's steps to implement the recommendations have curiously enough the white man's touch about them. There is surprisingly enough no reference to measures for reinstating of ratings discharged for mutiny… The tragic chapter in the RIN history could very well have become grim if the ratings had continued their resistance. They surrendered only after they were assured by eminent leaders now in the interim government that no vindictive action would be taken against them. Many were court martialled and many more were dismissed summarily.'

Aruna also added that the commission's conclusions suggest that the causes that led to RIN revolt were related to genuine grievances.

'This justification is further upheld by the government's somewhat reluctant admission that the mutiny "may not be entirely without good results". After having realized this, to ignore the men who risked their lives to revolutionize this denationalized branch of India's fighting services is to submit to the arguments of the White bosses of India.'

She further said, 'Left to himself the British Admiral would not have hesitated to destroy the entire Indian Navy for reasons of prestige. ...or again to be apologetic about these individuals who owing to war and post war strain acted mistakenly.'

In a narrow sense, the enquiry did lead to better service conditions for Indians on other ranks in the RIN. But it ignored the way in which the ratings had been mistreated, imprisoned and summarily dismissed, without receiving their dues.

REFERENCES

Report of the RIN Commission of Enquiry 1946, NAI.

EPILOGUE

PEOPLE, PLACES AND SHIPS

The naval mutiny of February 1946 involved thousands of people in actions across multiple locations. Some of them became admirals; others who played a prominent role were tossed into jail, or out into 'civvy street' and disappeared into obscurity.

The names of many of the ships and shore establishments changed after Partition and Independence. Even the names of the cities have changed. Here are the post-mutiny profiles of some of the main protagonists and brief notes on some of the ships and shore establishments whose names come up, again and again in this narrative.

B.C. Dutt

When Dutt was released from confinement on 18 February, the day he was dishonourably discharged, he was greeted like a hero by his fellow ratings. His name and exploits were splashed all over the nationalist press like the *Free Press Journal* and the *Bombay Chronicle*. But Dutt's hopes of being rehabilitated to serve in the navy again were dashed.

He was given six rupees upon discharge, while his legitimate dues after serving for five years, would have amounted to 600 rupees. He was ordered to be taken to Calcutta under police escort. But he had no intention of going to Calcutta since Bombay was his city. He gave his escorts the slip at Igatpuri Junction, got off the train, and returned to Bombay.

S. Sadanand, the founder-editor of the *Free Press Journal*, gave him a reporting job. In the *FPJ*, Dutt shared a room with the young cartoonist, Balasaheb Thackeray for three years. Eventually, he was disillusioned with journalism and left to join a leading advertising firm, Lintas, where he worked for around two decades. While at Lintas, he wrote his memoir *Mutiny of the Innocents,* with the help of his young copywriter colleague Shyam Benegal, who later became an acclaimed filmmaker.

A profile by Amita Shah in *Open* Magazine claims Dutt met twenty-seven-year-old Anusuya, a Punjabi from Ludhiana, while she was a member of Praja Socialist Party and he a journalist with *FPJ*. Anusuya, who had studied in Shanti Niketan, married him in 1955. She was a lawyer who specialized in family law, practising until her late eighties, and was considered one of the best legal minds in Bombay.

Dutt loved the good life and a drink, recalls Pradip Chanda, a trainee with Hindustan Lever at a time when Levers and Lintas had offices in the same building on different floors.

'At the end of the day, Balai would come down to the Lever's office on the fourth floor and together we would go looking for alcohol,' reminisces Chanda. 'We would often land up in an "aunty's" house and consume illegal hooch. Maharashtra was a dry state those days, you see.'

Dutt was also a fitness freak who would do yoga and head stands every morning. A voracious reader, he would never sleep before writing 2,000/3,000 words every day! His dream was to rejoin the navy of Independent India. But sadly, the government refused to give him that opportunity and the fact that he never sailed again hurt him deeply.

A socialist by inclination, he gravitated towards Ram Manohar

Lohia and Jayaprakash Narayan. He was also hugely influenced by Yusuf Meherally, who was elected Mayor of Bombay in 1942 despite being in Yerawada jail at the time. Dutt greatly admired Meherally, who is credited with coining the 'Quit India' slogan. Later, Dutt moved into the Yusuf Meherally Centre in Panvel and dedicated his time and energy in working on social causes. He was at the Centre when he passed away in 2009, at the age of eighty-six.

It took perseverance and snooping but I traced Anusuya Dutt to her flat in South Mumbai. I was given half an hour by her son Tanuj to talk to her one afternoon. A charming lady in her early nineties, she replied to most of my questions with a childlike smile.

I chatted with her until I was told that she was too tired and that she would have answers to all my questions if I could come the next day. But the next morning, I got a call from Tanuj that his mother could not sleep the whole night muttering incoherently about 'Mutiny' and had to be hospitalized. She passed away in 2017.

Rishi Dev Puri

Flamboyant, good looking and a daredevil, R.D. Puri was discharged from the RIN on 27 January 1946, three weeks before the mutiny, after the Navy Day episode and the subsequent inquiry.

His immediate family, who were quite influential, whisked him off to Shimla. 'Harry' was asked to run the famous Davicos restaurant on the Mall, which was owned by his family. There he perfected his piano-playing and became a *bon vivant*. Letters continued to flow not just between him and Shaila but also between him and Kusum and his fellow sailors back in Bombay, who believed him to be indispensable to the cause.

Many of Harry's colleagues felt that he had played a key role in the mutiny. Mathur [his first name is unknown], a naval rating who was part of the Ex-Servicemen Association, wrote to Harry on 31 March 1946, stressing the need for him to return. 'Your presence is urgently required [in Bombay] because everyone from our batch is insisting on this that if Dev will come, then only we will stay otherwise, we will search our way. So, my dear friend I advise you that if you will come to Bombay, you will see what we have done here and what more we can do. This is a last chance for us otherwise we are going to lose all that which we have done up to now.'

Harry, however, was given very different advice by the political leaders he met. Through Kusum and other contacts, he secured interviews with Pandit Nehru, Maulana Azad and Aruna Asaf Ali in the first week of May but their advice left him discouraged.

In a letter to a friend, he stated, 'I got into a little bit of a battle with Pt Nehru when I told him everything I did… He strongly advised me to keep out of party politics and preserve plenty of individual energy. He spent 35 minutes with me and out of all the three leaders, I found him the most obliging and kind.'

Harry would have carried on the struggle in some other way but his elder brother V.V. Puri and his family ensured he stayed out of further trouble.

A happy-go-lucky character, R.D. loved the good life. An attractive man with a rakish charm, he had women falling all over him. The India of the 1940s was too sedate for his tastes. In 1948, he smuggled himself out with the Indian Olympic team travelling to Wembley, London. He arrived in London penniless and became a professional piano player, performing in clubs and restaurants. Later, his brother set up a film distribution company for him in London. He was the distributor for the cult classic *Black Orpheus*, an international co-production, which won the Palme d'Or at the Cannes Film Festival.

He met his future wife Nicole, a Frenchwoman, in London. They had two daughters, Karina and Isabelle. Later, after he and Nicole divorced, R.D. returned to Delhi. His elder brother, father of Aroon Purie and Madhu Trehan, owned Living Media and many Delhi-ites will recall meeting him at the *India Today* office, for he worked with *India Today* in its formative years.

Madan Singh

Madan Singh was against the surrender but gave in to the majority view. He was dutiful, fiercely patriotic and committed to Independence. While M.S. Khan urged unconditional surrender, Vice President Madan determinedly led the anti-surrender group appealing to his comrades not to let the people of Bombay down. But ultimately, the anti-surrender group led by Madan yielded to the majority, a few minutes before the ultimatum expired.

He was held in solitary confinement for three and half months, after which he was discharged with 'disgrace'. He was escorted by armed policemen to the railway station, given a one-way ticket and put on a train to Ludhiana.

Like many others, Madan Singh struggled after discharge from the RIN. The cruellest blow came from his father, who was not pleased to see him return home and remarked to a neighbour that Madan had come back only for his money and live off him. Angered and hurt, he left his village for Bombay, where he tried his hand at journalism, the natural choice being the *Free Press Journal*.

But his nationalistic dreams died as he saw his stories killed in favour of British handouts. Angered, he once barged into the proprietor's room and launched into an emotional tirade. Sadanand replied calmly, 'You are absolutely correct, but I have eighteen ventures all blocked by the British. I have to keep one alive so I can at least point out some misdeeds of the British.'

Madan resigned the next day. It would take a while before he would find his feet. In 1948, he helped Biju Patnaik start Kalinga Airways, taking care of the technical side and managing it. He left Kalinga Airways in 1952 when it was nationalized.

In 1949, during a flight where people were being evacuated from Pakistan to India, he met his future wife, Pritam Kaur. The couple had three children – Vijay, Ranjit and daughter Annurag. In 1953, he flew to London, leaving behind his wife and children. He could barely afford a one-way ticket, but an opportunity to further his career with British Overseas Airlines Corporation (BOAC, a product of merger between British Airways and Imperial Airways) was irresistible. After extensive training in Avionics, Madan Singh was absorbed in BOAC as the second non-white employee, drawing equal pay to the Britishers of his rank.

He accepted an offer from Ghana Airways in 1963, directing the Avionics and technical side of the African airline from its headquarters in Accra. Thanks to his qualifications and position, Madan Singh and his family travelled all over the world. His daughter reminisces that their father did everything to broaden their education. 'He would take us to the best places. I think by the time I was five, I had done London, Paris, and New York. Been to the Louvre and all those kinds of things.'

She and her brother also recall how kind their father was. 'Once he was crossing a park in Bombay at night and a person came up to him and mugged him. Dad just stood there, not moving while it happened. Once it was done, he asked, "Is there anything else I can give you." That guy put everything back in dad's pocket.'

He was fond of Western and Indian classical music. He would take his children to Broadway shows. '*The King and I*, *My Fair Lady* and *Sound of Music* is what I remember,' says Annurag. 'He loved Mozart while we loved Beatles, but we would listen to the Beatles only in his absence.' He was also very fond of cooking, and his favourite cookbook was Larousse Guide to Gastronomy. Generous to the core, he once invited home the entire crew of an Indian ship anchored in Tema (Ghana). In 1990 he returned to India as a retiree. During his long years crisscrossing the globe, he maintained his Indian passport.

Rear Admiral (retd) Satyinder Singh wrote to him five times to apply for the status of freedom fighter. But Madan wrote back, 'It is not worth having it if it comes after asking.' He repeated this in an interview with *Tribune*.

When Beant Singh, former chief minister of Punjab, met Madan, his childhood friend, he was aghast to learn his fate and that of other mutineers. He pursued their case with the Ministry of Home Affairs and as Madan recalls: 'So finally I received a letter from Commodore Dina Bandhu Jena, VSM, inviting me to the induction ceremony on 26 February 1999 at Bombay when a ship was named SS Madan Singh. It does seem like a mirage after all these years but it's better late than never,' he confessed in an interview.

There is a hint of some bitterness though. He said, 'When history is written, it will show the mutiny was the immediate cause of India's freedom. The British were… shaken. Nevertheless, the role of the mutineers has been ignored and they were denied due recognition.'

Madan Singh passed away in 2007 at the age of eighty-seven, leaving behind his wife Pritam Kaur, who divides her time between her children. The eldest, Ranjit Singh Pender is retired in Spain, daughter Annurag Dhillon lives with her husband, an educationist and chairman of Dalhousie Public School, Dalhousie, and Dr Vijay Pratap Singh is a division leader of a well-known hospital in Central Valley, California.

Aruna Asaf Ali

Post-mutiny, she remained the only full-time politician as a member of the Socialist 'ginger' group or caucus in the Congress. Disillusioned with the Congress, she left in 1948 and joined the newly formed Socialist Party. She travelled with Rajni Palme Dutt to Moscow and officially joined the Communist Party in the early 1950s.

In 1953 her husband, the prominent Congress leader Asaf Ali died, but her work continued. In 1954, she was among the founders of the National Federation of Indian Women. Together with Kamala Devi Chattopadhyay she tirelessly worked for the upliftment of women. In 1956, she joined the women's wing of the Communist Party of India but left in 1956 after ideological disagreements with Moscow.

She was elected the first mayor of Delhi in 1958. In 1963, along with E. Narayanan, she started to publish *Patriot*, a daily newspaper under the Link publishing house, established in 1958 to publish *Link*, a weekly magazine. *Patriot* had the patronage and support of Jawaharlal Nehru, Krishna Menon, Biju Patnaik, et al, lending it prestige.

She rejoined the Congress in 1964 but opted to be less politically active. She remained very good friends with the socialist legends, Ram Manohar Lohia and Jayaprakash Narayan.

In 1965, she was awarded the Order of Lenin and the Lenin Peace Prize by the USSR. In 1992, she was conferred Padma Vibhushan, India's second-highest civilian honour. She was also the recipient of the Nehru Award for International Understanding. A stamp commemorating her life was issued in 1998. After her death, she was awarded the Bharat Ratna, India's highest civilian honour.

As a practising socialist, she believed in frugal living, staying in a one-bedroom apartment on Asaf Ali Road, named after her husband. She drove a 'battered blue Fiat…' according to her nephew, the well-known journalist, the late Abheek Burman.

Though she opposed the Emergency, she remained close friends with Indira Gandhi and the Nehru family. Her political career and her busy life meant that her battered blue Fiat became one of the most recognized vehicles in Delhi. She died on 29 July 1996, aged eighty-seven.

Kusum and P.N. Nair

Kusum was a star, something her husband 'Pano' Nair never became, despite thinking big. Post-mutiny, Pano apparently rejoined the army for a while and then struck out on his own.

But he was a failure in business. Ambitious projects were started, but due to bad luck or bad management, they never worked out. Family members say he once told them that he was a distant cousin to the Kapoors and had a Bollywood film project in mind. But he ran out of funding, so it wasn't completed.

He then discovered a technology for processing hardwoods (sal and bamboo) into paper pulp for the production of newsprint, after which he set up Nepa Mills in Madhya Pradesh as a private company with Kusum as a partner. Their ambition was to establish 'the largest paper mill in the world'.

Bad luck struck yet again. When they were to import the machinery, the rupee was devalued, and they could not raise the difference without the government stepping in and taking control. Pano didn't want to be a government employee, so he backed out. Nepa Mills continues to run now, as a Government of India undertaking that primarily recycles waste paper and manufactures newsprint.

'Pano' then moved to Delhi to start an engineering consultancy company. 'Their home in Jorbagh… was an intellectual salon with academics, officials, politicians, and diplomatic corps people as common visitors,' says their son-in-law, Barry Michie.

They had Delhi's Who's Who among their friends. Kusum and Pano eventually divorced, and after that, in 1968, Kusum left for the United States. She was estranged from her daughter Aruna for some time but they reconciled. Pano died in 2000.

Kusum continued to write columns under the nom de plume 'Birbal'. She was the founder of India's first private syndication agency, the National Press Syndication Agency. She and her husband 'Prano', as she called him, were also planning to start a publishing house for which she approached many politicians, including Nehru, to sit as directors. According to Kusum's sister Shaila, in a letter to R.D., though Nehru did not join the board, he assured them 'he would give them all the backing he could'.

According to Barry Michie, Indira Gandhi also asked Kusum to be her press secretary. However, she turned down the offer as 'she wanted to keep her independence as a journalist.'

Asoka Mehta, a member of the socialist wing of the Congress party and minister of planning, petroleum and chemicals, helped her research her first study, supported by the Planning Commission. This resulted in her first book, *Blossoms in the Dust*. That made her international reputation. The Planning Commission refused to endorse publication since the book was critical of India's economic/rural development efforts. It was eventually published by the reputed publisher, Duckworth and is acknowledged as a classic in the field of rural development.

Kusum continued her career as a researcher, author and visiting faculty at a number of US universities: Harvard, Michigan State, Chicago, Hawaii, Missouri and, finally, Kansas State. In addition, she carried out research in the US, China and Japan on rural and agricultural development issues. She indefatigably crisscrossed the globe to pursue her research into agro-economics and peasants and called herself an 'academic gypsy'.

Kusum's passion for rural economics resulted in many books and teaching offers in reputed American universities such as Harvard and Cornell.

Besides a few articles on the naval uprising, her book *Army of the Occupation* is among the most passionate accounts of what the ratings went through and what they achieved. Kusum was very active in her later years in Woodstock School, Mussoorie, as an honorary teacher of Indian music.

Kusum Nair passed away on 13 December 1993 at the age of seventy-four with an unfinished book relating to the agricultural history of the United States. Her obituary in the *Journal of Asian Studies*, said: 'Friend and critic of Nobel economists Gunnar Myrdal and Theodore Schultz, Kusum engaged everyone who met her with her deft wit, clarity of mind, and a preternatural intensity… always-fresh memories shared by those of us who knew her as a remarkable person, whose extraordinary life path had happily crossed ours.'

Commander Arthur Frederick King

After his disastrous handling of the *Talwar*, Commander King was not in disgrace as one might have expected. Though he went through a court martial, he was absolved of any wrongdoing. Instead, he was put in charge of the Mulund camp, where almost 400 ratings were held. King drove some of the prisoners he had personally known to the railway station in Thane, gave them a one-way ticket, and ordered them never to come back to Bombay.

Given his behaviour, one would have expected King to have been hated and shunned by both Indians and Pakistanis. Not a bit of it! After Independence, he was offered a senior position in the forces, by both India and Pakistan. This he declined and joined a private company, Phillips, Scott & Turner in Newcastle upon Tyne, manufacturing figs, syrups, salts and, above all, the well-known pain-relieving drug, Panadol. King worked in that company for thirty-four years and was awarded the Queen's Award for Industry for Exports.

He retired in 1982 to the New Forest, where he became captain of a golf club. He was one of the last surviving members of the Royal Indian Navy Association. In 1997, he organized the last 'Tamasha', as the grand reunion show of the RIN was called.

In 2004, after much persuasion, he visited India and was welcomed and felicitated by many of those ratings and officers who had risen to higher ranks; a few had even become admirals. Partly as a result of his visit, there is now a Seamen's War Memorial in Pune to commemorate Indian merchant seamen who died in the First and Second World wars. King passed away in November 2014, aged ninety-seven, and is survived by a daughter, Jennifer.

Admiral John Henry Godfrey

The Commission of Enquiry set up by the Government of India agreed on many points with Admiral Godfrey in their report. Patrick Beesly, the author of Godfrey's biography, *Very Special Admiral,* says, 'It was a sad end to Godfrey's 43 years in the Royal And Royal Indian Navies, but none of the many people with personal knowledge of India in 1946 whom the author has questioned would agree that Godfrey was to blame for the mutiny.'

Eventually, the mutiny was countered with excessive force, but Godfrey was replaced the next day and then faced the humiliation of having to report to his junior. Godfrey sailed for home on 9

May 1946. Three of his fellow officers, including the first officer of WRIN, wrote laudatory farewell messages.

Claude Auchinleck wrote: 'I admire most sincerely the way in which you have dealt with the problems which have confronted you and I am sorry that our partnership has come to an end.'

FOB Rear-Admiral Rattray, his immediate subordinate, sent a signal reading: 'We will not forget that you brought the Service to the threshold of a great future… on behalf of all in my command, I wish you a safe passage and many years of happiness in England.'

After his retirement, he was chairman of the Chelsea Hospital Management Committee. He also served on several important hospitals and founded a centre for spastic children in Chelsea. He was awarded the Order of the Nile of Egypt and made a chevalier of the French Legion d'Honneur, though sadly, he 'became the only officer of his rank in the Second World War to receive no official recognition (from Britain)' even though he contributed greatly to the Allied victory, says Beesly.

He was never bitter as he believed in the old naval adage that 'it was better to have incurred Their Lordships' displeasure than never to have come to Their Lordships' attention at all.'

Despite the strong persuasion of his former assistant, Ian Fleming, the 'son he never had', Godfrey refused to take the job of Naval Correspondent in the *Daily Telegraph*. He was not interested in journalism. However, he was immortalized as 'M' in the Bond thrillers.

'Godfrey celebrated his eightieth birthday in 1968, and from then on, his physical vigour began to decline,' writes Beesly. Admiral Godfrey died in Eastbourne, UK, on 29 August 1971, at age eighty-three. He was survived by his wife, Bertha Margaret, and three daughters.

The elusive M.S. Khan

M.S. Khan was one of the ringleaders of the naval mutiny, president of the NCSC, and a highly recognizable public face during and after the surrender. But he vanished without a trace, once he was discharged. All attempts by the author to trace him, or his family, proved that he was as elusive as the fictional Scarlet Pimpernel.

Here is what little is known. He was sent from Kalyan station to Gujranwala by Punjab Mail on Wednesday, 2 May 1946. According to IB records, his address for disembarkation was the care of his wife, Mrs Khursheed Jaw, and her address was listed as c/o Mr Alla Ditta, Daska, Distt Sialkot, Punjab.

The information supplied by the FOB to the director, IB, had this to say: 'As far as I know he is not connected with any political movement, but has expressed violent anti-British views on a number of occasions. During the mutiny he almost certainly came under the influence of subversive political elements. He has an unusual amount of control and command over large numbers of men, and undoubtedly averted several outbreaks of violence during the mutiny.'

Once it was established that he had moved to Pakistan, my attempts to trace his whereabouts intensified. But all attempts to trace him proved futile and costly.

I would have personally searched buildings in Daska, Sialkot, if there were no travel barriers between the two countries. I was led up the garden path by a former Pakistani *fauji* even though he came through a strong recommendation. Months were lost due to his glib assurances.

One of the most prominent Pakistani lawyers and former Cabinet ministre, Aitzaz Ahsan called several of his friends to establish my bonafides. I continued to see glimmers of light even while hitting one dead end after another.

My obsession for tracking down Khan increased directly in proportion to the number of dead ends. An intense internet search led me to an obituary of Admiral M.S. Khan, a former naval chief of Pakistan. Earlier I had read accounts which rumoured Khan had become Pakistan's naval chief. I hadn't believed them because 'my' M.S. Khan was not even a junior commissioned officer in 1946.

There was little chance of an ordinary rating being elevated to navy chief!

But this obituary suddenly gave flight to my hopes. Ah I thought! Finally, this will connect me to the person whose whereabouts had become an obsession. My friend in Pakistan, Aitzaz Ahsan was able to put me in touch with the daughter of Admiral M.S. Khan, the ex-navy chief.

I had a most cordial telephone conversation with his doting daughter, Turqain Zamaria, only to be told at the end of the pleasantries that her revered father, Adm. M.S. Khan, had no connection to the M.S. Khan of naval mutiny fame. However, the concrete benefit is a close digital friendship with Ms Zamaria.

Another acquaintance, Admiral Mian Zahir Shah (retd) told me how impossible it would be to trace a M.S. Khan. The Quaid-e Azam had forbidden the re-employment of the ratings discharged in disgrace.

I have a hunch, or rather a hope that my search for the elusive M.S. Khan may yield better results once this book is published. Perhaps, his friends or family will come forward. The quest continues.

SHIPS

HMIS *Hindustan*/PNS *Karsaz*

The HMIS *Hindustan* surrendered on 23 February 1946 after an intense exchange of artillery fire, which resulted in the heaviest casualties on any ship during the mutiny.

After the surrender, her armoury was secured, her decks cleaned of blood, and the injured and dead carried to hospital. The ship sustained serious damage. On the way to the hospital, the army convoy was stoned by angry mobs.

A few days after the mutiny, the HMIS *Hindustan* limped back to Bombay. After Partition, *Hindustan*, in 1948, was allotted to Pakistan. Due to its poor condition and its name, the Pakistanis assumed it was a deliberate insult. So they decided to pay it back in naval fashion.

As Admiral (retd) Mian Zahir Shah writes in his book *More Bubbles of Water:* 'a torpedo boat called "ML-420" (referred to as Char-Sau-Bees) went to India while an ailing sloop with the extraordinary name "Hindustan" came to Pakistan (rather reluctantly it seems, for she had to be towed all the way from Bombay to Karachi!)... Someone in the Armed Services Reconstitution Committee must have had a sense of humour!'

The *Hindustan* was indeed way past its sell-by date, having been commissioned in October 1930 even though it boasted two 4-inch guns, both suitable for use against a surface target, and four 1.9-inch saluting guns.

In Karachi, the ailing *Hindustan* could only be used as a harbour training ship for stokers. She was renamed *Karsaz* and lasted only about five years. HMIS *Hindustan*/PNS *Karsaz* was decommissioned by the Pakistan Navy in the late 1950s before being sold as scrap. Her guns still stand guard outside the administrative building of PNS *Karsaz*, the big naval engineering training establishment built later on in Karachi.

HMS *Glasgow*

HMS *Glasgow*, the powerful 9,100 tonne British cruiser, sailed into Bombay harbour at 1705 on Saturday, 23 February, almost twelve hours after the surrender. The C-in-C, Sir Claude Auchinleck, after frantic discussions with the viceroy and Prime Minister Attlee's office, had ordered it to sail at full speed from Trincomalee.

The *Glasgow*'s deployment was partly to rattle the mutineers but also as a morale-boosting exercise to show the British administration in India how seriously the mutiny was being taken.

Glasgow was a town-class (also known as Southhampton Class) cruiser, a formidable fighting machine with appropriate armament, including twelve 6-inch guns, anti-aircraft guns and machine guns in addition to deck-mounted torpedoes.

Glasgow was commanded by Captain Hubback, who came to Bombay with a reputation for being a very able officer with great public relations skills. Lt Gen. R.M.M. Lockhart, GOC-in-C, Southern Command, who was in charge of handling the Bombay mutiny superseding Admiral Godfrey, was highly impressed with Captain Hubback and gave him the responsibility of visiting all the RIN assets in Bombay. Hubback's offer to replace military guards with the guards of RN ratings was greatly commended. 'We sailors do not like to see sailors of a sister navy in trouble guarded by soldiers,' he wrote to Lockhart.

His PR skills were on full display when he threw open his ship to the public of Bombay and entertained a large party of non-official Indians and officers of the RIN, Army, RAF, and RIAF. This party did create an atmosphere of gaiety on a ship that had arrived to create terror.

The *Free Press Journal* (2 March 1946) wrote about the party that had taken place the previous evening. The headline was 'Munshis At Cocktail, Party Celebrates End of RIN Strike'.

The text below read: 'HMS *Glasgow* which entered the Bombay waters last Saturday (23/2/46) threw aboard a cocktail party this evening at which many citizens were present. Among the invitees were many titled men and women, Mr Mirchandani, the municipal commissioner, Mr and Mrs Munshi, Mr HE Butler, commissioner of police, Mr I.I. Chundrigar, President of the Bombay Muslim League Party. Mr Abu Jasdanwalla, Sir Charles Bristow, advisor to the governor of Bombay, were also present.

'The invited guests were taken around the cruiser and along with drinks were regaled with wartime stories. It was such a roaring party, mostly attended by the Bombay gentry. No one wanted to go home. In the wee hours, they were forced to disperse only after water cannons were unleashed upon them.' This was barely a week after the massacre of hundreds of civilians. To many Indians, it seemed like a shameful episode.

After its Bombay visit, *Glasgow* sailed around the Indian Ocean. She returned to Portsmouth in mid-1947 and was placed in the reserves. After refits and deployments in America and in the West Indies in 1952, it became the flagship of the Mediterranean fleet based at Malta under Admiral Earl Mountbatten of Burma. She was given the honour of taking part in the fleet review to celebrate the coronation of Queen Elizabeth II.

Post the Suez crisis, by the end of 1956, HMS *Glasgow* was decommissioned. Departing Portsmouth on 4 July 1958, she was towed to the shipbreaking yard in Blyth on 8 July, ending the saga of the most powerful ship brought to Bombay during the mutiny.

SHORE ESTABLISHMENTS

Castle Barracks

Castle Barracks was a storm centre. It witnessed the fiercest gun battle on the third day. About two months after the surrender, at 7.30 p.m. on 13 April, a powerful explosion shattered the peace there.

A confidential, secret report (file no. 391) filed by inspector of police, Palton Road Police station, on 15 April reads as follows: 'It was ascertained that the explosion had occurred on the verandah of Castle Barracks Annexe on the first floor. Near the railings of the verandah was found a large pool of congealed blood and about 10 feet away from this pool were found two other pools… Amongst the blood were found four pieces of metal. One piece of metal has been identified as the striker of the grenade, and downstairs on the parade ground was found the grenade lever.'

Among the casualties were one dead and four seriously injured. All were Muslims, and British authorities announced this accident took place while they were praying, though 7.30 p.m. is an unlikely time for prayers.

The report admitted, 'It is suspected that the deceased came into possession of the grenade during the recent RIN disturbance and that being a driver he did not know the mechanism of the grenade and while tampering with it, it suddenly exploded.'

This was not the isolated incident of violence at the Barracks post-mutiny. Several minor incidents had taken place after the day the ratings surrendered. A rattled administration seriously considered a recommendation made by Governor Colville as early as 27 February 1946 to Viceroy Wavell, where he argued, 'The two shore establishments which mutinied are situated in the south of the city, and the police problem, already a difficult one, becomes almost an impossible one if the loyalty, or at any rate, the good behaviour of these forces cannot be counted upon. I, therefore most earnestly urge… that these two establishments in Bombay city should either be pruned down to small numbers or moved outside the city.'

Similar recommendations were made by the various boards of enquiry investigating various shore establishments and ships. Accordingly, Castle Barracks was struck off from the list of naval shore establishments.

On 26 January 1950, Castle Barracks was renamed INS *Dalhousie*, a name that had been originally given to it in 1940. On September 1951, INS *Dalhousie* was renamed INS *Angre* in honour of Kanhoji Angre, the greatest Sarkhel (Admiral) India has known. INS *Angre* is presently the base depot establishment of Western Naval Command. It provides logistics and administrative support to all the ships and units based in Bombay and under the Western Command. The CO of INS *Angre* is a one-star officer (a commodore). The Manor House, since rebuilt, is now the seat of the Flag Officer Commanding Maharashtra Naval Area (FOMA) Naval Command, a two-star officer with the rank of Rear Admiral.

HMIS *Talwar*

Talwar, the epicentre of the uprising, continues to be used for meeting the training commitments of future generations of naval communicators, albeit in a different location. It was constructed at the site of the old railway terminal at Colaba, Bombay, and commissioned in 1939. It served as a signal school of the British Empire between 1939–46.

All signs of mutiny on the original site in Colaba have been completely erased. *Talwar* was completely sanitized after the surrender. The armoury was checked and secured, the kitchens were taken over, and the barracks cleaned. Even so, there were tell-tale signs of the turmoil at the time and, of course, many memories.

Immediately after the mutiny ended, the space where the communication school once stood was allocated to the Naval Transport Pool, which was set up as a centralized transport holding and management centre. Apart from catering to the transport requirements of the Western Naval Command, this also houses a workshop for carrying out repairs and maintenance of vehicles.

The signal school in Colaba, once the second-largest communication training facility in the British Empire, was 'paid off', and training facilities were shifted to temporary barracks in Cochin. This was housed in several temporary buildings around the present ceremonial parade ground in Cochin and simply called the Signal School.

On 23 June 1955, the foundation stone for a permanent building for the School in Cochin was laid by then-chief of naval staff, Admiral Sir Mark Pizey, KBE, CB, DSO. The building was inaugurated on 8 March 1958 by then-chief of naval staff, Vice Admiral Sir Stephen Carlill, KBE, CB, DSO. Even now at the Signal School in Kochi, HMIS *Talwar* is commemorated at the Talwar Hall, a state-of-the-art auditorium.

The legacy of HMIS *Talwar* was also carried forward by the Indian Navy, which commissioned a Type 12 frigate on 26 April 1960. This ship participated in the Liberation of Goa and then the Indo-Pakistan war of 1971. After she was decommissioned on 31 October 1985, her namesake, a Type 1135.6 frigate and the lead ship of her class, was commissioned on 18 June 2003. The new INS *Talwar* continues to serve in the Western Fleet of the Indian Navy.

Only old-timers would be aware that HMIS *Talwar* once stood on the space that serves as the Naval Transport Pool today and some of them still call it, Talwar.

PNS *Himalaya*, Karachi

There were three major shore establishments in Karachi in February 1946. HMIS *Chamak*, which first received the news of the mutiny, was a radar school. HMIS *Himalaya* was a gunnery school and training centre for diving. Post mutiny, of the three, only HMIS *Himalaya* retained its name and expanded its presence in Manora Island, Karachi, where it continues to be located.

After Independence, it became PNS *Himalaya* and further developed facilities for other professional naval schools. In the seventies, it started to train new entry sailors, while in the eighties, the diving section was upgraded to a school named PN Diving School.

Himalaya remains one of the most important shore establishments in Pakistan, offering 'Boot Camp Training' to new sailors. Besides diving training, it also conducts rescue operations during floods and other emergencies.

INDIAN OFFICERS

Admiral S.G. Karmarkar

Sadashiv Ganesh Karmarkar was thirty-three when he was asked to take command of HMIS *Talwar*, the shore establishment from where the mutiny broke out. He joined the RIN in 1927 and his batch trained on the HMIS *Dufferin* until 1930, when he graduated with merit. He was the course mate of Ram Dass Katari who later became the first Indian chief of the naval staff. Along with JRD Tata, Karmarkar was witness to the famous 'Bombay Victoria Docks Explosion' of 1944.

As Ranjit B. Rai wrote in the *Hindu* on 19 August 2013, 'SS Fort Stikine carrying a cargo of cotton bales, gold and ammunition including 1,400 tonnes of explosive, caught fire and exploded and broke into two. The explosion was so powerful, windows 12 km away in Bombay were shattered. Neighbourhoods close to the docks were wiped out… blasts and fires raged for two days. Showers of burning material set fire to Bombay's slums. Eleven vessels berthed close by were sunk or damaged and 800 deaths were reported. Witnessing the tragedy together and working together subsequently to minimize the loss and misery to citizens, JRD and Karmarkar became close in an association that lasted for decades.

Nearly two years later, Karmarkar was handed the difficult job of handling the *Talwar*, in the middle of the mutiny. Along with Ram Dass Katari and S.N. Kohli, he briefed Jawaharlal Nehru, the future prime minister, about the events.

His allegiance, like all RIN officers before Independence, was to the British. He was tasked with observing and reporting the activities of the mutiny ringleaders since he lived in a flat above Kusum and P.N. Nair in Riviera, Marine Drive. Though the ringleaders despised him, he became a popular officer after the mutiny ended, and India became Independent.

In 1947, Karmarkar became commander of INS *Hamla*, a logistic training establishment for both officers and sailors. He moved to Naval Headquarters in 1949 as chief of administration and performed dual duty as chief of material.

In 1950, Karmarkar became the second Indian to command INS *Delhi*, the flagship of the Indian Navy (he succeeded Adhar Kumar Chatterji). In September 1952, Karmarkar became captain, Indian Naval Barracks and CO of INS *Angre* in Bombay, and in 1954, Captain Superintendent Indian Naval Dockyard. He was promoted to commodore-in-charge Cochin in 1957. The first armament depot was opened under Karmarkar in 1958.

In 1960, Karmarkar was promoted to acting rank of rear-admiral and appointed flag officer Bombay. A few months later, his rank was confirmed and he continued as FOB for the next four years, followed by retirement on 16 June 1964.

Post-retirement, Karmarkar joined hands with JRD at the suggestion of then-defence-minister, Y.B. Chavan. From the Tata's Bombay House HQ, he started work on a project to decongest Bombay port. Around the same time, the Chowgules, who owned a shipping line, bought the sea frontage of Nheva Sheva and applied for permission to set up shipbuilding and repair facilities. Though the Chowgules employed Karmarkar with the blessings of Y.B. Chavan, the project did not find favour with the government and had to be abandoned. The Chowgule land was then taken over by the Jawaharlal Nehru Port Trust.

Sailors of the Indian Navy remember Karmarkar fondly as a gentleman officer. Admiral Karmarkar passed away in 1988 following surgery. He was cremated in Pune with full military honours.

Admiral Sourendra Nath Kohli

Lt Sourendra Nath Kohli was thirty when the mutiny broke out in 1946. Along with Lt S.M. Nanda he was posted in HMIS *Talwar*. He was a witness to Commander King's outburst against the ratings that sparked the rebellion.

Born in Amritsar, he graduated from St. Stephen's College, Delhi. Kohli joined the Royal Indian Navy Volunteer Reserve in 1936 and was commissioned as a sub-lieutenant in 1938 and promoted to lieutenant in 1941.

After Independence, he was one of the officers responsible for overseeing the expansion of the naval fleet. In 1948, he was sent to the United Kingdom in connection with the acquisition of destroyers. He was appointed CO of INS *Rana* after her purchase. In the mid-1950s, he became superintendent of the Naval Dockyard and twice served as the director of Naval Plans. In 1965, he was promoted to rear admiral, and from 1967 to '69 he commanded the Indian fleet, spearheaded by the aircraft carrier INS *Vikrant*. He was awarded the Param Vishisht Seva Medal (PVSM) and promoted to vice admiral on 14 February 1969. Kohli became flag officer commanding-in-chief of Western Naval Command in 1971. He was conferred the Padma Bhushan for his extraordinary leadership in the 1971 India-Pakistan war.

Admiral Kohli took over as chief of naval staff on 1 March 1973 and retired on 29 February 1976. He authored four books: *Sea Power And The Indian Ocean* (1978); *We Dared: Maritime Operations in the 1971 Indo-Pak War*; *The Indian Ocean and India's Maritime Security (1981)*; and *Indian Ocean: An Area of Tension and Big Power Pressures*. (The last two were expanded National Security Lectures.) He passed away, aged eighty, on 21 January 1997. He was survived by his three daughters.

Lt Admiral Sardarilal Mathradas (S.M.) Nanda

Admiral S.M. Nanda was born 10 October 1915 in Manora, Karachi. He hailed from Gujranwala, Punjab, and his father was employed as office superintendent in the Port Trust in Manora. He was the eldest of seven siblings, three boys and four girls. Married at age twenty-one to Sumitra, Nanda joined the Royal Indian Navy Volunteer Reserve in 1941 when he turned twenty-six, and was commissioned later in the same year as an acting sub-lieutenant in the executive branch. In 1942, he joined a communication course at HMIS *Talwar* and was posted there when the mutiny broke out.

Nanda played a vital role in liaisoning between the British, the ratings, and Congress leaders like Sardar Patel. He was appointed director of Personnel Services at Naval Headquarters in 1949. As commander of INS *Ranjit*, he participated in the coronation ceremony of Queen Elizabeth II in 1953.

In 1956, he was appointed commissioning CO of INS *Mysore* which was refitted in Liverpool. Sailing back from the UK, the *Mysore* paid an official visit to Split in erstwhile Yugoslavia, where he called on the president, Marshall Tito.

In 1958, he took over as the director general, Naval Dockyard Expansion Scheme. In 1961 he was selected to attend the Imperial Defence College and, in 1962, chief of material at Naval HQ. In May 1962, he became deputy chief of naval staff and, in 1964, was appointed as the managing director of Mazagon Dock Limited. In 1968, Nanda took over as the first flag officer commanding-in-chief, Western Naval Command, having been promoted to vice-admiral.

He became chief of the naval staff on 1 March 1970, succeeding Admiral Adhar Kumar Chatterji. In the 1971 Indo-Pak war, the Indian Navy attacked Karachi with missile boats in Operation Trident, which is recorded in detail in his memoirs, *The Man Who Bombed Karachi* (2004).

Nanda daringly deployed INS *Vikrant*, India's only aircraft carrier in the Bay of Bengal, to successfully blockade East Pakistan. This was a big factor in India's decisive victory which led to the creation of Bangladesh. Admiral Nanda retired on 30 August 1973. Post retirement, in 1974, he was appointed chairman and managing director of Shipping Corporation of India.

Admiral S.M. Nanda was much-decorated. Besides various service medals, he was awarded the Ati Vishisht Seva Medal (AVSM), General Services Medal, and the Param Vishisht Seva Medal (PVSM). In January 1972, he was conferred the Padma Vibhushan.

His family life was full of turbulence, though. His son, Suresh Nanda, became a controversial businessman, starting Crown Corporation, an arms trading company where Admiral Nanda played an executive role. Crown Corporation was mired in several controversies as it specialized in the supply of imported weapons to the armed forces.

Admiral Nanda's grandson, Sanjeev was subsequently convicted in a hit and run case that went all the way to the Supreme Court on appeal. On 2 January 2002, his daughter Beena, her husband Pradeep Mehra, and one of their three daughters were tragically killed in a helicopter crash. Admiral Nanda passed on 11 May 2009 in New Delhi. He was ninety-three.

Admiral Adhar Kumar Chatterji

Adhar Kumar Chatterji was born in Dacca in 1914. A few months before the mutiny, this alumnus of Presidency College, Calcutta, was appointed officer-in-charge of the radar school HMIS *Chamak*, the establishment in Karachi, which first received the news of the strike.

He was popular among the RIN ratings who saw him as a father figure. Post-mutiny, he was among the select few to attend the staff course at the Royal Naval College, Greenwich, UK. Upon his return to India, he was elevated to the rank of commander and served as director of Naval Planning at the Naval HQ.

In 1949, A.K. Chatterji was appointed commander (executive officer) of the flagship, INS *Delhi*, succeeding Commander Ram Dass Katari. In 1950, he handed over the command to S.G. Karmarkar.

He was then appointed naval advisor to the High Commissioner of India (first V.K. Krishna Menon and then B.G. Kher) in the UK. In 1953, he sailed from Portsmouth to Gibraltar in an armada consisting of ships from the Indian Navy, Royal Navy, Royal Australian Navy and the Royal New Zealand Navy to commemorate the coronation of Queen Elizabeth II.

In 1954, Chatterji became the commodore-in-charge of Bombay ('Combay'). He then attended Imperial Defence College in the UK and, upon his return in 1957, was appointed deputy chief of the naval staff.

In May 1962, Admiral Chatterji took over as the fourth flag officer commanding Indian Fleet. Upon the induction of aircraft carrier INS *Vikrant* in 1961, he flew his flag on the *Vikrant* as his flagship. He handed over the command to S.M. Nanda when he was appointed the second commandant of the National Defence College in 1964, being the first naval officer to hold that post.

In November 1965, Admiral Chatterji was appointed chief of naval staff. He became full admiral on 1 March 1968, again the first Indian officer to hold that rank. Admiral Chatterji retired from the Indian Navy on 28 February 1970. His famous words long after his retirement, 'Son, I may have long left the sea… But the sea has never left me,' still reverberates in the Indian Navy.

A versatile and analytical man, he was described as 'most mathematical minded' with 'considerable strategic acumen' and is remembered as the chief who brought technological advancement to the Indian Navy. As Commodore Srikant Kesnur says: 'Illustrating his versatility, post-retirement, he also became a gourmand cook bringing his perfectionist attitude to make a range of jams, jellies, pickles, kebabs, sandesh and other Bengali sweets... He was also a keen photographer, inveterate traveller and lover of nature...'

Admiral M.P. Awati, who is himself considered a legend in the Indian Navy described him as 'a giant of a man, bright, with an endearing Bengali accent'.

He passed away in New Delhi on 6 August 2001 and was survived by his daughters, Purabi and Prabhati.

Ali Ahmed Brohi

Ali Ahmed Brohi was most articulate in his deposition to the Commission of Enquiry. This twenty-five year old displayed knowledge and intelligence beyond his age and presented a statement that impressed the chairman, Justice Fazl Ali, no end.

Brohi was born on 11 November 1920 at Garhi, near Shikarpur Town in Sindh province, now in Pakistan. Brohi had ten siblings, two sisters and eight brothers.

His family was well-connected. His elder brother A.K. Brohi was in a celebrated legal partnership with Ram Jethmalani, and in 1960–61, he served as high commissioner of Pakistan in India. Their sister was married to Syed Qaim Ali Shah, who was chief minister of Sindh for three terms.

A.A. Brohi completed his matriculation from Bombay University and joined the RIN. He was joint secretary in the NCSC and among the ratings incarcerated in Mulund camp, and later transferred to Kalyan where the ringleaders were held. After being 'discharged with disgrace,' Brohi served as editor of the Sindhi dailies *Qurbani* and *Sada-e-Sindh* published from Karachi. He also worked for the Communist Party.

Brohi later served as Sindh information secretary and wrote several books on the history of Sindh. He also served as director-general of tourism in the West Pakistan Government. After his retirement in 1980, he took up the management of the well-known Sindhi newspaper *Hilal-i-Pakistan*. Among his most notable books is the extensively researched *History of Tombstones: Sindh and Balochistan*, which is a detailed account of the funeral rites of the tribal people of the area.

Brohi married twice, once at a very young age and the second time in 1960, when he was forty. He had six children from those two marriages, a son and two daughters from each marriage.

In 2001, Brohi started to participate in active politics and despite his age, became a prominent member of Muttahida Qaumi Movement (MQM) and an ardent supporter of its leader Altaf Hussain. Brohi passed away on 30 November 2003, aged eighty-three and is buried at Abdullah Shah Ghazi's shrine in Karachi.

RATINGS WHO DARED: DISHONOURABLE DISCHARGE AND DESTITUTION

The 396 ratings incarcerated in Mulund and Kalyan camps were discharged dishonourably. They were asked to return uniforms, kit and shoes issued to them six years ago even though they'd spent most of those years in war zones. Their dues were docked and their accounts debited for their inability to return these items in pristine condition.

They were thrust out of prison, penniless onto 'civvy street'. Many came from impoverished backgrounds, where they could barely support themselves and their families. There is no written record of the tragic course their lives subsequently took.

On 14 and 15 August 1947, India and Pakistan attained Independence. But this did not mean an end to their sufferings.

What hurt most was the abandonment by the political leaders who had persuaded them to surrender promising no victimization. They felt deeply disappointed and betrayed.

BISWANATH BOSE.

92 Nimoo Goswami Lane
Calcutta-5.

April 3, 1952.

Personal & Confidential.

Jawaharlal Nehru Esq.
The Hon'ble Prime Minister of India
Government of India
NEW DELHI.

My dear Jawaharlalji,

This letter would seem to you to be a strange and surprising, but I fervently hope this will receive your attention and due consideration to the facts mentioned herein.

In the first place I should like to introduce myself as an ex-Indian sailor with you, and consequently in the first step of my life I selected Navy and joined in the year 1943 on 25th October during the last great war. Although I was eldest son of my father and there was certain responsibility on my shoulder as I was a member of a very poor family I could not give up my hopes.

You may remember the time of disturbances throughout India and abroad created by the Indian sailors for the freedom of our country in the year 1946 on 18th February till 28th February, in which my name was also included as a leader and I was subsequently punished with the dismissal from the service and imprisonment for sometime. I was released from the Alipore Central Jail of Calcutta in the month of May 1946. Since my release from detention I have

contd' - - -

Facsimile of Biswanath Bose's letter to Prime Minister Jawaharlal Nehru, where he wrote: 'if there is any law for those who have been dismissed for taking part in

- 2 -

been trying to contact you for reappointment in the naval service, but all attempts so far been made by me did not bear any fruit.

However, I understand from the Captain of Indian Naval Barracks at Bombay that he is unable to recall me in the service. I should ask you for the reason of such action in the present days as we are aware that we have achieved full independence. If there is any law for those who have been dismissed from service for taking part in the mass movement for freedom of the country and that they cannot enter into their respective services then I must ask you to explain why yourself being a leader of Congress, a political party, should hold the post of a Prime Minister. But, at the same time I make an apology which I expect may be forbidden.

I anticipated while delivering speech in the public platform in several places in this city which formed by many eminent persons that you will duly consider changing law and reappointing the mutineers during British administration in our country, of course, for those who have been dismissed from service, but it was ignored.

In conclusion, I feel confident I am right in thinking, and you will not be so cruel to pass on your decision to this effect without delay. For your ready reference I hereby mention my official No.23627 A/B (s.s.). I apologize again for this writing.

Yours sincerely,

the freedom movement… then I must ask you to explain why yourself being a leader of Congress, a political party, should have the post of a Prime Minister!'

The Indians sent petitions to Prime Minister Nehru, Deputy Prime Minister Sardar Patel, Defence Minister Krishna Menon and others in positions of power. Their pleas for reinstatement were summarily rejected. In Pakistan too, the Quaid-e-Azam expressly forbade re-employment of the discharged ratings in the Pakistan Navy.

Their repeated appeals for reinstatement met with heartless stonewalling from the powers-that-be. One letter from the Ministry of Defence rejecting the application of a rating asking for re-employment read: 'The Government of India had after careful consideration decided not to enrol persons dismissed or discharged from the service on account of their participation in the RIN mutiny of February 1946. (Any person)… dismissed with disgrace from the Naval service, it is pointed out that he is ineligible even for any civil employment under the government.'

Lamenting, one of the ratings later wrote, 'We suffered quietly in the hope… But our hopes have been belied, our faith shattered… our only fault was that we loved our motherland and exhibited to the rest of the country that we too were with them in their struggle for freedom. If patriotism is a crime, we surely are guilty.'

Biswanath Bose, a discharged rating, in his book *RIN Mutiny: 1946,* revealed that he wrote a letter to Nehru, which said: 'My name was included as a leader [of the RIN mutiny] and I was subsequently punished with dismissal and imprisonment… since my release I have been trying to contact you unsuccessfully for reappointment in the Naval services… if there is any law for those who have been dismissed for taking part in the freedom movement of the country that they cannot enter into their respective services then I must ask you to explain why yourself being a leader of Congress, a political party, should have the post of a Prime Minister!'

This then was the tragic epilogue to the 1946 mutiny. A bunch of young men, some of them mere boys turned sixteen, ended up with their lives destroyed for the temerity of attempting

No.NL.02'0/NFQ/5520/N/D-2(a).
Government of India,
Ministry of Defence(Navy Branch).
New Delhi, the 6th November 1948.

MEMORANDUM.

Re-instatement of ratings removed from service
for participation in the R.I.N.Mutiny in February
1946 .

      With reference to his petition dated nil addressed to
Shri Madan Lal Mehta, the Assistant Private Secretary to
the Prime Minister, Shri O.P.Markandey is informed that the
Government of India have, after a careful consideration,
decided not to re-enrol persons dismissed or discharged from
the service on account of their participation in the R.I.N.
Mutiny of February 1946. There is, however, no statutory bar
to their re-employment under Government in civil employment
except where such dismissal was with disgrace.

                        (J.R.Mody)Major,
Under Secretary to the Government of India.

To

      Shri O.P. Markanday,
       (Ex-Sailor)
    P.o. & Village Rardas,
     Street Sonian,
      District Amritsar,
      East Punjab.

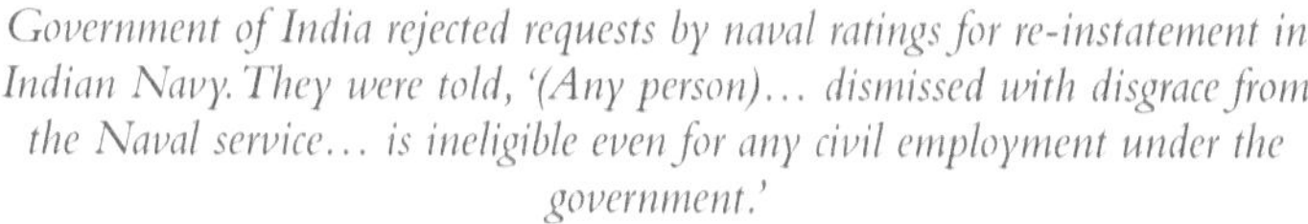

Government of India rejected requests by naval ratings for re-instatement in Indian Navy. They were told, '(Any person)… dismissed with disgrace from the Naval service… is ineligible even for any civil employment under the government.'

to free their motherland from tyranny. Not only did the British treat them inhumanely, those who assumed authority after the British departed refused to acknowledge their sacrifices, let alone make any redress.

For the discharged ratings – life post-Independence would come to resemble an ironic twist on the *Kallol* slogan *Cholchhe, Cholbe* – the injustice would go on.

SELECT BIBLIOGRAPHY

UNPUBLISHED SOURCES

Government Records
National Archives of India
Ministry of Defence: RIN Mutiny

Sr. No.   Brief Description
1. Vol. entitled Bombay Witnesses
2. Vol. entitled Delhi Witnesses
3. Vol. entitled Bombay Witnesses
4. Vol. entitled 'RIN Commission of Enquiry First Draft Report'
5. Vol. entitled 'Report of the RIN Commission of Enquiry 1946'
6. A bundle of old newspaper cutting bearing on the mutiny
7. Folder containing some memos etc.
8. Folder containing 'Memos of Witnesses Submitted to the Commission'
9. Folder entitled 'Karachi Statements'
10. Folder entitled 'RIN Commission Statements' Naval Headquarters (Naval Law Directorate)
11. File no. 3908, Police Document: Disturbances on Subhas Chandra Bose's birthday celebration, From 3.1.1946 to 27.1.1946, Head Police Office, Bombay

File No.   Subject
NL 0220 Reinstatement of ratings removed from service for participation in the RIN mutiny of February 1946
NL 9001 Directive concerning discipline in the mutiny. 348
NL9901 Board of Inquiry - HMIS VALSURA
NL9902 Board of Inquiry - ADEN W/T Station
NL9903 Board of Inquiry - HMIS HOOGHLY
NL9907 Board of Enquiry into Mutiny in HMIS AKBAR
NL 9908 Board of Enquiry into Mutiny in HMIS CHEETAH
NL9909 Board of Enquiry into Mutiny in HMIS MADRAS
NL9915 Discharge of ratings involved in the Mutiny in HMIS TRAVANCORE
NL9919 Board of Inquiry into Mutiny in HMIS ORISSA
NL9920 Board of Inquiry of 11 HMI Ships convened to investigate the circumstances of the Mutiny
NL9923 Mutiny in HMIS KUMAON
NL9924 Mutiny in HMIS JUMNA
NL9930 Report of Board of Inquiry into the causes of the Mutiny in HMIS TALWAR

NL9936 Courts-Martial of Mutineers at Karachi

NL9937 Board of Inquiry into the Mutiny in 37th MS FLOTILlA

NL9939 Board of Inquiry into the Mutiny in Castle BARRACKS

NL9942 Board of Inquiry into the Mutiny in HMIS NARBADA

NL9943 Board of Inquiry into the Mutiny in HMIS KHYBER

NL9945 Board of Inquiry into the Mutiny in HMIS MOTI

NL9946 Board of Inquiry into the Mutiny in HMIS DHANUSH

NL9947 Board of Inquiry into the Mutiny in KALABATI

NL9956 Board of Inquiry reg. the Mutiny in FORT BARRACKS

NL9958 Board of Inquiry relating to the Mutiny in HMIS KATHIAWAR

NL9959 Petition made by ratings in Malir Camp awaiting courts martial

NL9965 Charges and evidence of all ratings in category 'A' belonging
to HMI ships, DALHOUSIE, NARBADA, HAMLA, KHYBER, KATHIAWAR
  and DHANUSH

NL9967 Board of Inquiry into the Mutiny in HMIS MACHLIMAR

NL9976 Board of Inquiry into the Mutiny in HMIS CLIVE

NL9978 Board of Inquiry into the Mutiny in HMIS FEROZE

NL Board of Inquiry into the Mutiny in HMIS Humla

NL Board of Inquiry into the Mutiny in HMIS Chamak

NL Board of Inquiry into the Mutiny in HMIS Himalaya

NL Board of Inquiry into the Mutiny in HMIS Dalhousie

NL9982 General Instructions to deal with the persons involved in the Mutiny

NL9984 Details of mutiny courts-martial for the information of
HE the Viceroy & Governors of Bombay and Sind

NL9987 Mutiny Petitions

Home Political (Internal) Department

File No.   Subject

5/14/46 Mutiny in the RIN and Communal Disturbances in Sind

5/21/46 Disturbances in Bombay arising out of RIN Mutiny

18/2/46 Fortnightly Reports for the month of February 1946

21/2/46 Correspondence with the Secretary of State for India and Provincial
  Govts. about RIN Mutiny

21/8/46 Courts-martial arising out of the RIN Mutiny

33/4/46 Communist Publications - People's Age - Questions of the action to be
  taken against it for publishing objectionable articles and secret documents -
  policy regarding Govt's advertisements and grant of newsprint

Historical Section, Ministry of Defence

OTHER SOURCES

Report by General Sir Rob McGregor MacDonald Lockhart, National Army
  Museum ACC No 8310-154

MLS/10/1, Admiral Geoffrey Miles, Royal Indian Navy 1946-47.

(admmiles 004-017) Naval Headquarters comments, signed by Miles, on the Commission of Enquiry report.

'Naval Memoirs' (The Papers of Admiral John Henry Godfrey), Vol. 1, 1902-15, 1964, GBR/0014/GDFY 1/1 to Vol. 8, 1967, GBR/0014/GDFY 1/11. Churchill Archives Centre, Cambridge, 1967.

Imperial War Museum Transcripts.

PUBLISHED SOURCES

Ali, Aruna Asaf and GNS Raghavan, *Resurgence of Indian Women*. New Delhi: Radiant Publishers, 1991.

Ali, Aruna Asaf, *Fragments from the Past: Selected Writings and Speeches of Aruna Asaf Ali*. Delhi: Patriot Publishers, 1989.

Ali, Aruna Asaf, *Private Face of a Public Person: A Study of Jawaharlal Nehru*. Delhi: Radiant Publishers, 1989.

Azad, Abul Kalam, *India Wins Freedom*. Delhi: Orient Blackswan, 1988, Prabhat Prakashan, 2021.

Banerjee, Subrata, *The RIN Strike* (with a preface by E.M.S. Namboodiripad). New Delhi: People's Publishing House, 1981.

Bell, Christopher M. and Bruce A. Elleman, Ed., *Naval Mutinies of the Twentieth Century: An International Perspective*. Routledge Publication, 2005.

Bhagwatkar, V.M., *The Role of the RIN Mutiny of Feb. 1946 (Royal Indian Navy Uprising) in the Indian Freedom Struggle* (thesis approved for Ph.D. by Nagpur University).

Bose, Biswanath, *RIN Mutiny: 1946*. New Delhi: Northern Book Centre, 1988.

Bose, Sisir Kumar, *Netaji Subhas Chandra Bose*. Delhi: National Book Trust, 1986.

Chandra, Bipan et al. *India's Struggle for Independence 1857–1947*. New Delhi: Penguin Books (India) Limited, 1988.

Chattopadhyay, Gautam, 'The Almost Revolutions: A Case Study of India in February 1946', in B. De (ed.), *Essays in Honour of S.C. Sarkar*. New Delhi: People's Publishing House, 1976.

Collins, D.J.E. *The Royal Indian Navy* 1939–45 (ed. Bisheshwar Prasad).

Combined Inter-Services Historical Section, India & Pakistan, 1964

Council of State Debates, 1946, Manager of Publications, GOI, New Delhi

Das, Dilip Kumar, *Revisiting Talwar; A study in the Royal Indian Navy Uprising of February 1946*. Delhi: Ajanta Publications, 1993.

Das, Durga (ed.), *Sardar Patel's Correspondence,* Vol. III. Ahmedabad: Navajivan Publishing House, 1972.

Dutt, B.C. *Mutiny of the Innocents.* Bombay: Sindhu Publications Pvt. Ltd., 1971.

Dutt, Rajni Palme, *Freedom for India, The truth about Cabinet Mission's Visit.* Communist Party, 1946.

Dutt, Utpal, *Towards a Revolutionary Theatre*. Calcutta: Seagull Books, 2009.

Gandhi, Mahatma. *Collected Works,* Vol. LXXXIII. New Delhi: The Publications

Division, GOI, 1981. https://www.gandhiashramsevagram.org/gandhi-literature/mahatma-gandhi-collected-works-volume-89.pdf

Gourgey, Percy S., *The Royal Navy Strike of 1946*. Hyderabad: Orient Blackswan, 1996.

Grover, Varinder and Ranjana Arora (eds.), *Great Women of Modern India: Aruna Asaf Ali*. Delhi: Deep and Deep Publication, 1993.

Kaul, Triloki Nath, *Aruna Asaf Ali: A Profile*. Delhi: Prabhat Prakashan, 1990.

Khan, Maj-Gen. Shahnawaz, *My Memories of INA & its Netaji*. Delhi: Rajkamal Publications, 1946.

Khwaja, Aslam, 'Role of Karachi in the 1946 Naval Rebellion'. *Mainstream, 9* March 2016.

Krishnan, Vice Admiral N., *A Sailor's Story: An Autobiography*. Bangalore: Punya Publications, 2011.

Kulkarni, Prof. A.R., *Medieval Maratha Country*. Pune: Diamond Publications, 2008.

(Central) *Legislative Assembly Debates*, 1944, 1946–47, Manager of Publications, GoI, New Delhi

Low, C.R. *History of the Indian Navy* 1613–1863, 2 Vols. London: Richard Bentley and Son, 1877.

Madsen, Chris, 'The Royal Indian Navy Mutiny, 1946', 2003.

Majumdar, R.C., *History of the Freedom Movement in India,* Vol. III. Calcutta: Firma KLM Private Limited, 1977.

Mansergh, Nicholas (ed.), *The Transfer of Power* 1942–47, Vols. VI–VIII. London: Her Majesty's Stationery Office, 1976–79.

Menon, V.P., *The Transfer of Power in India*. Calcutta: Orient Longmans, 1957.

Meyer, John M., 'The Royal Indian Navy Mutiny of 1946: Nationalist Competition and Civil-Military Relations in Postwar India'. *The Journal of Imperial and Commonwealth History*, 45(1): 1–24, December 2016.

Moharir, V.J. *History of the Army Services Corps* (1939–1946). Sterling Publishers Private Ltd., 1979.

Mookherji, Radha Kumud, *A History of Indian Shipping*. Longman Green and Co., 1912.

Moon, Penderal (ed), *Wavell: The Viceroy's Journal*. London: Oxford University Press, 1973.

Moti Ram, *Two Historic Trials in Red Fort*: An Authentic Account of the Trial by The General Court Martial of Captain Shah Nawaz Khan, Captain PK Sehgal and Lt GS Dhillon and Trial by A European Military Commission of Emperor Bahadur Shah, proceedings of the first INA Trial, 1946.

Nair, Kusum, *The Army of Occupation*. Bombay: Padma Publications Ltd., 1946.

Nandurkar, G.M., *Sardar's Letters - Mostly Unknown,* Vol. I. Ahmedabad: Sardar Vallabhbhai Patel Smarak Bhavan, 1977.

Nandurkar, G.M. (ed.), *Calicut University Research Journal,* Vol. 8 Issue 1, August 2014.

Naravane, M.S., *Battles of the Honourable East India Company: Making of the Raj.* New Delhi: A.P.H. Publishing Corporation, 2006.

Nehru, Jawaharlal, *Selected. Works* (ed. S. Gopal), Vol. 15. New Delhi: Orient Longmans, 1982.

Nehru, Jawaharlal, *The Discovery of India.* First published 1946 by Signet Press, Nehru Memorial Fund, 1981.

Nehru, Jawaharlal, *An Autobiography.* Current edition published by Penguin Books with an Introduction by Sunil Khilnani. Originally published 1936.

Pandey, B.N., *Nehru.* Delhi: Rupa Publishing House, 1976.

Pannikar, K.M., *India and the Indian Ocean.* London: Allen & Unwin, 1951.

Papers on the India Government's Military Policy Officially Contributed to the Newspapers, GIPD, 1934.

Parliamentary Debates (Hansard) House of Commons, 1946, His Majesty's Stationery Office, London.

Prasad, Nandan, *Expansion of the Armed Forces and Defence Organization 1939-45* (ed. Bisheshwar Prasad), Combined Inter-Services Historical Section, India & Pakistan, 1956.

Priya P., Dissertation: *Royal Indian Navy Mutiny: A Study of its Impact in South India.*

Richmond, Herbert. *The Navy in India 1763–1783.* London: Earnest Benn Limited, 1939.

Sadasyula, Ratnakar, 'The Forgotten Naval Mutiny of 1946 and India's Independence', *Swarajya Magazine,* 19 February 2016.

Sarkar, Sumit, *Modern India 1885–1947.* Delhi: Macmillan India Limited, 1983.

Sarkar, Sumit, *'Popular' Movements & 'Middle Class' Leadership in Late Colonial India: Perspectives & Problems of a 'History From Below'.* Calcutta: KP Bagchi & Company, 1983.

Shah, Admiral Mian Zahir (Retd), *Bubbles of Water.* PN Book Club, Islamabad: The Army Press, 2001.

Shah, Admiral Mian Zahir (Retd), *Sea Phoenix: A True Submarine Story.* PN Book Club, 2005.

Shanin, Teodor (ed.), *Late Marx and the Russian Road.* London: Routledge & Kegan Paul, 1983.

Sharma, Lt Cdr G.D., *The Untold Story of Naval Mutiny: Last War of Independence.* Delhi: Vij Books, 2015.

Simha, Rakesh Krishnan, 'Forgotten Mutiny that Shook the British Empire'. *Swarajya Magazine,* February 2016.

Singh, Harkirat, *The INA Trial and the Raj.* Delhi: Atlantic Publishers & Distributors, 2003.

Singh, Satyindra. *Under Two Ensigns.* New Delhi: Oxford & IBH Publishing Co., 1986.

Some Facts and Figures About Indian Defence 1930–35, GIPD, 1935

(A) Summary of Important Matters Concerning the Defence Services in India 1935–36, 1936–37, 1937–38, 1938–39 & 1939–40, GIPD & GIPS, 1935–40.

Summary of Important Matters Connected with the Defence Services in India, 1933–34 & 1934–35, GIPS, 1934–35.

Sundaram, Lanka, *India's Armies and their Costs.* Bombay: Avanti Prakashan, 1946.

The Collected Works of Sardar Vallabhbhai Patel Vol X (1 January 1943–31 December 1946), Edited by P.N. Chopra & Prabha Chopra. Delhi: Konark Publishers, 1990.

The Indian Annual Register (ed. Nripendra Nath Mitra), 1946.

The Indian Annual Register, January-June 1946 vol. 1, published by The Annual Register Office, Calcutta.

Towards A People's Navy [CPI Memorandum to the RIN Enquiry Commission].

Tripathi, Amalesh, 'Bharater Swadhinata Sangrame Jatiya Congress', *Desh* (a Bengali weekly), 17 December 1988 and 18 March 1989.

Two Years of War Being a Summary of Important Matters Connected with the Indian Defence Services with Special Reference to the Year 1940–41, GIPD, 1941

Vaidya, K.B., *The Naval Defence of India.* Bombay: Thacker & Co., Ltd., 1949.

Walker, G.F., *Historical Background of the Royal Indian Navy* (with a foreword by J.F. Godfrey), GIPD, 1944.

NEWSPAPERS

Amrita Bazar Patrika
The Bharat Jyoti
The Bombay Chronicle
Dawn (Delhi)
The Free Press Journal
The Hindu
Hindustan Standard
The Hindustan Times
The Manchester Guardian
Morning News
The New York Times
The People's Age
The Statesman, Calcutta (late city edition) and Delhi
The Times
The Times of India
The Tribune

INDEX